The President as Leader

MICHAEL ERIC SIEGEL

Senior Education Specialist, The Federal Judicial Center and Adjunct Professor of Government at Johns Hopkins and American Universities, Washington, D.C.

D0913666

PEARSON

Boston   Columbus   Indianapolis   New York   San Francisco   Upper Saddle River
Amsterdam   Cape Town   Dubai   London   Madrid   Milan   Munich   Paris   Montreal   Toronto
Delhi   Mexico City   São Paulo   Sydney   Hong Kong   Seoul   Singapore   Taipei   Tokyo

Executive Editor: Reid Hester
Editorial Assistant: Emily Sauerhoff
Executive Marketing Manager: Wendy Gordon
Production Manager: Meghan DeMaio
Creative Director: Jayne Conte
Cover Designer: Suzanne Behnke
Cover Art: © Gary Blakeley/Fotolia
Project Coordination, Text Design, and Electronic Page Makeup: Murugesh Rajkumar/
    PreMediaGlobal
Printer/Binder/Cover Printer: Courier Companies

Copyright © 2012 by Pearson Education, Inc.

Library of Congress Cataloging-in-Publication Data

Siegel, Michael E.
    The president as leader / Michael Eric Siegel.
        p. cm.
    ISBN-13: 978-0-13-502407-2 (alk. paper)
    ISBN-10: 0-13-502407-2 (alk. paper)
    1. Presidents—United States—History—20th century.   2. Presidents—United States—History—21st century.   3. Political leadership—United States—History—20th century.   4. Political leadership—United States—History—21st century.   I. Title.
    JK511.S545 2012
    973.93092'2—dc23

                                                                                            2011030260

10 9 8 7 6 5 4 3 2 1—V013—14 13 12 11

ISBN-10: 0-13-502407-2
ISBN-13: 978-0-13-502407-2

BRIEF CONTENTS

DETAILED CONTENTS

iv

PREFACE

The intent of this book is to present readers with a novel, penetrating, and comparative view of the leadership skills of five US Presidents who have held office for at least one full term since Watergate. While there are many books on the presidency, and even a greater number on the subject of leadership, there are relatively few that combine a review of the experiences and decisions of recent presidents with a systematic analysis of their leadership strengths and weaknesses.

Building on the pioneering work of political scientist Fred Greenstein and others, the book argues that leadership in the White House is not ineffable but can be explained and assessed by using a consistent set of criteria to analyze presidential performance. The book argues that presidential leadership is exercised by real, flawed human beings, and not by superheroes or philosopher-kings beyond the reach of scrutiny or critique. By analyzing the leadership skills of five recent American presidents, the book intends to de-mystify the elements and dynamics of effective presidential leadership which our democracy has come to depend upon and value.

The analysis focuses on presidents who have served our nation since Watergate because of the author's strong view that that crisis precipitated monumental changes in the presidency, in Congress, and even in the media that cover the White House. The office that Jimmy Carter ascended to in 1977 was a substantially different one than the one Richard Nixon had inhabited from 1969–1974. Of course, a great many significant events had transpired between 1974 and 1976; however, more important than any particular event was the larger contextual transformation of the office itself, the "playing field" on which presidents were to exert leadership after Watergate had changed. Congress had become far more aggressive in its responsibilities of overseeing the executive branch of government and securing its rightful place within the founders' checks and balances system of government; the public had become more cynical, less trusting, of government in general and the presidency in particular; the judiciary had, perhaps experienced the accretion of its own powers and responsibilities to ensure the separation of powers among the three branches of government and the compliance of all branches with the rule of law; and the media, ever mindful of their identity as the "fourth branch of government" by many commentators, had increased their coverage of the presidency, incessantly searching for every possible act of imperfection or malfeasance in presidential behavior. As former President Gerald Ford famously observed, the "imperial" presidency had given way to the "imperiled" presidency.[1]

The book focuses on the strategies used by presidents since Watergate to overcome the Watergate legacy and create their own blueprint to lead the nation boldly into the future. The five men considered chose significantly different approaches stimulated, in the opinion of this author, less by the political party they represented than by their attitudes and capabilities along four dimensions of leadership:

(a) policy or vision—their goals and aspirations, the path forward they envisioned for the country;

(b) politics or strategy—their efficacy in translating their vision into reality through the staff they hired, their talent in negotiation and persuasion, and their ability to control an agenda;

(c) structure or management—their approach toward managing the White House and the executive branch, their preference for a "micro" or "macro" approach, the openness of their operation;

(d) process or decision-making—their ability to encourage dissenting opinions and listen actively to debate, while still making unambiguous decisions.

The core argument of the book is that effective presidents stay focused on a clear vision, in spite of temporary setbacks or failures. They surround themselves with talented people, professionals rather than friends, and give them the freedom they need to operate. They set up nimble and effective professionally run organizational structures. And they encourage conflict and dissenting opinions within their administrations as positive forces to help them make better decisions; nevertheless, they are not afraid of concluding ferocious internal debates by announcing clear and strong decisions. Of course, they also must be willing to examine the consequences of those decisions and make modifications along the way. Finally, effective presidents are not afraid to use power, but do they become intoxicated by it, as have the "imperial" presidents. Measured against the aforementioned criteria, at least two of the recent five presidents performed admirably in two or more categories, while two struggled in almost all categories.

The book argues that the success of the American polity in the 21st century and beyond is inextricably linked to the effectiveness of leadership in the White House. By examining the details of presidential leadership among our most recent presidents, the author hopes to familiarize students, voters, and

---

[1]Robert Dallek. **Hail to the Chief: The Making and Unmaking of American Presidents**, New York: Hyperion, 1996, Introduction. President Ford served from August 1974 (after Nixon's resignation) until January 1977.

political leaders with the strengths and weaknesses of recent presidents along four specific dimensions of leadership, and to suggest a model of presidential leadership for the future: one that is assertive, bold, daring, visionary, and effective; but one that also recognizes the inescapable constraints on presidential leadership imposed by our Constitution and by the checks and balances system of government that our founders created. Of course, the views expressed in this book are the author's personal views.

The author is indebted to the legions of undergraduate and graduate students who read and commented on earlier drafts of the manuscript; to Mr. Howard Goldblatt, a Washington DC lobbyist and former Congressional staffer who painstakingly reviewed every chapter and provided insightful and helpful commentary; to Ambassador Dennis Ross, a respected national security adviser and Middle East specialist in several recent administrations; to Mr. Ken Levine, who served as a high-level official in the Department of Health, Education and Welfare during the Carter Administration; to the staff of the Library of Congress, who are frequently unsung heroes to many scholars of this and other nations, in addition to ably serving members of Congress and their staffs; and mostly to his wife and daughter who tolerated endless family discussions of leadership and the presidents, faithfully attended the author's numerous lectures on the subject, and provided the kind of encouragement and sustenance that every author needs.

The author would like to express a special appreciation to his wife, Anne, the most courageous person on the face of the earth.

Introduction

The Presidency from the Beginning

T he presidency was created by a group of men "who had their fingers crossed," according to Professor Louis Koenig.[1] The professor's description of the founders' anxiety reveals the conflicting interests and objectives they had in creating the presidency. On the one hand, they wanted the president to lead the country with "energy," as Alexander Hamilton put it; on the other hand, they feared the return of a king. Indeed, the language of the Declaration of Independence contained attacks on the king himself for a "history of repeated injuries and usurpations, all having in direct object the establishment of an absolute tyranny over the states."

The fear of executive power was codified in early state constitutions. Pennsylvania, for example, had no chief executive at all, but entrusted a council of twelve popularly elected individuals to carry out selected executive functions. Except for New York, which provided for a stronger executive, the states made their executives weak and subordinate to the legislatures.[2]

On the national level, the fear of executive power manifested itself in the Articles of Confederation, the nation's first expression of a governing document adopted by the Continental Congress on November 15, 1777.[3] Under the Articles, there was no real executive power; supreme power was lodged in the hands of a congress of delegates from the states. The prevailing political culture in America during the early days of the republic was a distrust of concentrated power, particularly executive power, whether it was institutionalized in an elected office or a hereditary monarch.[4]

By 1787, however, leading thinkers and opinion makers had become disgruntled with what they perceived to be an abuse of power by aggressive

---

[1]Louis Koenig, *The Chief Executive*, 6th ed. (New York: Harcourt Brace, 1995), 1.

[2]Gary L. Gregg II, *Thinking about the Presidency: Documents and Essays from the Founding to the Present* (New York: Rowman and Littlefield Publishers, 2005), 4.

[3]Kenneth Janda, Jeffrey M. Berry, and Jerry Goldman, *The Challenge of Democracy: The Essentials*, 6th ed. (Boston: Houghton Mifflin, 1999), 64.

[4]Gregg, 4.

legislatures at the state level and an impotent government at the national level. James Madison wrote of the "legislative vortex" that had the tendency to suck all powers into it, whereas Thomas Jefferson in his "Notes on the State of Virginia" warned, "173 despots would surely be as oppressive as one."[5]

The absence of a strong executive was one reason, among others, for the failure of the Articles of Confederation. This scheme of government failed for at least four reasons:[6]

- The Articles of Confederation did not give the national government the power to tax, placing Congress in the awkward position of pleading for money from the states to pay for war debts and carry out the affairs of the new nation.
- The Articles made no provision for an independent leadership position to direct the government (the president was merely the presiding officer of the Congress).
- The Articles did not allow the national government to regulate interstate and foreign commerce. (When John Adams proposed that the confederation enter into a commercial treaty with Britain after the war, he was asked, "Would you like one treaty or thirteen, Mr. Adams?")
- The Articles could not be amended without the unanimous consent of all the state legislatures, giving each state the power to veto any changes to the confederation.

In short, once the Revolution had ended and independence was a reality, it was clear that the national government had neither the economic nor military power to function. The weaknesses of the government were further illustrated by the rebellion of debtors facing bankruptcy led by Daniel Shays, a Revolutionary War veteran. In 1786, Shays and his colleagues marched on a western Massachusetts courthouse with 1,500 supporters armed with barrel staves and pitchforks. They wanted to close the courthouse and prevent the foreclosure of farms by their creditors. Shays' Rebellion lasted for an entire year, until 1787. Massachusetts appealed to the confederation for assistance, and Congress approved a $530,000 requisition for the establishment of a national army. But the plan failed, as every state except Virginia rejected the call for money. In the end, the governor of Massachusetts called on the militia to restore order.[7]

Shays' Rebellion alarmed almost all American leaders, except for Thomas Jefferson, who delivered the following missive from Paris where he was serving as the American ambassador: "A little rebellion now and then is a good thing; the tree of liberty must be refreshed from time to time with the blood of patriots and tyrants."[8]

---

[5]Ibid.
[6]Janda et al., 65.
[7]Ibid.
[8]Ibid., 66.

Most political leaders were not persuaded by Jefferson's musings and turned their attention to constructing a stronger national government with an executive power. As Supreme Court Justice Robert H. Jackson observed some 150 years later, "While the Declaration of Independence was directed against an excess of authority, the Constitution (that followed the Articles of Confederation) was directed against anarchy."[9]

Fifty-five delegates arrived at the statehouse in Philadelphia to write a new constitution. For nearly four months, they debated many issues, including the nature of the executive branch. One proposal—the Virginia Plan—suggested an executive to consist of an unspecified number of people to be selected by the legislature for a single term.[10] Finally, however, the delegates agreed on a one-person executive who would be chosen by an electoral college.

Having no model on which to base their design, the framers created a presidency that was quite radical for the eighteenth-century world. According to Gary L. Gregg II, "Though we tend to take it for granted, to have an institution that would in some ways resemble a monarchy and yet would be limited in its power and influence and that would be elected periodically was something unheard of at the time."[11]

So what powers did the Constitution actually provide the president? The following is a summary of the executive article of the Constitution (Article II) and pertains to the conditions and terms of the office of the presidency, as well as the actual powers available to the president.

Section One of Article II spells out the *conditions and terms of office* as follows:

- The executive Power is vested in a President of the United States, and he will hold Office for a term of four years, along with the Vice President.
- Each state will appoint electors, in a manner determined by the legislature, and the number of electors will equal the number of Senators and Representatives that the state has in Congress. No Senator or Representative, however, may be an elector. The electors will choose the President and Vice President.
- Congress is to choose the actual day for the election.
- The eligibility criteria for election to the Presidency are that the candidate must be a natural born citizen of the United States, and 35 years of age.
- The Vice President will succeed the President in case of the Removal of the President from Office, or his death, Resignation, or Inability to discharge the Powers and Duties of the Office.
- The President's compensation (salary) may not be increased or diminished during his tenure.

---

[9]Robert H. Jackson, *The Struggle for Judicial Supremacy: A Study of a Crisis in American Power Politics* (New York: Alfred A. Knopf, 1941), 8.

[10]Janda et al., 67.

[11]Gregg, 5.

- The President, before he enters office, must take an oath to "preserve, protect, and defend the Constitution of the United States" (oath of affirmation).[12]

Section Two of Article II outlines the *powers of the office* of the president as follows:

- Commander-in-chief. The President shall be the commander-in-chief of the Army and Navy of the US, and of the militia of the several states when called into actual service of the US.
  He may require the opinions of officers in each executive department of government. And he has the right to grant reprieves and pardons for offenses against the US, except in Cases of Impeachment.
- Treaties and Appointment of Officers. The President has the power, with the advice and consent of the Senate, to make treaties (with two-thirds Senate concurrence) and to nominate and (with the advice and consent of the senate) appoint ambassadors, other public Ministers and Consuls, and Judges of the Supreme Court.
- Appointments during recess of the Senate. The President has the power to fill vacancies that may occur during a Senate recess by granting Commissions that expire at the end of the next session.
- Recommendations to Congress—Convene and Adjourn Congress—Receive Ambassadors—Execute laws. The President will deliver "from time to time" information on the state of the Union and recommend measures he judges are "necessary and expedient;" he may, on extraordinary occasions, convene both houses, or either of them; receive Ambassadors; take care that the laws be "faithfully executed" and commission officers of the US.
- Removal from Office. The President, Vice President and all civil Officers of the United States will be removed from Office on Impeachment for, Conviction of Treason, Bribery, or other high Crimes and Misdemeanors.[13]

Once the dust had settled, the commentary about the completed Constitution and presidential provisions began. At the Virginia ratifying convention, for instance, Governor Patrick Henry expressed the fears of some about the founders' creation of the presidency:

> This Constitution is said to have beautiful features but when I come to examine those features, Sir, they appear to me to be horribly frightful. Among other deformities it has an awful squinting; it squints toward monarchy, and does that not raise indignation in the breast of every American?[14]

---

[12]U.S. Constitution, Section One, Article II.

[13]U.S. Constitution, Section Two, Article II.

[14]Gregg, 8.

On the other hand, Alexander Hamilton, in the Federalist No. 70, refuted the allegations of "monarchy," and suggested that "energy" in the executive branch is a leading characteristic of good government. He added:

A feeble executive implies a feeble execution of the government. A feeble executive is but another phrase for bad execution; and a government ill executed, whatever it may be in theory, must be, in practice, a bad government.[15]

Whether or not the presidency, as created by the founders, had enough or too much power would be debated long after 1789. But there is no doubt that the office created in the late eighteenth century proved to be an imperfect guide for presidents who followed. The Constitution did not anticipate a civil war, two world wars, or a "cold war"; it did not anticipate a world saturated with nuclear weapons and other means of mass destruction; it could not envision a world transformed by global forces of transnational terrorism or environmental degradation. In this sense, as of this writing, it was the actions and decisions of the forty-three men who served in the office, building upon the pronouncements of the founders and philosophical insights of their contemporaries that primarily shaped the presidency.

THE EVOLUTION OF THE PRESIDENCY

During the more than 200 years of the presidency, the office grew far beyond the limitations imposed on it by the founders. In some cases, the accretion of power beyond those powers clearly delineated in the Constitution resulted from presidential responses to crises facing the county—including a civil war, imminent financial collapse, attacks on U.S. interests by foreign powers, and a myriad of other emergency situations.

One of the earliest examples of a president who was forced by circumstance to expand the powers of the presidency was Abraham Lincoln. When he entered the office in 1861, Lincoln faced the daunting challenge of the potential dissolution of the union. When Southern rebels fired on Fort Sumter in April 1861, Lincoln did not wait for Congress to return before taking steps to prevent the falling apart of the country. According to *Boston Globe* reporter Charles Savage, in his book, *Takeover: The Return of the Imperial Presidency and the Subversion of American Democracy*:

Without a declaration of war, Lincoln enlarged the Union Army and Navy, blockaded Southern ports, spent money not appropriated by Congress, and arrested Northerners suspected of being Southern agents without giving the legal rights—all exceeding the authority in federal law and the Constitution.[16]

---

[15]Ibid.

[16]Charles Savage, *Takeover: The Return of the Imperial Presidency and the Subversion of American Democracy* (New York: Little, Brown and Company, 2007), 17.

Lincoln acknowledged that his drastic steps were, in fact, outside of the constitutional framework of government. As soon as Congress reconvened, Lincoln asked for its authorization for his emergency actions, arguing they had been necessary to save the union.

Congress may have abided and even legitimated Lincoln's actions,[17] but the Supreme Court was emphatic in asserting that his actions should be viewed as a singular exception in American history, and not as a new definition of presidential power.[18] A year after the Civil War ended, the Supreme Court struck down a military tribunal Lincoln had used to prosecute Northern civilians, thereby limiting presidential power during an emergency. The Court's language in the case of *Ex Parte Milligan* (1866) is particularly instructive, and would be repeated in later years with other presidents:

> The Constitution of the United States is a law for rulers and people, especially in war and peace, and covers with the shield of protection all classes of men at all times, and under all circumstances. No doctrine involving more pernicious consequences was ever invented by the wit of man than that any of its provisions can be suspended during any of the great exigencies of government. Such a doctrine leads directly to anarchy or despotism.[19]

During the lugubrious days of the Great Depression, when unemployment in the United States reached higher than 25 percent of the working population and thirty-four states had closed their banks, influential voices in the United States, including columnist Walter Lippmann, called on newly elected President Franklin Delano Roosevelt to assume dictatorial powers.[20] Although Roosevelt eschewed pressures to assume "dictatorial" powers, he did not shy away from using a muscular approach to presidential leadership, including introducing far-reaching economic and social reform packages in the first hundred days of his presidency, establishing a committee on administration management (Brownlow Report) to provide more centralized administrative control by the White House over the executive branch of government,[21] and attempting to pack the Supreme Court with justices who would approve his programs.

As well, in 1940, President Roosevelt violated the recently enacted Neutrality Act by ordering the transfer of fifty U.S. Navy destroyers to Britain in exchange for the right to lease sites for naval bases. Roosevelt was responding to an entreaty from British Prime Minister Winston Churchill who notified the

---

[17]Matthew Crenson and Benjamin Ginsberg, *Presidential Power: Unchecked and Unbalanced* (New York: W.W. Norton and Company, 2008), 17.

[18]Savage, 17.

[19]Ibid.

[20]Jonathan Alter, *The Defining Moment: FDR's Hundred Days and the Triumph of Hope* (New York: Simon and Schuster, 2007), 5.

[21]Donald R. Brand, "The President as Chief Administrator: James Landis and the Brownlow Report," *Political Science Quarterly*, 123, no. 1 (Spring 2008), 70.

president that half of his country's destroyers had been lost and that Britain's capacity to protect its shipping from German U-boats was nearly defunct. Attorney General Robert Jackson argued that in spite of the apparent illegality of the exchange of destroyers for bases, Roosevelt's actions were sanctioned by his role as commander in chief. And in March 1941, Congress passed the Lend-Lease Act, which effectively ratified Roosevelt's actions.[22]

During the cold war between the United States and the Soviet Union, from 1945 to 1970, Congress actually added measures of power to the presidency through legislation enabling the president to lead the nation in the "containment" of Soviet powers; for instance, Congress passed the National Security Act of 1947 (Pub. L. 80-235, 1947), which substantially enhanced the president's leadership in the formulation and execution of national security policy by creating a single defense secretary responsible for all defense planning and the military budget. According to Crenson and Ginsberg, "By creating a more unified military chain of command and a single defense budget, the National Security Act diminished Congress's ability to intervene in military planning and increased the president's control over the armed services and national security policy."[23] The National Security Act also created the Central Intelligence Agency (CIA) and placed it under the direct supervision of the president. Presidents from 1947 to 1972 were more than happy to accept the elevated grants of power given to them by Congress and used these powers enthusiastically to protect the nation from communism.

Just as Congress empowered the presidency through legislation to conduct the "cold war," so too did Congress authorize President George W. Bush, within a week of the terrorist attacks of September 11, 2001, to "use all necessary and appropriate force against those nations, organizations, or persons he determines planned, authorized, committed or aided the terrorist attacks."[24]

Although this authorization for using military force was not a declaration of war, President Bush interpreted it as activating his full wartime powers as commander in chief, including the power to detain enemy combatants. Furthermore, claiming that the Taliban and al Qaeda were not entitled to procedural protections of the U.S. criminal justice system, nor to the humanitarian protections of the Geneva Conventions, the Bush administration asserted an entitlement to hold detainees indefinitely, to subject them to harsh methods of interrogation, and to try them in military commission instead of criminal courts.[25] These assertions by President Bush, in his pursuit of the "war on terror" and subsequently the war in Iraq, were challenged and in some cases reversed by the federal courts and to some extent modified by Congress. In a memorable quotation

---

[22]Crenson and Ginsberg, 224–225.

[23]Ibid., 248.

[24]Authorization for Use of Military Force against Terrorists, Pub. L. 107-40, 115 Stat. 224 (2001).

[25]Michael C. Dorf, "The Detention and Trial of Enemy Combatants: A Drama in Three Branches," *Political Science Quarterly*, 122, no. 1 (Spring 2007), 47.

from the U.S. Supreme Court case of *Hamdi v. Rumsfeld*, Justice Sandra Day O'Connor, writing for the majority, opined that, "A state of war is not a blank check for the President when it comes to the rights of the Nation's citizens."[26] In the Hamdi case, the Court decided that while the government could hold U.S. citizens in military custody, the Court would scrutinize the procedures used to determine whether someone is in fact an "unlawful combatant."[27]

The accumulation of presidential power also occurred because of the ambition, and even the feeling of grandiosity, held by some occupants of the office. Richard Nixon, who wanted to be the "architect of his times,"[28] took presidential power to entirely new heights, asserting that he knew the interests of the United States better than the public, Congress, and the courts, and that he could soar above all countervailing powers in protecting American interests both in Vietnam and domestically.[29]

Although the growth of presidential power was substantial, the acceptance of its growth by Congress, the courts, and the public was always tentative due to the details of U.S. constitutional framework. And yet, the expectations of presidential leadership and power became well established in the public mind. According to presidential scholar Fred Greenstein, "the president became the most visible landmark in the political landscape, virtually standing for the federal government in the minds of many Americans."[30] In their 2008 textbook, *Presidential Power: Unchecked and Unbalanced*, Johns Hopkins University political scientists Matthew Crenson and Benjamin Ginsberg assert, "Today whatever the travails of particular presidents, it is the presidency that dominates American government and politics."[31] In 1952, a period of relative tranquility, Supreme Court Justice Robert Jackson described the magnitude of the president's responsibilities as "the concentration of executive authority in a single head in whose choice the whole nation has a part, making him the focus of public hopes and expectations. In drama, magnitude and finality his decisions so far overshadow any others that almost alone he fills the public eye and ear."[32]

THE LIMITS OF PRESIDENTIAL POWER

Nonetheless, many presidents have expressed a different view on the actual exercise of power. In the words of President William Howard Taft, "The President cannot make clouds to rain, he cannot make the corn to grow, he

---

[26]*Hamdi v. Rumsfeld*, 542 U.S. 507, 569 (2004).

[27]Dorf, 51.

[28]Richard Reeves, *President Nixon Alone in the White House* (New York: Simon and Schuster, 2001), 14.

[29]Ibid.

[30]Fred I. Greenstein, *The Presidential Difference: Leadership Style from FDR to George Bush* (Princeton, NJ: Princeton University Press, 2004), 3.

[31]Crenson and Ginsberg, 9.

[32]Robert H. Jackson, *Youngstown Sheet & Tube Co. v. Sawyer*, 343 U.S. 579 (1952).

cannot make the business to be good."[33] Similarly, Thomas Jefferson opined that the presidential experience was a "splendid misery," and Andrew Jackson quipped that it was a "situation of dignified slavery."[34] A frustrated Lyndon Johnson once remarked, "The only power I've got is nuclear—and I can't use that."[35] Harry Truman, talking about Eisenhower, said, "He'll sit here and he'll say, 'Do this! Do that!' and *nothing will happen*. Poor Ike—it won't be a bit like the army. He'll find it very frustrating."[36]

Expressions of frustration on the part of past presidents underline the difficulty of leadership in the office. The challenges abound. First, as already discussed, the foundational design of the office was built on compromise, anxiety, and even reluctance. Rather than asserting the unequivocal need to "put someone in charge" of the government, the founders simply attempted to fix a structure where "no one was in charge" by assigning a modicum of leadership to a person they called president.

Furthermore, the founders, borrowing from the eighteenth-century French philosopher Baron de Montesquieu, insisted on the governing principle of "separation of powers," where no one branch of government would dominate the others. The executive, legislative, and judicial branches were meant to be equal and to keep one another in check, "ambition checking ambition," in the words of James Madison. In short, the president was to have "energy," but would be expected to operate in a collaborative leadership framework with Congress and the judiciary. In the area of foreign policy, for example, the approach of the founders to leadership was tantamount to "an invitation to struggle."[37] The president was given the role of commander in chief, but only Congress was allowed to declare war. The president could appoint ambassadors to represent U.S. interests in foreign countries, but his appointments required the "advice and consent" of Congress.

In addition, as the nation developed, political parties gained strength, as did powerful interest groups and, eventually, the media (known by some as a fourth branch of government). These forces would place yet more obstacles and limitations on presidential power.

In their well-regarded book, *The Paradoxes of the American Presidency*, Thomas Cronin and Michael Genovese observe that:

> We admire presidential power, yet fear it. We yearn for the heroic, yet are inherently suspicious of it. We demand dynamic leadership, yet grant only limited powers to the president. We want presidents to be

---

[33]Robert Dallek, *Hail to the Chief: The Making and Unmaking of American Presidents* (New York: Hyperion, 1996), Introduction.

[34]Ibid.

[35]"Lyndon Johnson: The Paradox of Power," *Time Magazine*, January 5, 1968.

[36]Richard E. Neustadt, *Presidential Power and the Modern President* (New York: Free Press, 1990), 9. Emphasis in original.

[37]Edward S. Corwin, *The President: Office and Powers*, 4th rev. ed. (New York: New York University Press, 1957), 171.

dispassionate analysts and listeners, yet they must also be decisive. We are impressed with presidents who have great self-confidence, yet we dislike arrogance and respect those who express reasonable self-doubt. We want leaders to be bold and innovative, yet we allow presidents to take us only where we want to go.[38]

Although compelling historical forces such as the Civil War, the Great Depression, World Wars I and II, and the Cold War contributed to the expansion of presidential powers, powerful forces during the 1960s and 1970s seemed almost to conspire to reduce presidential power and put the presidency back in check. In the wake of the Vietnam War, Congress passed legislation limiting the president's ability to sustain a long involvement in a foreign war absent the approval of Congress.[39] When specific details of Richard Nixon's abuse of presidential power during "Watergate" were revealed, Congress reacted again by limiting the president's ability to "impound" congressionally appropriated funds,[40] and gave itself a larger role in the formulation of budgetary policy in general.

According to historian Robert Dallek, the 1970s aftermath of Vietnam, which had driven Lyndon Johnson from power, and Watergate, which had compelled Richard Nixon's resignation, a theory arose about the "fragility of the American presidency."[41] The following book titles appeared: *The Tethered Presidency*, *The Post-Imperial Presidency*, and *The Impossible Presidency*. The impression arose of a "beleaguered and pathetic fellow sitting forlornly in the Oval Office, assailed by unprecedentedly intractable problems, paralyzed by the constitutional separation of powers, hemmed in by congressional and bureaucratic constraints, pushed one way and another by exigent interest groups, seduced, betrayed, and abandoned by the mass media."[42] In 1980, ex-President Gerald Ford said to general applause, "We have not an imperial presidency but an imperiled presidency."[43] And in 1996, former member of Congress and Defense Secretary (and future Vice President) Dick Cheney made the following statement at the awards ceremony for the Gerald R. Ford Foundation:

> I clearly do believe there have been times in the past, oftentimes in response to events such as Watergate and the War in Vietnam, where Congress has begun to encroach upon the powers and responsibilities of the President; that it was important to go back and try to restore the balance.[44]

---

[38]Thomas E. Cronin and Michael A. Genovese, *The Paradoxes of the American Presidency* (New York: Oxford University Press, 2004), 2.

[39]War Powers Act of 1973, Pub. L. 93-148, H.J. Res. 542 (1973).

[40]Congressional Budget and Impoundment Control Act of 1974, Pub. L. 93-344, 88 Stat. 297 (1974).

[41]Dallek, Introduction.

[42]Ibid.

[43]Ibid.

[44]Savage, 9.

In the aftermath of Vietnam and Watergate, Americans gazed at the White House with more skepticism than adoration, and Congress jealously guarded its powers vis-à-vis the presidency. The contemporary presidency, then, faces several obstacles to the exertion of leadership. The obstacles result from the perennial tensions in the exercise of power embedded in the founders' documents; from the recent history of the office, including the excesses of the "imperial presidency" of Richard Nixon (and to some extent Lyndon Johnson and perhaps even George W. Bush); and from the unrealistic expectations of Americans that a president can somehow ride into town on a white horse and in four years cure the nation of all its ills.[45]

HOW CAN PRESIDENTS LEAD EFFECTIVELY?

How do presidents overcome the obstacles to leadership and succeed in the exercise of power? The argument of this book is that they do so by mastering four key components of leadership. The components illustrate aspects of leadership that are not enunciated in the Constitution, but that constitute essential qualities of presidential job performance.

Building on the work of presidential scholar Fred Greenstein, who analyzed six qualities that influence presidential job performance,[46] this text focuses on four elements of leadership. The four components are chosen based on years of observation of presidential performance, twenty years of service in the federal government, and a model of the "strategic presidency" enunciated in a book by two veterans of the Carter administration titled, *Memorandum for the President: A Strategic Approach to Domestic Affairs in the 1980s*. The authors of this book, Ben W. Heineman Jr. and Curtis Hessler, served in high-level executive branch positions in the Carter administration—Heineman in the Department of Health, Education, and Welfare (subsequently the Department of Health and Human Services) and Hessler in the Department of the Treasury. Heineman and Hessler specify four core elements of a strategic approach to leadership in the White House, and this text has embellished their elements as follows:

policy—(vision), envisioned future, mission goals, objectives, purpose
politics—(strategy), persuasion, execution, implementation
structure—(management), internal organization, delegation, coordination
process—(decision making), conflict management, integrating diversity of
thought

Here is this book's central argument: Great position, including the presidency of the United States, sets up great potential for achievement, but does

---

[45]Hendrick Smith, *The Power Game: How Washington Works* (New York: Ballantine Books, 1998).

[46]Greenstein, 2004.

not guarantee it. Whereas a contemporary president enters an office of substantial power—according to Crenson and Ginsberg, it is "unchecked and unbalanced"—the obstacles to forceful leadership are formidable, and four years can pass by without significant presidential success.

A president can succeed, however, if he masters four aspects of leadership. He must enunciate a clear and compelling vision (policy); develop an implementation and influence strategy to execute his vision (politics); avail himself of an effective White House and cabinet management support system (structure); and employ effective decision-making techniques, including encouraging dissenting viewpoints, while managing conflict and arriving at clear, unambiguous decisions (process). Moreover, a president has to complete all of these activities while staying within the constitutional boundaries of his office. And he has to accomplish the four leadership functions quickly; according to Heineman and Hessler:

> A President has only four years to prove himself, less than that, actually since the campaign clock starts ticking well before the conclusion of his four-year term. It is important in this regard for the President to act quickly and decisively in pursuing policy objectives and redeeming campaign promises. If the President has a strong vision on what needs to be done he will be able to move things along, to shake the bureaucrats out of their complacency and the members of Congress out of their defensiveness and sell them all on a big cause.[47]

In short, a president has to develop a "strategy" of leadership that encompasses the four specified elements. The elements, or components, of presidential leadership work together in the following manner. (Each component of leadership will be detailed later.) When a president has a strong vision, he will be able to convey his policy objectives to the public and his own staff in a compelling manner; his staff will easily comprehend the president's priorities and channel their energy into the accomplishment of these goals; the president and White House staff will work hard to maintain control of their agenda, resisting the tendency of drift and internal, destructive personality conflicts; the president will organize the White House staff in a manner that supports the accomplishment of his vision and policy goals and provide adequate points of access and influence to his key staff members; and he will invite a diversity of views in the presidential decision-making process, but announce clear, unambiguous decisions. Of course, things will occasionally go off course, and the president must also utilize effective damage control techniques when necessary. Few presidents have been successful in all four areas of leadership, but some were. Abraham Lincoln, Franklin Delano Roosevelt, and Ronald Reagan in his first term are exemplars of success in all four areas of leadership. President George H.W. Bush provided strong leadership in the "politics" area, but came up short on "policy."

---

[47]Ben W. Heineman and Curtis A. Hessler, *Memorandum for the President: A Strategic Approach to Domestic Affairs in the 1980s* (New York: Random House, 1980), vi.

Jimmy Carter experienced difficulty in several aspects of leadership as defined here, and Bill Clinton showed significant achievement in "policy" and "politics," but proved wanting in the areas of "structure" and "process." Accordingly, we can also learn from the presidents who performed admirably in some aspects of leadership but failed in others.

The text will also suggest how the denouncement of the Nixon administration set the stage for the post-Watergate presidency, which is the reason for the selection of presidents who have served since Watergate. The book's major focus is a more in-depth comparison of the five most recent (post-Watergate) presidents—Jimmy Carter, Ronald Reagan, George H. W. Bush, Bill Clinton, and George W. Bush—along the specific dimensions of leadership adumbrated earlier: policy, politics, structure, and process. The analysis is driven not by partisan concern, but by the search for leadership acumen among the men who have served as president since Watergate. Hopefully, this analysis will also help students and American citizens generally sharpen their focus in estimating the potential abilities of candidates for the highest office in the land.

Policy (Vision)

The issue of "vision" is central to a president's objectives and goals.

> Questions a president or presidential candidate might ask under this component include:

- *Why am I running for office, anyway?*
- *Where do I want to lead the nation?*
- *What do I want to accomplish during the next four years?*
- *What are my most important goals or results? What is my purpose?*
- *How will my administration make a difference in the lives of American citizens?*
- *What do I want my legacy to be?*

"The first requirement of presidential leadership," according to historian Arthur Schlesinger Jr., "is to point the republic in one or another direction. This can be done only if the man in the White House possesses, or is possessed by, a vision of the ideal America."[48] In a very real sense, a visionary president can help to change the terms of political debate. In the words of historian Robert Dallek, "There is something almost magical in the mass appeal of presidents who are devoted to high-minded, broad-gauged purpose."[49]

Ray Smilor, author of the book *Daring Visionaries*, defined vision as, "the organizational sixth sense that tells us why we make a difference in the world."[50] Vision is a powerful instrument of presidential leadership because

---

[48]Arthur M. Schlesinger Jr., *The Imperial Presidency* (Boston: Mariner Books, 2004), 438.

[49]Dallek, Introduction.

[50]Ray Smilor, *Daring Visionaries: How Entrepreneurs Build Companies, Inspire Allegiance, and Create Wealth* (Cincinnati, OH: Adams Media Corporation, 2001), 12.

it helps a president clarify his purpose, goals, and most important priorities. Vision helps provide focus to presidential staff members and allows them to concentrate their energy and prevent drift. In the absence of a strong vision, a president will be pushed and pulled in a thousand directions; he will become the object of the political process, not its master. The president must control his agenda, enunciate clear priorities, and energetically focus on the execution of those goals as intimated in the aforementioned words of Alexander Hamilton.

George Washington, the nation's first president, demonstrated an embrace of vision when he assumed the office. Although few men began their presidency with more prestige than Washington,[51] no president entered an equally undefined office. From his behavior and decisions, it is clear that Washington understood the impact his actions would have in setting a precedent and creating a vision of how government would "administer national affairs for the foreseeable future."[52] President Washington also displayed a strong dedication to the vision of republican government, never losing sight of the fact that his legitimacy derived from the consent of the governed.[53] He showed an appreciation for the importance of his action to later generations, as reflected in the following statement:

> Many things which appear of little importance in themselves and at the beginning may have great durable consequences from their having been established at the commencement of a new general government. It will be much easier to commence the administration, upon a well adjusted system, built on tenable grounds, than to correct errors or alter inconveniences after they have been confirmed by habit.[54]

Showing strong determination for assertive leadership, Washington avoided, at all costs, "indecision, ambiguity, and vacillation" as undermining popular confidence in the competence of government. He also aimed to show his contemporaries that "the head of state can be powerful without endangering liberty."[55] President Washington adopted a methodical approach to decision making,[56] intervened actively in issues that were of importance to him, and demonstrated clear understanding that "successful presidential leadership greatly depended on a vision of purpose, which was necessary to inspire and unify a newly formed country divided by competing impulses that could have torn it apart."[57]

---

[51]Joseph J. Ellis, *His Excellency: George Washington* (New York: Vintage Books, 2005), 188.

[52]Dallek, 11.

[53]Ellis, 189.

[54]Dallek, Introduction.

[55]Ibid.

[56]Fred I. Greenstein, "The Presidential Difference in the Early Republic: The Highly Disparate Leadership Styles of Washington, Adams, and Jefferson," *Presidential Studies Quarterly*, 36, no. 3 (September 2006), 373–390.

[57]Dallek, 12.

President Abraham Lincoln confronted a nation that was literally tearing itself apart, but he had a strong vision of saving the union and ending slavery. He would not be dislodged from these beliefs, no matter how many crises he confronted during his years in office. They formed his core ideology and animated his presidency. Lincoln's dedication to saving the union and to ending slavery related to his profound belief in republican government. His strong vision helped clarify his purpose and helped mobilize his energy, and those around him, to the accomplishment of specific objectives. His vision also helped him deal with the persistent and numerous personality conflicts among his cabinet members and generals. Lincoln's vision helped him orbit around mission, not around ego.[58] With regard to the office of the president in particular, "He possessed an acute understanding of the sources of power inherent in the presidency, an unparalleled ability to keep his governing coalition intact, a tough-minded appreciation of the need to protect his presidential prerogatives and a natural sense of timing."[59]

President Franklin Delano Roosevelt, while demonstrating great flexibility and pragmatism, also reflected a strong vision born of the needs of America during the Great Depression. Roosevelt's visionary innovation helped to change the terms of the political debate in Washington. In his view, "government owed a definite obligation to prevent the starvation or other dire wants of its citizens."[60] And in terms of the presidency, he established the principle that action to help ordinary people was a part of the presidential job description.[61] President Lyndon Baines Johnson displayed vision when he called on America to overcome years of racial intolerance and hatred and to provide equal opportunities to all Americans. At a 1965 Howard University ceremony, Johnson reflected his vision of a highly active federal government when he said, "It is not enough for us to open up the gates of opportunity; we must push people through those gates." Johnson acted on his beliefs in the war on poverty—when he took office in 1964, 22.2 percent of Americans lived in poverty. When he left, only 13 percent were living below the poverty line—the greatest one-term poverty reduction in U.S. history.[62]

President Ronald Reagan also possessed a strong vision, in his case the vision related to cutting taxes, cutting social welfare spending, and increasing defense spending. His surpassing vision was a nation whose economy would be more robust once rid of the shackles of taxation and costly welfare spending, and a nation that would dare to lead the fight against the "evil empire"

---

[58]Ira Chaleff, *The Courageous Follower: Standing Up To and For Our Leaders* (San Francisco: Berret-Koehler, 1995).

[59]Doris Kearns Goodwin, *Team of Rivals: The Political Genius of Abraham Lincoln* (New York: Simon and Schuster, 2005), Introduction.

[60]Alter, 91.

[61]Ibid., 92.

[62]Joseph A. Califano Jr., "The Price of Forgetting a President," *Washington Post*, May 31, 2008, A13.

of communism. Reagan's vision helped him mobilize the energy of his staff to lobby Congress with great dexterity and focus. Though a Republican, Reagan was ultimately effective at persuading a Democratic House of Representatives to go along with many of his policy initiatives. In a May 26, 2008, issue of the *New Yorker*, author George Packer quotes Princeton historian Sean Willenz on Reagan's impact:

> Reagan learned how to seize and keep control of public debate. On taxes, race, government, spending, national security, crime, welfare and "traditional values," he made mainstream what had been the positions of the right wing fringe, and he kept Democrats on the defensive.[63]

If a president lacks a strong vision, he will be tossed around by events, pulled and tugged by powerful interest groups and congressional leaders, and paralyzed by the inevitable personality conflicts among his own staff members. President George H. W. Bush spoke mockingly of the "vision thing," and did not truly articulate a guiding vision for his administration. President Carter oriented his political campaigns around philosophical themes, such as honesty and integrity in government, but did not really articulate a compelling vision for Americans. In many respects, Carter campaigned on what he was and not on what he would do! As one journalist put it, "Carter seems to stand for everything and believe in nothing."[64] According to former New York City Mayor Rudy Giuliani, "Great leaders lead by ideas. . . . The people who work for you, those who look to you for answers, the media, even your rivals have a right to know how you see the world."[65]

Politics (Strategy, Political Savvy)

"Politics" captures the leader's ability to transform vision into reality, to get things done. As Mario Cuomo (former governor of New York) often says, "You can campaign in poetry, but you must govern in prose."[66]

There are several relevant questions a president must ask here:

- *How will I implement or execute my vision, my program?*
- *Upon whom will I rely to communicate my message?*
- *Who will manage congressional relations?*
- *What strategy will I use to influence the opposition party, or even members of my own party who may have their own political agendas?*
- *How will I lead or manage the executive branch of government of some 2 million people?*

---

[63]George Packer, "The Fall of Conservativism," *New Yorker*, May 26, 2008, 49.

[64]David Gergen, *Eyewitness to Power: The Essence of Leadership, Nixon to Clinton* (New York: Simon and Schuster, 2000), 167.

[65]Rudolph W. Giuliani, *Leadership* (New York: Hyperion Books, 2004), 171.

[66]Drum Major Institute for Public Policy, "Campaign in Poetry, Govern in Prose," http://www.dmiblog.com/archives/2007/09/campaign_in_poetry_govern_in_p.html, accessed June 17, 2009.

- *How will I work with the media?*
- *How will I stay true to my agenda, fulfill my campaign promises, and still have time to reflect and assess what I am doing?*
- *How many issues will I tackle at one time?*

Condoleezza Rice, who served as President George W. Bush's national security adviser and secretary of state, summed up the importance of "politics" in an interview with Richard Haass in 1994. At that time, Rice was the provost at Stanford University. She said, "You don't have a policy unless you can get it done. You can have the best policy in the world on paper; it can be intellectually beautiful and elegant, but if you can't get it done, it never happened."[67]

There are two critical aspects of "politics" for a president to master: the details of implementation and the "retail politics" or persuasion aspects of the job. First, the president must understand the requirements of policy implementation. A president cannot get things done alone. As Dwight Eisenhower observed at the end of his two-term presidency:

> The government of the United States has become too big, too complex, too pervasive in its influence for one individual to pretend to direct all the details of its important and critical programming. Competent assistants are mandatory; without them the Executive Branch would bog down. To command the loyalties and dedication and best efforts of capable and outstanding individuals requires patience, understanding, a readiness to delegate, and an acceptance of responsibility for any honest errors—real or apparent—those subordinates might make.[68]

A president relies on the other parts of the executive branch to implement his programs. President Harry Truman's commitment to recognizing the state of Israel in 1948 was made in a commitment to Chaim Weizmann, the future president of that country, that he would support partition. Truman was alarmed to learn that the American ambassador to the United Nations had voted for a UN trusteeship. Enraged, Truman wrote a note on his calendar that said, "The State Department pulled the rug from under me today . . . I'm now in the position of a liar and a double-crosser. I've never felt so low in my life." Truman's belief in recognizing Israel as the right thing to do, supported by his counselor Clark Clifford, was being undermined by third- and fourth-level bureaucrats at the Department of State (especially the director of UN Affairs, Dean Rusk, and the agency's counselor Charles Bohlen). It was also being opposed by the formidable "wise men" of the American foreign policy establishment—including George Marshall, James Forrestal, George Kennan, and Dean Acheson, who were looking at the practical matters of oil, numbers, and history. "There are 30 million Arabs on one side and about 600,000 Jews on the other," Defense

---

[67]Richard N. Haass, *The Power to Persuade: How to be Effective in Government, the Public Sector, or Any Unruly Organization* (New York: Houghton Mifflin, 1994), 52.

[68]Heineman and Hessler, 4.

Secretary Forrestal told Clark Clifford. "Why don't you face up to reality?" Through his persistence, and absolute dedication to the rightness of the decision to recognize Israel, and with Clifford's assistance, Truman prevailed; however, it was not accomplished through a simple presidential command.[69]

In a more recent example of the importance of policy implementation, once again demonstrating the president's inability to act alone, President George W. Bush experienced frustration in implementing his human rights vision. In a June 2007 speech in Prague (Czech Republic), Bush vowed to order U.S. ambassadors in unfree nations to meet with dissidents and lauded the fact that he had created a fund to help embattled human rights defendants. Nevertheless, the State Department never sent out a cable instructing ambassadors to sit down with dissidents until two months later. As of August 2007, not a penny had been spent on the program.[70]

We can glean an insight into the idea of bureaucratic defiance to the president through the following discussion between a Bush administration staff member and a State Department official shortly after Bush's Prague speech:

> **Bush Administration Staffer:** "It's our policy" (support of dissidents)
> **State Department Official:** "What do you mean?"
> **Bush Administration Staffer:** "Read the President's speech."
> **State Department Official:** "Policy is not what the president says in speeches. Policy is what emerges from interagency meetings."[71]

The second aspect of "politics" relates to a president's facility with persuasion and with "retail politics." For example, President Ronald Reagan displayed great dexterity in the art of persuasion, as he worked tirelessly in 1981–1982 to secure passage of his conservative political agenda in a Democratic-controlled House of Representatives. Reagan relied heavily on Washington insiders, including his Chief of Staff James Baker and Congressional Liaison Max Friedersdorf.

Reagan's legislative team met for long periods around a conference table in Chief of Staff James Baker's office, hammering out details of how to get key legislation tied up and passed on Capitol Hill.[72] They addressed important persuasion questions, such as Who needed to be stroked in Congress? How? With what arguments? What interest groups needed to be mobilized? To pressure whom? How should the issue be framed for the press? What columnist needed special attention? What must the president do? Can members of the cabinet take some of the load?

---

[69]Richard Holbrooke, "Washington's Battle over Israel's Birth," *Washington Post*, May 7, 2008, A21.

[70]Peter Baker, "As Democracy Push Falters, Bush Feels Like a 'Dissident'," *Washington Post*, August 20, 2007, A1.

[71]Ibid.

[72]Lou Cannon, *President Reagan: The Role of a Lifetime* (New York: Simon and Schuster, 1991), 182.

The Reagan team displayed a legislative acumen that was absent from the Carter administration. Reagan's team was completely dedicated to their cause, but also understood the importance of the interests of those they were trying to convince, and tailored their persuasive appeals accordingly. Carter's team believed that the justness of the cause itself, which was never totally clear to begin with, would help the president prevail.

In an interesting exchange with House Speaker Tip O'Neill, an old-style Democratic politician whose basic instinct was to help a Democratic president, President Carter explained how he "handled the Georgia legislature by going over their heads directly to the people." O'Neill replied, "Hey wait a minute—you have 289 guys up there [House Democrats] who know their districts pretty well. They ran against the Administration and they wouldn't hesitate to run against you." Carter replied, "O really!"[73]

Negotiating, bargaining, influencing, building coalitions, enlisting the support of competent people—all of these are requisite skills of a successful strategic president. According to political scientists Robert Dahl and Charles Lindblom in their classic text, *Politics, Economics, and Welfare*, "Because he is a bargainer, a negotiator, the politician does not often give orders. He can rarely employ unilateral controls. Even as a chief executive or a cabinet official he soon discovers that his control depends on his skill in bargaining."[74]

Structure (Management)

Structure is setting up an effective organizational structure: an efficient White House operation.

Questions a president might ask under this component include:

- *How will I organize the White House?*
- *What management structure will I utilize?*
- *Will I have a chief of staff?*
- *Will I have an open or closed operation?*
- *Will I favor micro or macro management of White House staff?*
- *How will I assure the alignment of the management with my policy agenda?*

There is nothing in the Constitution that mandates an organizational structure for the presidency. Presidents have wide latitude in the kind of management design they choose, and, as of this writing, the forty-three men who have served in the office have certainly taken full advantage of this flexibility. One of the fundamental choices a president must make, for example, is whether to have a chief of staff. President Jimmy Carter decided against including a

---

[73]Betty Glad, *Jimmy Carter: In Search of the Great White House* (New York: W.W. Norton and Company, 1980), 420.

[74]Robert A. Dahl and Charles E. Lindblom, *Politics, Economics, and Warfare* (New York: Harper and Row, 1953), 333–334.

chief of staff in his White House initially, but was persuaded to add the position later in his administration.[75] Carter believed that he could replace the traditional White House hierarchy with a "spokes of the wheel" management structure—the president at the center of the wheel and the spokes radiating in and out with great ease. He favored a management style that political scientist Edwin Hargrove described as "collective collegiality."[76] But the loose structure proved problematic, enabling cabinet members to articulate public positions that were actually at odds with administration proposals and to initiate meetings with individuals with whom Carter had not authorized contact.[77]

The importance of the chief-of-staff position is aptly illustrated in the transition between the first and second Reagan administrations. In the first Reagan administration, James Baker served President Reagan deftly and even protected the president from his own blind spots.[78] In deciding to replace Baker with Donald Regan as chief of staff during the second term, however, President Reagan clearly underestimated the impact this would have on his presidency.

To amplify Reagan's blind spot in this instance, he casually and spontaneously accepted a proposal that Donald Regan (his first-term treasury secretary) and James Baker (his first-term chief of staff) change jobs. Baker was attracted to the switch because he knew it would place him at the center of Reagan's continuing interest in cutting taxes and also provide him more access to foreign policy decisions. For his part, Regan liked the idea of becoming chief of staff, because it would place him at the very core of power and give him increased access to the president.[79] But these men were not the same, and the change amounted to a breakup of the team that had been largely responsible for Reagan's first-term success.[80] As Lou Cannon explains:

> No presidency has ever undergone such a thoroughgoing transformation in management as Reagan's did under his new chief of staff, Donald T. Regan. Where Baker was collegial, Regan was directive. Where Baker was cautious, Regan was bold. Baker preferred to operate behind the scenes, forging a political consensus and framing it in terms that Reagan could endorse. Regan charged ahead, dismissing arguments he disagreed with as readily as he had dismissed contrary opinions at Merrill-Lynch.[81]

Baker and his deputy chief of staff Michael Deaver had been particularly protective of Reagan to a fault, always sensitive to the possibility of self-inflicted wounds. Reagan had some serious blind spots, as most leaders do, and Baker was

---

[75]Greenstein, 2004, 7.

[76]Erwin Hargrove, *Jimmy Carter as President: Leadership and the Politics of the Public Good* (Baton Rouge: Louisiana State University Press, 1988), 24.

[77]Glad, 449.

[78]Cannon.

[79]Ibid., 557–559.

[80]Ibid.

[81]Ibid., 561.

willing to confront his boss as a "courageous follower."[82] But Donald Regan had been groomed mostly in the private sector and was unskilled in the arts of diplomacy and retail politics. He expressed surprise, for instance, about the fact that Baker would consistently return phone calls and did not understand that "strong political capital in Washington is as important as accumulating financial assets on Wall Street, and he had no resources to draw upon when crises struck."[83]

Process (Decision Making)

This dimension of leadership relates to the methods a president uses to make and announce decisions. The leader must consider whether he wants a great diversity of opinion, or a more narrowly drawn range of options. The following questions are relevant to decision making:

- *How will I make and announce decisions?*
- *Will I deliberately encourage dissenting opinions?*
- *How will I handle conflict among my own advisers?*
- *How will I apply "damage control" when needed?*

In the spring of 2005, President George W. Bush described the office he held as follows: "It is a decision-making job, when you're dealing with a future president, you ought to say, 'How do you intend to make decisions? What is the process by which you will make large decisions and small decisions? How do you decide?' "[84] A year later, he described himself as the "decider."

Decision making is central to presidential job performance and presidents need to develop processes, techniques, and strategies for effectiveness in this area. One vital aspect of effective decision making is the president's interest in hearing a diversity of views. The research on "group-think," about how groups can quickly form the illusion of consensus and block out any dissenting opinions, has been applied to presidential decision making by psychologist Irving Janis. Janis uses the Bay of Pigs incident to illustrate the dangers of group-think.[85] In that case, Kennedy's advisers were much too quick to reinforce the president's notion that we could "liberate" Cuba by sending in U.S. troops and fomenting a "revolution" against Castro. Realizing that mistakes had been made in the decision-making processes of the Bay of Pigs incident, President Kennedy took specific measures to ensure that there would be an open and honest debate among members of the Executive Committee during the Cuban Missile Crisis; one measure he took was to leave the room during various stages of the Committee's deliberations.[86]

---

[82]Chaleff.

[83]Cannon, 567.

[84]Alexis Simendinger, "Bush's 'Aha' Moments," *National Journal*, July 23, 2005, 2358.

[85]Irving L. Janis, *Groupthink: Psychological Studies of Policy Decisions and Fiascoes* (Boston: Houghton Mifflin, 1982).

[86]Robert F. Kennedy, *Thirteen Days: A Memoir of the Cuban Missile Crisis* (New York: W.W. Norton and Company, 1999).

President Kennedy had learned an important lesson from the Bay of Pigs fiasco: that many, even most, presidential advisers will give the president the advice they think he wants to hear, not the advice he needs. Most people want to please their boss.

It is equally clear that the boss, in this case the president of the United States, can have great influence on the ability of his aides to express diverse opinions. A president can actively solicit diverse points of view, consider them seriously, and then reach a clear decision. Kennedy did this in the Cuban Missile Crisis and Lincoln did it during the Civil War.[87]

Alternatively, a president can signal impatience with dissenting views and seek closure on issues prematurely. One example of this tendency in presidential decision making is the decision by George W. Bush to introduce a massive tax cut in his first administration. During the 2000 campaign for president, Bush had promised to cut taxes, and he meant to deliver on that promise quickly and unambiguously. Early in his first term, he proposed a $1.6 trillion tax cut over ten years that included reducing the top brackets, eliminating the estate tax, reducing the marriage penalty, and increasing child credits.[88] Democrats objected to the plan, but following rounds of negotiations, the Senate and House eventually agreed on a cut of $1.35 trillion, amounting to a significant victory for Bush.[89]

As the president's proposal was making its way through the scrutiny of his own advisers, however, Paul O'Neill, secretary of treasury, and Alan Greenspan, chairman of the Federal Reserve Board, raised concerns about the extent of the cuts. O'Neill and Greenspan feared that Bush was making unduly optimistic assumptions about the extent of the budget surplus over the next ten years, and underestimating the potential ripple effects on the economy of a tax cut this large, particularly its potentially negative effect on the deficit.[90] O'Neill was publicly less enthusiastic about the size of the Bush tax cuts, and there was growing concern in the administration about his loyalty to the president. In a one-on-one conversation with President Bush in O'Neill's office, the treasury secretary laid out his concerns and ideas about the tax cut. Bush responded by saying, "I won't negotiate with myself. It's that simple."[91] In short, the decision had been made, and the time for discussion had ended in the mind of the president. He was no longer open to dissenting opinion. This tendency to close off debate—in service of being a "decider"—would hurt Bush in many aspects of his presidency, including the War in Iraq.[92]

---

[87]Goodwin.

[88]James P. Pfiffner, "Introduction: Assessing the Bush Presidency," in Gary L. Gregg II and Mark J. Rozell II, eds., *Considering the Bush Presidency* (New York: Oxford University Press, 2004), 4.

[89]Ibid.

[90]Ron Suskind, *George W. Bush, the White House, and the Education of Paul O'Neill* (New York: Simon and Schuster, 2004), 38–51.

[91]Ibid., 117.

[92]Bob Woodward, *Plan of Attack* (New York: Simon and Schuster, 2004).

By the end of his two terms, the federal deficit had mushroomed to almost $400 billion, and the War in Iraq was considered highly unpopular. It is possible that Bush would have arrived at better decision had he been more open to dissenting views.

In the case of Iraq, the dissenting view was expressed forcefully by Secretary of State Colin Powell. In a private meeting with the president, Secretary Powell expressed his concerns about the imminent war in Iraq:

> Don't let yourself get pushed into anything until you are ready for it or until you think there's a real reason for it. This is not as easy as it is being presented, and take your time on this one. Don't let anybody push you into it. You are going to be the proud owner of 25 million people. You will own all their hopes, aspirations, and problems. (Privately Powell called this the Pottery Barn rule: You break it, you own it.) It's going to suck the oxygen out of everything. This will become the first term. Iraq has a history that is quite complex. The Iraqis never had a democracy. So you need to understand that this is not going to be a walk in the woods.[93]

Presidential aides must summon the courage to give their boss honest and direct advice, as articulated by Ira Chaleff in a compelling book titled, *The Courageous Follower: Standing Up To and For Our Leaders* (1995). Chaleff argues that we all serve our bosses more effectively by telling them the truth, and not by currying favor through deceit or half-truths.

Dean Acheson served as secretary of state under President Harry Truman, and he described the sort of relationship needed as follows:

> It is important that the relations between the President and the Secretary of State be quite frank, sometimes to the point of being blunt. And you just have to be deferential. He is the President of the United States, and you don't say rude things to him—you say blunt things to him. Sometimes he doesn't like it. That's natural, but he comes back, and you argue the thing out. But that's your duty. You don't tell him only what he wants to hear. That would be bad for him and everyone else.[94]

With these four aspects of presidential leadership in mind, subsequent chapters of this text will assess the performance of four recent presidents to derive "lessons" of leadership. But first a review of the Nixon presidency and its demise will set the context for the presidents who served full terms after Watergate.

---

[93]Ibid.

[94]Haass, 80.

Richard Nixon, Watergate, and the Transformation of the Presidency

R ichard Nixon wanted to be the "architect of his times," according to Elliot Richardson, who held three cabinet posts under Nixon and resigned from the last one instead of following Nixon's orders to dismiss a Watergate special prosecutor.[1] Though he possessed the intellectual power and strategic insight to be an architect, Nixon did not possess many of the traits normally associated with successful politicians. Remarkably, he was uncomfortable with people and in groups and was "in his element, alone with his yellow pad and thoughts."[2] Nixon sometimes referred to himself as an "introvert in an extrovert's business."[3] Political science professor James David Barber, author of the pioneering book, *The Presidential Character*, said that, "In essaying Nixon's personal style the easiest place to begin is with the elimination of personal relations as a primary focus of his energy in adapting to political roles."[4]

Indeed, Nixon, who ascended to the presidency in January 1969, structured the White House and the executive branch of government in ways that reinforced his preference for isolation and his predilection for centralized power. For instance, only four people had walk-in access to the Oval Office,[5] and anyone else, including his cabinet secretaries, who sought an audience with the president would have to arrange an appointment through Nixon's chief of staff, Bob Haldeman.[6] The culture of isolation had many costs, however; according to Nixon's biographer Richard Reeves, "In the beginning the idea was to make the President's world secure from outsiders; in the end, even the insiders themselves could no longer penetrate the reality."[7]

Nixon considered himself an outsider to the political (and social) Establishment, in spite of the fact that he had been a naval officer, Duke Law School graduate, a member of Congress, Wall Street lawyer, and vice president of the United States.[8] He believed that the executive branch of government—that sprawling mass of about 3 million government employees who toil in huge cabinet agencies—opposed him, because, after all, it had been in the clutches of Democratic presidents for twenty-eight of the previous thirty-six years.[9] Accordingly, Nixon felt he needed to protect himself and his ambitions by shoring up power in the White House, and placing his loyalists in the executive departments to tame the existing employees.

In campaigning for the presidency in the tumultuous year of 1968, Richard Nixon promised to "bring us together" and to restore a sense of law and order

---

[1]Richard Reeves, *President Nixon: Alone in the White House* (New York: Simon and Schuster, 2001), 14.

[2]Ibid.

[3]Ibid., 11.

[4]Ibid., 140.

[5]Ibid., 125.

[6]Ibid., 31.

[7]Ibid., 5.

[8]Ibid., 51.

[9]Andrew Rudalevige, *The New Imperial Presidency* (Ann Arbor: University of Michigan Press, 2005), 60.

to a country that was, in many respects, "coming apart at the seams."[10] The lingering war in Vietnam, the persistence of racism and discrimination against minority groups in the United States, and the clamoring of women for equality and liberation were contributing to a mood of fundamental challenge to the status quo. In 1969, there were 602 bombings or bombing attempts in the United States; in 1970, there were 1,577. Many of these cataloged bombings occurred on college campuses, and in the spring of 1969 alone, over 300 colleges experienced demonstrations.[11] In the fall of 1970, Boston University had to evacuate buildings on 80 occasions because of bomb threats, and 175 threats were made at Rutgers University that same year.[12]

During the 1968 campaign, Nixon had repeatedly promised to do something about the lawlessness and to get tough with political extremists, criminals, and black and other ethnic militants. Early in his administration, on February 27, 1969, he wrote to the president of Notre Dame University about the "small irresponsible minority" of students with "an impatience with democratic processes, and intolerance of legitimately constituted authority, and a complete disregard for the rights of others."[13] Less publicly, the president ordered the intensification of the activities of the Central Intelligence Agency (CIA), Federal Bureau of Investigation (FBI), National Security Agency (NSA), and military intelligence to monitor and harass campus radicals.[14] This proclivity for surveillance and suppression would permeate Nixon's White House operations for years to come.

And yet, in his 1969 inaugural address, Nixon laid out a more moderate, conciliatory vision. As the gathering forces of violence and frustration enveloped larger numbers of campuses and attracted greater amounts of media attention, Nixon called on Americans to "lower our voices." He delivered the following words of reconciliation:

> In these difficult years, America has suffered from a furor of words; from inflated rhetoric that promises more than it can deliver; from angry rhetoric that fans discontents into hatreds . . . We cannot learn from one another until we stop shouting at one another—until we speak quietly enough so that our words can be heard as well as our voices.
>
> For its part, government will listen. We will strive to listen in new ways to the voices of quiet anguish, the voices that speak without words, the voices of the heart—to the injured voices, the anxious voices, the voices that have despaired of being heard. Those who have been left out, we will try to bring in.[15]

---

[10]Melvin Small, *The Presidency of Richard Nixon* (Lawrence: University Press of Kansas, 1999), 157.

[11]Ibid.

[12]Ibid.

[13]Ibid., 158.

[14]Ibid.

[15]"Inaugural Address. January 20, 1969," in *Public Papers of the Presidents of the United States, Richard Nixon, 1969* (Washington, D.C.: U.S. Government Printing Office, 1971), 2.

Nixon had also campaigned against President Lyndon Baines Johnson's Great Society programs of the 1960s. He promised a smaller, less intrusive government. His rhetorical assault on the growth of the "Washington bureaucracy," especially the proliferation of welfare and poverty programs, resonated with many Americans.[16] On the other hand, the Democrats had maintained control of Congress, which made it hard for Nixon to dismantle the Great Society, although he could help scale it back.

But Nixon also antagonized conservative Republicans, who were never totally secure with him in the first place, when he proposed a guaranteed annual wage for poor Americans, which was presented as "welfare reform." And when he proposed several programs that placed him in the middle of the road, he was called an Eisenhower, and even a Rockefeller, Republican.[17] Nixon hired Daniel Patrick Moynihan, a Democrat and Harvard professor, to head up his Council for Urban Affairs. Nixon suggested to Moynihan that he (Nixon) was a conservative social reformer in the tradition of Benjamin Disraeli.[18] Together they concocted a Family Assistance Plan (FAP) and announced it in August 1969 in a presidential address that also dealt with job training, revamping of the Office of Economic Opportunity, and a revenue salary proposal under the umbrella concept of a "new federalism."[19] The plan amounted to a national income of $1,600 a year plus a food stamp allotment for a family of four.[20] The states would be allowed to supplement, allowing a family of four to secure a combined income of $3,900 in wages and FAP support. This proposal would have made 1.3 million more Americans eligible for federal aid. Nevertheless, his plan drew strong opposition from conservative Republicans (who thought it was overly generous) and from liberal Democrats (who thought it was stingy). In addition, Nixon failed to consult with congressional leaders in advance of introducing the legislation.[21] Subsequently, the Senate Finance Committee revived the idea and sent the legislation back to the White House with instructions to the president to increase benefits for poor families. Nixon, however, had lost his enthusiasm. Still, Congress approved a revised version of the FAP in October 1972, thereby introducing the supplemental security income (SSI) to people who were blind and disabled and could not find work. The 6.2 million citizens eligible for this aid became the first recipients, aside from veterans, of federally guaranteed unions.[22]

Nixon's approach to welfare policy typified many of his other policy approaches, which were described by biographer Melvin Small as schizophrenic.[23]

---

[16]Small, 185.

[17]Ibid.

[18]Reeves, 45.

[19]Small, 88.

[20]Ibid.

[21]Ibid.

[22]Ibid., 189.

[23]Ibid., 162.

For instance, the president believed in ending legal segregation but opposed forced school integration. He was a life member of the National Association for the Advancement of Colored People (NAACP), and as vice president (under Eisenhower) he had invited Martin Luther King Jr. to the White House. He had also opposed the poll tax and supported anti-lynching laws.[24] But in private, he referred to African Americans, as he did to Jewish Americans, in disparaging terms.[25]

His real love, however, was foreign policy, and in this realm he was more consistent and more strategic. Nixon once mused that domestic policy could run itself, but that the president was vitally needed to provide leadership in foreign policy. And leadership he did provide. Nixon began a policy of détente with the USSR and an opening of diplomatic contacts with the People's Republic of China.[26] But he was also persistent in continuing the Vietnam War. He believed that he could not simply abandon the South Vietnamese.

To help him accomplish his great strides forward in American foreign policy, Nixon centralized the formulation and execution of foreign policy under National Security Adviser Henry Kissinger. The opening of contacts with China, the Vietnamization program, and détente with the USSR were run out of the National Security Council (NSC), not from the State Department. During the first Nixon administration, the NSC staff increased from eighteen to fifty members and its budget tripled.[27] Kissinger even took over budget review functions for the State and Defense departments.[28]

President Nixon then started to more aggressively use the powers of his office to pursue his policies. For example, in 1971, Congress passed a defense authorization act, stating it was new U.S. policy to "terminate at the earliest date" American involvement in Vietnam.[29] When he signed the bill, Nixon issued the following signing statement:

> I have today signed H.R. 8687, the military procurement authorization act of 1971.
>
> To avoid any possible misconception, I wish to emphasize that Section 601 of this act—the so-called Mansfield Amendment—does not represent the policies of this Administration. Section 601 urges that the President establish a "final date" for the withdrawal of all forces from Indochina, subject only to the release of US prisoners of war . . .
>
> Section 601 expresses a judgment about the manner in which the American involvement in the war should be ended. However, it's

---

[24]Ibid., 161.

[25]Ibid., 161; and Reeves, 42–43.

[26]Small, 97.

[27]Rudalevige, 61.

[28]Ibid.

[29]Ibid., 63.

without binding force or effect, and it does not reflect my judgment about the way in which the war should be brought to a conclusion. My signing of the bill that contains this section, therefore, will not change the policies I have pursued and that I shall continue to pursue toward this end.[30]

Whatever Nixon thought he might want to accomplish domestically, and whatever vision he wished to apply toward the expansion of presidential power, he became consumed with the idea of knowing the truth about American security better than anyone else did. He became increasingly insecure and defensive, believing that the Congress, the media, the universities, and even his own government opposed him. He had reason for concern. In April 1970, the Senate refused to confirm his appointment of G. Harold Carswell to the Supreme Court, the second rejected nominee in six months. In May, many Americans refused to accept his rationale for the invasion of Cambodia, setting off a tumult across the country that culminated in the deadly fusillade that killed four students at Kent State University. "These twin uprisings by the President's 'enemies,'" according to journalist J. Anthony Lukas, "marked a turning point in the Nixon administration."[31] And then in the midterm elections of November 1970, Nixon's Republican Party gained two seats in the Senate, but lost twelve in the House. It also lost eleven governorships and some key state legislatures.[32] Nixon felt he was on the defensive. According to journalist Lukas, "By the spring of 1970 the White House was pervaded by what one aide called the 'us vs. them' outlook. It was real confrontational politics."[33]

The negative events of 1969–1970 only added urgency to the actions Nixon had already begun to initiate to assure his continual electoral success. As early as 1969, Nixon sought to use the Internal Revenue Service to curtail the activities of left-leaning groups. The administration created a Special Services Staff to collect information on some 11,000 organizations and individuals and conducted 200 audits. In 1972, John Ehrlichman, the domestic policy chief, demanded information on the tax records of Lawrence F. O'Brien, chairman of the Democratic National Committee (DNC). Meanwhile, at around the same time, White House Council John Dean gave Internal Revenue Service Commissioner John Walters a list of nearly 500 people active in South Dakota Democratic Senator George McGovern's 1972 presidential campaign, insisting that they be investigated.[34]

---

[30]"Statement on Signing the Military Appropriations Authorization Bill. November 17, 1971," in *Public Papers of the Presidents of the United States, Richard Nixon, 1971* (Washington, D.C.: U.S. Government Printing Office,1972), 362.

[31]J. Anthony Lukas, *Nightmare: The Underside of the Nixon Years* (New York: The Viking Press, 1976), 3.

[32]Ibid., 1–2.

[33]Ibid., 11.

[34]Rudalevige, 64.

During the early 1970s, White House political aide Charles Colson began putting together an opponents list as part of a "political enemies project." The list would become known as the "enemies list," and included some 200 people and 18 organizations. A few of the names—Jane Fonda (a politically outspoken liberal-leaning actress); Dick Gregory (a politically outspoken liberal-leaning comedian); Ramsey Clark (a former liberal-leaning attorney general of the United States); Bella Abzug and Shirley Chisholm (former members of Congress with liberal-voting records); the Black Panthers; and the Institute of Policy Studies—could be regarded as enemies of Richard Nixon.[35] Others, such as Edward Kennedy, Edmund Muskie (liberal-leaning Democratic senator from Maine), Walter Mondale (liberal-leaning Democratic senator from Minnesota and vice president of the United States under Jimmy Carter), and Birch Bayh (liberal-leaning Democratic senator from Indiana), were at least political enemies.[36] There were many other names on the list—including presidents of Yale, Harvard Law School, MIT, and the Ford Foundation; ex-cabinet members; Gregory Peck (a prominent somewhat politically outspoken actor); and Joe Namath (a well-known football star with occasional political involvements).[37] Some people got on the list for doing nothing more than contributing to Democratic candidates. Professor Hans Morgenthau was placed on this list because he was confused with Robert Morgenthau, the former U.S. attorney in New York City.[38]

To deal with such enemies, in March 1969, John Ehrlichman, then counsel to the president, called John Caulfield, a New York City police officer, and asked him to set up "a private security entity in Washington for the purpose of providing investigative support for the White House."[39] Caulfield brought another member of the New York Bureau of Special Services, Anthony Ulasewicz, and together the ex-New York cops conducted several investigations, first for Ehrlichman and later (after July 1970) for White House Council John Dean.[40]

The investigators worked with particular alacrity on the trail of Senator Teddy Kennedy. Hours after the Chappaquiddick incident—in which Senator Kennedy drove his car off a bridge in Chappaquiddick, Massachusetts, and his companion, Mary Jo Kopechne, drowned—Ehrlichman directed Caulfield to send Ulasewicz to the scene. The White House sleuth spent four days on the island posing as a reporter, and at news conferences, he frequently asked questions that would embarrass Kennedy. He did everything he could to dig up dirt on Senator Kennedy, including allegedly tapping the phones of Kopechne's roommates.[41] Nixon demanded an even more powerful approach to Kennedy, who

---

[35]Lukas, 12–13.

[36]Ibid., 13.

[37]Ibid.

[38]Ibid.

[39]Ibid., 14.

[40]Ibid., 15.

[41]Ibid., 16.

was highly critical of Nixon's Vietnam War strategy. Nixon asked his aides to assign "one of our best people to the Teddy Kennedy fight."[42]

In May 1971, the Nixon administration ordered the military to arrest several thousand Vietnam War protesters in Washington, D.C., in a move that amounted to a dragnet (or military operation) and detained them in a way that violated their constitutional rights. Colson even promised to send teamster thugs to assist the police. In 1975, the courts ruled that most of the arrests had been illegal and awarded monetary damages to 1,200 of the detainees.[43]

Under Nixon's guidance, government agencies were working to provide systematic intelligence on "subversive" organizations and people the president perceived to be a threat to domestic tranquility. Nixon asked the CIA to investigate foreign links to domestic protesters.[44] The CIA conducted a domestic surveillance program, named CHAOS, from 1969 to 1974; its fifty staffers compiled dossiers on 7,200 American citizens.[45] CHAOS also made use of a large CIA "mail intercept program," which for some twenty-four years had opened and examined mail between American citizens and communist countries.[46]

Other presidents, including Lyndon Baines Johnson, had been enthusiastic consumers of surveillance; however, none sought to redefine the inherent power of the president or to engage in that activity to the same extent as Nixon did. In a June 1969 memorandum, Nixon's attorney general, John Mitchell, claimed that unilateral presidential power extended to wiretapping any group whose purpose was to "attack and subvert the government by unlawful means."[47] An internal White House memo said that the Justice Department should "work for the President," and not for its own bureaucratic interests.[48]

In the spring of 1970, staff Tom Huston was told to begin developing a new domestic security program.[49] Beyond his service in army intelligence, the twenty-nine-year-old Huston brought no experience to this new assignment. But he took to it with gusto![50] He wanted to organize a tough line against dissenters.

In July 1970, Huston drafted a proposal, which became known as the "Huston Plan"; it called for (1) intensified electronic surveillance of "domestic security threats" and foreign diplomats, (2) monitoring of American citizens using international communications faculties, (3) an expansion of "mail coverage"

---

[42]Ibid., 17.

[43]Small, 86.

[44]Rudalevige, 66.

[45]Ibid.

[46]Lukas, 29.

[47]Ibid., 68.

[48]Ibid., 69.

[49]Ibid., 30.

[50]Ibid., 31.

(the examination of envelopes to determine sender, postmarks, etc., and in some cases opening and reading mail), (4) more informants on college campuses, (5) the lifting of restrictions on surreptitious entry, (6) and the establishment of an interagency group on domestic intelligence and internal security with representatives from the White House, FBI, CIA, NSA, DIA (Defense Intelligence Agency), and the three military counterintelligence agencies.

Huston's plan, however, met stiff resistance from FBI Director J. Edgar Hoover, and Nixon chose not to challenge Hoover. Instead, he and his advisers turned to the CIA, which proved to be more amenable to implementing the Huston Plan.[51]

For instance, the CIA intensified domestic surveillance programs, as noted earlier. By 1974, CHAOS had compiled 13,000 files—including individual folders on 7,200 Americans. The agency conducted physical surveillance, installed wiretaps, opened mail, and carried out at least two break-ins against American citizens during the Nixon administration.[52] The Secret Service accumulated intelligence files on some 47,000 persons considered to be potential threats to Nixon. Other signs that the Huston Plan was implemented included a rash of burglaries reported of radicals and dissident groups between 1970 and 1972. The robbers generally did not take cash or valuables, but focused on absconding files, correspondence, and other documents.[53] Among those who reported such burglaries were Mark Rudd, a leader of students for a Democratic Society at Columbia University; Charles Garry, a California attorney for Huey Newton, Bobby Seale, and Angela Davis; Eqbal Ahmed, a Pakistani scholar who was a leading opponent of the Vietnam War; and Dan Rather and Marvin Kalb, reporters for CBS News.[54]

In June 1971, when the Pentagon's encyclopedic secret history of the U.S. involvement in Vietnam, known as the Pentagon Papers began appearing in print, Nixon decided that an aggressive response was necessary.[55] Nixon and Kissinger feared that the leaks would jeopardize negotiations underway with North Vietnam, China, and the USSR, especially their ability to keep the talks confidential. Nixon sought an injunction to prevent the publication of the Pentagon Papers, but he was denied by the Supreme Court. Then former staffer David Ellsberg was identified as the leaker, and Nixon's attention turned to him. Nixon instructed Colson to stop the leaks, saying, "I want it done, whatever the cost."[56]

Enter the "Plumbers," with an assignment to find out all they could about Ellsberg—his life, motives, and associates.[57] The main operatives were former

---

[51]Ibid., 36.
[52]Ibid., 37.
[53]Ibid.
[54]Ibid.
[55]Rudalevige, 72.
[56]Lukas, 71.
[57]Rudalevige, 73.

FBI agent G. Gordon Liddy and former CIA operative E. Howard Hunt. For Hunt, this would be more of the same, as he had been on the White House payroll since the summer of 1972 as a consultant to Colson. Hunt had worked on forging cables claiming to show that the Kennedy White House had provoked the assassination of South Vietnam President Ngo Dinh Diem in 1963. In addition, he had dug into the Bay of Pigs operation and into Chappaquiddick and other aspects of Senator Ted Kennedy's personal life.[58]

In a July 1971 memo, Hunt directed the Plumbers to "neutralize Daniel Ellsberg." The means he chose to accomplish this neutralization was to obtain a CIA psychological profile of Ellsberg and seek Ellsberg's files from his psychiatric analyst.[59] The CIA complied with Hunt's request, despite rules that ostensibly precluded it from performing such evaluations of American citizens at home. Nevertheless, the Plumbers were unhappy with the profile's conclusion that Ellsberg was sane. They sent it back, demanding revisions, and received a slightly juicier version (the leaks were an "act of aggression at his analyst, as well as the President and his father").[60] Not yet satisfied, the Plumbers went to Ehrlichman proposing a "covert operation" that would examine the medical files still held by Lewis Fielding, Ellsberg's psychiatrist. Ehrlichman agreed on the proviso that the job would not be traceable, and later claimed that Nixon himself approved the plan.[61] In his memoirs, however, Nixon denied any prior knowledge, but admitted that "it was at least in part an outgrowth of my sense of urgency about discrediting what Ellsberg had done and finding out what he might do next."[62]

Hunt and Liddy recruited a team of burglars, mostly Cuban exiles trained by Hunt in his CIA days in the Bay of Pigs operation. The project was paid for by money obtained by Colson from the dairy lobby, though the donors had no knowledge of this use of the money. The duo supplied with information from the CIA; however, the subsequent operation failed. Although they were supposed to leave no traces, they left so many that the office had to be trashed to make the entry resemble an ordinary robbery. In addition, they were able to obtain only a fraction of the information they needed, and Hunt and Liddy urged a raid on Ellsberg's apartment as well.[63] This request was denied.

But other operations went forward. For example, in May 1972, the Plumbers broke into the Chilean embassy in Washington to gain information on the plans of the socialist Allende government. They installed wiretaps, most notably on a navy officer—who, rather ironically, had been spying on the Nixon NSC on behalf of the Joint Chiefs of Staff.[64] At this point, according to

---

[58]Ibid.
[59]Lukas, 91.
[60]Rudalevige, 73.
[61]Ibid., 73–74.
[62]Ibid., 74.
[63]Ibid.
[64]Ibid.

Lukas, "The White House had moved across the line from . . . prodding other agencies into direct operations more appropriate to a secret police force."[65]

Nixon was emphatic in claiming a right to keep these and other operations secret under the rubric of executive privilege. He justified his argument in a 1973 statement as follows:

> To ensure the effective discharge of the executive responsibility, a President must be able to place absolute confidence in the advice and assistance offered by the members of his staff. And on the performance of their duties for the President, those staff members must not be inhibited by the possibility that their advice and assistance would ever become a matter of public debate . . . Otherwise, the candor with which advice is rendered and the quality of such assistance will inevitably be compromised and weakened.[66]

The secrecy certainly extended to Nixon's conduct of the war in Southeast Asia. In March 1969, Nixon approved a plan to bomb enemy sanctuaries inside Cambodia. The initiative was kept secret, and a procedure was devised to conceal the bombing. The procedure involved briefing pilots on night missions over Vietnam, then diverting them via ground control instruction over Cambodia; false reports on each mission were filed through normal channels, while real reports were filed separately and secretly. The public had no awareness of the 4,000 sorties that were flown until they were revealed in late May 1970.[67]

But another Nixon policy in Cambodia was fueling the fire of protest in America. After a March 1970 coup brought a pro-American faction to power there—removing the neutral regime of Prince Sihanouk—Nixon approved the use of South Vietnamese troops to drive the North Vietnamese into the arms of Cambodian troops. Instead, as North Vietnamese troops moved further into Cambodia, North Vietnam began full-scale support for the murderous Khmer Rouge guerillas fighting the new Cambodian government. In late April, Nixon secretly ordered the use of 32,000 U.S. ground troops in assaults into Cambodia. In an Oval Office address, the president claimed that the operation was not an invasion but an incursion for Cambodia's benefit as the North Vietnamese had disrespected Cambodia's neutrality and built military sanctuaries all along the Cambodian frontier with South Vietnam.[68] And, Nixon claimed that in the past two weeks North Vietnam had stepped up its activity and sent thousands of soldiers to invade the country from the

---

[65]Lukas, 94.

[66]"Statement about Executive Privilege. May 12, 1973," in *Public Papers of the Presidents of the United States, Richard Nixon, 1973* (Washington, D.C.: U.S. Government Printing Office, 1975), 76.

[67]Rudalevige, 81.

[68]"Address to the Nation on the Situation in Southeast Asia. April 30, 1970," in *Public Paper of the Presidents of the United States, Richard Nixon, 1970* (Washington, D.C.: U.S. Government Printing Office, 1971), 406–407.

sanctuaries. Cambodia, in turn, sent out a call for help from the United States. Rejecting the alternatives of doing nothing or of supplying Cambodia with military assistance, Nixon announced that U.S. forces, in cooperation with the armed forces of South Vietnam, were launching attacks "to clean out the major enemy sanctuaries in the Cambodia-Vietnam border."[69] He boldly stated that, "we take this action not for the purpose of expanding the war into Cambodia but for the purpose of ending the war in Vietnam and winning the just peace we all desire."[70] And placing it into a bigger context, the president opined, "If, when the chips are down, the world's most powerful nation, the Untied States of America, acts like a pitiful, helpless giant, then forces of totalitarianism and anarchy will threaten free nations and free institutions throughout the world."[71]

Nixon also anticipated the possible fallout from his actions, and in his concluding remarks stated, "Whether I may be a one-term President is insignificant compared to whether by our failure to act in this crisis the United States proves itself to be unworthy to lead the forces of freedom in this critical period in world history."[72] If anything, President Nixon understated the reaction. Widespread demonstration broke out across the nation, and at Kent State and Jackson State universities protestors were killed by nervous National Guardsmen and police.[73] Congress also reacted angrily and even Senate Minority Leader Hugh Scott (R-PA) reproached Nixon for having kept him in the dark.[74] In June, the Senate voted to repeal the Tonkin Gulf Resolution and to pass the Cooper-Church Amendment denying funds for military operations in Cambodia—though carefully written to allow the president "to protect the lives of US armed forces whenever deployed."[75]

In the short term, Nixon defused the political crisis by removing most American troops from Cambodia by the end of June; however, privately he reacted defensively to public criticism by beginning work on the aforementioned Huston Plan.[76] The administration defended the prerogatives of the president to act unilaterally in foreign policy. Administrative sources agreed that the president's constitutional authority included "the power to deploy American forces abroad and commit them to military operations when the president deems such action necessary to maintain the security and defense of the United States." Assistant Attorney General William Rehnquist (who later became chief justice of the U.S. Supreme Court) cited authority under Supreme Court precedent as well as the tactical decision-making power granted the commander in chief.[77]

---

[69]Ibid., 407.

[70]Ibid., 408.

[71]Ibid., 409.

[72]Ibid., 410.

[73]Rudalevige, 81.

[74]Ibid., 82.

[75]Ibid.

[76]Ibid.

[77]Ibid.

In May 1972, Nixon announced he had approved a naval blockade of North Vietnam and the mining of Haiphong Harbor, to accompany a renewed escalation of the bombing campaign. A week before the 1972 election, Kissinger proclaimed that "peace is at hand"; the public and Congress were surprised to find that the most massive bombing of the war had begun on December 18, after Nixon's landslide electoral victory. Thirty-six thousand tons of bombs were dropped on Hanoi and other Northern cities in ten days.[78] Legislation seeking to end the war began moving through Congress when it reconvened in January 1973. Later that month a peace agreement was announced.[79]

But the end of the war did not end the use of unilateral presidential power. For instance, though military action in Cambodia was now forbidden by law, in early 1973 American bombing resumed (this time against rebels battling the Lon Nol government). Covert actions continued unabated around the globe. Within Vietnam, the Phoenix Program of pacification within South Vietnam sought to weed out Vietcong sympathizers lurking in the ground population. Military, State Department, and CIA personnel set up interrogation centers in all 235 districts of the country.[80] Then came intervention in Iraq, Iran, and Chile, all predicated on Nixon's anti-communist instincts.[81]

To the end, Nixon remained unrepentant in his unilateral exercise of foreign policy power. His veto of the War Powers Resolution (WPR; to be discussed later) claimed that its restrictions "upon the authority of the President" (it would require a stronger congressional role in deciding to *keep* American troops abroad and consultation on *sending* them) were both "unconstitutional and dangerous to the best interests of our nation."[82] And a White House "Vietnam White Paper," touting the peace agreement and distributed to members of Congress in January 1973, condemned the "incessant attacks from the US Congress . . . No president has been under more constant and unremitting harassment by more who should drop to their knees each night to thank the Almighty that they do not have to make the same decisions that Richard Nixon did."[83]

But by then, as political scientist Andrew Rudalevige suggests, "Legislators seemed more inclined to bring Richard Nixon to his knees instead."[84] One important area in which they would do so was over the matter of the president's habit of "impounding" (refusing to spend) congressionally authorized and appropriated funds. Impoundment had been used by other presidents, but Nixon was far more aggressive in his use, which was characterized by one observer as "unprecedented in scope, severity, and truculence."[85] Again Nixon

[78]Ibid.

[79]Ibid.

[80]Ibid., 83.

[81]Ibid., 83–84.

[82]Ibid., 85.

[83]Ibid.

[84]Ibid.

[85]Ibid., 89.

upped the ante by defending his powers as inherent and non-negotiable. Nixon impounded $15 billion by 1973, 20 percent of all discretionary spending. He also targeted specific programs for elimination—such as the Office of Economic Opportunity—in spite of the fact that they had been funded by Congress.[86]

Nixon had never really forgotten that he prevailed in 1968 with only 43 percent of the popular vote, and that the Democrats retained a solid edge nationally in voter registration.[87] He was determined to win big in 1972; however, polls throughout 1971 showed Nixon running behind potential challenger Democratic Senator Edmund Muskie of Maine. And in early May 1972, polls showed him ahead of the actual Democratic candidate Senator George McGovern of South Dakota.[88] Those around the president, his true believers, shared this goal of re-electing Nixon by a wide margin. Charles Colson wrote his staff members a memorandum a few months before the presidential election that displayed the intensity of the cause: "There are only 71 days left and every one counts. Ask yourself every morning what you are going to do to help re-elect the president today."

Nixon's aides unleashed a full-scale "dirty tricks" campaign: first to discredit and eliminate Edmund Muskie as a candidate and later to go after McGovern and his left-wing supporters. The dirty tricks campaign was directed largely by Donald Segretti (the word *segretti* means *secrets* in Italian).[89] Segretti fabricated Muskie campaign literature alleging that the Senator and Vice President Hubert Humphrey had been arrested for drunk driving in the company of a prostitute.[90] The Committee to Re-Elect the President (CREEP) paid a retired Washington, D.C., tour driver to volunteer to drive Senator Edmund Muskie's car—the man was code-named "Sedan Chair"—and paid $1,000 a month to report on what he heard and saw.[91] Ken Clawson of the White House Press Office was most likely responsible for sending a letter to the *Manchester Union Leader* falsely accusing Senator Muskie's wife of using a derogatory term in public and of being emotionally unstable. Muskie defended his wife's honor in an emotional speech in front of the *Union Leader*, during which he appeared to shed tears. Some voters expressed doubt about a man running for president who would shed tears so easily.[92] During the Florida primary, Republican agents mailed forged letters under the heading "Citizens for Muskie," accusing Washington Democrat Senator Henry (Scoop) Jackson, a rival for the nomination, of fathering an illegitimate child

---

[86]Ibid.
[87]Ibid., 92.
[88]Ibid.
[89]Small, 254.
[90]Rudalevige, 93.
[91]Reeves, 424.
[92]Small, 254–255.

and of having been arrested on charges of homosexuality.[93] In 1974, Segretti was indicted on the counts of distributing illegal campaign material and sentenced to four-and-a-half years in jail.[94]

But the main activity, understated by the Nixon camp, one that would ultimately lead to the first resignation of a president in U.S. history, was the break-in at DNC headquarters in the Watergate apartment and commercial complex during the early morning hours of June 17, 1972.[95] District of Columbia police apprehended five men wearing surgical gloves and carrying tear-gas fountain pens, walkie-talkies, and new $100 bills—resources to help them plant electronic surveillance equipment in DNC offices.[96]

Four of the men caught in the Watergate complex were Cubans who had worked for the CIA; the fifth, James McCord, was a former CIA agent, who was chief of security for CREEP. The two men coordinating the operation from a Howard Johnson hotel across the street were E. Howard Hunt and G. Gordon Liddy.[97]

On June 19, *Washington Post* reporters Bob Woodward and Carl Bernstein wrote a story about links between the break-ins and the White House; they discovered the links in police investigation reports of Hunt and Liddy's hotel room. Three days later, President Nixon assured the nation that the White House had not been involved in the particular incident.[98] In a subsequent October 10 *Washington Post* article, Woodward and Bernstein described the break-in as part of a massive, nationwide campaign of habitual spying and sabotage conducted in behalf of the president's re-election efforts and directed by CREEP.[99]

The allegations about the Nixon White House gave evidence to Democratic challenger McGovern's claim that the "Nixon Administration is the most corrupt administration in our nation's history."[100] McGovern was an uncharismatic, World War II bomber pilot with a Ph.D. in history, who had served in the Kennedy administration, was director of the Food for Peace Program, and was elected to serve as South Dakota's senator in 1963.[101]

Meanwhile, Representative Wright Patman (D-TX), chair of the House Banking Committee, demanded hearings to examine the murky financial dealings surrounding the Watergate principals. Nixon, however, refused to allow his staff to appear before the committee and a coalition of Republican and Southern Democrats helped Nixon prevent Patman from issuing subpoenas for the staff to appear.

---

[93]Ibid., 255.

[94]Ibid.

[95]Ibid.

[96]Ibid.

[97]Ibid.

[98]Ibid., 256.

[99]Katherine Graham, *Personal History* (New York: Vantage, 1998), 465–466.

[100]Small, 260.

[101]Ibid., 258.

Nixon expressed no remorse about the revelations stemming from the Watergate break-in and told Haldeman to "play it tough."[102] By June 23, he had approved a plan to have the CIA obstruct the FBI investigation into the burglary, claiming that it was a matter of national security.[103] The cover-up strategy focused on silencing the burglars and on White House staff misleading investigators, shredding documents, and committing perjury. Hunt's White House safe was cleared out by Ehrlichman, and Dean told FBI Director Patrick Gray to destroy the Ellsberg materials, and Gray surprisingly complied with the request.[104]

Nixon became increasingly agitated and threatened to deny the *Washington Post*'s renewal of its television license through the Federal Communication Commission.[105] He went after Jewish supporters of McGovern and wanted to intensify his program of using the IRS to investigate Jewish contributors to the Democratic Party, a program he had started in 1971. The only problem, much to Nixon's chagrin, was that the IRS was filled with Jews![106]

The chronology of events leading to Nixon's resignation has been widely described, but the following represents a summary for contextual purposes. The summary is drawn largely from Michael Schudson's book, *Watergate in American Memory: How We Remember, Forget and Reconstruct the Past.*[107]

- Shortly after the Watergate break-in, the press reported that one of the burglars, James W. McCord Jr., had been a CIA employee and was presently employed by President Nixon's campaign organization, the Committee to Re-Elect the President (officially abbreviated as CRP but more commonly known as CREEP). As mentioned, the *Washington Post* actively pursued the story and linked CREEP activity to many White House staff members. The White House retorted that Democrats and liberals in the media were exaggerating the importance of the Watergate incident—characterized by White House Press Secretary Ron Ziegler as a "third-rate burglary"—to gain political advantage in the election.

- Five months later, Nixon was re-elected by a landslide victory over Democratic challenger George McGovern. In the first few months of 1973, the Watergate burglars and two of the organizers—Hunt and Liddy—were found guilty of wiretapping and conspiracy in the U.S. District Court for the District of Columbia. The trial judge, U.S. District Court Judge John J. Sirica, imposed stiff sentences but characterized them as "provisional," holding out the possibility that he would reduce them if the convicted burglars cooperated with federal investigators. There was

---

[102]Rudalevige, 93.

[103]Ibid.

[104]Ibid., 94.

[105]Graham, 480–481.

[106]Small, 262.

[107]Michael Schudson, *Watergate in American Memory: How We Remember, Forget and Reconstruct the Past* (New York: Basic Books, 1992), 16–20.

suspicion that some of the burglars who had shifted their pleas from "not guilty" to "guilty" were being paid or pressured by higher authority in the Nixon campaign to keep quiet. The White House was paying E. Howard Hunt for his continued silence with President Nixon's knowledge and approval.[108]

- In February, Senate Confirmation Hearing of L. Patrick Gray to head the FBI revealed that White House counsel John Dean had sat in on FBI interviews when the FBI was investigating Watergate and had received copies of FBI investigative reports. This suggested a collusion to protect White House staff. In March, James McCord, hoping for a reduced sentence, wrote to Judge Sirica that political pressure had been applied to Watergate defendants to plead guilty and remain silent, that defendants had perjured themselves at trial, and that other people who helped plan the Watergate break-in had not been indicated during the hearing.
- In April, allegations that Nixon's two closest aides, Chief of Staff H. R. Haldeman and Domestic Affairs Adviser John Ehrlichman, were involved in the cover-up of the Watergate affair, along with John Dean, led to the resignations of all of them. Attorney General Richard Kleindienst also resigned, and Nixon named Secretary of Defense Elliot Richardson to replace him.
- In May, Richardson appointed Harvard Law School Professor Archibald Cox to be the special Watergate prosecutor. Shortly thereafter, the Senate Select Committee on Presidential Campaigning Activities was set up by a unanimous vote of 77–0 in the Senate. In February, public, televised hearings began under the leadership of Senator Samuel J. Ervin (D-NC).
- During the Senate hearings, John Dean directly implicated Nixon in the Watergate cover-up. And Alexander Butterfield, a White House aide, revealed that President Nixon had tape-recorded conversations in the Oval Office.

According to Schudson,

The senate inquiry made public not only White House involvement in the Watergate cover-up but other abuses of power prior to and unconnected with the Watergate break-in. This included revelations that President Nixon used the Internal Revenue Service to harass political opponents; that the White House kept an "enemies list" of journalists, intellectuals, politicians, lower end union leaders, and others; and that the White House had established a "Plumbers Unit" to investigate leaks to the press—a group that among other things burglarized Daniel Ellsberg's psychiatrist's office.[109]

- During the summer of 1973, the Senate Committee and the special prosecutors sought access to the White House tapes. Nixon stonewalled repeatedly, citing executive privilege as a justification. The White House

[108]Ibid., 17.
[109]Ibid., 18.

also refused the Senate's subpoena of the tapes, sending the Senate and the special prosecutor to court.

- Meanwhile, Attorney General Richardson informed Nixon that Vice President Spiro Agnew was under investigation for corrupt practices during his term as governor of Maryland. By October, the investigation of Agnew led to a plea bargain where Agnew pleaded no contest for one charge of income tax evasion and paid $40,000 fine in return for resigning as vice president of the United States.[110] In October, President Nixon nominated Michigan Republican Congressman Gerald Ford as the new vice president, and Ford was sworn in two months later.
- Failure to workout a compromise over prosecutor Cox's access to the tapes led the president to ask Attorney General Richardson to fire Cox, which Richardson refused to do and resigned instead. William Ruckelshaus, Richardson's deputy, also refused and was fired. Solicitor General Robert Bork, third in command at the Justice Department, carried out the order. These events, popularly known as the Saturday Night Massacre, led to the first serious consideration of impeachment by Congress.[111]
- The new special prosecutor, Texas lawyer Leon Jaworski, worked out a deal where Nixon would turn over nine tapes that Cox had subpoenaed to Judge Sirica. But the president's lawyer revealed two of those tapes did not exist, one with Nixon's first discussion with former attorney general and CREEP chairman John Mitchell after the break-in, and a second one between the president and John Dean on April 15. Another tape, carrying a conversation between the president and Chief of Staff Haldeman the day after the break-in, turned out to have a mysterious eighteen-minute gap.
- In February 1974, the House Judiciary Committee voted by a margin of 410–4 to begin an impeachment investigation. In March, the Watergate grand jury returned indictments charging John Mitchell, H. R. Haldeman, John Ehrlichman, Charles Colson, and others with a criminal conspiracy to obstruct justice. Both Jaworski and the House Judiciary Committee issued subpoenas for additional White House tapes, setting a deadline for the end of April.
- On April 29, Nixon announced he would not release the tapes but would provide 1,200 pages of edited manuscripts. When these transcripts were released to the public, people were astonished and outraged at the language used by the president and his advisers. The president's talk was "foul, vengeful, and full of ethnic slurs."[112]
- In July, the House Judiciary Committee approved three articles for impeachment: the first listed nine counts of obstruction of justice; the second abuse of power, including the use of the IRS, CIA, and FBI so as to be "subversive" of constitutional government; and the third for failure to comply with congressional subpoenas during the

---

[110]Ibid., 18–19.
[111]Ibid., 19.
[112]Ibid., 20.

investigation.[113] A third of the Republican members joined a unanimous Democratic majority. The Supreme Court, with four sitting members appointed by Nixon, voted 8–0 that President Nixon was obligated by law to turn over all of the subpoenaed tape recordings. Days later the president's attorney revealed a tape recording from June 23, 1972, capturing a communication between Nixon and his aides, where the president is asking them to use the CIA to disturb the FBI's investigation of Watergate. This became known as the "smoking gun tape." And shortly after its release, all members of the House Judiciary Committee, including Nixon's most zealous supporters, declared they now pursued impeachment. Knowing that he had little support left in the U.S. Senate, two months later on August 9, 1974, President Nixon resigned.

The meaning of Watergate will be debated for years to come,[114] but there is no debate that it caused a very strong reaction in the American political system. Here is how *Washington Post* editor Katherine Graham summarized the meaning of Watergate:

> Even today, some people think that the whole thing was a minor peccadillo, the sort of thing engaged in by lots of politicians. I believe Watergate was an unprecedented effort to subvert the political process. It was a pervasive, indiscriminate use of power and authority from an administration with a passion for secrecy and deception and an astounding lack of regard for the normal constraints of democratic politics. To my mind, the whole thing was a very real perversion of the democratic system—from firing people who were good Republicans but who might have disagreed with Nixon in the slightest, to the wiretappings, to the breaking and entering of Ellsberg's psychiatrist's office, to the myriad dirty tricks, to the attempts to discredit and curb the media. As I said in a speech at the time, "It was a conspiracy not of greed but of arrogance and fear by men who came to equate their own political well-being with the nation's very survival and security."[115]

And for the particular focus of this book—the presidency—Watergate had a profound effect. According to historian Arthur Schlesinger Jr.:

> Watergate's importance was not simply in itself. Its importance was in the way it brought to the surface, symbolized and made politically accessible the great question posed by the Nixon Administration in every sector—the question of presidential power. The unwarranted and unprecedented expansion of presidential power, because it ran through the whole Nixon system, was bound, if repressed at one point, to break out at another. This, not Watergate, was the central issue.[116]

---

[113]Committee on the Judiciary, House of Representatives, *Impeachment of Richard M. Nixon President of the United States* (Washington, D.C.: U.S. Government Printing Office, 1974).

[114]Schudson, 21–25.

[115]Graham, 504.

[116]Arthur Schlesinger Jr., *The Imperial Presidency* (New York: Houghton Mifflin, 1973), 275.

During the remainder of the 1970s and entering into the 1980s, Congress passed a plethora of laws, resolutions, and statutes aimed at curtailing the absolute power of the presidency and restoring the role of the legislative branch in the U.S. government.[117] Professor James Sundquist referred to this burst of activity as the resurgence of Congress.[118] In April 1973, on the floor of the House of Representatives, Representative Gillis Long (D-LA) said, "The president has outstripped the authority of his office in the actions he has taken. Congress will not stand idly by as the president reaches for more and more power."[119] Senate Majority Leader Mike Mansfield (D-MT) proclaimed, "The people have not chosen to be governed by one branch of government alone."[120]

One of the first legislative actions reflective of congressional resurgence was the War Powers Resolution of 1973. Passed in November 1973 over Nixon's veto, the WPR started with a statement of purpose that the president's power as commander in chief applied only after a declaration of war, or some other form of authorization, by Congress, or if American armed forces were under attack.[121] The next section stipulated that the president shall "consult with Congress" before initiating the use of force in every possible instance and continue consultation until the troops are "out of harms way." Unless war was declared (by Congress), the president was required to report on each troop deployment within forty-eight hours, and justify the circumstances. Congress reserved the right to require at any time by concurrent resolution that the engagement close. And in the absence of a congressional authorization or motion, the troops were to be withdrawn from hostility within sixty days.[122] The chief sponsor of the legislation, Senator Jacob Javits (R-NY) said, "There would be no more presidential wars!"[123]

Congress also addressed the intelligence issue in reaction to the CIA's support of the White House Plumbers, providing disguises for the burglars of Ellsberg's psychiatrist, and the excesses of the Huston Plan. In 1974, Congress passed the Hughes-Ryan Amendment to the foreign aid bill. The CIA would be required to brief six (later eight) separate congressional committees on covert action that was underway. The president would be required to issue a written "finding" justifying each covert action as "important for US national security."[124]

In 1973, the new CIA Director James Schlesinger, wanting to know his personal liability in light of the CIA Plumbers revelations, directed that all

---

[117]Rudalevige, 101.

[118]James L. Sundquist, *The Decline and Resurgence of Congress* (Washington, D.C.: Brookings Institution), 1981.

[119]Rudalevige, 102.

[120]Sundquist.

[121]Rudalevige, 118.

[122]Ibid., 119.

[123]Ibid.

[124]Ibid., 120.

potentially embarrassing agency actions be compiled in a single report. The resulting 693-page report detailed 900 major covert projects and several thousand lesser ones since 1961.[125] The projects included plots to assassinate foreign leaders, attempts to test illicit drugs on unsuspecting American citizens, and multiple uses of wiretaps.[126]

President Ford, who replaced Nixon in 1974, appointed a blue-ribbon commission on domestic abuses by the CIA, under the leadership of Vice President Nelson Rockefeller. Other members of the commission included the American Federation of Labor and Congress of Industrial Organizations (AFL-CIO) president Lane Kirkland, Kennedy cabinet member Douglas Dillon, and former California governor Ronald Reagan.[127] The commission found that the majority of the CIA's domestic activities were in compliance with statutory authority, but some actions were "plainly unlawful."[128]

Congress convened its own hearings on intelligence and CBS News correspondent Daniel Schorr testified about numerous assassination attempts undertaken by the CIA. The Senate created the Church Committee, chaired by Democratic Idaho Senator Frank Church (officially titled the Select Committee to Study Covert Operations with Respect to International Activities). The House founded a similar committee under the leadership of Representative Otis Pike (D-NY).[129]

Frank Church's bipartisan Senate Committee interviewed more than 800 officials and held twenty-one public hearings, uncovering widespread intelligence abuses by the CIA and FBI.[130] In April 1976, the Church Committee released a six-volume report, consisting of thousands of pages on foreign and military intelligence, domestic operations, and many other aspects of the intelligence community. The report was critical of the FBI and CIA. Presidents Ford and Carter felt pressure to clean house. President Ford issued a February 1976 executive order that banned political assassination, created an Intelligence Oversight Board, and demanded that the CIA remain out of domestic activity and prevented human subjects research.[131] The policies continued under Carter, especially because Vice President Walter Mondale served on the Church Committee.

The Foreign Intelligence Surveillance Act (FISA) of 1978 sought to provide oversight over what presidents claimed as their "inherent authority." FISA limited foreign intelligence information to information related to clandestine international activities, sabotage, terrorism, or hostile acts carried out by foreign agents or powers. The legislation created a special FISA court

---

[125]Ibid., 121.

[126]Ibid.

[127]Ibid.

[128]Ibid.

[129]Ibid.

[130]Jonathon Mahler, "After the Imperial Presidency," *New York Times,* November 9, 2008, 49.

[131]Rudalevige, 122.

to review applications for surveillance linked to such investigations and required the attorney general of the United States to sign off on each application. The standard for issuing warrants was set at a low level, compared to the one used in criminal courts, and the drafters intended this to be a wall between information obtained from FISA investigators and information obtained from criminal prosecutors. The wall became a controversial issue, however, after 9/11. It became clear that battling the terrorists would require tearing down the strict wall of separation between intelligence and law enforcements; however, in the days following Watergate, Congress was determined to restrict the executive's freedom of motion in the intelligence arena in many different ways.

In the Budget Reform and Impoundment Control Act of 1974, Congress re-inserted itself directly into the budget and spending process. The act declared that the president could no longer impound congressionally appropriated funds, but could rescind or defer funds with congressional input.[132] The act also created budget committees in both houses of Congress with responsibility for formulating an overall budget ceiling. Strict deadlines were arranged for every step of this budget process, and a Congressional Budget Office was set up to provide Congress with budgetary expertise independent of the executive branch.[133]

The Congress also passed the Ethics in Government Act (EGA) in 1978, arguing that Congress had not tried to usurp executive functions, but simply sought a workable mechanism for dealing with allegations of executive corruption.[134] The EGA contained a variety of requirements designed to curb malfeasance and prevent conflicts of interest, largely by making them more transparent: All federal officials at high levels, senior staff, Senate-confirmed appointments (including federal judges), and presidential candidates would be required to file public financial disclosure forms detailing income and investment information. Any gifts valued over $35 would have to be disclosed, and formal and informal lobbying contacts between ex-federal employees and their former agencies were prohibited for two years. An Office of Government Ethics was created to monitor compliance.[135]

But the best known provision of the EGA was Title VI, the special prosecutor provision, which became known as the Independent Council Act (ICA).[136] There had been grave concern over Nixon's removal of Archibald Cox from office, and members of Congress saw Title VI as a means to remove politics from the administration of justice. The executive branch could simply not be trusted to police itself.[137]

---

[132]Ibid., 128.

[133]Ibid., 130.

[134]Ibid., 136.

[135]Ibid., 133–134.

[136]Ibid., 134.

[137]Ibid., 135.

The independent counsel law provided a three-stage process for initiating an investigation once the attorney general received information alleging that a high-level federal official had violated federal law.

- The attorney general would conduct a preliminary investigation.
- Unless the attorney general found "no reasonable grounds to warrant further investigation," he or she would apply to a Special Division of the U.S. Court of Appeals, a panel of three judges serving two-year terms on the panel.
- The panel would name and appoint the independent counsel and define his or her jurisdiction.[138]

Before the act's expiration in 1999, twenty cases were brought, employing twenty-nine independent counsels at a cost of over $175 million.[139] Charges ranged from allegations of drug abuse by White House aides to perjury, bribery, fraud, and influence peddling by cabinet secretaries. Some fifty convictions resulted. The Iran-Contra investigation led to eleven convictions and two pretrial pardons; the Whitewater probe, through considerable expansion of the independent counsel's authority into areas ranging from suicide to sex, led to some fifteen convictions and to the impeachment of President Clinton.[140]

In 1988, the Supreme Court upheld the ICA's constitutionality despite its odd amalgamation of a judicial employee into the executive branch, in the case of *Morrison v. Olson*.[141] The majority agreed with an assertion made by the Senate in 1978: Congress had not tried to usurp executive functions but simply sought a workable mechanism for dealing with allegations of executive corruption.[142]

Justice Antonin Scalia vigorously dissented, pointing out that the ICA "deeply wounds the President, by substantially reducing the President's authority to protect himself and his staff." Scalia bristled at the idea that the law provided a low "trigger mechanism" for those who wished to attack the president, and that presidential accusers were empowered to bring criminal charges with little evidence but much potential for damaging the White House. In Scalia's opinion:

> The institution of the independent counsel enfeebles him more directly in his constant confrontations with Congress, by eroding his public support. Nothing is so politically effective as the ability to charge that one's opponent and his associates are not merely wrongheaded, naïve, ineffective, but, in all probability, "crooks." And nothing so effectively gives and appearance of validity to such charges as a Justice Department investigation and, even better, prosecution. The present statute provides ample means for that sort of attack.[143]

---

[138]Ibid.

[139]Ibid., 136.

[140]Ibid.

[141]*Morrison v. Olson*, 487 U.S. (654) 1988, 705, 711, 713F.

[142]Ibid.

[143]Ibid.

For Congress on the other hand, the institution of the independent counsel was "the grandest moment to its victory of Richard Nixon and the Imperial Presidency."[144] It was part of a new edifice erected to protect Congress and the nation from the reappearance of an imperial president.

The resurgence regime, according to legal scholar Gerhard Casper, was underpinned by "framework statutes," laws designed not to solve a specific problem but "to support the organizational skeleton of the Constitution by developing a more detailed framework for governmental decision making . . . and attempts to stabilize expectations about the ways in which governmental power is exercised."[145] Statutes such as the Congressional Budget and Impoundment Act and the WPR are aimed at channeling information—and authority—through new procedures and veto panels. The framework of statutes was designed to push back against the president's two-century long expansion of prerogative authority, according to Professor Andrew Rudalevige.[146] Throughout the 1970s, adds Rudalevige, "The efforts by Congress to regain the powers of the purse and the sword, along with its generally instituted standing were extensive and ambitious."[147]

Presidents serving in the wake of Nixon and Watergate, according to political scientists William W. Lammers and Michael A. Genovese, "have been affected by a series of limiting influences, including greater public skepticism about government, greater capacities for independent action in Congress, the proliferation of interest groups, economic problems, more fragile electoral coalitions, and a far more adversarial press."[148] This was the political milieu that awaited the first full-term Watergate president, Jimmy Carter, following a brief healing period of quiet, humble leadership exercised by President Gerald R. Ford.

---

[144]Suzanne Garment, *Scandal: The Crisis of Mistrust in American Politics* (New York: New York Times Books, 1991), 83.

[145]Gerhard Casper, "The Constitutional Organization of the Government," *William and Mary Law Review* 26 (Winter 1985), 187–188.

[146]Rudalevige, 136.

[147]Ibid.

[148]William W. Lammers and Michael A. Genovese, *The President and Domestic Policy: Comparing Leadership Styles, FDR to Clinton* (Washington, D.C.: Congressional Quarterly Press, 2000), 351.

The Presidency of James Earl Carter

Jimmy Carter announced his candidacy for the 1976 presidential election on December 12, 1974, and began his full-time campaign the following year.[1] Some would say he presented a thin set of credentials for the highest office in the land, having served only one term as governor of Georgia and two terms in the Georgia State Senate. On the other hand, Carter had the confidence, energy, and ambition, along with the political acumen, to attain victory in his race for the White House. Many years earlier, he told his high school friends he would be governor one day, and as a young naval officer he aspired to become the chief of naval operations.[2] Carter also believed that he had succeeded in his largest initiative as governor of the state of Georgia: the reform and reorganization of the executive branch of state government. As well, he claimed credit for having introduced "zero-based budgeting" to the Georgia state government. Under this process, agencies were asked to justify their budgets in entirety each year anew, instead of merely relying on their last year's budget as a base of estimates for the coming year.[3] Still he was not the Democrat whom most party regulars would have predicted would be their nominee in 1976, nor the man whom they guessed would actually be elected president in the November 1976 race against incumbent President Gerald Ford.

EARLY LIFE

James Earl Carter Jr. was born on October 1, 1924, in Plains, Georgia. His father, James Earl Carter Sr., a farmer, and his mother, Lillian Gordy Carter, a registered nurse, raised him in the community of Archery, Georgia. He was the eldest of four children.[4] His childhood was marked by a strong emphasis on peanut farming, talk of politics, and devotion to the Baptist faith. Carter attended Georgia Southwestern College and the Georgia Institute of Technology, and received a B.S. degree from the United States Naval Academy in 1946.[5]

The same year he graduated from the United States Naval Academy, he married Rosalynn Smith, who was also from Plains. They subsequently had four children: John William "Jack," James Earl III "Chip," Donnel Jeffrey "Jeff," and Amy Lynn.[6]

In 1946, Carter was commissioned as an ensign and served aboard the *USS Wyoming*, a battleship that had been converted into a floating laboratory to test electronics and gunnery equipment. He served as radar officer and Combat Information Center officer. When the *USS Wyoming* was

---

[1]Gregory Paul Domin, *Jimmy Carter, Public Opinion and the Search for Values* (Macon, GA: Mercer University Press, 2003), 8.

[2]Betty Glad, *Jimmy Carter: In Search of the Great White House* (New York: Norton and Company, 1980), 46, 57.

[3]Ibid., 179.

[4]"Biography of Jimmy Carter," http://www.jimmycarterlibrary.gov.

[5]"Biography of Jimmy Carter," http://www.whitehouse.gov/about/presidents/jimmycarter/.

[6]"Biography of Jimmy Carter," http://www.jimmycarterlibrary.gov.

decommissioned in August 1947, Carter was immediately assigned to the *USS Mississippi*, a ship with a similar function to the *Wyoming*, as Training and Education officer.[7] These events occurred when he was a candidate for a Rhodes Scholarship, though he would ultimately not receive it.[8] In June 1948, he was accepted to the USN Submarine School, Submarine Base, New London, Connecticut, for a six-month officer's course. After completing this course, he spent two years aboard the *USS Pomfret*, where he was promoted to lieutenant, junior grade, in 1949.[9]

In 1952, Jimmy Carter was selected for duty with Shipbuilding and Naval Inspector of Ordinance in Groton, Connecticut, as a prospective engineering officer on the *USS K-1*, which would later become the *USS Seawolf*, a nuclear submarine.[10] Admiral Hyman Rickover personally appointed Carter to this position following a personal meeting and interview. While in Groton, he was promoted to lieutenant in June 1952. Rickover and Carter did not spend much time together in Connecticut, but Rickover's work ethic and expectation of his men were influential. The admiral's emphasis on dedication, hard work, responsibility, and performance was known throughout the navy, and had also been a subject that he discussed with Carter during their first meeting.[11] Rickover assigned him to the nuclear submarine program in Schenectady, New York, at the U.S. Atomic Energy Commission, Division of Reactor Development, Schenectady Operations Office. While in New York, Carter attended graduate courses at Union College in reactor technology and nuclear physics.[12]

In 1953, following the death of his father, Carter resigned his naval commission and returned to Plains, where he took over the Carter farms. He and Rosalynn also opened Carter's Warehouse, a seed and farm supply company. After returning to Plains, he got involved in the local community serving on the education, hospital authority, and library supervisory boards.[13]

POLITICAL CAREER

His political career began in 1962 when he was elected to the Georgia Senate. In 1966, Carter ran his first bid for governor of Georgia. Because Georgia state law restricts governors from succeeding themselves, the incumbent was

---

[7]"Jimmy Carter's Naval Experience," http://www.jimmycarterlibrary.org/documents/jec/jcnavy.phtml.

[8]Kenneth E. Morris, *Jimmy Carter American Moralist* (Athens: University of Georgia Press, 1997), 103.

[9]"Jimmy Carter's Naval Experience."

[10]Ibid.

[11]Francis Duncan, *Rickover: The Struggle of Excellence* (Annapolis, MD: U.S. Naval Institute Press, 2001).

[12]http://www.jimmycarterlibrary.gov.

[13]Ibid.

unable to seek re-election. The race consisted of a former governor; a former lieutenant governor; Jimmy Carter, who was a state senator at the time; and two businessmen who were known segregationists in the Democratic primary.[14] Through a series of runoffs, Jimmy Carter did not receive the party's nomination, although the election was ultimately decided by the state legislature because neither the Republican nor Democrat candidate received a majority of the votes.[15] Despite this loss, the race brought Carter's name to statewide prominence that he would need and benefit from during his 1970 bid for governor of Georgia.

During his second campaign for governor, his main opposition for the Democratic nomination was Carl Sanders, former governor of Georgia (1963–1967). During the campaign, segregation and racial overtones were issues around which Carter treaded lightly. Sanders was a moderate while Carter ran as a populist, forcing a runoff for the Democratic nomination. During his campaign, Carter assembled a group of advisers, including Hamilton Jordan, Jody Powell, Bert Lance, Stuart Eizenstat, and Gerald Rafshoon, who would remain with him through his term as governor as well as his presidential campaign and his time in the White House. Together they helped Carter campaign across the state, appealing to blue-collar, middle-class, predominantly white voters who were also segregationists. According to E. Stanly Godbold, "Carter himself was not a segregationist in 1970. But he did say things that the segregationists wanted to hear."[16] Carter would not only defeat Sanders in the Democratic runoff, but eventually defeat Republican Hal Suit in the general election by an almost 20 percent margin.[17]

Jimmy Carter was sworn in as governor of Georgia on January 12, 1971. Carter generally ran on a more conservative note, carefully not treading too hard on conservative Georgians' toes; but in his inauguration speech as he began his governorship, he announced, "I say to you quite frankly that the time for racial discrimination is over." This dedication to equal rights for all races and genders became a staple of his time in power and he did everything he could to assure equality in government as well as everywhere else, appointing several black people and women to high government positions.[18]

As governor, Carter focused on the reorganization of the Georgia state government. This effort took all four years of his governorship and resulted in a restructuring effort that moved 265 agencies, boards, bureaus, and commissions into twenty line agencies. Grouping divisions with similar agendas and resources allowed for the reduction in agency numbers as well as eliminating

---

[14]"GA Governor – D Primary," http://www.ourcampaigns.com/RaceDetail. html?RaceID=382413.

[15]"GA Governor – 1966," http://www.ourcampaigns.com/RaceDetail.html?RaceID=40398.

[16]"People & Events: James Earl ('Jimmy') Carter Jr. (1924–)," http://www.pbs.org/wgbh/amex/carter/peopleevents/p_jcarter.html.

[17]"GA Governor – 1970," http://www.ourcampaigns.com/RaceDetail.html?RaceID=40401.

[18]"American President: Jimmy Carter, Life before the Presidency," Miller Center of Public Affairs, http://millercenter.org/academic/americanpresident/carter/essays/biography/2.

duplication. Efficiency in government also went up through this restructuring by aligning groups that would consistently work together. Although restructuring of government is usually met with mixed reviews, Carter received heavy criticism for the creation of three "super agencies," the departments of administrative services, natural resources, and human resources.[19]

As discussed earlier, Jimmy Carter also proposed budget reform within the state government through what was referred to as his zero-based budgeting plan. This plan redesigned the method by which budget proposals were structured. Yearly budgets for agencies and departments are usually based off of the previous year's budget and adjusted accordingly depending on expenditures. In zero-based budgeting, Carter pushed for agencies to begin at zero and write a new budget proposal from scratch each year, forcing them to explain and justify the money that was requested.[20]

Jimmy Carter was a strong supporter of education, an issue that he had addressed as a city councilman, state senator, governor, and president of the United States. Reform of the state's education program was named "Adequate Program for Education in Georgia," and was designed to provide funds for career-focused education and smaller classes and to equalize funding across districts. Funding was also increased for preschool education that would lead to a statewide kindergarten program.[21]

Carter then addressed the criminal justice system. He proposed unification of the court system to consolidate the courts, similar to the reorganization of his state agencies and departments. In choosing judges from around the state, Carter implemented a merit system of selection to ensure that the judges who were placed on the bench had the necessary qualifications to handle the requisite caseload. Promoting judges on the basis of merit was then followed with a constitutional method of regulating conduct within the judicial branch.[22] The criminal justice reform was rounded out by penal reform in which the death penalty was replaced by life in prison.[23]

In Carter's gubernatorial campaign in Georgia from 1969 to 1970, he found themes that he believed would resonate in 1975 with a larger, national political audience, especially in the wake of Watergate: the need for honesty and high ethical standards among all government officials, transparency in government operations, efficiency in government management, and government leaders who would serve the needs of the people and the "common good," instead of the selfish needs of organized interests.[24] Carter presented himself to the voters of

---

[19]Glad, 180–181.

[20]Ibid.

[21]"Education in Georgia," 2008–09 Edition Education Policy Primer, 13, http://www.gpee.org/fileadmin/files/pdf/Education_in_GA.pdf.

[22]Ibid.

[23]Craig Brandon, *The Electric Chair: An Unnatural American History* (Jefferson, NC: McFarland & Company, 1999), 242.

[24]Edwin C. Hargrove, *Jimmy Carter as President: Leadership and the Politics of the Public Good* (Baton Rouge: Louisiana State University Press, 1988), 4.

Georgia as a man of the people, as an outsider who was not beholden to special interests, and as a courageous leader who had the audacity and wherewithal to challenge the status quo. He had evolved a leadership style described by some as "stylistic populism."[25] In his autobiography, *Why Not the Best?*, Carter reflected on his state government experience and expressed his notion of the common good and his disdain for conventional political arrangements:

> It is difficult for the common good to prevail, especially against the intense concentration of those who have a special interest, especially if decisions are made behind locked doors. . . . The 250 members of the legislature were almost all good honest men and women. A tiny portion were not good or honest. In the absence of clear and comprehensive issues, it is simply not possible to marshal the interest of the general public, and under such circumstances legislators respond to the quiet and professional pressures of lobbyists.[26]

Carter's presidential campaign began on December 12, 1974. He was little known on a national level despite serving as the Democratic National Committee's campaign chairman for the congressional and gubernatorial elections in 1974.[27] He began a grassroots campaign taking on the problems of government that were still fresh in the public's mind from Watergate. Carter promoted his status as a Washington outsider, including his religious values and southern roots that could rebuild the public's faith in the White House. His supporters, known as the Peanut Brigade, traveled to the host states for the primaries and campaigned vigorously, helping him win more than half of the states.[28] He would win the nomination on the first ballot at the Democratic National Convention in 1976, having gained enough delegates to win before the convention began.[29]

After the Republican convention, President Gerald Ford was heavily involved with America's Bicentennial celebration and chose to remain at the White House rather than campaign. It was not until October 1976 that Ford began actively campaigning against Carter. Immediately after the convention, Carter held a 33 percent lead in the polls; however, this number decreased during the months before Ford began campaigning.[30] The 1976 presidential campaign saw the return of televised presidential debates for the first time sine the 1960 election. A poll taken after the first debate showed that Carter had clearly won and remained ahead in the race. During the second debate, Ford commented that Europe, and specifically referenced Poland, was not dominated by the

[25]Glad, 139.

[26]Jimmy Carter, *Why Not the Best?* (New York: Bantam Books, 1976), 101.

[27]http://www.jimmycarterlibrary.gov.

[28]"Election of 1976, an Outsider Prevails," 2003 Teachers Fellows for C-Span.org, http://www.c-span.org/classroom/govt/1976.asp.

[29]"US President – D Convention – July 16, 1976," Our Campaigns, http://www.ourcampaigns.com/RaceDetail.html?RaceID=58483.

[30]"Election of 1976, an Outsider Prevails."

Soviets, nor would it be allowed to happen under a Ford administration.[31] Ford's apparent confusion on important foreign policy issues caused a halt in his momentum in the polls that would only be hurt more after Bob Dole made a controversial remark during the vice presidential debate.[32] Despite an increase in poll numbers, Ford would never catch up to Carter. In addition, President Ford decided to pardon President Richard Nixon, a move that probably cost him votes in the 1976 election.[33] Carter's popularity and the new face he presented to the government and the White House would carry him into the election and led to him to victory on November 2, 1976.[34]

Using the four-part leadership framework will help analyze the accomplishments and limitations of the Carter presidency.

POLICY

The themes Jimmy Carter used in his successful gubernatorial campaign in Georgia in 1970 would find strikingly strong resonance in his 1975–1976 campaign for the presidency. Carter's biographer, Betty Glad, summarized the themes as follows:

> refusal to accept ideological labels; avoidance of controversy; emphasis on personality, morality, and integrity; preference for concrete proposals over broad political issues; ability to corral a network of talented and energetic supporters as well as disciplined, effective staff; and willingness to go for the jugular of his opponents when the circumstances seemed to demand it.[35]

Hamilton Jordan, who had served as Governor Carter's chief of staff and would later serve him in the White House, believed that Jimmy Carter was particularly equipped to run a successful presidential campaign and told reporter Jules Whitcover that:

> With the Vietnam war coming to a close, domestic problems and issues were apt to be a more important consideration, the problem solving ability of the American government was very much in question and someone outside of Washington, and outside the Senate, a governor who had proved that problems could be dealt with effectively in the state, could win.[36]

---

[31]"1976 Carter/Ford Debates," http://www.pbs.org/newshour/debatingourdestiny/1976.html.

[32]"Vice-Presidential Debate of 1976," Newshour with Jim Lehrer, http://www.pbs.org/newshour/debatingourdestiny/interviews/mondale.html.

[33]Fred I. Greenstein, *The Presidential Difference: Leadership Style from FDR to George W. Bush* (Princeton, NJ: Princeton University Press, 2004), 116.

[34]http://www.jimmycarterlibrary.com.

[35]Glad, 107.

[36]Jules Whitcover, *The Pursuit of the Presidency, 1972–1976* (New York: Viking Press, 1977), 109–110.

Jordan wrote a seventy-two-page memo on November 4, 1972, that strongly influenced Carter's presidential campaign. He advised Carter to spend the subsequent three to four years studying the issues of the day, boning up on foreign policy matters in particular. He also recommended that Carter study previous presidential administrations and expand his contacts with Washington and the Eastern Establishment. Jordan advised Carter to concentrate on running in primaries in states, such as New Hampshire and Florida, where he could show a good, early lead.[37] Finally, in what would become the hallmark of the Carter campaign, Jordan counseled Jimmy Carter to cultivate his Kennedy smile and emphasize his personal qualities—competence, honesty, and outsider status. Carter was advised, in short, to "run against Washington."[38]

By all accounts, Carter took Jordan's advice quite seriously and immediately began to act on his recommendations. Apparently, one of Carter's first actions was to read *The Presidential Character: Predicting Performance in the White House*, the well-regarded book on previous presidents by Duke University political scientist James David Barber.[39] In that book, Barber developed typologies of U.S. presidents along the variables of how much energy they put into the job (active or passive), and what kind of affect they had toward the job and the presidential experience (positive or negative). Barber concluded that the "active-positive" presidents were more successful overall in the White House, and during the 1976 campaign Carter used Barber's terminology to predict that he would be "active and positive in approach as president."[40]

In addition, Carter increased his contacts and relationship-building efforts with Establishment figures such as former secretaries of states Dean Rusk and William Rogers; sought advice from his mentor, Navy Admiral Human Rickover; and became involved with the Trilateral Commission where he met Zbigniew Brzezinski, Michael Blumenthal, and Cyrus Vance, all of whom would subsequently be invited to join his cabinet.[41]

But the main efforts Jimmy Carter undertook were based on Jordan's advice regarding stylistic issues. By June 1975, Carter had traveled more than 50,000 miles, visited 37 states, delivered more than 200 speeches, and appeared on 93 radio and television programs.[42] On the road, he made it a point of staying with friends and avoiding fancy hotels or other trappings of privilege. Setting the tone of his campaign, Carter told a group of supporters in Berlin, New Hampshire, that, "It is time for someone like myself to make

---

[37]Kandy Stroud, *How Jimmy Won: The Victory Campaign from Plains to the White House* (New York: William Morrow and Company, Inc., 1977), 185–187.

[38]Glad, 211.

[39]James David Barber, *The Presidential Character: Predicting Performance in the White House* (Englewood Cliffs, NJ: Prentice-Hall Publishers, 1972).

[40]Glad, 487.

[41]Ibid., 224–225.

[42]Ibid., 233.

a drastic change in Washington. The insiders have had their chance, and they have not delivered."[43]

In that statement, the essence of the Carter campaign and leadership approach can be discerned. He presented himself, as he had done before, as the outsider, and as an outsider he alone could restore a sense of honor and integrity to the White House. After all, the nation was still in shock over the revelations of the imperial tendencies of Richard Nixon, as exemplified most dramatically in the Watergate crisis, and American citizens were searching for a different kind of leadership. In many ways, Jimmy Carter was the perfect candidate to appeal to voters in the aftermath of Watergate. He was an outsider, not part of the tainted Washington Establishment; he was a self-described "man of the people," not an elitist; he was a farmer and engineer by background and training; and he exuded wholesomeness and integrity.

Responding to the condition of alienation and fear that many Americans felt in the months and years after Watergate, Carter campaigned for the presidency on the themes of honesty and integrity, and "giving America a government as good as its people." In fact, he wrote a book with that title.[44] In the course of his presidential campaign, Carter did discuss some specific issues. For instance, he opposed President Ford's tax plan (to slash taxes by $28 billion) and he proposed gas rationing and tax increases on oil imports.[45] In addition, he called for a comprehensive energy conservation program, renewed commitment to the protection of the environment, tax reform, and a reorganization of the federal bureaucracy.[46] But the bulk of his campaign for the presidency was thematic, not programmatic. Carter presented himself as Nixon's opposite. According to his biographer, Betty Glad, "Many of Carter's issue stands were not stands at all, but abstract statements of principle to which few could object."[47] According to *Washington Post* reporter Bob Woodward:

> But Carter . . . was not Nixon. He was not a lawyer. He had never held office in Washington—the seat of a government few any longer trusted. He was an outsider, and he would tell the truth—always. He would divest himself of the trappings of the imperial presidency. He promised to remain close to the people. He would do what he deemed right, not what was politically expedient. Carter had fashioned a powerful message in the aftermath of Watergate. He was able to use Watergate as both whipping boy and selling point. The diagnosis was that government was corrupt to the core. The remedy was to make the government as good as he was by electing him.[48]

---

[43]Ibid., 250.

[44]Jimmy Carter, *A Government As Good As Its People* (New York: Simon and Schuster, 1977).

[45]Glad, 317.

[46]Hargrove, 12.

[47]Glad, 305.

[48]Bob Woodward, *Shadow: Five Presidents and the Legacy of Watergate* (New York: Simon & Schuster, 2000), 42.

Jimmy Carter recognized correctly that the president is the symbolic head of American government. According to previously cited presidential scholar James David Barber, the presidency is "the focus for the most intense and persistent emotions in the American polity."[49] As a presidential candidate, Jimmy Carter sought, above all, to reassure the American public that their government maintained its integrity, and that its leaders could once again fulfill the responsibilities of the office with dignity and honor. He wanted to reassure the people that he would project a different, more humble leadership approach, that random and evil forces would not be allowed to destroy their precious Constitution, and that he could be trusted with the reins of power that he would put to good use. To show his resolve to maintain an honorable administration, at many of his campaign stops Carter made the same statement, "I want a government that's as truthful and honest and decent and fair and compassionate and filled with love as the rest of the American people."[50] To emphasize his humility in his elevated position, he often said, "I have never claimed to be better or wiser than any other person. I think my greatest strength is that I am an ordinary man, just like all of you."[51]

Jimmy Carter was really not a visionary. He suffered from what historian James Macgregor Burns once called "strategic myopia."[52] Carter lacked a grand vision, a compelling picture of the nation's future beyond the simple restoration of trust. He proved to be an effective critic of the recent past and an avowed enemy of the "imperial presidency"; however, he was almost mute on the subject of the future policy direction for America. Carter possessed a considerable set of skills for attacking the status quo, but a more meager set for charting out a future course of governing. According to Carter's speechwriter, James Fallows, Carter's speeches became more passionate when he talked "about the subject that most inspired him—not what he was prepared to do, but who he was. Where Lyndon Johnson boasted of schools built and children fed, where Edward Kennedy holds out the promise of the energies he might mobilize and the ideas he might enact, Jimmy Carter tells us that he is a good man."[53]

Carter won the 1976 presidential election by 1.7 million votes. He received 50.1 percent of the popular vote compared to Gerald Ford's 48 percent. He won eleven of the thirteen states in the South and the few Northern states that he needed to win: New York, Ohio, Pennsylvania, Massachusetts, Wisconsin, and Minnesota. The electoral college vote was 297–240; the smallest winning total since Woodrow Wilson's victory over Charles Evans Hughes in 1916.[54]

---

[49]Barber, 4.

[50]Stroud, 424–425.

[51]Ibid., 425.

[52]Burns presentation at the University of Maryland, College Park, Maryland, October 1988.

[53]James Fallows, "The Passionless Presidency: The Trouble with Jimmy Carter's Administration," *Atlantic Weekly*, May 1979, http://www.theatlantic.com/unbound/flashbks/pres/fallpass.htm.

[54]Glad, 400.

America was about to experience a presidency that was "outside the familiar mold," as described by James Sterling Young in his foreword to the book *Jimmy Carter as President: Leadership and the Politics of the Public Good*:

> Carter was the first president to be elected from the Deep South since before the Civil War, the first to be elected under the new presidential selection system of the 1970's, and the first true outsider—having no previous experience in Washington—to be elected since Woodrow Wilson. If the ways of Washington were new to Jimmy Carter and most of his Georgia lieutenants when they came to the White House, the ways of their president were new to Washingtonians too.[55]

POLITICS

Watergate proved to have a profound influence on the American polity. Not only did President Nixon's excesses create fear among American citizens, a fear that Jimmy Carter was particularly adept at addressing, but they also caused the Congress to reinsert itself more aggressively in the scheme of government and to begin to scrutinize the executive branch more consistently and aggressively than before. With the 1974 election of the "Watergate Babies," seventy-five Democrats newly elected to office three months after the resignation of Richard Nixon, the Congress would change in fundamental ways. These newly elected Democrats presented a different profile than did their counterparts of earlier years; they were newer to the institution, more activist in orientation, and more willing to charter new territory for policy initiatives and to challenge presidential leadership. They were less likely to play the traditional role of new members—apprenticeship—and more likely to demand full participation in the activities of Congress, including having a full voice in the legislative process and a strong presence in the oversight of the executive branch of government.[56] In Massachusetts, for example, Paul Tsongas was the first Democrat to be elected from his district in the twentieth century, and Les AuCoin was the first Democrat elected to the House of Representatives from Oregon's northwest corner since the 1800s. The dramatic changes in Congress after Watergate proved to be problematic for Jimmy Carter, especially in light of the absence of an effective congressional relations strategy in his administration, which will be detailed later. According to Gregory Paul Domin, "Ironically, it was the genuineness of Carter's anti-Washington position, so formidable with the public that hindered his effectiveness once in the nation's capital."[57]

---

[55]Hargrove, Foreword.

[56]Ben W. Heineman Jr. and Curtis A. Hessler, *Memorandum for the President: A Strategic Approach to Domestic Affairs in the 1980s* (New York: Random House, 1980), 92; and Roger Davidson and Walter J. Oleszek, *Congress and Its Members*, 11th ed. (Washington, D.C.: Congressional Quarterly Press, 2007).

[57]Domin, 65.

A second set of political obstacles faced by Jimmy Carter when he assumed the presidency: The nation's economy was experiencing a period of hyperinflation, serious energy problems were looming, and the traditional ideas of the Democratic Party were inadequate to address these kinds of issues.[58] Indeed, Carter emphasized that he would stake out different ground and failed to be constrained by the practices and policies of previous Democratic presidents. According to James Sterling Young:

> After Roosevelt's New Deal, Truman's Fair Deal, Kennedy's New Frontier, and Johnson's Great Society, here was a Democrat who not only spurned labels but presented a large legislative agenda with a drastically conservative cast. Carter moved to retrench and reform— not to extend—the welfare state that other Democrats had built; to curb and roll back the regulatory state that other Democrats had built; to reduce intervention in the private sector as a way of solving public problems in the long run; to deregulate and start relying on market forces in order to achieve desired revenue ends.[59]

Carter moved quickly, but not strategically, to achieve his policy objectives. The day after his swearing in, he issued his first executive order to pardon Vietnam draft dodgers, suggesting he would be faithful to his campaign promises. This enraged Senator Barry Goldwater of Arizona, who called Carter's order, "the most disgraceful thing that a president has ever done."[60] In early February, he announced that by March, he would send plans for a new Energy Department to Congress,[61] and he promised to have a comprehensive energy program ready for delivery to a joint session of Congress by April 20.[62] At a March 9 press conference, President Carter offered a large number of domestic programs and foreign policy departures including a Youth Conservation Corps program, a Middle East settlement idea, gradual withdrawal of U.S. troops from South Korea, and arms negotiations with Russia. He also revealed his tax rebate program, his plan to reorganize the federal government, and his opposition to "wasteful" water projects in the West.[63]

The problem was that President Carter had not assigned levels of priority or urgency to these multifarious legislative proposals. They were sufficiently

---

[58]Hargrove, 21–22.

[59]Ibid., Foreword.

[60]Burton L. Kaufman and Scott Kaufman, *The Presidency of James Earl Carter, Jr.* (Lawrence: University Press of Kansas, 2006), 35.

[61]Jimmy Carter, "Reorganization Plan Authority Remarks on Transmitting Proposed Legislation to the Congress," February 4, 1977; and John T. Woolley and Gerhard Peters, *The American Presidency Project* (Santa Barbara: University of California), http://www.presidency.ucsb.edu/ws/index.php?pid=7522&st=&st1=.

[62]Jimmy Carter, "The Energy Shortage Remarks on Returning from the Trip to Pittsburgh, Pennsylvania," January 30, 1977; and Woolley and Peters.

[63]Jimmy Carter, "The President's News Conference of March 9, 1977," in *Public Papers of the Presidents of the United States of America, 1977, Book I January 1 to June 30, 1977* (Washington, D.C.: Government Printing Office, 1977), 340, 348.

numerous to overwhelm the process that was available to deal with them. According to Ben Heineman Jr. and Curtis Hessler:

> The President sent a flotilla of major proposals to Congress in the first eighteen months of his administration—cuts in water projects, social security finance, a tax rebate scheme, hospital cost containment legislation. . . . Many of these proposals went to the tax-writing committees of Congress: Senate Finance and House Ways and Means. And because the President had overloaded the Congress and those committees with reforms that would not command ready assent, because he was not able to marshal the Administration's resources and develop political support for the major battles that were required, and because many of his top political lieutenants were untutored in the ways of Congress, most of these proposals were either sunk or badly damaged.[64]

Not only was Jimmy Carter's agenda expansive, but he also moved quickly on specific matters without doing his political homework. For instance, he selected Theodore Sorensen to be director of the CIA without consulting key members of Congress, such as Senate Majority Leader Robert Byrd. Sorensen had requested draft exempt status earlier in his career and had given depositions opposing the over-classification of national security documents in the Pentagon Papers (1971) and Daniel Ellsberg (1973) cases. When Sorensen's actions became known, he came under attack by Republicans and Democrats alike. Conservatives asked for the withdrawal of his nomination, and Byrd suggested there would be "difficulty" with it. Carter took an ambiguous stand on the matter, which forced Sorensen to eventually withdraw his name from nomination.[65]

Carter showed insensitivity to Democratic leaders by failing to consult them on appointments from their states. He chose Republican John Ellis of Ohio as deputy commissioner of education without consulting Ohio Senator John Glenn, one of Carter's most enthusiastic supporters. President Carter also upset Speaker of the House Thomas "Tip" O'Neill when he appointed Nixon's attorney general, Elliott Richardson, a Republican from O'Neill's home state of Massachusetts, as a U.S. representative to the Law of the Sea Conference. Richardson was expected to run for governor of Massachusetts against O'Neill's oldest son. In addition, Carter failed to touch base with House Whip John Brademas (D-IN) on a proposal to revamp the U.S. Department of Health, Education, and Welfare (HEW). Brademas had been deeply involved in developing many of the programs that would be affected by the reorganization.[66]

On February 21, in his 1978 budget revisions, Jimmy Carter axed nineteen water projects. Members in the affected districts were not consulted in

---

[64]Heineman and Hessler, Preface.

[65]Glad, 448

[66]Ibid., 418–419.

advance. Once the decision to eliminate the projects was made, Carter's team made phone calls and sent memos to the relevant members of Congress, but they arrived so late in the week that many of the members had already gone home for the weekend and learned of the cuts from local newspapers! Jody Powell, Carter's assistant, remarked that the members of Congress had been "basically" informed.[67] Senators such as Butler Derrick (R-SC) and Gary Hart (D-CO) were outraged; Hart stated that he had been "blindsided" by Carter's actions. The Senate voted 65–24 to stop Carter's cutoff of the water projects.[68] According to Senator Robert Byrd (D-WV), had the president talked to the senators the outcome might have been different. Said Byrd, "At least the Senators would have felt that they had been consulted and heard."[69] Eventually, President Carter was able to prevail with a modified list of cuts, but the damage had been done. Astonishingly, Frank Moore, the president's director of congressional liaison, claimed that he never knew it was traditional to tell people what was going to be in the budget "before it was released."[70]

Even in instances when Carter identified strong priorities, and attached these to legislative proposals, he failed to adequately lobby for his position, or to engage in what journalists call "retail politics." A telling example of this oversight comes from a book by Tip O'Neill.[71] On February 2, 1977, Jimmy Carter delivered an energy speech on national television wearing a cardigan sweater. (In some respects, Carter was trying to emulate President Franklin Roosevelt and his "fireside chats.") Carter eloquently explained to the nation how the energy crisis demanded sacrifices of all Americans and that the White House was no exception. He told Americans that he had ordered all the thermostats at the White House to be set at lower temperatures, which was why he was wearing a sweater.[72] Carter explained that importing large quantities of foreign oil was a concern and that America "must face the fact that the energy shortage is permanent."[73] The president also explained a series of cutbacks on expenditures for the White House such as eliminating luxuries like door-to-door limo service for all staff, cutting staff size for the members of his cabinet, and asking the public not to mail gifts to the White House, implying that although he knew the intentions behind them, it was a financial expenditure people should not face.[74] He also mentioned that he had an energy bill before Congress and that he would appreciate Congress acting on it.[75]

---

[67]Ibid.

[68]Ibid.

[69]Ibid., 419–420.

[70]Ibid., 420.

[71]Tip O'Neill, *Man of the House* (New York: St. Martin's Press, 1988).

[72]Jimmy Carter, "Report to the American People—Remarks from the White House Library," in *Public Papers of the Presidents of the United States, 1977*, 71.

[73]Ibid., 70.

[74]Ibid., 73.

[75]Ibid., 74.

Once again, the energy bill had been developed largely behind closed doors under the direction of Secretary of Energy James Schlesinger.[76] The key provisions of the bill included a tax on gasoline pegged to rise with consumption, a tax on gas-guzzling automobiles, several conservation measures including tax credits for investments in greater fuel efficiency of buildings, taxes on domestic crude at the wellheads to increase domestic process to world levels with a revenue rebate to the public, federal control of intrastate natural gas sales, tax incentives for industries to shift to coal, and an end to gasoline price controls.[77] The president wanted Congress to consider 113 interlocking provisions in one package. Yet no attempt had been made to build a coalition in Congress while these proposals were being developed.[78]

Five minutes after the speech, Speaker O'Neill rang to compliment Carter on his speech and then asked that the president call all the chairpersons of the committees who would be dealing with the energy bill. Carter responded that he did not feel that was necessary, as all the committee chairs had heard the speech.[79]

President Carter's reaction to Speaker O'Neill's request reveals several dimensions of persuasion (and leadership) ineptitude. First, it is more than likely that each member of Congress who heard the energy speech may have actually heard a unique version of the speech, a version tailored to fit his or her own perceptions and needs. For example, the senator from Texas probably heard a different speech than did the senator from New Jersey, given the different levels of oil production in the two states. According to Professor Hargrove, the plan was too liberal for conservatives with its idea of continuing price controls and too conservative for liberals in its price increase proposals.[80]

Furthermore, people are rarely mobilized to action based on speeches alone. Presidents need to engage in retail politics, and follow the broad appeal of a legislative agenda with a "selling" strategy tailored to the individual needs of members of Congress. Years later, the Clinton health care program would falter because of a similar dynamic: Hillary Clinton and Ira Magaziner failed to practice retail politics with key stakeholders in that debate.[81]

Finally, Carter failed to recognize that follow-up calls by the president to members of Congress also help demonstrate the president's personal commitment to his program or proposal. President Lyndon Johnson, for instance, called resistant Southern senators at all hours of the night (and into the early

[76]Hargrove, 50–51.

[77]Bob Rankin, "Carter's Energy Plan: A Plan of Leadership," *Congressional Quarterly Weekly Report*, April 23, 1977, 727–728.

[78]Hargrove, 51.

[79]O'Neill.

[80]Hargrove, 51.

[81]David S. Broder and Haynes Johnson, *The System: The American Way of Politics at the Breaking Point* (Boston: Little Brown and Co., 1997).

morning hours) to personally lobby them for his civil rights bills.[82] Johnson liked to say "Nothing convinces like conviction."

One aspect of the congressional relations problem stemmed from Carter's own disdain for retail politics, as described by one of his aides:

> We used to always joke that the worst way to convince the President to go along with your position was to say this would help you politically, because . . . he wanted to be a different kind of President. He was elected somehow to be a different kind of President. He was running against the sort of system of inside deals and so forth. He saw himself above that system. He did not enjoy politics per se in the same way that a Humphrey or a Johnson did . . . It's not something that came naturally to him.[83]

Another aspect of the problem stemmed from the fact that Jimmy Carter surrounded himself with mostly Washington outsiders, men and women who were not well tutored in the norms of Capitol Hill. For the key White House positions, he chose Georgian political intimates. Carter named his old friend and political ally, Bert Lance, as director of the Office of Management and Budget. He named the director of the Georgia Office of Planning and Budget, James McIntyre Jr., as deputy director.[84] Jody Powell was named Press Secretary, and Hamilton Jordan as special assistant to the president. Robert Lipshutz, the financial campaign manager in 1976, was named legal counselor to the president. The main adviser on domestic issues, and a man who did have some Washington experience, was Stuart Eizenstat (who was later named the domestic policy adviser). Carter appointed his Georgia friend, Frank Moore, to the post of director of congressional liaison; however, Moore was particularly unfamiliar with the inside workings of Congress.[85]

His White House aides lacked direction and focus. A former White House aide described the early meetings of Carter's senior advisers as follows: "We all looked at each other and asked who should run the first meeting? Maybe Bob Lipshutz because he is the oldest among us."[86] James Fallows, Carter's speechwriter, described the Carter presidency as passionless, due to the president's lack of passion focused on a single issue or set of issues and his resulting inability to inspire passion among staff.[87]

His cabinet selections represented more connection to the Washington Establishment. For instance, Joseph Califano, Carter's secretary of HEW, had served in the Johnson administration, and Patricia Harris and Michael

---

[82]Robert Dallek, *Flawed Giant: Lyndon Johnson, 1960–1973* (New York: Oxford University Press, 1998).

[83]Hargrove, 17.

[84]Glad, 414.

[85]Ibid., 414–415.

[86]Hedrick Smith, *The Power Game: How Washington Works* (New York: Ballantine Books, 1988).

[87]Fallows.

Blumenthal had also served various Democratic administrations.[88] Cecil Andrus had served as Democratic governor of Idaho and had an active presence in the Democratic National Committee. Nonetheless, there were gaps in communication and coordination between the White House staff and the cabinet. President Carter had a particular aversion to the control of cabinet agencies by the White House staff, which will be explained later.

Finally, Carter undervalued the importance of one-on-one time with key members of Congress and presidential advisers. Bob Woodward presents a telling example of this tendency in his book, *Shadow*.[89] Carter scheduled a tennis game one Sunday afternoon and invited Senator Lloyd Bentsen, among others, to join him in a game of doubles. They played only a few sets, and immediately after the game, Carter walked off the courts and the three senators were sent home. Bentsen could not believe it. He was shocked! How many times do I get to spend one-on-one time with the president, he wondered to himself? Senator Bentsen was so upset that he called the White House the following day and inquired about why he was not invited to have lemonade with the president after the game. The response that came back from the White House was, "The President thought you would want to go home and spend time with your families."[90] In most cases, this would be sound advice, but not in the case of denying yourself a chance to meet informally with the president of the United States. Jimmy Carter was underestimating the incredible value of one-on-one time with an important congressional leader. And it works both ways. A leader can influence a follower (though senators hate to call themselves followers), and a follower can influence a leader. Former Secretary of State Colin Powell learned about the importance of one-on-one time with a boss. According to a more recent Woodward book, Powell heard that the vice president (Dick Cheney) and secretary of defense (Donald Rumsfeld) were having private dinners with President George W. Bush—and he was not. He demanded equal time, and through the good offices of Condoleezza Rice, Powell also had the chance for a one-on-one dinner with President Bush.[91] There is speculation that perhaps the only reason the United States even *tried* the diplomatic route to resolve the Iraq crisis was due to Powell's demand for one-on-one time with his boss.

In spite of Carter's troubles, he had a moderately successful first year legislatively speaking. President Carter's proposals for the creation of a Department of Energy, for authority to reorganize the government, and for building a natural gas pipeline from Alaska were approved as was his economic stimulus package and a major public works program.[92] Carter's legislative success rate was 75.4 percent, however, compared to other Democratic presidents

---

[88]Glad, 415.

[89]Woodward, 2000, 55.

[90]Ibid.

[91]Bob Woodward, *Plan of Attack* (New York: Simon and Schuster, 2004), 167.

[92]Glad, 423.

that score was not overly impressive, especially because Carter was working with a Democratic Congress. During President Kennedy's first year, he had achieved a legislative success rate of 81 percent, and Lyndon Johnson had scored 88 percent![93]

By 1978, the administration recognized some of its problems and addressed them. For instance, Carter added three new members, who were Washington insiders, to the congressional liaison staff. He cut the number of legislative priorities from sixty down to thirty.[94] His legislative score went up slightly, to 78.3 percent in 1978; however, this was, again, a lower figure than that achieved by Kennedy (85.4 percent) and Johnson (93 percent) in their second years as president.[95] His tax bill and energy bills had been shredded beyond recognition and he did not find a way to address the economic downturn.[96]

Looking back on the Carter administration, where he served as secretary of state, Cyrus Vance ruminated about the absence of "political" savvy in Jimmy Carter, saying, "I think [Carter] should have involved himself much more with the Congress than he did, and he should have used his White House staff more effectively in dealing with the Congress. The master at this . . . was Lyndon Johnson; he was superb."[97] Lyndon Johnson was a president who knew how to persuade Congress. He described the need for the president to persuade Congress to his biographer, Doris Kearns Goodwin, in this fashion:

> There is but one way for a President to deal with Congress, and that is continuously, incessantly, and without interruption. If it's really going to work, the relationship between the President and Congress has got to be almost incestuous. He's got to know them even better than they know themselves. And then, on the basis of this knowledge, he's got to build a system that straddles from cradle to the grave, from the moment a bill is introduced to the moment it is officially enrolled as the law of the land.[98]

STRUCTURE

Jimmy Carter was a detailed-oriented person who prided himself on his ability to master the intricacies of public policy. According to Edwin Hargrove, "He wished to understand thoroughly the issues for which he assumed primary responsibility and he characterized his cognitive processes as those of an

---

[93]Ibid.

[94]Ibid.

[95]Ibid., 425.

[96]Ibid.; and Heineman and Hessler.

[97]Cyrus Vance, "Carter's Foreign Policy: The Source of the Problem," in Kenneth W. Thompson, ed., *The Carter Presidency: Fourteen Intimate Perspectives of Jimmy Carter* (Lanham, MD: University Press of America, 1990), 135–144.

[98]Dallek.

engineer."[99] According to Carter's domestic policy adviser, Stuart Eizenstat, "He's one of the brightest political officials with whom I have dealt, and indeed one of the brightest men—extremely analytic, very incisive, just a very, very intelligent man."[100]

This habit of mind led Carter to personally read every bill that came before the Georgia legislature and to spend many a night reading through drafts of bills and copies of government reports. In the 1976 presidential campaign, Carter worked with Eizenstat on issue stances. Carter apparently moved through the alphabet from "Abortion" to "Zaire," choosing the issues not on the basis of importance, but in alphabetical order.[101] According to Betty Glad:

> He lacks, it seems, a well thought-out conceptual framework to guide his concrete political choices. He immerses himself in the technical details of programs that interest him, testing various strategies and rhetorical appeals. Yet he fails to bring the components together in an integrated approach that would give him a sense of direction and set up priorities for his various programs.[102]

The engineer's mentality led Carter down the path of micromanagement with regard to his own staff and operation. Indeed, President Carter wanted to closely manage everything. His supervisory purview included the White House tennis courts, whose schedule he apparently kept in a folder on his desk right beside folders containing material on strategic arms talks and Middle East Peace.[103] Carter himself described his tendencies to micromanage in a 1982 interview, "I'm an engineer at heart, and I like to understand details of things that are directly my responsibility."[104]

Carter's management "style" was influenced by another staff memo, this time from Patrick Caddell, who wrote a fifty-six-page missive to Carter in 1976. Caddell advised Carter to compensate for his rather narrow electoral victory over Gerald Ford by emphasizing style over substance in the early days of the administration. He also advised Carter to "use the honeymoon period to reassure and win over broad segments of the American public."[105]

And so he did. Carter sent out 300,000 invitations to the inauguration, many to people whom he had met on the campaign trial and to whom he

---

[99]Hargrove, 5–6.

[100]Stuart Eizenstat, "Interview with Stuart Eizenstat," in James Sterling Young et al., eds., *Jimmy Carter Presidential Oral History Project* (Charlottesville, VA: Miller Center, 1982), http://webstorage3.mcpa.virginia.edu/poh/transcripts/ohp_1982_0129_eizenstat.pdf.

[101]Ibid., 4.

[102]Glad, 476.

[103]Fallows.

[104]Jimmy Carter, "Interview with Jimmy Carter," in Young et al., http://webstorage3.mcpa.virginia.edu/poh/transcripts/ohp_1982_1129_Carter.pdf.

[105]Domin, 40.

had promised an invitation.[106] For the swearing-in ceremony in front of the Capitol, Carter wore an ordinary three-piece suit and used his campaign name, "Jimmy Carter," rather than his formal name of James Earl Carter. He surprised many observers, in addition to the security detail of the Secret Service, by walking down Pennsylvania Avenue to the White House with his wife, Rosalyn, at his side.[107]

President Carter enrolled his daughter in a predominantly African American public school near the White House, eliminated chauffeur service for several White House aides, and scaled back many other perks of office. He asked that the traditional musical rendition of "Hail to the Chief" not be played when he entered a room, because it gave the impression of an imperial presidency.[108]

Carter insisted on an open administration and eschewed the erection of barriers between him and the public. He was influenced by Stephen Hess' book, *Organizing the Presidency*, that argued that successive presidents had permitted the White House assistants to crowd out cabinet officers and become their principal advisers (a tendency especially pronounced in the Nixon administration where cabinet secretaries were intercepted by White House staff when they attempted to see the president).[109] According to Bob S. Bergland, Carter's secretary of agriculture, "[Carter] stated early in the formation of his new administration that he was going to use Cabinet government, and he kept his word."[110] Bergland never felt that presidential staff blocked his access to the president, "I had direct telephone access to the President in his Oval Office. I didn't come through the White House Switchboard. I came through the secretary who sat just outside the Oval Office. If the President was busy, he would always call me back."[111]

Carter evolved a White House staff structure termed "spokes of the wheel," with the president at the center and the advisers arrayed around him in a circle.[112] There was no chief of staff, and presidential assistants would no longer give direction to cabinet officers. Carter preferred a more informal policy development process referred to as "collective collegiality."[113] Hamilton Jordan appearing on CBS's "Face the Nation," in mid-November said, "The concept of a chief of staff is alien to Governor Carter and those around him. He's always had a strong team effort."[114] President Carter explained his rationale for operating without a chief of staff in a 1982 interview with James

---

[107]Domin, 37–38.

[108]Ibid., 38–39.

[109]Stephen Hess, *Organizing the Presidency* (Washington, D.C.: Brookings Institute, 1976).

[110]Bob S. Bergland, "Politics and Agriculture: Lessons of the Carter Presidency," in Thompson, 115–131.

[111]Ibid.

[112]Hargrove, 24.

[113]Ibid., 26.

[114]Glad, 411.

Sterling Young, "I have never wanted a person under me to whom all my chief advisors had to report and then have that one person report to me . . . I wanted but seven or eight of my staff members to have unimpeded, direct access to me and not feel that they ever had to go through a chief of staff."[115]

Hamilton Jordan later reflected on the loosely defined managerial style that Carter administration employed, including the decision to not have a strong chief of staff and to "compartmentalize" issues:

> The mistake the President made was that he and his staff tended to compartmentalize problems and issues in the White House too much. Our organization reflected that. We also overreacted to some of the excesses of the past. As a result of the Nixon experience, it became a campaign statement that we would not have a powerful chief of staff in the White House. "I'm going to be the President and I'm going to make decisions and run things." We never sat down and talked about whether Jimmy Carter should make that statement or not. That was a political reaction to the excesses of the Nixon administration. It was also the kind of hands-on President he thought he would be.[116]

Nonetheless, Carter's more loosely designed management structures contributed to the escalation of problems for the administration. Carter and his staff were unable to exercise damage control during a period of intense questioning of Bert Lance's banking practices. Carter's popularity took a nosedive during the Lance affair, and it seriously challenged his claim to moral superiority.[117] Carter's ambassador to the UN, Andrew Young, traveled around the country making inflammatory statements. In May 1977, he told reporters on a trip to London that "the old colonial mentality is still strong in Britain" and that the "Russians and Swedes are racists."[118] Young finally went too far when he held an unauthorized meeting with the Palestine Liberation Organization (PLO) representative Zehdi Labib Terzi. He resigned shortly thereafter.[119]

In the summer of 1978, Carter appeared to be in deep trouble when a Harris Poll showed a 61 percent negative rating on the president's ability to improve confidence in the White House.[120] In June 1979, Carter and his closest advisers, including Powell, Rafshoon, and Caddell, were whisked away in a helicopter to Camp David for the purpose of reinvigorating the administration. From July 6 to 16, Carter brought people from politics, the media, the civil rights movement, and labor unions to meet with him. He announced that Caddell had been warning him about his findings that a majority of Americans believed for

---

[115]Carter, 1982, 8–9.

[116]Hamilton Jordan, "Interview with Hamilton Jordan," in Young et al., http://webstorage3.mcpa.virginia.edu/poh/transcripts/ohp_1981_1106_jordan.pdf.

[117]Kaufman and Kaufman, 73.

[118]Glad, 440.

[119]Kaufman and Kaufman, 184.

[120]Glad, 443.

the first time that their children's "lives may not be better than their own."[121] *Washington Post* columnist Meg Greenfield described the event in this fashion:

> It is a highly personal anti-institutional method, and it combines in some odd proportions humbleness and notions almost of royalty. Carter is the plain fellow asking your opinion and submitting himself to criticism. But he is, in addition somehow the benevolent Shakespearean duke, the ruler figure on whom all authority reposes, along with all the capacity to bring peace and blessing to the duchy—the majestic leader who goes freely and willingly among his people.[122]

PROCESS

In an unusual attempt to build diversity into his foreign policy apparatus, Jimmy Carter named two very different men to the highest foreign policy posts in government. Carter appointed Cyrus Vance, an accomplished Wall Street lawyer and a conciliator and mediator by temperament and training, to be secretary of state. And Zbigniew Brzezinski, irascible by nature and tempered by a horrific personal experience with the USSR, was appointed as national security adviser (Details provided to author buy Carter White House adviser Mark A. Siegel). Mark A. Siegel was special liaison to the Jewish community in the Carter White House for 1976. He had previously served as chairman of the Democratic National Committee.

On almost all policy decisions that arose during the Carter presidency, Vance and Brzezinski took diametrically different positions. Typically, Vance favored negotiating with the Soviets, working out compromises in international conflicts, and relying on the UN and other international organizations to resolve regional disputes. Such a stance was evident in emphasis on the importance of the SALT (Strategic Arms Limitation Talks) treaty.[123] Brzezinski almost always disagreed and favored a tougher, more muscular policy vis-à-vis the Soviet Union. To him, America could negotiate with the Soviet Union only from a "position of strength."[124]

When a president is confronted with two aides who constantly disagree, he must find ways to resolve tough issues; frequently this means having to side with one person over the other, or at least with one idea over the other. Not so with Jimmy Carter. During a speech given at the U.S. Naval Academy in June 1978, Carter sought to define U.S. policy toward the Soviet Union in the midst of differing statements from Brzezinski and Vance on the issue. He then asked his advisers, most notably Brzezinski and Vance, to submit their opinions on what the tone and content of the speech should be. In his speech, he tried to blend both their positions into one composite position, though "It had an obvious

---

[121]Ibid., 445

[122]Ibid.

[123]Fallows.

[124]Kaufman and Kaufman, 43–44.

break in the middle."[125] Out of this amalgam, Carter presented numerous schizophrenic proclamations on foreign policy issues; his speeches and pronouncements were half Vance and half Brzezinski. In the words of one member of Congress, "Jimmy Carter had both feet firmly planted in mid-air!" Only when the Soviets invaded Afghanistan did Carter finally decide to side with Brzezinski, and shortly thereafter, Vance left the administration in opposition to the Iranian hostage rescue mission. According to Deputy Secretary of State Warren Christopher, when Vance found out that Carter had given the green light on the rescue mission, the secretary's "reaction was volcanic—the angriest I've ever seen him. Not only did the idea of a rescue mission infuriate him, but also that a matter of such moment had been raised and decided in his absence."[126]

Why, in the end, did Carter defer to the advice of Brzezinski over that of Vance? Part of it had to do with Carter's distrust of the bureaucracy of the State Department and his more favorable opinion of the National Security Council (NSC). Carter believed that the NSC provided a better setting for developing, analyzing, and debating strategic policy, and this showed in how he tried to balance the bureaucracy of the State Department with the "intellectual ferment of the NSC."[127] In his own words, Carter described how he viewed the State Department's role in his administration:

> I used the State Department as kind of an anchor or screen to hold us back from doing things that were ill-advised, to point all the reasons why something wouldn't work, and to make sure that we didn't take any radical steps.[128]

Carter clearly did not view the policy-making authority of the State Department in the same way that Cyrus Vance did.

Additionally, both Brzezinski's attitude and closer relationship with the president may also have influenced Carter to defer more so to the National Security Agency's advice. Said Carter, "When [Brzezinski] would say something, though, because of his appearance, because of his attitude, his statement which [Vance] could have made in a non-provocative way became provocative."[129] The two had a very close relationship since Brzezinski had long been a supporter and adviser to Carter.

SUMMING UP

As construed herein, Jimmy Carter was not a strategic president. He did have his accomplishments, however. He was directly responsible for mediating a peace process between Israel and Egypt and helped those adversaries agree to

---

[125]Fallows.
[126]Kaufman and Kaufman, 213.
[127]Ibid., 44.
[128]Carter, 1982, 39.
[129]Ibid.

sign the Camp David Peace Treaty in 1978. Carter was able to convince Israel's Prime Minister Menachem Begin and Egypt's President Anwar Sadat to move beyond their deadlock over "positions" and toward agreement on the fulfillment of "interests." Although Israel and Egypt demanded control of the Sinai Peninsula, which the Israelis had captured in the 1967 "Six-Day War," Carter and his mediation team helped reconcile the Israeli interest in security with the Egyptians interest in sovereignty.[130] He successfully negotiated the Panama Canal Treaty—a feat several presidents prior to him had failed to accomplish. He placed the issue of human rights on the international agenda, and perhaps his influence led to the release of political prisoners in Argentina and other countries. Finally, he was responsible for nominating more women and minorities to the federal bench than any other president before him.

Despite his achievements, this Democratic president had trouble leading a Democratic-controlled Congress, did not establish clear policy objectives, presided over a huge economic downturn (interest rates reached 17 percent and inflation stood at 12.5 percent), and failed to rally the nation to particular causes of importance in many respects.[131] His practice of telling the nation the truth, as he defined it, proved unsuccessful. The most famous case of Carter's straightforward speaking to America is now known by a word he didn't use in his speech. In 1979, he gave what is now known as the "malaise" speech. This speech is memorable because of the nature of Carter's remarks. He pointed out flaws and shortcomings in himself and the nation as a whole. Some of his comments blamed the public and how they valued themselves compared to others in terms of materialism.[132] The speech itself was very positively received and many Americans felt a connection with the president; however, in the end, Carter's poll numbers suffered as cabinet members were asked to resign and left the public with a sense of uncertainty in the president's plans and programs.[133]

President Carter also was demonstrably lacking in several fundamental leadership qualities: consulting with key stakeholders in any change effort, influencing and persuading people to go along with proposed programs, spending adequate one-on-one time with key constituents and colleagues, articulating a vision to galvanize attention and resources, and limiting goals but focusing on them "like a laser beam" (to quote President Bill Clinton). In the words of presidential adviser David Gergen, "Carter attempted too much and accomplished too little."[134]

[130]Roger Fisher and William Ury (with Bruce Patton), *Getting to Yes: Negotiating Agreement without Giving In* (New York: Penguin Books, 1991), 41–42.

[131]"Jimmy Carter: American Experience," PBS.org, http://www.pbs.org/wgbh/amex/carter/tguide/index.html.

[132]Jullian E. Zellzer, "What Carter Had Right," Politico.com, July 15, 2009, http://www.politico.com/news/stories/0709/24918.html.

[133]Andie Coller, "Was Carter Right?" Politico.com, July 15, 2009, http://www.politico.com/news/stories/0709/24944.html.

[134]Lou Cannon, *President Reagan: The Role of a Lifetime* (New York: Simon and Schuster, 1991), 111.

Perhaps the major failing of President Carter was his attempt to personalize the office, projecting the illusion that power politics can somehow be transcended by good people.[135] Carter presented himself as purer than all the interest groups, members of Congress, and other players in U.S. dynamic political process. As he said, "I owe nothing to special interest groups. I owe the people everything."[136] According to Betty Glad, Carter suggested that, "The President with a mythic tie to the people, becomes the central actor in the political system—the sole spokesman for the public interest. It is an old idea and politically dangerous in some ways. Those with access to the media and a superior ability to touch the right psychological button can create a following."[137] This concept is rich in irony, because in some ways Carter's approach to leadership, as described by Glad, harkens back to the imperial presidency that he so avidly sought to demolish.

[135]Glad, 506.
[136]Stroud, 424.
[137]Glad, 506.

The Presidency of Ronald Reagan

Ronald Reagan was inaugurated as the fortieth president of the United States on January 20, 1981, amid political conditions that could not have been more cleverly scripted for the former actor. Radical Iranian students held fifty-two American hostages for the 444th day, and, somewhat meaningfully, released them only hours after Reagan's inauguration.[1] A theocratic regime in Tehran, whose devotees had kidnapped the American hostages and whose influence appeared to be spreading throughout the Persian Gulf, threatened to disrupt the stability of the region. The Soviet Army occupied Afghanistan and Ethiopia, and was poised to enter Poland to put down anti-communist strikes and demonstrations; and Cuban troops had intruded on three African countries.[2]

Domestically, almost all major economic indicators were pointing in the wrong direction: inflation was at 12.5 percent, interest rates hovered around 16 percent, and the unemployment rate had climbed to 7.1 percent.[3] In his first inaugural address at the West Front of the U.S. Capitol, President Reagan put the economic problem at the center of his concerns when he said:

> These United States are confronted with an economic affliction of great proportions. We suffer from the longest and one of the worst sustained inflations in our national history. It distorts our economic decisions, penalizes thrift, and crushes the struggling young and the fixed-income elderly alike. It threatens to shatter the lives of millions of our people.[4]

According to the final report of the Initial Actions Project, a political guide to action prepared for Reagan by pollster-strategist Richard Wirthlin, "No American president since Franklin D. Roosevelt had inherited a more difficult economic situation."[5] The miserable condition of the American economy prompted James Baker, a Reagan aide and future White House chief of staff, to declare, "We ought to have three goals, and all of them are economic recovery."[6]

These economic times were the perfect stage whereon Reagan could make his big debut. Having come from an underprivileged background, he could understand the plight of the poorest of the poor. However, his experience with General Electric (GE) and other major companies also gave him insight into what businesses and the economic middle to upper classes needed.

---

[1]Alexandra Cosgrove, "Iran Hostage Anniversary," CBS News, January 18, 2001, http://www.cbsnews.com/stories/2001/01/18/iran/main265244.shtml.

[2]Alexander Haig, *Caveat, Realism, Reagan and Foreign Policy* (New York: MacMillan Company, 1984), 10.

[3]Lou Cannon, *President Reagan: The Role of a Lifetime* (New York: Simon and Shuster, 1991), 20.

[4]Ronald Reagan, *Speaking My Mind: Selected Speeches* (New York: Simon and Shuster, 1989), 59.

[5]Cannon, 1991, 107.

[6]Ibid.

EARLY LIFE

Ronald Reagan was born on February 6, 1911, in Tampico, Illinois. He was born to a poor man of Irish descent—Jack Reagan—and his wife—Nelle Reagan. Jack was a shoe salesman who moved from town to town and tried to make a living for his family between drinking bouts.[7] However, the family eventually settled down in Dixon, Illinois, where the Reagan boys attended high school, and where Ronald Reagan always considered home. This "small universe" of Dixon made a lasting impression on Reagan, and he always had fond feelings for it.[8]

Nevertheless, there was a darker side to Reagan's childhood. In addition to his father's drinking problem and associated difficulty with finding employment, Reagan's family was hit particularly hard during the Depression and Reagan's mother had to go to work at a dress shop to keep the family going.[9] However, in his characteristically optimistic style, Reagan generally described his childhood as a very happy time. Reagan learned the virtue of hard work and tenacity from his mother. These humble beginnings allowed Reagan to connect with the American people, even during economic crisis.

Reagan's mother was a devout Christian and she taught her boys to be the same. Ever since he was a young boy, Reagan read the Bible and learned its teachings. He always claimed it to be one of his favorite books.[10] Reagan had a particularly strong faith in the goodness of people, which stemmed from the optimistic faith of his mother and the Disciples of Christ faith, which he was baptized into in 1922.[11] He later attended the Presbyterian Church and always maintained his Christian values, being swayed by the influences that came along with them. Reagan was a deeply religious man, but unlike other presidents did not wear his religion on his sleeve.

During high school, Reagan was a very athletic boy, tall and muscular like his father, so he was involved in many sports.[12] Reagan participated in basketball, football, and track, and was later elected student body president of his high school. Reagan expressed talents in many areas, not only being involved in sports and student government but also being heavily involved in drama.[13] After high school, he attended Eureka College in Illinois, where he participated in the football, track, and swim teams, and was a reporter for the school newspaper.[14] He also served as student body president, and was

---

[7]Lou Cannon and Carl M. Cannon, *Reagan's Disciple: George W. Bush's Trouble Quest for a Presidential Legacy* (New York: PublicAffairs, 2008), 2.

[8]Ronald Reagan, *An American Life* (New York: Simon & Schuster, 1990), 27.

[9]Cannon and Cannon, 2.

[10]Reagan Presidential Library and Foundation, http://www.reaganlibrary.com.

[11]Paul Kengor, *God and Ronald Reagan: A Spiritual Life* (New York: HarperCollins, 2004), 16.

[12]Lou Cannon, *Governor Reagan* (New York: PublicAffairs, 2005), 21.

[13]Reagan Presidential Library and Foundation, "1911–1934: Dixon High School," http://www. reaganlibrary.com, accessed November 9, 2009.

[14]National Archives, http://www.reagan.utexas.edu/archives/reference/reference. html#Ronald_Reagan.

a member of the Tau Kappa Epsilon fraternity. He graduated in 1932 with a B.A. in economics and sociology.

Even though Reagan graduated during the depths of the Depression, he searched for a job with characteristic optimism. His charisma, voice talent, and ability to re-create a Eureka College football game in an exciting way entirely from memory landed him a job as a sports announcer for WOC radio. Later he moved to station WHO in Des Moines, where, as sportscaster "Dutch Reagan," he became popular throughout the state for his broadcasts of Chicago Cubs baseball games. Because the station could not afford to send him to Wrigley Field in Chicago, Reagan was forced to improvise a running account of the games based on sketchy details delivered over a teletype machine.[15]

Reagan got his big break in 1937 when he went to Catalina, California, to cover the spring training of the Chicago Cubs. He was able to do a screen test for Warner Brothers.[16] The studio hired him and he began to act, mostly in B movies as the easy-going, good-looking, and amiable guy whom everybody loved.[17] The skill he brought into playing these characters was carried over into his presidency in abundance, especially because, as many people noted, "Reagan was playing the heart-warming role of himself."[18] He also acted in a few major movies such as *King's Row* and *Hellcats of the Navy*, and he always received good reviews.

Reagan married actress Jane Wyman in 1940. They had two children and adopted one more. By 1948, however, Jane filed for divorce, and by 1949 it was finalized, later making Reagan the only president to have been divorced.[19] Jane spoke little of the marriage while harboring no ill feeling toward Reagan.[20] Shortly after his death, she commented, "America has lost a great president and a great, kind, and gentle man."[21]

In 1937, Reagan joined the Army Enlisted Reserve.[22] Because of his poor eyesight, he was never able to go overseas but instead was assigned domestically; he mostly made war movies to inform the public and to recruit more soldiers.[23] After his army service, he returned to the acting world and assumed the role of president of the Screen Actors Guild. He was president during some of the most tumultuous times in Hollywood, when some, including Reagan, suspected the industry had been compromised by the infiltration of communists. Reagan worked tirelessly to save the reputation of the innocent and to

---

[15]Cannon, 1991, 22.

[16]Cannon, 2005, 48.

[17]Cannon, 1991, 27.

[18]Lou Cannon, "Why Reagan Was the Great Communicator," *USA Today*, June 6, 2004, http://www.usatoday.com/news/opinion/editorials/2004-06-06-cannon_x.htm, accessed November 9, 2009.

[19]Cannon, 2005, 73.

[20]Ibid., 74.

[21]http://www.cnn.com/2004/ALLPOLITICS/06/11/reagan.friday2/index.html.

[22]Army Reserve 100th Anniversary, http://www.armyreserve100th.com/faces.php.

[23]Cannon and Cannon, 111–112.

root out what he called the "evil" of communism.[24] It was in this capacity that he met his future wife, Nancy Davis, when she contacted him after she was mistaken for another Nancy Davis on the communist blacklist. They fell in love and were married in 1952.

The relationship between Nancy and Ronald was described as "close, real, and intimate" by all who knew them.[25] They were truly in love. In an interview with BBC after Reagan's death in 2004, Nancy told the reporter, "Our relationship is very special. We were very much in love and still are. When I say my life began with Ronnie, well, it's true. It did. I can't imagine life without him."

Although Reagan turned out to be a champion of conservatism in his later years, his political history was not completely one-sided. Reagan cast his first vote in a presidential election for Franklin Delano Roosevelt, who would remain his hero for the rest of his life.[26] He was a Democrat through his high school and college years, and even into his career as an actor. However, in the 1950s, his views began to change as he began to believe in a more limited federal government. As the spokesperson for GE, Reagan delivered hundreds of speeches each year. These speeches became increasingly pro-business and pro-conservative values. Eisenhower was the first Republican presidential candidate whom Reagan supported, and he officially became a Republican in 1962.[27] The turning point for his political involvement was in 1964, when he delivered a televised speech, "A Time for Choosing," for Barry Goldwater. This rousing, Republican speech launched him into public view and catapulted him onto the national scene. He became governor of California three years later.

POLITICAL CAREER

Reagan's previous political success and his focus on the economy made him the ideal candidate in the 1980 presidential race. The problems confronting the nation demanded forceful leadership, and the major role that Ronald Reagan was eager to fill in January 1981 was that of a president riding tall in the saddle once again. When *Time* magazine chose Reagan as its "Man of the Year" for 1980, the cover story observed that Jimmy Carter was "bitterly resented by Americans for reducing their high hopes down to the size of a presidency characterized by small people, small talk, and small matters. He [Carter] made Americans feel two things they are not used to feeling and will not abide. He made them feel puny and he made them feel insecure."[28]

There was nothing small about Ronald Reagan's vision of restoring American greatness, however. He was dedicated to economic recovery and the

---

[24]Kengor, 23.

[25]Michael Bechloss, "Ronald Wilson Reagan: The Great Communicator," in *American Heritage: Illustrated History of the Presidents* (New York: Crown, 2007), 296.

[26]Cannon, 2005, 37.

[27]Reagan, 1990, 27.

[28]Cannon, 1991, 103.

re-establishment of respect for America among nations of the world. Years of serving as president of the Screen Actors Guild, hosting GE's radio show, and serving two terms as governor of California had prepared Reagan to assume the responsibilities of power. He exerted leadership with confidence and enthusiasm, and Americans appreciated it. When voters went to the polls in 1984 to re-elect Ronald Reagan by the largest electoral vote landslide in U.S. political history, carrying 49 of 50 states, many of them told exit pollsters that they approved of his policies.[29] But 40 percent of the Reagan voters told the pollsters that what they liked most about Reagan was the fact that he was a "strong leader."[30]

As with other presidents this book has considered, many of Reagan's contemporaries underestimated his capacity for leadership. Edmund G. Pat Brown, the incumbent governor of California in 1966, was one who underestimated Reagan when he challenged Brown for the governor's position. Brown characterized Reagan as a know-nothing actor and ran a negative campaign focused on Reagan's ineptitude for leadership. In one television advertisement, Brown was seated in a schoolroom telling a group of young children, "I'm running against an actor and you know who shot Lincoln, don't cha?"[31]

Governor Brown's campaign strategy backfired, and Reagan defeated him by a million votes. In countering Brown's negative advertisements, Reagan expressed the view that actors are frequently among the noblest people on earth, because they are able to understand the feelings and motivations of other people and truly comprehend the requirements for connecting effectively to an audience. He also suggested a practical benefit of acting as preparation for politics; after all, quipped Reagan, being an actor teaches people how to face a camera and how to handle tough questions from the press.[32]

Another factor in Reagan's defeat of the incumbent governor was the growing turmoil of the 1960s. California campuses had erupted in protests to the Vietnam War, there were riots in Watts (a neighborhood of Los Angeles), and citizens were demanding change. According to Lou Cannon, Governor Brown, who had succeeded as a welfare state Democrat and had built freeways and universities, "could not comprehend that the world was changing."[33] Reagan's handlers, by contrast, portrayed Reagan as a "citizen-politician," an everyman who was slow to anger but willing to fight for just causes and correct wrongdoing when it occurred.[34] He was an amiable optimist, "Illinois comes to California."[35] Reagan's campaign was heavily financed by entrepreneurs such

---

[29]Charles O. Jones, "Ronald Reagan and the U.S. Congress," in *The Reagan Legacy: Promise and Performance* (Chatham, NJ: Chatham House Publishers, 1988), 63.

[30]David Gergen, *Eyewitness to Power: The Essence of Leader Nixon to Clinton* (New York: Simon and Shuster, 2000), 193.

[31]Johanna Neuman, "Former President Reagan Dies at 93," *Los Angeles Times*, June 6, 2004.

[32]Cannon, 1991, 152.

[33]Ibid., 48.

[34]Neumann.

[35]Cannon, 1991, 41.

as Alfred Bloomingdale, heir to the Bloomingdale department store Fortune, was a close friend of Reagan and served as a member of the U.S. Advisory Commission on public diplomacy; Jack Warner, a prominent film executive, was the driving force behind Warner Brothers; and Lewis Wassermann was an American talent agent and the manager of Music Corporation of America, and by a roster of Hollywood stars including Jimmy Stewart, John Wayne, and Bob Hope.[36] Reagan's smile and self-deprecating campaign style gave Californians assurance that he would take on problems directly and restore a sense of calm to California's universities and streets. In her award-winning book, *Way Out There in the Blue: Reagan, Star Wars and the End of the Cold War*, author Frances Fitzgerald describes Reagan's campaign style as follows:

> Throughout his political career, Reagan presented himself as a citizen-politician, an amateur who ran for office to restore common sense and common decency to a government, which had grown too big, too complex, and too removed from the concerns of average Americans. There was always a populist and anti-intellectual theme to his rhetoric. The solution to the crime problem, he once said, would not be found in the social worker's files, the psychiatrist's notes, or the bureaucrat's budget. It is a problem of the human heart.[37]

As governor of one of the largest states, Reagan was "distant from the government in Sacramento over which he now presided."[38] As comfortable as he was with himself, Reagan was uncomfortable with the rudiments of political procedure. He did not know how budgets were prepared or how bills were passed. He was unprepared for the "everydayness of governance."[39] Upon entering office, he was asked what his first priority as governor would be. He replied, "I don't know, I've never played a governor."[40]

Reagan's approach to governing California was animated by a belief in cutting the size of government. In Sacramento, he set out to "squeeze, cut, and trim the cost and size of government."[41] Reagan demanded a 10 percent across-the-board cut in state budgetary allocations; however, the executive order could not be universally applied, because many programs were legally mandated or pegged to specific revenue streams. But to the extent that the cut was implemented, it cut into all programs indiscriminately, causing disruptions and delays in service delivery. State workers were asked to voluntarily work on some national holidays (e.g., Lincoln's birthday) and were virtually

---

[36]Frances Fitzgerald, *Way Out There in the Blue: Reagan, Star Wars, and the End of the Cold War* (New York: Touchstone, 2000), 60.

[37]Ibid., 28.

[38]Cannon, 1991, 47.

[39]Ibid.

[40]Dinesh D'Souza, *Ronald Reagan: How an Ordinary Man Became an Extraordianry Leader* (New York: Simon and Shuster, 1999), 65.

[41]Ronald Reagan, "Inaugural Address," Sacramento, CA, 1967.

barred from traveling out of state.[42] He fought hard with the Board of Regents of the University of California and reduced its funding requests by 15 percent. But many entitlements were pegged at specific amounts, and a 200-million-dollar deficit remained from Governor Brown. The growing deficit finally forced Reagan to raise taxes, which was abhorrent to him, and he reluctantly presided over one of the largest tax increases in California's history.

In his re-election bid for governor in 1970, Reagan ran against Jesse Unruh, speaker of the California assembly. He won the race by a half-million votes, once again relying on the citizen-politician rhetoric. Assisted by able staff members Ed Meese, William Clark, and Lyn Nofziger (all of whom would join him later in Washington), Reagan passed a landmark welfare reform bill that added eligibility and job training requirements and raised benefits for the truly needy.[43] Welfare rolls decreased by 300,000, a 15 percent decline.[44] His eight years as governor presaged his future presidency. According to Fitzgerald:

> In his eight years in Sacramento, Reagan never worked long hours or spent evenings drinking with legislators; he left the office every afternoon at five, went home to a quiet dinner with Nancy, and was usually in bed by ten. He worked hard on his speeches and on certain major issues, but the day-to-day work of governance did not interest him, and he left a great deal of it to Clark and Meese. As a result, he remained ignorant of much of what went on in the governor's office.[45]

In the 1980 presidential campaign, Ronald Reagan was able to use incumbent President Jimmy Carter's own technique against him. In his successful 1976 presidential campaign, Carter had developed a "misery index" to measure economic conditions—a combination of inflation and unemployment. When Carter ran for office, the misery index stood at 13.5, and he used that figure to attack Gerald Ford's presidential performance. But when Carter ran against Reagan almost four years later, the misery index had climbed to 20.6, and Reagan took great delight in revealing this figure to America, asking the question, "Are you better off or worse off than you were four years ago?"[46]

The Reagan campaign recruited former Michigan Congressman David Stockman, who proved to be a key player in the election bid. Originally sought because of his stance as a staunch fiscal conservative, Stockman had also worked as a staff assistant to increasingly popular Independent Party presidential candidate John Anderson. Reagan agreed to debate Anderson on national television, and put Stockman to the task of mimicking the statements and questions that Anderson would pose. The preparation worked, as Reagan used the debate to comfortably pronounce his wishes of making America once

---

[42]Fitzgerald, 62.

[43]Ibid., 67.

[44]D'Souza, 69.

[45]Fitzgerald, 64.

[46]Gergen, 154.

again a "shining city on a hill" while taking effective jabs at Jimmy Carter, who refused to debate Anderson.[47]

In the larger election campaign, Reagan decried Carter's mismanagement of the economy and his weakness in foreign policy, and railed against the dangerous idea that America's best days may be behind it. He connected Carter to the Democratic Party's moribund social welfare policies of the past twenty-five years, which had originated in good intentions but had ossified and grown into an immovable bureaucratic morass. In short, Reagan represented the voice of the conservative movement in the United States demanding its turn to run the country. According to Reagan aide Martin Anderson, "Reagan combined the personal appeal of Barry Goldwater and the political skill of Richard Nixon."[48]

He won with 50.75 percent of the popular vote in the three-way race, taking forty-four states. Reagan swept the mega states on both coasts, the Midwest, and nearly all of the Sunbelt. Carter won only Georgia, Maryland, West Virginia, Rhode Island, Minnesota, Hawaii, and the District of Columbia. He was the first incumbent president to be ousted since Herbert Hoover.[49]

Journalist Laurence Barrett provided a compelling description of the context for Reagan's 1980 victory:

> It is also vital to understand the larger landscape of 1980. Over the previous dozen years or so the great highways of American politics had devolved into a trackless savanna. Assassinations, racial turmoil, Vietnam, Watergate, the energy crisis, inflation, and a series of shocks had softened America's confidence in their system and their leaders. Their sense of direction, pointing them only toward better times since World War II, had become muddled. At home the citizenry found itself stuck in the ooze of stagflation. Looking abroad, Americans saw only frustration, burdens, danger. Their elected guides seemed to have led them into one swamp after another. On real estate of that kind, any high ground seemed inviting. Reaganism offered firm footing, refuge from the mush.[50]

POLICY

There were two basic components to Reagan's vision, as described by his speechwriter, Peggy Noonan, "Reagan wanted to do two things. His vision was of a freer and more peaceful world, and of an America in full and vibrant possession

---

[47]1980 Presidential Debate, http://www.debates.org/pages/trans80a.html.

[48]Martin Anderson, *Revolution: The Reagan Legacy* (Stanford, CA: Hoover Press Publication, 1990), Prologue.

[49]Gergen, 164.

[50]Barrett Lawrence, *Gambling with History: Reagan in the White House* (New York: Penguin Books, 1984), 47.

of its economic freedoms."[51] Noonan's statement underlines the two vital thrusts of the Reagan vision—economic recovery and global power and leadership in support of a more peaceful world. In both these areas, Reagan developed vision, accompanied by policies and strategies that could be easily characterized as non-conventional: He would repudiate the philosophical underpinnings of the welfare state and the doctrinal foundations of nuclear deterrence.

Some critics allege that Reagan was intellectually lazy and ignorant of the fine points of governance. Indeed, Clark Clifford, a pillar of the Democratic Party Establishment, described him as an "amiable dunce." Others asserted that Reagan was merely a puppet under the control of his staff. The record, however, indicates otherwise. According to his biographer, Lou Cannon:

> Reagan arrived in Washington for the first act of his presidency equipped with a familiar script of his own devising and accompanied by a production team that was determined to make him a star . . . But it was the script that was compelling, and it was Reagan who wrote it. While he would become the most highly managed president in the history of the republic, Reagan did not depend on his managers for political inspiration. He had found his ideas for himself, drawing on the resources of his life and the requirement of his performances, and shaped them into a story that would become the screenplay of his presidency.[52]

The ideas for the script began to take shape in the 1950s when Ronald Reagan played host for television's popular *General Electric Theater* and traveled the country giving speeches at GE plants. He visited a total of 135 plants and spoke to nearly 250,000 employees.[53] The script that emerged from this corporate-sponsored odyssey was "patriotic, antigovernment, anticommunist, and pro business."[54] It became known as "The Speech." GE eventually dismissed Reagan, because his speeches had taken on too much of a political tone, but he preserved the outline and focus of "The Speech" and used it in a rousing performance on behalf of Republican presidential candidate Barry Goldwater in 1964.

The basic idea of "The Speech" was that the federal government was too big, too bothersome, and too anti-business.[55] Reagan opined that government does not solve problems, but merely subsidizes them. It stifles individual freedom and restricts profits; overall, government is inimical to freedom.[56]

Reagan believed that government was sapping the energy from America's productive enterprise. He was strongly influenced by the research of David Stockman (who later became Reagan's Office of Management and Budget [OMB] director) that demonstrated the increasingly large outlays for social

---

[51]Peggy Noonan, "Ronald Reagan," in Robert A. Wilson, ed., *Character Above All: Ten Presidents from FDR to George Bush* (New York: Simon and Shuster, 1995).

[52]Cannon, 1991, 88.

[53]Ibid. 59.

[54]Ibid.

[55]Ibid., 90.

[56]Ibid.

welfare programs—known as "entitlements." In fact, Stockman's numbers indicated that 48 cents of every government dollar was going to pay for social security, pension, and welfare programs.[57]

Stockman had previously worked for Daniel Patrick Moynihan while Moynihan was a professor at Harvard. (Moynihan served as an economic and labor policy adviser to President Nixon.) Stockman attracted a great deal of interest from Reagan and his colleagues with his 1975 article "The Social Pork Barrel" in the *Public Interest*. Stockman analyzed the congressional budget process and claimed that:

> Special interest groups and advocates in this bureaucracy had made Congress a weak buffer group with revenues fully committed for years in advance. The federal budget process, potentially the basic forum for serious policy choices, has been reduced to a mere annual retreat of account juggling.[58]

Reagan also believed that Americans were paying excessive taxes. As a movie star, Reagan made $3,500 a week before World War II, and he paid 91 percent in income tax on much of that money. He claimed that the American tax structure was created by Karl Marx, and promised to change it.[59] When he took office, the marginal tax rate (rate at which the last tax dollar of income is taxed) was at 70 percent. When he left, under his 1981 tax bill and 1986 tax reform measure, the marginal rate was down to 33 percent.[60]

Married to his critique of the existing budgetary and tax arrangements was his belief in "supply-side economics," the idea that cutting taxes would benefit all Americans, because citizens with more disposable income would invest in productive enterprises and all Americans, even those at the lower rungs of the economic pecking order, would benefit. The ideological inspiration for supply-side economics came from two books—Jude Wanniski's *The Way the World Works* (1978) and George Glider's *Wealth and Poverty* (1981)—which were championed by Congressman Jack Kemp (R-NY) and other Reagan enthusiasts. Both books held out the hope of unprecedented economic growth for the United States and predicted that once tax rates were reduced, increased productivity would generate so much new wealth that government revenues would actually increase.[61]

Soon after he won the Republican nomination, Reagan commissioned Martin Anderson, a top adviser, to draw up an economic agenda for his first term in office. Anderson worked with Alan Greenspan, then running his own economic consulting firm in New York, and they drafted a speech Reagan

---

[57]Ibid., 241.

[58]Ibid., 237.

[59]Richard Reeves, *President Reagan: The Triumph of Imagination* (New York: Simon and Shuster, 2005), 11.

[60]Cannon, 1991, 277.

[61]Ibid., 236.

gave in Pittsburgh in September 1980. The speech set the tone for Reagan's first administration: It pledged a 30 percent cut in income taxes, a significant reduction in social welfare spending, a scaling back of government regulations, and a balanced budget.[62]

The basic blueprint of Reaganomics reflected the Pittsburgh speech and was summarized in a 281-page message submitted from the White House to Congress on February 18, 1981, titled, "America's New Beginning: A Program for Economic Recovery." The document proposed:[63]

- A budget reform plan to cut the rate of growth on federal spending.
- A series of proposals to reduce personal income tax by 10 percent a year over three years and to create jobs by accelerating depreciation for business investment in plants and equipment.
- A far-reaching program of regulatory relief.
- In cooperation with the Federal Reserve Board, new commitments to monetary policy that will help restore a stable economy and healthy financial markets.

In short, Ronald Reagan wanted to inspire an economic recovery concomitant with a reduction in the size and scope of government. His vision was strong, and he believed that he could reduce taxes significantly, cut social welfare spending, increase military spending, and still balance the budget. In many ways, this analysis was flawed and all of its goals, taken together, were unachievable. But this never deterred Reagan from continuing to believe in them. According to political scientist Erwin Hargrove, "Reagan had become a true believer in the supply side theory and saw no contradictions in its claims."[64] Although he struggled through a severe recession in 1982, the later years of his first term did start to see an incredible burst of economic expansion and growth. According to journalist Lawrence Barnett, "Out of the debris of the 1981–1982 recession, which Reagan's policies had caused, a recovery was blooming."[65]

The second part of Reagan's vision related to foreign policy. Reagan strongly believed that the United States had let its guard down under Carter and previous presidents and had suffered an illness called the "post-Vietnam syndrome." Americans had dropped their focus on military preparation and in consequence had failed to adequately back up their diplomatic interventions with military might, or perceived might. To Reagan and others, the Iranian hostage crisis was a glaring demonstration of the veracity of the post-Vietnam syndrome argument.

---

[62]Gergen, 164.

[63]Office of the Press Secretary, 1981.

[64]Erwin Hargrove, *The President as Leader: Appealing to the Better Angels of Our Nature* (Lawrence: University Press of Kansas, 1988), 142.

[65]Barrett, Introduction.

Indeed, although President Reagan was determined to cut domestic spending programs and personal income taxes, he favored increasing military spending. According to Laurence Barnett, "A refurbished military establishment, with new nuclear weapons systems, remained central to his theory on how to deal with the Soviet Union."[66] Military strength, he reasoned, symbolized the power of the nation, not the authority of its government, and was crucial to the pursuit of cherished national goals. He ignored Republicans who told him the Pentagon was rife with "fraud, waste, and other abuse," and he ignored Nixon's recommendation, delivered in the form of a sixteen-page handwritten memo as Reagan entered office, for a 10 percent cut in Pentagon staffing.[67]

Reagan believed staunchly in the power of freedom. He abhorred communism—based partly on his personal recollections of the communists' attempt to infiltrate the American film industry when he was president of the Screen Actors Guild—and was convinced that the communist system was antithetical to the will of God and to the highest aspirations of humankind.[68] He also believed that the Soviets could not compete with the United States in the marketplace. In his book, *Revolution*, Martin Anderson summarized Reagan's views on U.S.-Soviet relations to six basic premises:[69]

- A belief that a U.S.-Soviet nuclear war would have devastating consequences for both sides.
- A commitment to the reduction of nuclear arms instead of a limitation of the increases or a freeze at current levels.
- A moral revulsion to the doctrine of "mutual assured destruction" (MAD) that had been U.S. national nuclear defense policy for some twenty years.
- A belief that the Soviet Union was an "implacable foe" and the center of an "evil empire."
- A belief that the productive power of the U.S. economy was vastly superior to that of the Soviet economy. If the United States began a drive to upgrade the power and scope of its military forecast, the Soviets would not be able to keep up with it.
- A skepticism about arms control treaties, based on a book that argued that nations kept their treaty obligations only when it was in their interest to do so.

In short, Reagan believed that to achieve a freer and more peaceful world, the United States would have to confront the USSR through a position of strength.[70] Convinced that the Soviets represented an "evil empire," Reagan

---

[66]Ibid.

[67]Cannon, 1991, 92.

[68]Ibid., 281.

[69]Anderson, 72–74.

[70]Noonan, 204.

thought he could marshal the resources of the country to influence the Soviets to pursue negotiations and cooperate with the United States in finding a more stable world order. At its core, the belief had integrity and was expressed in many of Reagan's speeches, perhaps most famously at the Berlin Wall in June 1987 when he said, "Mr. Gorbachev, tear down this wall."[71] On its outer fringes, however, Reagan's defense strategy contained some radical assumptions based more on ideology and the movies than on empirical science. For instance, on March 23, 1983, he announced that after consultation with the joint chiefs of staff, he had decided to embark on a long-range research and development effort to counter the threat of Soviet nuclear missiles. He also believed that the United States could eventually make the Soviet missiles "impotent and obsolete" through a missile defense program that became known as "Star Wars" or Strategic Defense Initiative (SDI).[72] The notion was that the United States could erect a protective shield over itself, and through laser technology or otherwise, it could disable incoming Soviet missiles before they reached their targets, causing them to explode in space. In spite of the deep skepticism of most scientists about the viability of this program—which is one reason Richard Nixon had abandoned it during his presidency—Reagan, animated more by his vision than by reality, persisted in thinking it could happen and devoted large sums of government money to its achievement. Ultimately, though, the program worried Soviet officials and served as a useful bargaining chip for Reagan in negotiations with Soviet General Secretary Mikhail Gorbachev. Alexander Bessmertnykh, former foreign minister of the Soviet Union, stated that Reagan's SDI program accelerated the collapse of the Soviet Union.[73]

Many argue that Reagan's firmness toward the Soviets in the early years of his presidency paved the way for the profound changes that emerged in U.S.-Soviet relations, particularly in his second administration.[74] It is clear that Reagan's successes in negotiating with Gorbachev and encouraging the Russian leader's domestic reform initiatives known as *perestroika* helped accelerate the dissolution of the Soviet empire, which technically occurred in 1991, during the administration of Reagan's successor, President George H. W. Bush.

Overall, President Reagan was a visionary who held strong beliefs and used those beliefs as a guide to decision making. Like other visionaries, Reagan was convinced that his ideas could help make a positive difference in American society and even in the world. Though he was unsophisticated in his understanding of every detail of his own policy recommendations, he was

---

[71]Reagan, 1989, 352.

[72]Fitzgerald, 17.

[73]Alexander Bessmertnykh, *A Retrospective on the End of the Cold War*, Remarks at Princeton University Conference, February 23, 1993.

[74]James Mann, *The Rebellion of Ronald Reagan: A History of the End of the Cold War* (New York: Viking Adult, 2009), 278.

passionate about the core beliefs and willing to fight hard for their political expression. Americans admired him for being resolute and for the ease and comfort with which he communicated his beliefs.[75]

POLITICS

Ronald Reagan was sixty-nine years old on November 4, 1980, when he was elected president. Most of his friends were not Washington insiders, and he brought many Californians with him to govern. But Reagan was not going to repeat Carter's mistakes. He understood almost immediately that his political success would be closely linked to his acceptance in Washington.[76] He was sensitive to the idea of retail politics.

In a telling illustration of the different leadership styles of Carter and Reagan, author Lou Cannon describes an hour-long meeting in the White House between the outgoing and incumbent presidents on November 20, 1980. Carter meandered through a lengthy laundry list of issues that included China, South Korea, Western Europe, Poland, U.S. nuclear forces, and the B-1 bomber. Reagan did not ask many questions or display much of a reaction at all, which puzzled and frustrated Carter. On the other hand, Reagan asked Carter for a copy of the index cards that Carter had used to communicate the information to Reagan's staff. As Cannon suggests, Carter's interests were so broad that he seemed to lack focus even in a private conversation. Reagan's range was narrow, says Cannon, but his agenda was compelling. He simply wanted to cut domestic spending and build up the military.[77] He considered all other issues peripheral.

Reagan wasted no time in pursuing his focused agenda. He hit the ground running. He named James Baker as his chief of staff, and Baker tapped several Washington insiders to staff the transition process.[78] It was apparent that Baker understood Reagan's policy objectives and clearly prepared administration recruits for what they would be doing. Ed Meese, counselor to the president, told newcomers, "We all know what the President wants, and our job is simply to go out and do it."[79] This provides a strong contrast to the confusion that marked the early days of the Carter administration.

Reagan staff member David Gergen and pollster Richard Wirthlin drafted an "Early Action Plan" for the first hundred days of the Reagan presidency. The plan was based on research that Gergen's team had conducted on the first hundred days of five previous presidents who had been freshly elected (non-incumbents): Roosevelt in 1933, Eisenhower in 1953, Kennedy in 1961,

---

[75]Michael Siegel, "Lessons in Leadership from the Three American Presidents," *Journal of Leadership Studies*, 8, no. 1 (2001), 41.

[76]Cannon, 1991, 101.

[77]Ibid., 106.

[78]Gergen, 165.

[79]Reeves, 27.

Nixon in 1969, and Carter in 1977.[80] They studied how each president had managed his first hundred days in office (as Roosevelt had established the importance of that period), including the legislative proposals, executive orders, symbolic gestures, meetings with Congress, introduction to the Supreme Court, speeches, and press conferences. The group drew three conclusions:[81]

- The public makes a fresh evaluation of the president the day he takes office. Until then, they have only known the candidate. Now he holds the reins of power and people must judge anew: Is he really up to the job? Do people trust him? Does he know where he wants to go? Does he have a central focus? "In short, do we like what we see—or suffer from buyer's remorse?"[82]
- The Carter experience revealed the need for focus. Taking charge in 1977, Carter had attempted to emulate Roosevelt by sending up stacks of legislation in the early months (as described in Chapter 3), but his ideas had no internal coherence. By the end of Carter's first hundred days, puzzled reports could not make sense of what he was trying to accomplish. One of them quipped, "He seems to stand for everything and believe in nothing."[83]
- The early months provide an opportunity for a president to put a firm thematic stamp on his administration. Roosevelt called himself "Dr. New Deal," whereas Nixon invoked the theme of this inaugural address—"Bring Us Together." Reagan would have to move fast to put his stamp on the presidency.[84]
- It was also apparent that the first hundred days were a time of great peril for previous presidents. Kennedy had the Bay of Pigs; Ford had his pardon of Nixon; and Carter had the disastrous proposal to cut water projects.

The Early Action Plan (or Initial Actions Project) would have been impossible to carry out had Reagan—along with Meese, Anderson, and other policy advisers—not first worked out a substantive agenda for his presidency well before the election.[85] Reagan assembled a team that relied heavily on longtime loyalists at the core of his administration. It included Ed Meese, Michael Deaver (communications director), Lyn Nofziger, Martin Anderson, Casper Weinberger (defense secretary), William Clark (national security adviser), Ed Rollins (assistant to the president for political affairs), and Craig Fuller (cabinet secretary)—all from California. But he also included a sizable band of Washington insiders, who were more identified with the Ford-Bush wing of the Republican Party: James Baker, Richard Darman (deputy chief of staff), Max Friedersdorf (congressional liaison), Kenneth Duberstein (congressional relations), Elizabeth

---

[80]Gergen, 166.

[81]Ibid.

[82]Ibid.

[83]Ibid., 167.

[84]Ibid.

[85]Ibid., 168.

Dole (head of outreach), and James Brady (press secretary). Reagan also gave David Gergen the "anomalous title" of White House director.[86]

Several of the Washington people were seen as moderates, but as David Gergen suggests they were, more importantly, "realists." The conservatives insisted that "people are policy," but Reagan understood the need for a mix of ideological "purists" and political "professionals."[87] According to David Gergen, "the coalition government that Reagan created at the White House in his early years (joining ideologues with pragmatists) was one of the strongest teams in the past fifty years."[88]

And so the persuasion process began. Central to the president's lobbying operation was James Baker, who immediately identified a powerful ally in Senate Majority Leader Howard Baker (R-TN). Howard Baker had become majority leader with the takeover of the Senate by the Republican Party in 1980, on Reagan's coattails. Senator Howard Baker was a "bottomless store of knowledge on the vanities, divisions, and weaknesses of the Senate."[89] Howard Baker would also rely on the insight and guidance of Republican Senator Paul Laxalt, a Reagan loyalist and one of the few people in Washington who called the president by his first name.[90] To help Reagan's lobbying effort in the House, where the Democrats maintained a majority, Reagan leaned heavily on Max Friedersdorf, who was assisted by Kenneth Duberstein.

During the first hundred days of the Reagan presidency, Reagan personally conducted sixty-nine meetings with 467 members of Congress, prompting one member to say that he saw more of Reagan in the first four months of his presidency than he had seen Carter in four years.[91] James Baker worked sixteen-hour days, tirelessly explaining Reagan's vision to members of Congress. Reagan's easy-going style and natural ability for negotiation impressed Republican members of Congress and even the Democrats. Tip O'Neill, Speaker of the House, put it this way:

> Republicans like him as an individual and he handles the media better than anybody since FDR, even Jack Kennedy. There's just something about this guy people like. They want him to be a success. They're rooting for him, and of course they're rooting for him because we haven't had any Presidential success for years—Kennedy killed, Johnson with Vietnam, Nixon with Watergate, Ford, Carter and all the rest.[92]

On February 18, 1981, in a speech to a joint session of Congress, Reagan revealed his plan for economic recovery. He relied on inspiration from Lincoln

---

[86]Ibid., 169.

[87]Ibid.; and Nelson W. Polsby and Aaron Wildavsky, *Presidential Elections: Strategies and Structures of American Politics*, 12th ed. (New York: Rowman and Littlefield Publishers, 2008).

[88]Gergen, 169.

[89]Cannon, 1991, 113.

[90]Ibid.

[91]Ibid., 114.

[92]Ibid., 116.

and themes from his 1964 Goldwater speech. He asked Congress to join him in "restoring the promise that is offered to every citizen by this, the last best hope of man on Earth."[93] President Reagan called for cutting $41 billion from the Carter budget and making mild to fatal reductions in eighty-three federal programs. He attacked waste and fraud in the federal government and asked for a 30 percent tax reduction over three years along with an increase in military spending. It was a stunning speech and two-thirds of respondents across the nation said they agreed with the president's messages.[94] Nonetheless, some contemporary observers, such as the *New York Times'* Steve Roberts, raised some concerns. According to Roberts, "President Reagan's economic program represents a daring gamble that a sweeping application of an untested economic theory can improve the economy radically and quickly."[95]

The Reagan team dismissed such skeptics and lobbied intensely to achieve its objectives. As he trimmed and focused his legislative program, the president delegated heavily to the skillful troika of James Baker, Ed Meese, and Michael Deaver. They relied on David Stockman to convince members of Congress of the economic soundness of the program, on James Baker to assess the political dynamics, and on Reagan himself to sell his program. The whole agenda was limited to only three major objectives: tax cuts, cuts in domestic spending programs, and increases in defense appropriations.

In addition, Richard Darman, one of Baker's assistants, advocated the creation of a Legislative Strategy Group (LSG) to assure coordination and consistency in the Reagan legislative approach. Darman was concerned that the treasury, OMB, and the White House were going in slightly different directions to achieve the president's goals, and he insisted on tighter coordination.[96] The LSG expanded beyond the troika to include other players who were critical to the president's agenda: Richard Darman, Craig Fuller, David Stockman, Max Friedersodorf, Elizabeth Dole, David Gergen, Press Secretary Larry Speakes, and as needed political heavyweights such as Martin Anderson or Treasury Secretary Donald Regan.[97]

The group met for long periods of time around a conference table in James Baker's office, hammering out details of how to get key legislation tied up and passed on Capitol Hill.[98] They addressed important persuasion questions, such as Who needed to be stroked in Congress? How? With what arguments? What interest groups needed to be mobilized? To pressure whom? How should the issue be framed for the press? What columnist needed special attention? What must the president do? Can members of the cabinet take some of the load?

The political landscape at the time was not totally hospitable to Reagan. In spite of the fact that the Republicans took control of the U.S. Senate in the 1980 elections, and in doing so defeated prominent liberal Democrats such as Birch

---

[93]Ibid., 118.
[94]Reeves, 22.
[95]Ibid.
[96]Barrett, 89.
[97]Cannon, 1991, 182.
[98]Ibid.

Bayh (D-IN), Frank Church (D-ID), and John Culver (D-IA), the Democrats held a fifty-three-seat advantage in the House of Representatives of the ninety-seventh Congress.[99] A sizable number of the Democrats were conservative, known as "Boll Weevils," and the Reagan team practiced a strong bipartisan approach for change. Starting with President Reagan and cascading down to almost all of his aides, the Reagan team emphasized a common cause in expressions such as, "Our aim is to increase our national wealth. Let us join in a new determination to re-build the foundation of society. I'm here tonight to ask you to join me in making our plan work."[100] Reagan's aides brought small groups of members of Congress to the White House to chat with Reagan, sometimes over coffee, sometimes for lunch, and sometimes for state dinners with distinguished visitors from aboard.

In addition, Reagan's lobbying team prepared him effectively for the telephone calls he would make on behalf of his economic reform program. Max Friedersdorf prepared call lists for Reagan accompanied by a short biographical and political summary of each congressional member Reagan intended to persuade. For example, for the call with Margaret Heckler, a Massachusetts Republican, Friedersdorf's notes said:

> North Suburbs of Boston and Veterans' Affairs Committee . . . Peggy wants to support the President but feels vulnerable because her district is likely to be reapportioned and she will be pitted against Barney Frank, a liberal Democrat.[101]

After his conversation with Heckler, Reagan wrote a note reflecting empathy for her situation:

> Has a very real problem . . . Many of our cuts are extremely sensitive in her area. There is no doubt of her personal support and desire to be of help. We need to give her good rational explanations re: the cuts such as college loans, etc.[102]

The Reagan team displayed a legislative acumen that was absent from the Carter administration. They were completely dedicated to their cause, but also understood the importance of the interests of those they were trying to convince, and tailored their persuasions accordingly. Carter's team believed that the justness of the cause itself, which was never totally clear to begin with, would help the president prevail.

The Reagan team achieved remarkable results, as Congress passed an 8.5 percent cut in domestic spending programs in the Gramm-Latta Omnibus Reconciliation Bill/1981 that was sponsored by Representative Phil Gramm (D-TX) and Delbert Latta (R-OH). On July 16, 1981, the House approved the administration's military buildup by a vote of 354–63, joining the Senate in approving a $136 billion military appropriations bill. The legislation approved $426.4 billion more (around 8 percent) than was spent the year before,

---

[99]Barrett, 146.

[100]Ibid., 149.

[101]Reeves, 52.

[102]Ibid.

which amounted to the largest single military authorization bill in history.[103] And Reagan achieved his tax cuts with the passage of the Economic Recovery Tax Act (ERTA) of 1981. Sponsored by Congressman Jack Kemp (R-NY) and Senator William Roth (R-DE), the ERTA phased in a 25 percent cut in individual taxes over several years, accelerated business depreciation deductions, indexed individual income tax parameters (to guard against "bracket creep" through inflation), reduced windfall profit taxes, and allowed all working taxpayers to establish individual retirement accounts (IRA).[104]

The ERTA tax cuts were the most sweeping since the 1921 Mellon cuts, and amounted to nearly a trillion dollars during Reagan's eight years in office. Amid criticisms that the tax cuts were a "great day for the aristocracy"—a giveaway to the rich—the reductions shifted the load of taxation to the top of the income bracket, increasing the top 1 percent's tax payments by 51 percent.[105] Meanwhile, the share of income taxes paid by the bottom 50 percent of taxpayers dropped significantly. The decrease in tax rates also had the pleasing effect of reducing temptations of the wealthy to finesse tax laws, thus exposing more total income to taxation. Much of the economic act's final and lasting success was its system of tax credits that created incentive for businesses to expand and develop. It was Reagan's most practical application of his supply-side beliefs. The system of tax credits served to nearly eliminate taxes on business investments and research, opening room for innovation and laying groundwork for jobs. Of the tax cuts, President Clinton's 1994 Council of Economic advisers stated, "It is undeniable that the sharp reduction in taxes in the early 1980s was a strong impetus to economic growth."[106]

The effects of the Reagan economic program, however, were not instantly positive. Legislative victory did not quickly translate into economic success. The short-term effect of the Reagan program for economic recovery was a decline in social services for the most truly needy Americans. In 1981, a recession struck. According to the Bureau of Labor Statistics (U.S. Department of Labor), unemployment levels in 1982 ranged from 9.8 to 10.8 percent. There were 17,000 business failures in 1981, the largest number since the Great Depression.[107] In the 1982 mid-term elections, the Republicans lost twenty-two seats in the House and seven governorships, though they maintained control of the Senate.[108] Reagan stuck to his guns and resisted pressure from many, including friends such as Senator Laxalt, to raise taxes.[109] His belief in

---

[103]Ibid., 76.

[104]Office of Tax Analysis, United States Department of the Treasury, Revenue Effects of Major Tax Bills, Working Paper 81, 12, http://www.ustreas.gov/offices/tax-policy/library/ota81.pdf, accessed November 10, 2009.

[105]Christopher Frenze, *The Reagan Tax Cuts: Lessons on Tax Reform. April JEC Report: The Joint Economic Committee of the United States' Congress*, 1996, 2, http://www.house.gov/jec/fiscal/tx-grwth/reagtxct/reagtxct.htm.

[106]Ibid., 1.

[107]Cannon, 1991, 233.

[108]Barrett, 5.

[109]Ibid., 234.

the "magic of the marketplace" and his dogged resiliency paid off. The economic recovery that began in 1983 continued through Reagan's second term and carried over to the Bush administration, providing the biggest economic expansion in U.S. history until that time. Eighteen million new jobs were created; inflation was brought down to 4.4 percent, and unemployment stood at around 5.5 percent.[110] One negative trend, however, loomed on the horizon: the increasingly large budget deficits ($190 billion by 1984) that Stockman continued to sound the alarm on, mostly to deaf ears in the administration.[111]

As he took great pleasure in his legislative achievements, Reagan also had to ultimately exert damage control over his administration. The need for damage control centered around Reagan's first secretary of state, Alexander Haig, who attempted to expand the president's agenda in directions that were not acceptable to Reagan, Meese, or Baker.

When Reagan had hired Haig (who was strongly recommended to him by Richard Nixon in the same memo alluded to earlier), Reagan said, "You will be my spokesman. And you will be the integrator of foreign policy in my administration."[112] Reagan added, "I will look to you for guidance and leadership in this area."[113]

In his first press conference at the State Department, Haig described himself as the "vicar" of foreign policy, an unfortunate choice of words by his own admission.[114] His imperial tendencies and quest for domination were beginning to frighten Meese, Deaver, and Baker; however, it was equally clear that Haig found the Reagan leadership process to be mysterious. In his book, *Caveat*, he expressed it this way:

> To me the White House was as mysterious as a ghost ship; you heard the creak of the rigging and the groan of the timbers and sometimes even glimpsed the crew on the deck. But which of the crew had the helm? Was it Meese? Was it Deaver, or was it someone else? It was impossible to know for sure.[115]

The Reagan team found Haig equally inscrutable, but knew that he wanted to push Reagan into a more aggressive stand against the growing Soviet influence in South America. For his part, Reagan was focused on the domestic agenda, specifically on economic recovery. (Nixon's sixteen-page memo to Reagan, described earlier, advised him to not leave the country for the first five months of his presidency.) Indeed, Reagan approved a three-week delay in the release of a State Department "White Paper," documenting the flow of military weapons from communist countries to El Salvador. When the report was finally released, attention shifted from Stockman and the economic program to Haig and his proclamation of the administration's determination to resist

---

[110]Ibid., 275.

[111]Reeves, 211.

[112]Cannon, 1991, 194.

[113]Haig, 12–13.

[114]Ibid., 53.

[115]Ibid., 185.

"Cuban adventurism." But it was actually Haig's "adventurism" that prompted Baker—with President Reagan's blessing—to ask Haig to limit his television appearances.[116]

Another incident helped seal the fate of Haig, and it began with a defining moment of the Reagan presidency—John Hinckley's assassination attempt on Ronald Reagan on March 31, 1981. As David Gergen suggests, the assassination attempt, and particularly its aftermath, solidified the image of Reagan as a hero to many Americans and strengthened his bond with American citizens.[117] After all, it takes a strong and centered person to take a bullet and walk into George Washington University Hospital and say to the emergency room doctors, "I hope you're all Republicans!"

While Ronald Reagan was on the operating table where doctors were trying to remove a bullet that had lodged within an inch of the president's heart, Vice President Bush was flying back from Texas. Haig was seated in the White House Situation Room with Caspar Weinberger, arguing inconclusively about the status of U.S. military forces.[118]

Simultaneously, Larry Speakes, who had become the administration's press secretary when James Brady became disabled from the Hinckley attack, stood at a podium in the White House Briefing Room. A reporter asked whether Bush would become the "acting president" if Reagan was under anesthesia, and Speakes answered that he did not know.[119] At that point, Haig ran to the Briefing Room with such alacrity that his colleagues thought he would have another heart attack (Haig had suffered a heart attack years earlier). He replaced Speakes at the podium and proceeded to conduct a highly efficient briefing, but then said words he would live to regret:

> Constitutionally, gentlemen, you have the President, the Vice President and the Secretary of State in that order and should the President decide that he wants to transfer the helm to the Vice President, he will do so. He has not done that. As of now, I am in control here, in the White House, pending return of the Vice President, and in close touch with him. If something came up, I would check with him of course.[120]

Haig had gotten the order of succession wrong. The twenty-fifth amendment to the Constitution, ratified in 1967, provides the following order of succession to the president: vice president, speaker of the house, and president pro tempore of the Senate. By making this error, and extending a nervous and excited state of mind, Haig made people more, not less nervous, about the condition of the nation during Reagan's surgery.[121]

And yet, Reagan continued to endure Haig's eccentricities until the two men traveled to Europe together several months later. On that trip, the president was

---

[116]Cannon, 1991, 196.

[117]Gergen, 176.

[118]Cannon, 198.

[119]Ibid.

[120]Barrett, 118.

[121]Ibid.; and Cannon, 1991, 199.

appalled at Haig's display of temper over what seemed to be trivial matters. In addition, Haig complained about his accommodations in Air Force One, when Deaver placed him in the third compartment instead of the second one directly behind the president's quarters.[122] Haig's most self-destructive act was giving diplomatic instructions to U.S. Middle East negotiator Phillip Habib without Reagan's approval. Finally, Reagan, always reluctant to address staff discordance, ended Haig's tenure as secretary of state.[123]

The Reagan political effort was very strong in the first administration. Reagan clearly communicated his beliefs and objectives, recruited talented staff and allowed them the freedom to maneuver, and they negotiated with confidence and determination on a limited agenda. The president maintained clear control of his agenda and found ways to exert damage control when events or personalities threatened to derail him. This would change in the second administration, however.

STRUCTURE

During his tenure as governor of California, Reagan used a management approach that was described by his aide Lyn Nofziger as "macro-management." Reagan focused on the big picture, the large objectives and general direction of his administration, but eschewed the details of implementation. He carried the same philosophy to Washington. In an interview with Lou Cannon, Reagan put it this way, "You get the people that you believe in and that can do things that need doing. The decisions about policy are mine, and I make them."[124]

This approach worked remarkably well in Reagan's first presidential term, according to Cannon, because Reagan's 1980 campaign had unambiguously laid out an agenda of lowering taxes, increasing defense spending, and cutting domestic spending programs. Reagan set the tone, but delegated the details. He was a "9 to 5" president.[125] As Reagan explained to *Fortune* magazine, "Surround yourself with the best people you can find, delegate authority, and don't interfere as long as the policy you've decided is being carried out."[126]

He developed a notion of cabinet councils to manage the cabinet. The technique had been employed by Ed Meese in California. Meese had assigned a small "super cabinet" at the point of the pyramid, presiding over policy to be carried out by individual departments. As envisioned for Washington, the "top stone" would consist of the three to four of the most senior cabinet offices—perhaps state, defense, treasury, and justice—and a similar number

---

[122]Cannon, 1991, 200.

[123]Ibid., 202.

[124]Ibid., 182.

[125]Robert Hershey, "Politics Not Business, as a Model for Government," *New York Times*, October 18, 1983.

[126]Reagan Quotes from PBS's the American Experience, http://www.pbs.org/wgbh/amex/reagan/sfeature/quotes.html, accessed November 9, 2009.

of White House aides. This elite would be the board of directors over which Reagan would preside as chair.[127]

James Baker was skeptical of this idea and saw it as an invitation to administrative gridlock. He could not imagine the secretaries of state and

▶ FIRST REAGAN ADMINISTRATION[128]

INAUGURATION: January 20, 1981, the Capitol, Washington, D.C.

VICE PRESIDENT: George H. W. Bush

SECRETARY OF STATE: Alexander M. Haig Jr.; George P. Shultz (from July 16, 1982)

SECRETARY OF THE TREASURY: Donald T. Regan

SECRETARY OF DEFENSE: Caspar W. Weinberger

ATTORNEY GENERAL: William French Smith

SECRETARY OF THE INTERIOR: James G. Watt; William P. Clark (from November 21, 1983)

SECRETARY OF AGRICULTURE: John R. Block

SECRETARY OF COMMERCE: Malcolm Baldridge

SECRETARY OF LABOR: Raymond J. Donovan

SECRETARY OF HEALTH AND HUMAN SERVICES: Richard S. Schweicker; Margaret M. O'Shaughnessy Heckler (from March 9, 1983)

SECRETARY OF HOUSING AND URBAN DEVELOPMENT: Samuel R. Peirce Jr.

SECRETARY OF TRANSPORTATION: Andrew L. Lewis Jr.; Elizabeth H. Dole (from February 7, 1983)

SECRETARY OF ENERGY: James B. Edwards; Donald P. Hodel (from December 8, 1982)

SECRETARY OF EDUCATION: Terrel H. Bell

97th CONGRESS (January 3, 1981 to January 3, 1983):

SENATE: 53 Republicans; 46 Democrats; 1 Independent

HOUSE: 191 Republicans; 244 Democrats

98th CONGRESS (January 3, 1983 to January 3, 1985):

SENATE: 55 Republicans; 45 Democrats

HOUSE: 163 Republicans; 272 Democrats

Election of 1976

Candidates	Electoral Vote	Popular Vote
Ronald Reagan (Republican)	489	43,903,230
James Earl Carter (Democratic)	49	35,480,115

---

[127]Barrett, 72.

[128]http://www.millercenter.virginia.edu/academic/americanpresident/carter.

defense, for instance, spending long hours considering decisions in the domain of interior, labor, or education. Instead, Baker instituted a series of "modified cabinet councils," or subcommittees of the cabinet, where heads of departments with related concerns would refine options for President Reagan. Similar to the functions of the National Security Council, each body would comb information and tease up proposals for the president, who is spared from the details of analysis.[129]

In the end, the White House established seven cabinet councils as follows:[130]

- Economic Affairs—chaired by the treasury secretary
- Natural Resources and the Environment—chaired by the commerce secretary
- Human Resources—chaired by the secretary of health and human services
- Food and Agriculture—chaired by the secretary of agriculture
- Legal Policy—chaired by the attorney general
- Management and Administration—chaired by Ed Meese

More important than the structures that Reagan's team developed, however, was the loyalty of the men and women around him to the causes he believed in. The Reagan aides and cabinet secretaries were focused and determined to advance the twin visions of economic prosperity and military strength previously discussed. They were largely united, in spite of some temporary setbacks and lively disagreements. In fact, Reagan's cabinet secretaries and political lieutenants were frequently more loyal to Reaganism and its policy aspirations than they were to the mission of the agencies over which they presided. A glaring example is James Watt, whose enthusiasm for environmental protection paled in comparison to his élan for the Reagan crusade against government regulations.[131]

PROCESS

Like President Franklin Delano Roosevelt, Reagan believed that the decisive aspect of presidential leadership was inspirational rather than programmatic. The president's responsibility, in this construction, is to lead the way in restoring a sense of hope and national pride. Reagan, to an even greater extent than Roosevelt, was unaware of the details of governance. According to Lou Cannon:

> The paradox of the Reagan presidency was that it depended totally on Reagan for its ideological inspiration while he depended totally on others for all aspects of governance except for his core ideas and his powerful performances . . . He left to others what he called the

---

[129]Ibid.
[130]Ibid., 72–73.
[131]Cannon, 1991, 526.

"details" of government, a category that included the preparation for a budget, the formulation of foreign policy, the translation of ideas into legislative proposals, and the resolution of conflicts among his principal advisers.[132]

And yet, one of the details of governing, as seen in the administration of Jimmy Carter, is dealing with conflict among presidential advisers. Unlike Carter who attempted to blend the wildly diverging positions of Secretary of State Vance and National Security Adviser Brzezinski into a consolidated amalgam of policy initiatives, Reagan's approach was to steer clear of conflict, to step aside and hope the principles would work things out on their own. President Reagan was uncomfortable with staff conflict and mostly tried to avoid it. According to Laurence Barrett, "Reagan so despised turmoil in the ranks that he tended to deny, even to himself, that it existed so that he might have to impose order."[133]

On the other hand, when he really cared about an issue, Reagan proved to be a surprisingly deft negotiator, as he was in his role of president of the Screen Actors Guild. Meg Greenfield, the late editor of the *Washington Post* editorial page, took note of Reagan's bargaining skill in a 1982 *Newsweek* essay, titled, "How Does Reagan Decide?" Greenfield observed that Reagan made decisions the way a labor leader does:

> . . . the long waiting out of an adversary, the immobility meanwhile, the refusal to give anything until the last moment, the willingness— nonetheless—finally to yield to supreme personal force or particular circumstances on almost everything, but only with something to show in return and only if the final deal can be interpreted as furthering the original Reagan objective.[134]

The Soviets would learn of this negotiating style in arms control negotiations at Geneva and Reykjavik. A Russian note taker who watched Reagan closely in the summits told American negotiator Jack Matlock that Reagan reminded him of an "old lion, lazily watching an antelope on the horizon, taking no interest, dozing a bit. He doesn't move when the antelope stops only ten feet away, that's too far. At eight feet the lion suddenly comes to life!— Reagan the negotiator suddenly fills the room."[135]

It is clear that Reagan accomplished a great deal during his first term. He had certainly shifted the political debate in Washington and revived the conservative movement in America. He challenged some of the basic assumptions of the twenty-five-year Democratic-controlled Congress and introduced new fiscal and tax policies, significantly changed social welfare

---

[132]Ibid., 94.

[133]Barrett, 37.

[134]Reeevs, 333.

[135]Ibid.

policies, and initiated a return to military strength and leadership. He even challenged some of the basic doctrines of U.S. defense policy, such as MAD, and envisioned a world with vastly reduced nuclear arsenals. According to Laurence Barrett:

> He had begun to restore, in small but highly significant ways, older ideas. Reagan had removed a few of the bricks in the wall of the welfare state; he hoped to extract more. He had added steel to the military machine and implanted backbone in the country's posture abroad; he wanted to continue that. He had reduced the government's role in many ways—as policeman of the strong, guardian of the environment, protector of the weak, wet nurse of the hungry—and he wanted to make that stick.[136]

Ronald Reagan operated from a clear vision and assured its achievement by piecing together a highly functional and accomplished political team that could negotiate effectively with the Republican Senate and the Democratic House. Reagan eschewed the details of governance to an alarming degree, but his team possessed the expertise necessary to carry out his objectives vigorously. He taught them his vision, and got out of their way. He even devised methods for damage control with people such as Haig and, less successfully, Stockman, who in different ways challenged the administration's goals. President Reagan kept his team focused on a limited policy agenda and assured success in achieving his political objectives through an effective negotiation style and delegation of power to highly competent aides.

President Reagan persisted in the face of great obstacles and temporary setbacks, such as the October 1983 massacre of 241 U.S. Marines stationed in Lebanon by a Shia Muslim commando unit with ties to the Iranian Revolutionary Guards. Reagan had sent the Marines to Lebanon to help stabilize that country during a bitter conflict between the mostly Christian Lebanese government and the disaffected Islamist elements there.[137] The murder of the Marines hit Reagan hard and bitterly reminded him of the fragility of a superpower's strength. But he put the incident behind him and persevered with the upbeat, confident demeanor the nation had come to expect of him. Neither the assassin's bullet nor the terrorist's deadly deeds would stop this president from accomplishing his objectives and bringing his vision to fruition.

THE SECOND TERM

In his campaign for a second presidential term, Ronald Reagan ran against a formidable Democratic opponent in Walter Mondale, who had served as Jimmy Carter's vice president for four years and as a two-term member of the U.S. Senate from Minnesota. Mondale was well versed on policy issues, and a

---

[136]Barrett, Introduction.

[137]Reeves, 197.

good deal younger than President Reagan who, at seventy-three years of age, was starting to show some fatigue. He tried to focus his campaign on the widening economic disparities that had emerged during Reagan's first term and pointed to economic facts and figures that supported his claims. For instance, yearly income for the average American family (using 1982 dollars) had risen 3.5 percent during Reagan's first term (about $700 a year). Typical middle-class family income rose at about 1 percent a year. But the average income of the most affluent Americans rose by 9 percent from $37,618 to $40,888.[138] Mondale keyed heavily on the ballooned deficits, which were now at an astonishing 6 percent of the gross national product.[139]

Reagan countered Mondale's gruesome facts with numbers of his own. Taxes were down 25 percent across the board, interest rates were down 10 points, average personal earnings up $3,000, and "more men and women are [going] to work than ever before in our country's history."[140] Reagan's poor performance during the first of two debates with Mondale in Louisville, Kentucky, however, led to concern among his staff and campaign team. Indeed, Reagan's advisers called on the communications talents of Roger Ailes (who would become the owner of Fox News) to coach and recharge Reagan for the next debate in Kansas City.

In the Kansas City debate, Reagan's age came up as an issue. Henry Trewhitt of the Baltimore Sun observed that Reagan was the oldest president in U.S. history and noted that members of his staff said the president looked tired after the Louisville debate. Trewhitt remarked that President Kennedy had gone for days on end without sleep during the Cuban Missile Crisis and asked Reagan if he had any doubts about being able to function in such circumstances. Without missing a beat, Reagan replied, "Not at all, Mr. Trewhitt, and I want to let you know that also I will not make age an issue of this campaign. I am not going to exploit for political purposes, my opponent's youth and inexperience!"[141]

Reagan's overwhelming media presence, as much as anything, dominated Mondale's bid for the presidency. Pristine scenes of American flags waving, smiling men going to work, and children leaving for school aired throughout the country. He succeeded in portraying himself as the cheerful leader of a prospering country, while imputing Mondale with the woes of the Carter years. "Why would we ever want to return to where we were less than four short years ago?" Reagan asked.[142]

[138]Cannon, 1991, 516.

[139]Bureau of Economic Analysis, NIPA Tables 1.1.5 and 3.2, http://bea.gov/national/nipaweb/SelectTable.asp?Selected=N, accessed November 10, 2009.

[140]J. David Woodward, *The America That Reagan Built* (Westport, CT: Greenwood Publishing Group, 2006), 84.

[141]Commission on Presidential Debates, 1984 Debate Transcript, http://debates.org/pages/trans84c.html.

[142]Woodward, 2006, 84.

The advertisements, and the campaign's title of *Prouder, Stronger, Better*, were the product of San Francisco adman Hal Riney. Upon arriving in Washington in June 1984, Reagan's aides briefed Riney on the accomplishments of the first term, specifying only that Nancy Reagan had not liked the combative nature of the 1980 campaign's advertisements. With no other specific instructions, the campaign team set Riney to work.[143] The result was two of the most successful political advertisements in the television era: *Bear in the Woods* and *Morning in America*. They conveyed a strong, convincing message cloaked in a softer approach. *Bear in the Woods* showed a bear, representing the Soviet Union, wandering in a forest and asked, "isn't it smart to be as strong as the bear?" *Morning in America* listed figures that helped combat Mondale's while reassuring Americans of the future, "This afternoon 6,500 young men and women will be married, and with inflation at less than half of what it was just four years ago, they can look forward with confidence to the future."[144] Riney, who would later be inducted to the Advertising Hall of Fame, became a serious contributor to the Reagan re-election bid.

At the Democratic Convention, July 19, 1984, Walter Mondale announced that he would raise taxes if he were to be elected president. He said, "I mean business. By the end of my first term, I will cut the deficit by two-thirds. Let's tell the truth. Mr. Reagan will raise taxes, and so will I. He won't tell you. I just did."[145] Mondale's fate was sealed. Reagan won in a landslide, garnering the highest electoral vote total in the history of the republic.

Reagan won forty-nine states and 525 electoral votes to 10 (Mondale carried his home state of Minnesota by less than 1 percent). Flush with a resounding electoral victory, Ronald Reagan began his second term with great expectations of continued political and legislative success. And yet, the human foundations of his first administration's success began to change, and the president even encouraged key personnel changes without full awareness of the profound impact they would have on his success

Reagan did not have to wait very long for his first small crisis. It occurred regarding a planned trip to a German military cemetery at Bitburg to lay a wreath in honor of the fallen soldiers. Among the fallen buried at Bitburg, however, were forty-nine Waffen SS troops. The idea of Reagan effectively honoring Nazi SS soldiers provoked great outrage among the American Jewish community, and reached one of its most eminent leaders, Holocaust survivor and Nobel Prize winner Elie Wiesel. The president was determined to solidify his relationship with West German Chancellor Helmut Kohl, who had been unwavering in his support for the siting of new American missiles in Europe, and was not willing to change his plans.[146] Reagan's staff was split on the issue,

---

[143]George Raine, "Creating Reagan's Image," *San Francisco Chronicle*, June 9, 2004, http://www.sfgate.com/, accessed November 9, 2009.

[144]Woodward, 2006, 84.

[145]Jack Germond and Jules Witcover, *Wake Me Up When It's Over: Presidential Politics of 1984* (New York: Macmillan Publishing Company, 1985), 413.

[146]Ibid., 573; and Reeves, 249.

Nancy Reagan expressed concerns about the visit, and compromises were attempted. (One, a stopover at a concentration camp while the president was en route to Bitburg was considered and then rejected.) In the end, Reagan went as planned. According to Lou Cannon:

> By his stubborn insistence on going through with this ceremony after its negative implications had been pointed out to him by the world Jewish community, Republican leaders, and Nancy Reagan, Reagan inflicted needless political damage on his presidency in the critical opening months of his second term.[147]

But the biggest crisis of the second Reagan administration was the Iran-Contra affair. Operating cooperatively with the Israelis, and later through a covert U.S. initiative managed by National Security Council staff member Oliver North, the Reagan administration from late summer 1985 through mid-autumn of 1986 supplied anti-tank and anti-aircraft weapons to Iran in violation of its proclaimed policy of withholding weapons from nations that sponsored terrorism. What Reagan hoped to accomplish through these actions was the release of American hostages being held in Lebanon. The Iranians had strong influence over Hezbollah, the group holding the hostages in Lebanon.[148] In addition, the Iranians were overcharged for the weapons and the proceeds went to support the rebel forces in Nicaragua, the Contras—whom Reagan called "freedom fighters." The Contras were fighting against the Marxist-oriented Sandinista regime. This, however, was in violation of a congressional ban on such support through the Boland Amendments.[149]

Many questions about the situation, and the extent of President Reagan's involvement and/or knowledge, remain unanswered because of the death of the then director of the CIA William Casey on May 21, 1987. The Tower Board, chaired by former Texas Senator John Tower who was charged with investigating the Iran-Contra affair, concluded that Reagan's advisers had traded arms for hostages in violation of administration policy and singled out chief of staff Regan for criticism.[150]

But the Tower Commission did not exempt President Reagan from criticism with regard to his conduct in the Iran-Contra affair, noting in particular deficiencies in his management style:

> The President's management style is to put the principal responsibility of policy review and information on the shoulders of his advisers. Nevertheless, with such a complex, high risk operation and so much at stake, the President should have ensured that the NSC (National Security Council) system did not fail him. He did not force his policy to undergo

[147]Cannon, 1991, 573.

[148]Ibid., 589.

[149]Ibid.

[150]Bob Woodward, *Shadow: Five President and the Legacy of Watergate* (New York: Touchstone, 1999), 120.

the most critical review of which the NSC participants and the process were capable . . . the most powerful functions of the NSC system— providing comprehensive analysis, alternatives, and follow-up—were not utilized.[151]

Democratic Senator Daniel Inouye of Hawaii put the matter even more bluntly when he said, "They ran a government outside government. They conducted a secret foreign policy and concealed it through a concerted campaign of dishonesty and deception. And when the affair began to unravel, they attempted to cover over their deeds."[152]

Author Lou Cannon suggests that the Iran-Contra affair revealed some underlying developments in the second Reagan administration that prevented it from matching the first in performance.[153] These factors also relate the general principles of presidential leadership this book has been exploring:

- Reagan's landslide election in 1984 may have contributed to a diminished sense of political accountability.
- President Reagan felt deeply frustrated at his inability to respond to terrorism or rescue American hostages in Lebanon. Many future presidents would share this frustration.
- The strong view of the CIA and NSC staff that Iran was strategically important and vulnerable to Soviet influence. This was particularly the view of CIA Director William Casey.
- President Reagan's emotional commitment to the Nicaraguan "contras" and his instructions to Bud McFarland (the fifth NSC adviser) to keep together "body and soul" after Congress restricted aid to the rebels.
- There were opportunities for profits from the arms sales for various arms dealers.
- The reduced political competence of the White House staff. According to Cannon, the Iran initiative would have been "inconceivable" during Reagan's first term when the president was surrounded by aides who guarded his public approval ratings and by former Californians accustomed to protecting Reagan from himself. Reagan had casually cut himself off from the political moorings that had protected him from drifting astray during the first term. Gone were Baker, Deaver, and Darman, the team of pragmatists responsible for most of his political success. The pragmatists would have seen the folly of selling weapons to Iran in this manner. Reagan's own political instincts were dulled by the magnitude of his re-election victory.[154]

---

[151]Tower Commission, *President' Special Review Board Report* (New York: Bantam Books, 1987), 79–80.

[152]Reeves, 430.

[153]Canon, 1991, 593.

[154]Ibid., 593–594.

Nonetheless, in his second administration, President Reagan managed to achieve another important legislative victory in the Tax Reform Act of 1986. And he engaged Gorbachev in meaningful discussions about placing limits on nuclear weapons.

The second term featured a drastic tempering of policy toward the Soviet Union. In 1988, Reagan walked through Red Square and responded to concerns about his use of the title "evil empire." "I was talking about another time, another era," he replied.[155] The change initiated when Margaret Thatcher, whom Reagan highly regarded, said to him of Gorbachev, "we can do business together." Reagan believed Thatcher and his first meeting with Gorbachev confirmed the assessment. Reagan came to recognize him as a fresh mind, the first Soviet leader who came from the post-Stalin generation, and was pleased with his references to God and Jesus Christ in public statements.

Reagan was impressed with Gorbachev's sense of humor and used levity to leverage his human side. During one encounter, Reagan told of a debate between a Russian and an American. The American said, "Look, I can go into the Oval Office, pound on the president's desk and say: Mr. President, I don't like the way you're running our country." And the Russian responded, "I can do that." The American said, "You can?" The Russian replied, "Sure. I can go into the Kremlin, into the general secretary's office, and say: Mr. General Secretary, I don't like the way that President Reagan is running his country."[156] Reagan also sensed Gorbachev's sincerity, a trait that many in America questioned. "I think I'm a good judge of acting," he once said. "I don't think he's acting."[157]

Reagan ultimately was a focused negotiator who was unwilling to budge from his stated intentions: pressure the immoral Soviet system to change. In the course of their discussions during the first meeting in Geneva in 1985, Reagan and Gorbachev took a walk to the Paul house on Lake Geneva and Reagan delivered an interesting few sentences: "Mr. General Secretary, here we are, two men born in obscure rural hamlets, both poor and from bumble beginnings. Now we are the leaders of our countries, and probably the only two men who can start World War III, and possibly the only two men . . . who can bring peace to the world."[158] Gorbachev expressed that he felt threatened about the prospect of an SDI missile defense and warned that the Soviets would, in response, have to expand their offensive and defensive systems. Reagan stood firm, "We won't stand by and let you maintain weapon superiority over us. We can agree to reduce arms, or we can continue the arms race, which I think you know you can't win."[159] Reagan knew that the staggering Soviet economy was unable to match an American armament.

---

[155]D'Souza, 185.

[156]Ibid., 178.

[157]Ibid., 186.

[158]Reeves, 289.

[159]D'Souza, 189.

While the November 1985 Geneva Summit between Reagan and Gorbachev produced relatively few concrete results—agreements on cultural exchanges, civil air safety procedures, and new consulates—it did help to connect the two men personally and they agreed "to accelerate the work . . . to prevent an arms race in space and to terminate it on earth . . . including the principle of 50 percent reductions in the nuclear arms of the US and USSR appropriately applied."[160]

At the October 1986 Reykjavik summit, Gorbachev surprised State Department officials by handing Reagan a printed summary of Soviet proposals in the form of actual instructions to Soviet ministers:

- An agreement on a 50 percent reduction in the strategic offensive weapons of the Soviet Union and the United States.
- An agreement on the complete elimination of U.S. and Soviet medium-range missiles in Europe.
- An agreement pledging not to use their right to withdraw from the anti-ballistic missile (ABM) systems for ten years.[161]

It was the third provision that gave Reagan pause, because it directly threatened his cherished SDI. Reagan reiterated his belief that the SDI was defensive in nature and even proposed to share its operational details with the Soviets. Gorbachev reacted coolly, sarcastically saying that the Americans would not even share agricultural secrets with the Soviets.[162] Gorbachev insisted that the proposals were meant to be a package and refused any alteration of the defense provision. The two men went home without an agreement.

Reykjavik, British Prime Minister Margaret Thatcher said, was the turning point in the Cold War. In the months that followed, Gorbachev realized that with Reagan he had only two options: push forward into a hopeless arms race that the Soviet economy could not afford, or come humbly back to the negotiating table. In December 1987, Gorbachev came to Washington and signed the Intermediate-Range Nuclear Forces (INF) Treaty, rescinding his previously stated "non-negotiable" demand that the United States abandon SDI. Under the treaty, the superpowers agreed to reduce intermediate-range nuclear missiles to zero. For the first time in history, the United States and the Soviet Union agreed to abolish a whole class of nuclear weapons.[163]

The INF Treaty was the major act of surrender in the Cold War. It set the table for the Strategic Arms Reduction Talks (START) Treaty, a treaty finally signed in 1991 that cut Soviet strategic missiles in almost exactly the ratios that Reagan had advocated. It effectively ended the Soviet threat, whose elimination had been one of the top three priorities of Reagan's presidency.

---

[160]Reeves, 294.

[161]Ibid., 343.

[162]Ibid., 344.

[163]D'Souza, 191.

The big legislative achievement of the second administration was the Tax Reform Act of 1986. In his 1986 State of the Union Address, the president declared his intention "to simplify the entire tax code so all taxpayers, big and small, are treated fairly."[164] Despite a fierce lobby from the groups that benefited from the loopholes, on October 22, 1986, Reagan signed into law a tax reform bill that simplified and condensed the tax code. It pared down the number of tax brackets to just three: 15 and 28 percent for individuals and 36 percent for corporations.[165] The tax reform increased the personal exemption and standard deduction, removing millions of low-income taxpayers from the rolls. It provisioned an alternative minimum tax that ensured that wealthy taxpayers could not escape paying taxes altogether.[166]

SUMMING UP

In a June 22, 1986, *New York Times* magazine essay entitled, "The Reagan Legacy," White House correspondent Bernard Weinraub summarized Reagan's legacy in this fashion:

> It is clear that his impact, like Franklin Delano Roosevelt's, rests in large part on restoring the primacy of the Presidency as an institution after nearly two decades of White House disarray marked by Vietnam, Watergate, and the hostages in Iran.[167]

One of Ronald Reagan's most powerful critics, Democratic Massachusetts Senator Edward Kennedy, affirmed Weinraub's analysis by saying, "He has contributed a spirit of goodwill and grace to the Presidency and American life generally and turned the Presidency into a vigorous and forceful instrument of national policy."[168] Charles O. Jones, the former president of the American Political Science Association, defined Roosevelt and Reagan as "bookend presidents," saying, "One pushed in the direction of more government, and trying to make the system work. This one is trying to make it work in the sense of less government. They're both radical, but in totally different directions."[169]

The strength of Reagan's legacy is evident in the number of streets, airports, schools, and federal buildings named for him. Reagan appointed the first female Supreme Court justice, Sandra Day O'Connor, who brought a lasting moderating influence to the judiciary. In advising Senator John McCain (R-AZ), the 2008 Republican presidential nominee, on how to conduct himself, L. Brent Bozell, founder and president of the Media Research Center, put

---

[164]Ibid., 122.

[165]Reeves, 359.

[166]D'Souza, 124.

[167]Bernard Weinraub, "The Reagan Legacy," *New York Times*, June 22, 1986, Politics page 1.

[168]Reeves, 325.

[169]Ibid.

it bluntly, "It is time for McCain to be Reagan."[170] And in the course of the hotly contested 2008 Democratic contest to chose the party's nominee, candidate Barack Obama, former Democratic senator of Illinois, said this on the campaign trail:

> I think Ronald Reagan changed the trajectory of America in a way that Richard Nixon did not and in a way that Bill Clinton did not. He put us on a fundamentally different path because the country was ready for it. I think they felt like with all the excesses of the 1960s and 1970s and government had grown and grown but there wasn't much sense of accountability in terms of how it was operating. I think people, he just tapped into what people were already feeling, which was we want clarity we want optimism, we want a return to that sense of dynamism and entrepreneurship that had been missing.[171]

There is no doubt of the importance of Ronald Reagan's legacy. Applying the framework used in this book, one would have to conclude that his first term demonstrates the almost complete mastery of the four dimensions of leadership specified. Reagan had a strong vision and conveyed this vision convincingly to his aides and to the American public, organized his administration for political and managerial success, used his values to make decisions and to chose priorities, and exerted damage control when necessary to implement his agenda. He overcame formidable obstacles, including an attempt on his own life, a worsening economy early on, and the tragic deaths of U.S. Marines in Lebanon. Nonetheless, he accomplished a great deal legislatively and completed the translation of vision into policy.

The second administration was not quite as successful, although Reagan still left office with high approval ratings. The president's macro-management style showed vulnerabilities in the easy acceptance of a major staff change (Regan-Baker) that would have enormous negative political and managerial consequences, and in the concomitant policy disasters such as Iran-Contra. The team he had put together in the first administration—an agile combination of ideologues and politicians, Californians, and Washingtonians—was gone. Reagan was thrown upon his own devices, and he came up short as age and his natural limitations began to show their mark. Nonetheless, Reagan achieved a significant tax cut and a highly meaningful improvement in relations with the Soviet Union, leading to important arms reductions and peace talks. Henry Kissinger called Reagan's achievements in dealing with the Soviets "the greatest diplomatic feat of the modern era."[172]

---

[170]Brent Bozell, "From the Right, He Looks Too Blue," *Washington Post*, March 9, 2008, B1.

[171]Mary Kate Cary, "Is Barack Obama the Next Ronald Reagan?" *US News and World Report*, April 3, 2009, http://www.usnews.com/blogs, accessed November 9, 2009.

[172]Henry Kissinger, Video Commemoration of Ronald Reagan, Republican National Convention, San Diego, CA, August 13, 1996.

Reagan's pronouncing, "It's morning again in America," did not apply equally to all Americans. Some of his domestic spending cuts caused great despair and hardship among disadvantaged Americans. And some considered his huge tax cuts, resulting in accumulating federal budgetary deficits, highly irresponsible.[173]

Nevertheless, above all else, Reagan restored the power and integrity of the White House as an instrument of positive change in America. He certainly gave great voice to the conservative movement, and in the words of his close adviser:

> When Reagan was reelected in 1984 by the largest electoral vote margin in history, it became clear that something serious was happening. It was no longer possible to dismiss his presence and political virtues as some mysterious, unexplainable accident of nature, or to blame it on his charm, good looks and sense of humor. No, it was something in scope and power equivalent to an intellectual earthquake that would shake the political establishment of the United States—and the world—for some time to come.[174]

---

[173]Matthew Dallek, "Not Ready for Mount Rushmore: Reconciling the Myth of Ronald Reagan with the Reality," *American Scholar*, Summer 2009, http://www.theamericanscholar.org/, accessed November 10, 2009.

[174]Anderson, 6.

The Presidency of George H. W. Bush

W hen asked at the beginning of his unsuccessful bid for the 1980 Republican Party presidential nomination why he thought he would be elected president, George Bush replied, "I've got a big family and lots of friends."[1] Bush's sardonic reply revealed the foundation of his political style: personal, practical, and experiential. Bush believed deeply in the importance of personal contacts and loyalty as a platform for political leadership. Indeed, as expressed by *New York Times* columnists Thomas Friedman and Maureen Dowd, "His very ideology is friendship . . . People, not ideas or issues, drive him."[2] In *A World Transformed*, the book chronicling the end of the Cold War that he co-authored with his National Security Adviser Brent Scowcroft, Bush said, "I believe that personal contact would be an important part of our approach for both diplomacy and leadership of the alliance and elsewhere . . . For me, personal diplomacy and leadership went hand-in-hand."[3] This preference for personal diplomacy and keeping and utilizing a vast network of friends and family was something he manifested his entire life, even in his earlier days.

EARLY LIFE

George H. W. Bush was born on June 12, 1924, in Milton, Massachusetts, into a long line of financially successful people. His maternal grandfather, George Herbert Walker Sr., was the founder and director of G. H. Walker & Co., a private Wall Street banking firm. His father was a wealthy investment banker, who later became a U.S. senator from Connecticut (1952–1963). Despite the affluence and prestige of the Bush family, young George H. W. was always taught to work hard and give back to the community and society.[4] His mother instructed him about the importance of humility and the dangers of self-importance as an approach to life.[5] Nevertheless, some believe that because he was raised in a white-collar, upper-class, private school atmosphere, he could never really connect with the American people, especially the lower classes.[6]

Later in his life, Bush attended Phillips Academy Andover, a private boarding school in Massachusetts for grades 9–12. There, he was captain of the soccer and baseball teams, and senior class president.[7] He graduated on

---

[1] Richard Ben Cramer, *What It Takes: The Way to the White House* (New York: Vintage Books, 1992), 12.

[2] Maureen Dowd and Thomas L. Friedman, "The Fabulous Bush and Baker Boys," *New York Times,* May 6, 1990.

[3] George H. W. Bush and Brent Scowcroft, *A World Transformed* (New York: Vintage Books, 1999), 60.

[4] "George Herbert Walker Bush," Miller Center of Public Affairs, University of Virginia, http://millercenter.org/academic/americanpresident/bush, accessed June 19, 2009.

[5] Herbert S. Parmet, *George Bush: The Life of a Lone Star Yankee* (New York: Simon and Schuster, 1997), 23.

[6] "Biography of George Herbert Walker Bush," the White House, http://www.whitehouse.gov/about/presidents/georgehwbush/, accessed November 20, 2008.

[7] "School House to White House: The Education of the Presidents," National Archives, http://www.archives.gov/publications/prologue/2007/spring/schoolhouse.html, accessed November 20, 2008.

June 12, 1942, and immediately enlisted in the navy. He served in the navy during World War II from 1942 until September 1945. When he became a pilot in July 1943, he was the youngest pilot in the navy.[8] He flew torpedo bombers in the Pacific theater, and went on fifty-eight combat missions during the war. On September 2, 1944, while flying a mission to bomb an enemy radio site, his plane was shot down by Japanese fire. Bush had to bail out over the ocean and was later rescued by a submarine. He was awarded the Distinguished Flying Cross for heroism under fire.[9]

During a Christmas break in Greenwich, Massachusetts, George met his future wife, Barbara Pierce. Barbara also came from a wealthy family—her father was the president of McCall Corporation, a publisher of popular magazines. They were married while Bush was still in the navy, on January 6, 1945. They had six children: George Walker; Robin, who died of leukemia at the age of four; John Ellis "Jeb"; Neil; Marvin; and Dorothy.[10] Jeb Bush served as governor of Florida from 1999 to 2007, and George Walker Bush served as president of the United States from 2001 to 2009.

In September 1945, Bush left the navy to pursue his education. He attended Yale University from 1945 until he completed his undergraduate degree in economics in 1948 as part of an accelerated program that allowed him to graduate in three years. Bush was active in campus life, playing on the baseball team and eventually becoming the captain. He was also part of the Skull and Bones society, a secret and very exclusive society.[11]

After graduating from Yale, Bush used one of his many family connections to gain employment in the oil industry, working for Dresser Industries in Midland, Texas. In 1950, Bush and a friend formed an oil development company in Midland. Three years later, they merged with another company to create Zapata Petroleum. In 1954, Bush became president of Zapata Off-Shore Company, which developed offshore drilling equipment. Soon after that he relocated the company and his family to Houston, Texas.[12] Bush continued to use this deal-making, personal style for the rest of his life, which later catapulted him onto the national political stage.

POLITICAL CAREER

George Bush would successfully run for president in 1988 as the ultimate insider, typifying the approach of a dealmaker who is devoid of missionary zeal.[13] He had practiced the deal-making, pragmatic style of politics over

[8]"History's Youngest Naval Aviator: George H.W. Bush," Mid-Atlantic Air Museum, http://www.maam.org/flightsim/news/tbm_history.htm, accessed November 20, 2008.

[9]Miller Center of Public Affairs.

[10]"Biography," George Bush Presidential Library and Museum, http://bushlibrary.tamu.edu/research/bio_ghwbush.php, accessed November 19, 2008.

[11]Miller Center of Public Affairs.

[12]Ibid.

[13]Collin S. J. Campbell, "The White House and Presidency under the 'Let's Deal' President," in *The Bush Presidency: First Appraisals* (Chatham, NJ: Chatham House, 1991), 185.

thirty years, which began when he was chairman of the Republican Party in Harris County, Texas, and ended in the White House. In between, he advanced to two terms in the U.S. House of Representatives, where he represented the constituents of Houston (1966, 1968); continued in public service as the U.S. ambassador to the United Nations during the Nixon administration (1971–1973); served as chairman of the Republican National Committee during the tumultuous days of Watergate (1973–1974); served as the head of the American liaison office in the People's Republic of China (1974–1975); served as director of the Central Intelligence Agency (CIA) for a brief period (1975–1976) under Gerald Ford; and finally served as a loyal vice president to Ronald Reagan (1981–1989).

In his mostly triumphal strides in politics—with the exception of two defeats for a U.S. Senate seat for Texas in 1964 and 1970—Bush evinced a positive, non-ideological, and tactical political disposition.[14] As chairman of the Harris County Republicans, for instance, he proved to be the hardest-working person ever to occupy that position. According to biographer Tom Wicker, "He was enthusiastic and optimistic, raised money, organized precincts, brought in recruits, found volunteers, computerized the voter rolls, moved the committee to better quarters, and stayed right on top of the paperwork. . . . Everything Chairman Bush touched seemed to succeed."[15]

In the course of his political education, George Bush also learned how to display great flexibility in his policy preferences (cynics might use the term *zig and zag*) and to curry favor with the prevailing political forces. For instance, during the early 1960s, as Barry Goldwater was gathering considerable popularity for the rebirth of American conservatism, Bush decided to oppose the 1964 Civil Rights Act, thinking that would put him in good stead to be elected to Congress from Texas. When he campaigned in 1965, Bush lambasted his opponent, Democrat Ralph Yarborough, for being a liberal and voting to cut off a filibuster on the Civil Rights Act. He also said that the United States should pull out of the United Nations, because it had recently admitted Communist China.[16] Years later, when the national political winds had shifted in the direction of a more liberal civil rights agenda, he voted for the 1968 Open Housing Bill as a member of the House of Representatives.[17] Another biographer, Timothy Naftali, suggested that to many observers, Bush's adaptability was a "sign of weakness."[18] Indeed, after losing the 1966 Senate race in Texas, Bush confided to his pastor, "You know, John, I took some of the right positions to get elected. I hope I never do it again. I regret it."[19]

---

[14]Fred I. Greenstein, *The Presidential Difference: Leadership Style from FDR to George Bush* (Princeton, NJ: Princeton University Press, 2004), 160.

[15]Tom Wicker, *George Herbert Walker Bush* (New York: Penguin Books, 2004), 15.

[16]Cramer, 419.

[17]Wicker, 21.

[18]Timothy Naftali, *George H.W. Bush* (New York: Henry Holt and Company, 2007), 14.

[19]Wicker, 18.

As he advanced in his political career, George Bush continued to show a strong preference for loyalty and friendship as a basis of political acumen; however, he showed strong courage when, in a cabinet meeting shortly after Watergate, Bush advised President Richard Nixon to resign. It was, as Tom Wicker asserts, one of his most unguarded and honest political moments.[20]

During the early days of the 1980 presidential election, Bush campaigned for the Republican Party nomination in Pennsylvania as the anti-Reagan and coined the term *voodoo economics* to describe Reagan's plan for cutting taxes, increasing defense spending, cutting domestic spending, and balancing the budget. He impressively won the Iowa caucuses, but faltered in New Hampshire, the first primary state. Perhaps the key event of the campaign was a pre-primary debate scheduled between front-runners Bush and Reagan. The other GOP candidates were excluded from the debate, but they showed up and demanded to participate. In his establishment-oriented style, Bush acceded to the agreed-upon rules, whereas Reagan invited the others to join in the debate, exclaiming, "I paid for the microphone." The incident seemed to define the differences between the Republican front-runners: Bush, quietly sitting, asking that the rules be abided; Reagan seizing the political moment with perfect timing.[21] Bush lost the nomination, but his strong showings impressed Reagan enough to choose him as the vice presidential candidate. Bush once again appeared to define himself by the nature of his new position.[22] On the Republican ticket with Reagan, he was able to change course quickly. According to Timothy Naftali:

> Bush agreed, performing the trick of the political chameleon. He was a Goldwater Republican again. It had been sixteen years since he had presented himself as a man of the hard RIGHT, but he knew how to do it. Bush had his supporters put their ERA (equal rights amendment) signs away, and he announced his personal opposition to abortion.[23]

As Reagan's vice president, Bush wore the Reagan label well. He refused to separate himself from the president on issues as controversial as the deficit and friendly negotiations with Mikhail Gorbachev.[24] Building on a precedent established by Jimmy Carter and his vice president, Walter Mondale, Bush was given unusually easy access to Reagan, as they held a private lunch together every Thursday.[25] Also, Bush continued to excel in the art of making friends and repeatedly demonstrating great loyalty to President Reagan, earning the reputation as the ultimate team player.[26]

[20]Ibid., 35.

[21]Ryan J. Barilleaux and Mark J. Rozell, *Power and Prudence: The Presidency of George H. W. Bush* (College Station: Texas A&M University Press, 2004), 17.

[22]Ibid.

[23]Naftali, 39.

[24]Ibid., 42.

[25]Wicker, 64.

[26]Ibid., 63.

On one occasion, however, Bush was forced to publicly disagree with President Reagan. In 1988, the Reagan Justice Department indicted Panamanian dictator Manuel Noriega for drug trafficking and racketeering. Nevertheless, U.S. Department of Justice lawyers could not devise a way to bring Noriega to the United States for trial. Secretary of State George Schultz proposed a deal: The indictment and sanctions against Noriega would be lifted, and in return Noriega would leave Panama for good. Bush initially backed the idea, but began to have doubts when Daryl Gates, the Los Angeles chief of police, convinced him that dismissing the Noriega indictment would represent a betrayal of law enforcement officials who had given their lives in the "war on drugs." Bush subsequently renounced the deal and recommended that Reagan forsake it. But on this matter, Reagan was immovable, and he went ahead with the plan. Noriega dismissed the deal, negotiations collapsed, and Noriega remained in place.[27]

In the Iran-Contra scandal that enveloped the second Reagan administration, Bush was clearly present during the important decisions and planning activities in the "arms-for-hostages" deal. He was present on January 11, 1986, when Reagan signed a presidential "finding," lending support to anti-Sandinista activities underway. According to reporter Richard Ben Cramer:

> He [Bush] knew, for starters, the administration shipped arms to Iran. In fact, he was for it, in a quiet, barely traceable way, not because he thought it would work, but it might . . . *and the President was for it.* He knew that if the deal went down as hoped ("planned" was too grand a term), then US hostages would come home. He knew Bud McFarlane, Ollie North, and John Poindexter were running the show. He knew the Israelis had started the whole deal, were in it up to their eyeballs, in it for their own reasons, not mostly those of the U.S. And he knew the President didn't quite grasp the details of the operation.[28]

Bush tried to warn President Reagan about the inadvisability of appearing on national television to discuss the Iran-Contra affair before he was truly prepared; however, his advice went unheeded, and Reagan experienced one of his few defeats on television. Ultimately, Bush claimed that he had been "out of the loop on the Iran-Contra affair," but the facts prove otherwise.[29]

Bush's apparent paralysis during the Iran-Contra affair may have reflected, more than anything else, an institutional reality of the American polity until the 1990s and early years of the twenty-first century: The vice president had always been somewhat constrained in his ability to shift presidential policy in one direction or the other. In their book *Men of Zeal*, William Cohen (who served as secretary of defense under President Clinton) and George Mitchell (U.S. senator from Maine and the Senate majority leader during the

---

[27]Ibid., 71.
[28]Cramer, 117. Italics in original.
[29]Ibid.

Clinton years), expressed the institutional weaknesses of the vice president in policy deliberations:

> A vice president lacks the flexibility to express his views on a controversial issue and not only because of loyalty and confidentiality he owes the president. Even in cabinet sessions, when deep divisions exist, for the vice president to advocate any position might undercut the administration should the president reject it or compromise the president's flexibility in reaching a decisions by forcing him to avoid embarrassing his own vice president.[30]

In 1987, when George Bush announced his candidacy for the 1988 Republican Party presidential nomination, his strongest challenge came from Senate Republican leader Robert Dole of Kansas.[31] Dole had served honorably as a Republican senator from Kansas, was a war hero (whose right arm was shattered in combat), and came from a working-class background. Dole's personal and political characteristics presented strong contrasts to those of George Bush, who came from a privileged family and was variously described as "wimpish" or "preppy" by his opponents.[32] During the primary race with Dole, there were echoes of Iran-Contra and Bush's ambiguous role in that scandal. Moreover, evolving problems in the later days of the Reagan administration would prove troubling to Bush. Reagan's close adviser and attorney general in the second administration, Ed Meese, was forced to resign amid allegations of ethical lapses in some of his business dealings. Disgruntled Chief of Staff Donald Regan, who had resigned from the Reagan White House, wrote a book revealing, among other things, Nancy Reagan's heavy reliance on an astrologer for personal guidance and counseling.[33]

As the Bush/Dole competition intensified, Bush displayed continual loyalty to his mentor, Ronald Reagan. Former New York Governor Mario Cuomo, who was considering a run for the Democratic presidential nomination, proposed a bipartisan commission on the budget. When Cuomo brought the idea to Bush in September, Bush replied, "Wouldn't it be a tax increase commission?"[34] Bush issued a press release opposing the idea; however, Dole accepted Cuomo's commission idea, suggesting it would be antidote for a deteriorating economic situation. Subsequently, Dole nearly doubled Bush's 19 percent of the vote in Iowa, creating great anxiety in the Bush camp.

Then in the New Hampshire primary, Bush's nearly twenty-point lead disappeared quickly. He began to perceive that his relatively mild-mannered approach to campaigning, almost premised on a kind of "noblesse oblige,"

---

[30]William Cohen and George J. Mitchell, *Men of Zeal* (New York: Penguin Books, 1989), 264, 271.

[31]Michael Beschloss, *American Heritage Illustrated History of the Presidents* (New York: Crown Publishers, 2000), 492.

[32]Wicker, 87.

[33]Ibid., 80.

[34]Naftali, 52.

would have to give way to a more aggressive posture. Accordingly, Bush ratcheted up his anti-tax rhetoric and solidified an 11 percent win in New Hampshire, effectively ending the contest for the Republican nomination. The Bush victory in New Hampshire was given substantial assistance from the state's governor, John Sununu, who would be rewarded with an appointment as Bush's White House chief of staff.[35]

Bush's Democratic opponent was Massachusetts Governor Michael Dukakis. Dukakis was taking credit for the "Massachusetts Miracle" of economic revitalization, which fit well with his pro-business pragmatic liberalism. Dukakis was a man of solid policy credentials and accomplishment, having introduced a bill to create the first condominiums in Massachusetts when he served in the state legislature, championed insurance reform in that state, and made a name for himself with the "no-fault" insurance initiative.[36] Like Jimmy Carter, Dukakis probed every bill for its government implications and voted on the merits.[37] Dukakis gained momentum as Bush became increasingly embroiled with Panama's dictator Noriega.

By mid-May, Bush was trailing Dukakis by sixteen percentage points, prompting Ed Rollins (Reagan's 1984 campaign manager) to say, "How an incumbent vice president who wrapped up his party's nomination in March [six weeks before the Democrats] can be an underdog is amazing to me."[38] When Bush selected Republican Indiana Senator Dan Quayle as his running mate, the media criticized Quayle for not having served in Vietnam while others of his generation had. Quayle performed miserably on a nationally televised debate with the Democratic vice presidential candidate, Texas Senator Lloyd Bentsen. When Quayle tried to compare himself to another young, relatively inexperienced senator running for national office—John Kennedy—Bentsen quipped, "I served with Jack Kennedy. I knew Jack Kennedy. Jack Kennedy was a friend of mine. Senator, you're no Jack Kennedy!"[39]

Bush won his party's nomination and, as pressure mounted for him to deliver a powerful acceptance speech at the Republican National Convention, he enlisted the services of Reagan's speechwriter, Peggy Noonan. She helped Bush craft one of the most memorable, and memorably violated presidential promises in American political history. Bush stated his opposition to taxes in unequivocal terms, "My opponent [Governor Dukakis] won't rule out raising taxes. But I will. And Congress will push me to raise taxes, and I'll say, 'No!' And they'll push, and I'll say 'No' again. And they'll push again and I'll say: 'Read my lips, no new taxes!' "[40]

---

[35]Beschloss, 492.

[36]Cramer, 503.

[37]Ibid., 509.

[38]Naftali, 60.

[39]Beschloss, 493.

[40]George Bush, "Acceptance Speech," Address at Republican National Convention, New Orleans, LA, August 18, 1988, George Bush Presidential Library and Museum, http://bushlibrary.tamu.edu/research/pdfs/rnc.pdf, accessed June 19, 2009.

Subsequently, the presidential campaign became heated and ugly. Bush felt increasing pressures to overcome a significant lead the Democrats had developed, according to polls. Then in the first presidential debate, Dukakis displayed an almost total lack of debating acumen. Bernard Shaw of CNN asked Dukakis a question about one of the most volatile and emotional issues in American society: crime and punishment. Dukakis's maladroit answer may have cost him the election at that particular moment:

> **Shaw:** Governor, if Kitty Dukakis were raped and murdered, would you favor the death penalty?
>
> **Dukakis:** No, I don't Bernie. And I think you know that I've opposed the death penalty all my life. I don't see any evidence that it's a deterrent, and I think there are better and more effective ways to deal with violent crime. We've done so in my own state . . . one of the reasons why we have had the biggest drop in crime in any industrial state.[41]

Democratic Party officials were astounded. How could their candidate have been so calm and pedantic about a highly emotional issue involving his own wife? How could he have missed an opportunity to show America that he cared about Kitty Dukakis and also about crimes that many Americans feared?[42]

Bush continued to press Dukakis on issues of crime, and portrayed the Massachusetts governor as soft on crime and as a card-carrying member of the American Civil Liberties Union.[43] Bush's campaign adviser, Lee Atwater, described strong focus group responses to an advertisement featuring Willie Horton, an African American parolee in the state of Massachusetts, who, after receiving a weekend pass, went out and committed rape. Bush operatives informed focus groups viewing the spot that Dukakis had opposed the death penalty, voted against the "Pledge of Allegiance," and opposed prayer in public schools. Focus group results showed that within ninety minutes of the viewing experience, 50 percent of the audiences had shifted their support to Bush.[44] According to journalists Michael Duffy and Dan Goodgame:

> Atwater's approach . . . transformed the campaign from a race about issues into a race about values. For most voters, Atwater believed, choosing a president came down not to position papers and issue proposals, but to the cultural and personal cues a candidate transmits to explain to voters who he is and how he thinks.[45]

Bush's negative campaigning did damage to Governor Dukakis, who appeared unwilling to respond to Bush's charges.[46] He announced the theme

---

[41]Wicker, 95.

[42]Ibid.

[43]Michael Duffy and Dan Goodgame, *Marching in Place: The Status Quo Presidency of George Bush* (New York: Simon and Schuster, 1992), 25.

[44]Cramer, 997.

[45]Duffy and Goodgame, 26.

[46]Wicker, 104.

of the campaign to be "competence," which proved quite weak in relation to the portrayal of him by Bush as a "bleeding heart liberal," which most Americans believed to be true. Bush was the opposite of Dukakis, according to Tom Wicker, "What the voters saw in Bush, on the other hand, was not brilliance or even strength, and certainly not vision. At least in 1988 they saw a man who shared their instincts and their most enduring values—one of which was winning. George Bush had learned how to win."[47]

And win he did. Bush defeated Dukakis, carrying 53 percent of the popular vote, forty states of the union,[48] and 426 of the 538 electoral votes.[49] President Bush was the first president elected to succeed a predecessor of his own party since 1928 and the first sitting vice president to be elected since 1836.[50] Yet, his victory, though decisive, was not as stunning or impressive as Reagan's, especially in the farm states. And his victory came at a cost, according to Tom Wicker:

> Polls showed that people blamed Bush for the negative tone (some even thought racist, owing to Willie Horton's black skin) of the 1988 campaign. If the campaign was unenlightening on important issues, moreover, that was largely because Willie Horton and the Pledge of Allegiance were *not* important national issues. Besides, Bush's triumph did not give him much of a "mandate" to do anything, other than what might come routinely into the Oval Office. He had not, after all, campaigned to do much of anything—only on the proposition that he was a tried and experienced leader, a man of conventional virtue, while his opponent was not to be trusted.[51]

Bush's victory in 1988 did not amount to a mandate for change; it was not really a *clarifying* election in the same way that Reagan's 1980 and 1984 elections were. According to Duffy and Goodgame, "Bush emerged from the campaign not so much as a spokesman for the country's aspirations, but as a shrewd oracle of its uncertain mood and conflicting desires."[52] In many ways, the elections turned on perceptions of toughness on issues such as crime and security and did not really point the nation in one direction or the other. According to political scientist Bert Rockman, "Political contests that are not turbocharged with big ideas are fertile territory for symbolic appeals and innuendos. The 1988 campaign, precisely because it was so devoid of policy ideas (unlike 1980), fed on symbols and innuendos."[53]

---

[47]Ibid.

[48]Beschloss, 494.

[49]Duffy and Goodgame, 33.

[50]James P. Pfiffner, "Establishing the Bush Presidency," *Public Administration Review* (January/February 1990), 64.

[51]Wicker, 105. Italics in original.

[52]Duffy and Goodgame, 32.

[53]Bert A. Rockman, "The Leadership Style of George Bush," in *The Bush Presidency: First Appraisals*, 9.

The *Washington Post* may have best described the significance and context of the Bush victory in 1988. In its editorial page on November 14, 1988, it summarized aptly the challenges that would confront George Bush and the ironic conclusion that his governance would focus mostly on his competence, the theme that Michael Dukakis was criticized for using:

> The truth of the matter is that the whole argument over the nature of Mr. Bush's mandate is in a sense merely incidental to a much larger and more immediate issue: How, on the basis of his campaign rhetoric and whatever the voters consider his mandate to be, a newly installed President Bush will handle the challenge of creeping Gramm-Rudman deadlines, burgeoning federal government costs and a Democratic Congress not exactly bursting with enthusiasm to help him out of the fiscal and financial pressures that are intensifying. His mandate in this poorly focused election may not have been to fix the budget deficit, but until he does, he can do little else. Given all this, we expect Mr. Bush's plans cannot be grandiose; his claims and demands will not be dramatic. He will reveal himself as a man whose hope is to make the so-called Reagan revolution work, to somewhat extend its social sympathies and to vindicate the past eight years in the next four. He will also be doing a lot of bailing out. If you will pardon the expression, in this context we think the Bush presidency is more likely to be about competence than ideology.[54]

Turning to the four-part leadership framework will help illustrate significant differences between the presidency of George H. W. Bush and those of Carter and Reagan.

POLICY

George Bush's political style had always been highly pragmatic, personal, and incremental. He frequently expressed a measure of discomfort in waxing eloquent about his aspirations or the strategic intent of his political activities. According to Dennis Ross, who served as director of the State Department's Policy Planning Staff and later as special envoy to the Middle East in the Bush administration, President Bush was uncomfortable in a world of philosophical absolutes.[55] Bush commented a number of times that he did not think in terms of grandiose objectives and that he did not operate out of some large-scale blueprint for reforming society.[56] Bush was hesitant to use dramatic language and often deleted phrases from his speeches while delivering them.[57] As he put it in *A World Transformed*, "It was difficult for me to give dramatic

---

[54]"The Great Mandate Hunt. . .," *Washington Post,* November 14, 1988, A10.

[55]Dennis Ross, interview by author, December 1, 2008, Washington, D.C.

[56]Barilleaux and Rozell, 9.

[57]Duffy and Goodgame, 77.

speeches on my vision for the nation. I was certain that results . . . would be far better than trying to convince people through rhetoric."[58] Nevertheless, he was guided by important principles, values, and beliefs, as he explained in the same work:

> Even if I could not express it as well as Reagan, I knew what I hoped for our country and for the world. I wanted to tackle the big problems facing us, such as lingering superpower confrontation. I was determined to do what I could to make the world a better, safer place, where people would no longer fear imminent nuclear war . . .
>
> I too had my own guiding principles and values. Everything I learned from history, from my father, Prescott Bush, everything I've learned from my service in the US Navy reinforced the words "duty, honor, country." I believe one's duty is to serve the country. This can mean not only military service, especially in a time of war, but also opportunities for elective offices. I think it is important to put something back into the system—to get in the arena, not simply to carp and criticize from the sidelines.[59]

Clearly, Bush was raised to think of politics as a high calling.[60] His family provided the experiences, support, and values to encourage him to pursue elective office. And he took the notion of "duty, honor, and country" quite seriously. On top of his vaunted notion of the political enterprise, Bush, as mentioned earlier, also believed in the importance of the personal relationships—indeed, the friendships—that would lead to effectiveness diplomatically and politically. According to Dick Cheney, who served as President Bush's secretary of defense (and would later serve as vice president for George W. Bush), "The personal relationships that the President had acquired over the years was another ingredient that contributed to the administration's success. Basically, he knew everyone."[61] Even when he had been an oilman in Texas, he believed that "business rested entirely on personal relations."[62]

In the realm of foreign policy, it is clear that President Bush understood the fundamental and rapid transformations occurring in the global environment. Bush recognized the significant changes that were underway in the Soviet empire, accelerated by the rise to power of Mikhail Gorbachev in 1985 and the impact those changes would have on U.S.-Soviet relations. Several significant changes occurred during the Bush years, as summarized by presidential scholar Fred Greenstein, "The first three years of George H.W. Bush's presidency

---

[58]Bush and Scowcroft, 17.

[59]Ibid.

[60]Dowd and Friedman, 34; Parmet, 31.

[61]Dick Cheney, "The Bush Presidency," in Kenneth W. Thompson, ed., *The Bush Presidency, Part Two: Ten Intimate Perspectives of George Bush* (New York: University Press of America and the Miller Center, UVA, 1998), 10.

[62]Cramer, 323.

witnessed the collapse of communism in Eastern Europe, the demise of the Soviet Union, and the dramatic military triumph of a US-led military coalition over the forces of Saddam Hussein's Iraq."[63]

In the first year of his presidency, Bush gave several speeches that signified a shift in direction in U.S. policy and suggested innovative ideas regarding U.S.-Soviet relations. He spoke about going beyond the "containment" policy emblematic of the Cold War, seeking integration of the Soviets into the "community of nations," and making a commitment to match Soviet moves toward greater peace with "moves of our own."[64] He added that words would have to be matched by deeds and that the Soviets would have to take positive steps, such as reducing their conventional forces concentrated in Europe, permitting self-determination in all of Eastern Europe (already well underway in Poland), working with the United States to effect practical measures for diplomatic resolutions of regional disputes, and joining the United States in addressing global problems such as drug trafficking and environmental degradation.[65]

According to political scientists Barilleaux and Rozell, Bush's worldview was "founded in his resume."[66] Unlike most of his predecessors, Bush shared with President Eisenhower the credentials to claim status as a foreign policy professional. Through his experiences as a U.S. ambassador to the United Nations under Nixon, head of the American liaison office in the People's Republic of China, and CIA director under Ford, Bush schooled himself in the intricacies of international diplomacy and the outlook of its practitioners. Indeed, Barilleaux and Rozell suggest, "he identified more with foreign affairs managers than domestic political operatives."[67]

President Bush's comprehension of the complexities of international relations led him to embrace the value of order and stability in world affairs, good personal relations among national leaders, and sensitivity to the interests and views of other countries.[68] The philosophy that emerged from this amalgam of views amounted to what Barilleaux and Rozell characterize as a "conservative internationalism": a desire to promote the classical and universal values associated with the American system—such as liberty and democracy—but to do so through means that ensure security and stability in the international arena.[69]

Bush's embrace of conservative internationalism was evident in his cautious reaction to the breakup of the Soviet Union's East European empire and to the fall of the Soviet regime itself. As the United States and its European allies worked to manage the winding down of the Cold War, Bush met frequently with British Prime Minister Margaret Thatcher, French President

---

[63]Greenstein, 160.

[64]Bush and Scowcroft, 15–16.

[65]Ibid., 53.

[66]Barilleaux and Rozell, 115.

[67]Ibid., 117.

[68]Ibid.

[69]Ibid., 118.

François Mitterrand, and West German Chancellor Helmut Kohl. Following one particular meeting with Kohl, Bush explained his thinking to reporters in the following way, "The enemy is unpredictability, the enemy is instability."[70] Although many Germans were eagerly pursuing unification of East and West Germany, Bush counseled a gradual approach that would allow the unification of Germany to occur while still preserving the country's membership in the North Atlantic Treaty Organization (NATO). In April 1989, Kohl issued a public call for negotiating on reducing the number of short-range nuclear weapons in Europe in response to domestic pressure in his country. Bush feared that this action would undermine NATO's defensive capability in the face of a potential attack from the Warsaw Pact. Bush's reaction to Kohl's proposal was vintage Bush: He invited Kohl to a discussion at Camp David. Kohl could not attend, due to competing responsibilities at home, but sent his foreign policy adviser, NATO Security General Manfred Worner (a former German defense minister and political ally of Kohl). The discussions between Bush and Worner resulted in a plan for reductions in NATO and Warsaw Pact conventional forces, thereby reducing the risk of an invasion that might trigger the use of nuclear weapons.[71]

Bush reacted calmly, and not boisterously, when the Berlin Wall came down in 1989, recognizing the difficult position he would have created for Soviet President Mikhail Gorbachev by a more visual and emotional display of jubilation. When asked by reporter Lesley Stahl if he was excited about the fall of the Berlin Wall, Bush replied, "I'm not an emotional kind of guy."[72] U.S. senators had been advising President Bush to go to Berlin and "dance on the wall"; however, Kohl told him how inappropriate and foolish this would have been.[73]

In December 1991, only a short time after the fall of the Berlin Wall, Bush met with Gorbachev on two warships near the Mediterranean island of Malta. The meeting resulted in a process of consultations that within a year led to the reunification of Germany almost entirely on Western terms.[74] At a May 31 White House meeting, Gorbachev explicitly accepted Germany's reunification and its continued membership in NATO. In return, Bush offered Gorbachev a series of well-meaning proposals, emphasizing a consultative role for the Soviets in fashioning a cooperative global strategy to replace the Cold War divisions. He even held out the idea of financial aid for the Soviet Union.[75]

President Bush may have been overly optimistic when he referred to a "new world order" emerging from his discussions with Gorbachev, but it is evident that his clear-headed thinking about preserving order in the midst of

---

[70]Ibid.

[71]Ibid., 124.

[72]Bush and Scowcroft, 149.

[73]Ibid., 151.

[74]Zbigniew Brzezinski, *Second Chance: Three Presidents and the Crisis of American Superpower* (New York: Basic Books, 2007), 57.

[75]Ibid.

a rapidly changing international environment was important. According to Zbigniew Brzezinski, professor of International Relations at Columbia University and National Security Council Adviser under Jimmy Carter:

> It is impossible to overestimate the importance of the peaceful reunification of Germany in October 1990 that followed this (May 31) meeting. The fall of the Berlin Wall a year earlier made reunification seem inevitable, but only if there was no regressive Soviet reaction to the Wall's removal. The Soviet army was still in East Germany, and while the East German regime was demoralized and confused by Gorbachev's apparent acquiescence, a change of mind in the Kremlin (or simply a change in the Kremlin) could have unleashed Soviet forces . . .
>
> Bush's performance deserves the highest praise. He cajoled, reassured, flattered, and subtly threatened his Soviet counterpart. He had to seduce Gorbachev with visions of a global partnership while encouraging his acquiescence to the collapse of the Soviet empire in Europe. At the same time, Bush had to reassure his British and French allies that a reunited Germany would not threaten their interests.[76]

Bush's conservative internationalism was also evidenced in his reaction to the Chinese government's harsh crackdown on student demonstrators in Beijing's Tiananmen Square in 1989. Chinese authorities ordered soldiers to attack a peaceful crowd of a hundred thousand student demonstrators who had occupied Tiananmen Square, killing hundreds, wounding thousands, and arresting thousands more.[77] The president's response was muted; it included a strong denunciation—"I deeply deplore the decision to use force"—but was offset by his desire to preserve the relationship the United States had with China.[78] Secretary of State James Baker, sensitive to public and congressional opinion, urged Bush to issue a more forceful rebuke for the Chinese action, accompanied by at least limited sanctions. But at a press conference two days after the massacre, Bush said, "This is not the time for an irrational response, but for a reasoned, careful action that takes into account our long-term interests and recognition of a complex internal situation in China."[79] He decided not to cut off the commercial relationship because he did not want to punish the people, but to suspend military sales and contracts, government-to-government sales, commercial exports of weapons, and visits between U.S. and Chinese military leaders.[80] However, he encouraged continued humanitarian aid and medical assistance through the Red Cross.[81] He also made no move against the exports that were part of China's $12 billion trade

---

[76]Ibid.

[77]Duffy and Goodgame, 182.

[78]Bush and Scowcroft, 101.

[79]Duffy and Goodgame, 182.

[80]Bush and Scowcroft, 89.

[81]Ibid., 90.

surplus with the United States.[82] In the end, Bush commented, the difference in cultural perceptions could not be ignored. The Americans interpreted the Tiananmen Square crisis in the context of their ideals of freedom and human rights, whereas the Chinese considered its impact on security and stability.[83]

Even in his reaction to Saddam Hussein's invasion of Kuwait in August 1990, Bush reflected his conservative internationalism. After learning of the Iraqi action, Bush almost immediately issued a statement condemning the invasion as "naked aggression" and called for the "immediate and unconditional withdrawal of all Iraqi forces." He recognized that Hussein's actions amounted to a threat to world order, not to mention to the world's oil supply.[84] Later that night (August 1), he signed executive orders banning all trade with Iraq and freezing Iraqi and Kuwait assets.[85] But he used cautious language and moved with great care on the military side of things, prompting British Prime Minister Thatcher to admonish him about the dangers of "going wobbly" when they met in Aspen, Colorado, shortly after the Iraqi invasion.[86] Bush advised continued attempts at diplomatic initiatives and economic sanctions against Hussein and signaled his willingness to continue to negotiate, while methodically preparing for the possibility of war by securing agreements with other nations about military basing operations and obtaining financial commitments to the war effort. When he announced that he was sending troops to Saudi Arabia on August 8, Bush indicated that their purpose was defensive in nature.[87] Ultimately, he chose to confront Saddam through force, but he did so with some hesitancy and with adequate preparation. The careful management of policy was evident, and the preparation bore tremendous fruit.

President Bush effectively forged an international coalition against the Iraqi government of Saddam Hussein that included countries as diverse as Saudi Arabia, China, and Israel, secured economic sanctions against Iraq, and obtained a passage of a UN resolution authorizing the use of military force to restore Kuwait's freedom. The Soviet Union joined the coalition after Bush convinced Saudi Arabia to give a billion dollars in aid to the Kremlin.[88] Bush managed to build a military force of 771,000 troops to rescue Kuwait, and 230,000 of those troops were non-U.S. soldiers.[89] According to Duffy and Goodgame, "It remains difficult to overstate the diplomatic virtuosity that Bush displayed in accommodating the interests of coalition members large and small and keeping them united behind an effective policy."[90]

---

[82]Duffy and Goodgame, 182.

[83]Bush and Scowcroft, 110.

[84]Duffy and Goodgame, 135.

[85]David Mervin, *George Bush and the Guardianship Presidency* (New York: St. Martin's Press, 1996), 177.

[86]Barilleaux and Rozell, 125.

[87]Mervin, 178.

[88]Barilleaux and Rozell, 30.

[89]Brzezinski, 71.

[90]Duffy and Goodgame, 152.

In short, President Bush's conservative internationalism was based on the premise that it was important to maintain a semblance of order and stability within the context of a rapidly changing international environment. He was careful in managing delicate relationships and shifting power configurations. Although he cautioned the Germans about moving too fast toward the reunification of their nation, he admonished British Prime Minister Thatcher about the dangers of going too slow.[91] Bush believed that political skills are largely personal and that political leaders are guided less by ideological zeal than by personal relationships and the unyielding effect of friendships. As the Soviet empire was unraveling and Eastern European nations were throwing off the shackles of communism and Soviet domination, Bush perceived his major role to be one of facilitating, encouraging, and managing these processes. He proved deft at arranging diplomatic relationships needed to guarantee stability in the middle of these titanic shifts of power and influence.

On the other hand, according to Zbigniew Brzezinski, Bush did not fully realize the strategic implications of the changes in world politics. For instance, although Bush appreciated the significance of the reunification of Germany, he was "caught unawares" by the escalating Yugoslav crisis.[92] Yugoslavia's failure to redefine the central government's powers created a head-on collision between the dominant Serbian republic and two major components of the federation, Croatia and Slovenia. Their declaration of independence in June 1991 led to a Serbian invasion that started a long bloody war.[93] Furthermore, according to Brzezinski, Bush did not give adequate thought to developing a comprehensive program for political and economic reform within Russia that would help link that country to Europe. Monetary aid flowed in a mindless way and without a strategy for economic or financial reform. Finally, he failed to convert the impressive military victory over Saddam Hussein into lasting political reform in Iraq, or to a reinvigoration of the Israeli-Palestinian peace process.[94] As expressed by Brzezinski:

> The world that the Bush team faced was coming asunder, a definable and historically comprehensible era (the Cold War) was coming to an end. But the right course to pursue was not self-evident. Bush needed to define his priorities, look beyond just today and tomorrow, and act accordingly. This he never quite did. He focused primarily on the delicate task of peacefully managing the dismantling of the Soviet empire and then on cutting Saddam Hussein's excessive ambitions down to size. He brilliantly achieved both but exploited neither.[95]

President Bush was less willing to articulate a vision on domestic policy. In many respects, he intended to continue the Reagan policies, but reduce the

---

[91]Ross.
[92]Brzezinski, 59.
[93]Ibid., 60.
[94]Ibid., 60–64.
[95]Ibid., 71.

most severe aspects of those policies on the poor, reaching for a "kinder, gentler" approach. In a June 1991 speech, President Bush called for a "synthesis of all Reagan-era market economics and community-based social action."[96] He identified specific priorities in the areas of deficit reduction, education reform, and drug control policy; however, his approach was one of moderation, which Barilleaux and Rozell describe as "disjointed incrementalism."[97] His notion was to take one step at a time and guide the nation toward improvement. In his inaugural address, President Bush emphasized the policy limits imposed by a large budget deficit. He said that new programs and increased government spending were not the answers to the nation's problems. He opined that the United States had "more will than wallet" and it needed to limit its aspirations for major changes in domestic public policy. Instead, he called on the nation to renew its commitment to private acts of charity and "a thousand points of light" for the improvement of society.[98]

Bush did not see himself as an innovator, but as a "guardian" in domestic policy and as a "steward" president in general.[99] According to political scientist David Mervin, guardians are largely satisfied with the status quo, even though they may recognize a need for marginal change.[100] To a guardian, leadership is not about crusading, nor about working to a blueprint, but it is about problem solving on a case-by-case basis. As Bush said in the ending of his 1989 inaugural address, "Some see leadership as high drama and the sound of trumpets calling, and sometimes it is that. But I see history as a book with many pages, and each day we fill a page with acts of hopefulness and meaning."[101]

Although he achieved important legislative victories with the passage of the 1990 Americans with Disability Act and the 1990 Clean Air Act, in many cases he settled for half-measures or a slight lurch forward with respect to domestic policies. And because he was not driven by strong conviction, he could be easily persuaded to abandon or shave policy objectives.

A good example of Bush's tendency to scale down policy objectives was in the area of drug control policy. Shortly after taking office, Bush told reporters that he knew from his leadership of President Reagan's anti-drug effort that education, treatment, and other demand-side solutions were more likely to reduce drug use than supply-side strategies, such as interdiction and punishment. Bush's notion was reinforced by Treasury Secretary Nicholas Brady (whose job included overseeing the Customs Service), who concluded privately in an early drug strategy meeting that efforts aimed at attacking supply were

---

[96]Andrew Rosenthal, "Bush Outlines an Attack on Domestic Ills," *New York Times,* June 13, 1991.

[97]Barilleaux and Rozell, 12.

[98]George H. W. Bush, Inaugural Address, January 20, 1989, http://bushlibrary.tamu.edu/research/public_papers, accessed August 9, 2011.

[99]Ross.

[100]Mervin, 32.

[101]Bush, inaugural address.

doomed as long as there was a high demand for drugs. But by the time Bush announced his grand strategy on drug control—in his first prime-time television address from the Oval Office in September 1989—he shifted gears to advocate a crackdown on drug shipments and drug crime. This was (in part) due to the insistence of Chief of Staff Sununu, who possessed polls showing most Americans favored "get-tough" measures instead of education and treatment strategies.[102]

Overall, George Bush was not a visionary, but a skillful practitioner of power politics in the international arena[103] and a proponent of a modified "Reaganism" on the domestic front. He saw himself as a problem-solver and relationship-builder—not a visionary. According to Mervin, "Governance for a president like Bush was a low key, low profile affair with little room for ideology or flamboyant rhetoric. He preferred the term 'doer' to 'dreamer,' and expressed cynicism about the more lofty and even public aspects of the presidency."[104] According to Duffy and Goodgame:

> Because he had campaigned as a caretaker and arrived in office with only the most modest marginal mandate for change, Bush had no need to carve out a large public role for himself. A high-profile presidency would only raise public expectations at a time when any president would be hard-pressed to satisfy the country's complex and conflicting political demands. Bush instead sought to dial back his exposure, particularly on substantive issues, trimming the role of the presidency in the lives of most Americans. In this way he was making a virtue of necessity: his inability to affect a swaggering leadership style dovetailed with his minimalist agenda.[105]

In some respects, Bush was an effective leader. He understood that he served as president during a time of profound change. In many ways, he was the last Cold War president, and he was also practically driven to confront the mounting budgetary deficits the country confronted in the early 1990s. According to Barilleaux and Rozell:

> Bush saw his mission as being to guide the country effectively during a period of transition, rather than precipitating large-scale changes. He managed events competently, he protected the powers and prerogatives of his office, and he effectively minimized the influence of his opinions. None of these accomplishments sounds particularly stirring or likely to inspire future references in studies of presidential "greatness." But some times calls for boldness, whereas others require quiet leadership and perhaps defensive action.[106]

---

[102]Duffy and Goodgame, 104.

[103]Brzezinski, 46.

[104]Mervin, 27.

[105]Duffy and Goodgame, 45.

[106]Barilleaux and Rozell, 106.

The effect of Bush's approach to leadership is that American unity is best preserved through the sense of a caring collective conveyed by leaders whose main purpose is "not to steer the ship of state in a particular direction, but to keep it on an even keel while nurturing the gentle arts of civility."[107] And none are better qualified to do this than those who have devoted their lives to public service and being part of the government.

But the absence of a grand vision would take its toll, especially after the Gulf War when George Bush, with an unusually large groundswell of popular support—nearly 90 percent popularity—could not translate this support into policy accomplishment or programmatic direction in domestic policy. He was still "guarding," but the country was sliding into a recession and demanding more forceful leadership. This vision and performance gap was effectively exploited by Bush's opponent, Arkansas Governor Bill Clinton, in the 1992 presidential race.

POLITICS

President Bush entered the White House in an atmosphere of relatively low expectations. He had no obvious mandate to carry out, a residue of bad feelings from the unusually negative campaign he had conducted, a looming budget deficit (which by 1989 had grown to $155 billion, twice what it had been eight years earlier),[108] and a Democratic-controlled Congress.[109] Perhaps the inauspicious circumstances reinforced his previously described proclivity to go slow and take careful, measured steps in governance. According to political scientist Charles Jones, Bush "hit the ground limping."[110] According to presidential scholar James Pfiffner:

> The new Bush Administration was marked by a preference for competence, not ideology. The president's style was one of reactive problem-solving, not strategic vision. His approach to Congress was one of compromise, not confrontation. His approach to policy was personal communication rather than "going public."[111]

Bush's transition process fit the incrementalist theme. Lacking a compelling set of urgent policy objectives, Bush downplayed the importance of a 100 days agenda. According to Barilleaux and Rozell, "As one elected to continue with existing policies, Bush came to the presidency with a perspective unusual for an American Chief Executive: he did not feel a compelling sense

---

[107]Kerry Mullins and Aaron Wildavsky, "The Procedural Presidency of George Bush," *Political Science Quarterly*, 107, no. 1 (Spring 1992), 12.

[108]Barilleaux and Rozell, 195.

[109]Charles O. Jones, "Meeting Low Expectations: Strategy and Prospects of the Bush Presidency," in *The Bush Presidency: First Appraisals*, 55.

[110]Ibid.

[111]Pfiffner, 70.

of urgency to put his mark on policy through decisive victories in the early months in office."[112]

Bush selected mostly moderate insiders. He did not surround himself with "big ideas" people in the conservative movement who were attached to Reagan.[113] He preferred experienced, competent individuals instead of ideological crusaders, and he tapped associates from nearly every phase of his career.[114] From his early days in Texas, he appointed James Baker as secretary of state and Nicholas Brady as treasury secretary; he drew associates from the Ford administration, including National Security Adviser Brent Scowcroft, Defense Secretary Dick Cheney, and U.S. Trade Representative Carla Hill. From his years with Ronald Reagan, he appointed Office of Management and Budget Director Richard Darman.

◥ THE ADMINISTRATION OF GEORGE H. W. BUSH[115]

INAUGURATION: January 20, 1989, the Capitol, Washington, D.C.

VICE PRESIDENT: J. Danforth "Dan" Quayle

SECRETARY OF STATE: James A. Baker III; Lawrence S. Eagleburger (from December 8, 1992)

SECRETARY OF THE TREASURY: Nicholas F. Brady

SECRETARY OF DEFENSE: Richard B. Cheney

ATTORNEY GENERAL: Richard L. Thornburgh; William P. Barr (from November 20, 1991)

SECRETARY OF THE INTERIOR: Manuel Lujan Jr.

SECRETARY OF AGRICULTURE: Clayton K. Yeutter; Edward Madigan (from March 7, 1991)

SECRETARY OF COMMERCE: Robert A. Mosbacher; Barbara H. Franklin (from February 27, 1992)

SECRETARY OF LABOR: Elizabeth H. Dole; Lynn M. Martin (from February 22, 1991)

SECRETARY OF HEALTH AND HUMAN SERVICES: Louis W. Sullivan

SECRETARY OF HOUSING AND URBAN DEVELOPMENT: Jack F. Kemp

SECRETARY OF TRANSPORTATION: Samuel K. Skinner; Andrew H. Card (from January 22, 1992)

SECRETARY OF ENERGY: James D. Watkins

SECRETARY OF EDUCATION: Lauro F. Cavazos Jr.; Lamar Alexander (from March 14, 1991)

SECRETARY OF VETERANS AFFAIRS: Edward J. Derwinski

SUPREME COURT APPOINTMENTS: David H. Souter (1990); Clarence Thomas (1991)

---

[112]Barilleaux and Rozell, 133.

[113]Ibid., 13.

[114]Mullins and Wildavsky, 41.

[115]Beschloss, 495.

Ten of his sixteen-member cabinet had known him for at least ten years.[116] He added a few movement conservatives to important positions: Jack Kemp as secretary of housing and urban development, Drug Czar William Bennett to head the White House Office of National Drug Control Policy, and James Pinkerton as deputy director of policy and planning.[117]

As in all administrations, there were tensions among the Bush appointees between the "incrementalists" and the "warriors." The warriors wanted an aggressive campaign to promote a conservative agenda over the objections of Democrats and moderate Republicans. Their ideas were championed in Congress by Newt Gingrich, the Republican whip, and by conservative journalist Patrick Buchanan (who would challenge Bush in the 1992 primaries for not being adequately conservative). Inside the White House, warriors included Domestic Policy staffer James Pinkerton, Office of Policy Development member Charles Kolb, and Housing and Urban Development Secretary Jack Kemp.[118] On the other side were those who shared Bush's belief in gradualism and caution, including Richard Darman, Nicolas Brady, Roger Porter (assistant to the president for domestic affairs), and John Sununu.

In March 1989, Sununu outlined what he would consider a "successful presidency":

> By putting together a solid record of accomplishment on which to campaign in 1992; a checklist of bills passed that major constituents would applaud, of bills vetoed that the other constituency—especially conservatives—had despised; and a tally of presidential actions taken, crises handled, and opportunities seized.[119]

Central to the Bush quest for a successful presidency was cooperation with congressional Democrats to make incremental progress on a wide range of issues: curbing the use of illegal drugs, stabilizing the banking and credit industry (looming savings and loan crisis), and reducing the federal budget deficit.[120]

Bush started out with a conciliatory tone toward Congress in his inaugural address:

> To my friends, and yes, I do mean friends—in the loyal opposition and, yes, I mean loyal—I put out my hand. I am putting out my hand to you, Mr. Speaker, our differences ended at the water's edge. And we don't wish to turn back time, but when our mothers were young; Mr. Majority Leader, the Congress and the Executive were capable of working together to produce a budget on which this nation could live. Let us negotiate

---

[116]Ibid.

[117]Barilleaux and Rozell, 21.

[118]Ibid., 134.

[119]Mervin, 159.

[120]Barilleaux and Rozell, 137.

soon and hard. But in the end, let us produce. The American people await action. They didn't send us here to bicker. They ask us to rise above the merely partisan.[121]

Having served in the House and presided over the Senate, Bush had many friends in both chambers and on both sides of the aisle. During the first half of 1989, virtually all the senators and almost half of the house members had been invited to the White House for some function or ceremony.[122] President Bush also reached out to the executive branch of government. Twenty days after his inauguration, he gathered hundreds of the government's senior career executives at Daughters of the American Revolution (DAR) Constitution Hall to praise their dedication and ask for their help in governing. President Bush said:

> I'm coming to you as president and offering my hand in partnership. I'm asking you to join me as full members of our team. I promise to lead and to listen, and I promise to serve beside you as we work together to carry out the will of the American people. Our principles our clear: that government service is a noble calling and a public trust.[123]

Meanwhile the Democratic Party faced its own set of challenges, in spite of being the majority party. For example, the majority leader of the Senate, Robert Byrd of West Virginia, decided to step down, and the Democrats elected George Mitchell of Maine as his replacement, bypassing two of the presumptive candidates for the position. Furthermore, two prominent Democrats, House Majority Whip Tony Coelho of California and Jim Wright, the feisty speaker of the house from Texas, were forced to resign due to questions about their ethics.[124] On June 6, 1989, Thomas Foley of Washington was elected speaker and over the next two weeks a completely new House Democratic leadership team was put in place: Richard Gephardt of Missouri became majority leader and William Gray of Pennsylvania became whip.[125]

Bush was able to work successfully with Congress in the early weeks and months of his presidency to solve the savings and loan crisis. Due to the absence of government regulation and guidelines, numerous savings and loan institutions made exuberant but sometimes careless investments, and were losing a great deal of money, creating the need for a monthly infusion of $1 billion from the federal government to keep them operating. In August 1989, Bush and the Democratic Congress agreed on a $157 billion bailout for the industry under the Financial Institution Reform, Recovery, and Enforcement Act.[126]

---

[121]Bush, inaugural address.

[122]Pfiffner, 70.

[123]Max Stier, "A Lesson for Obama on Reaching Out to the Federal Workforce," *Washington Post,* December 26, 2008.

[124]Jones, 55–56.

[125]Ibid., 56.

[126]Wicker, 109.

But the capacity for cooperation between the two branches of government was seriously undermined in March 1989, when the Senate rejected President Bush's nominee for secretary of defense, John Tower. The rejection of a cabinet nominee was only the ninth in the history of the republic and the first since 1959.[127] John Tower had served four terms as a U.S. senator from Texas, had served as President Reagan's chief negotiator in the SALT (Strategic Arms Limitation Talks) treaty, and had been a strong supporter of George Bush during the 1988 presidential election campaign. Moreover, the commission that Tower chaired to investigate the activities of high-level government officials during the Iran-Contra affair did not directly implicate Vice President Bush.[128]

On the other hand, Tower was somewhat unpopular in the Senate because of his dictatorial ways of managing the Senate Armed Services Committee and his reputation as a drinker and womanizer. Furthermore, there were charges that Tower was too close to certain defense contractors and had been paid $750,000 in consulting fees.[129]

Bush realized that the nomination was in trouble when the sitting chairman of the Senate Armed Services Committee Senator Sam Nunn (D-GA) said, "I cannot in good conscience vote to put an individual at the top of the chain of command when his history of excessive drinking is such that he would not be selected to command a missile wing, a strategic air command bomber, or a Trident submarine."[130]

Nevertheless, Bush refused to back down and asserted his right as president to fill his cabinet with his people of his own choosing. The Senate rebuked him, defeating the Tower nomination, mostly along party lines, by 11–9 in the Armed Services Committee and by 53–47 in the full chamber.[131] According to James Pfiffner:

> The crucial decision on the part of the Administration was to let the issue escalate from the fitness of John Tower to head the Department of Defense to the credibility of the President. Once the president's power became the issue, the Republicans had to fall into ranks. The stakes were raised considerably, and the fight became much more partisan. If the president lost, it would be more than merely not having a particular man as Secretary of Defense, it would be a serious blow to the President's credibility.[132]

Bush recovered quickly by naming an alternative candidate, Dick Cheney, who had previously served as President Ford's chief of staff and a five-term

[127]Mervin, 90–91.

[128]Wicker, 110.

[129]Ibid., 109–110.

[130]Ibid., 110–111.

[131]Ibid., 111.

[132]Pfiffner, 71.

Republican member of Congress from Wyoming, within twenty-four hours of the Tower defeat. Cheney was confirmed in one week.[133]

Perhaps the biggest disappointment of President Bush's political perform-ance was revising his "no new taxes" pledge with November 5, 1990, signing of the Omnibus Budget Reconciliation Act of 1990. The bill, which resulted from several months of closed-door negotiations among Bush, fellow Republicans, and congressional Democrats, stipulated the following package: $137 billion in revenue increases, including a rise in the marginal income tax rate for in-dividuals from 28 to 31 percent and limitations on tax deductions for the wealthy over a four-year projection period; an increase in gasoline prices by 5 cents per gallon and a cut in Medicare by $42.5 billion.[134] When he signed the bill into law, President Bush described it as the "centerpiece of the largest deficit reduction package in history."[135] However, in March 1992—after losing his bid for re-election to the White House—Bush stated that his turnaround on the tax pledge was his worst mistake as president.[136]

What happened to cause George Bush to reassess his own decision and to criticize himself for pursuing deficit reduction, a goal he described as vital in various speeches and announcements? The answer provides a clue about the political problems confronted by a president who operated in a closed-door, deal-making style and was less sensitive, in fact somewhat oblivious, to the public aspects of the presidency.[137]

In his 1988 acceptance speech, George Bush promised a "kinder, gentler America," and pledged to improve education, protect the environment, and reduce the federal deficit. But he also promised to do all these things without raising taxes.[138] Indeed, in December 1988, Bush rejected a deficit reduction plan proffered by the National Economic Commission—a group formed in the waning days of the Reagan administration to deal with the quickly grow-ing federal deficit—because that plan included tax increases. He was able to achieve agreement with Congress on a "slide-by" budget for fiscal year 1990, which included a modest $15 billion deficit reduction package and excluded a capital gains tax cut proposed by Bush and opposed by congressional Democrats.[139]

The 1990 slide-by budget, however, was merely a Band-Aid over a deep defi-cit problem, and the Gramm-Rudman-Hollings amendment called for a balanced budget by 1993. Bush, influenced by Richard Darman, felt enormous pressure

---

[133]Cheney, 6.

[134]Duane Windsor, "The 1990 Deficit Reduction Deal," in Richard Himelfarb and Rosanna Perotti, eds., *Principle over Politics? The Domestic Policy of the George H. W. Bush Presidency* (Westford, CT: Greenwood Publishers, 2004), 30.

[135]George Bush, "Statement at Signing Ceremony for 1990 Omnibus Budget and Reconciliation Act," Congressional Almanac, 1990 (Washington, D.C.: Congressional Quarterly, 1991), 166.

[136]Mervin, 156.

[137]Barilleaux and Rozell.

[138]Windsor, 28.

[139]Ibid., 29.

to deal with the deficit problem, and in May 1990 invited the Democratic leadership to participate in a budget deficit summit. By extending the invitation, Bush promised to deliberate without precondition and in an atmosphere of "goodwill, statesmanship and respectful agreement on the merits."[140] The negotiations were held in secret, and at the insistence of the Democratic leadership Bush issued the following statement after a few days of talks:

> Both the size of the deficit problem and the need for a package that can be enacted require all of the following: entitlement and mandatory program reform, tax revenue increases, discretionary spending reductions, orderly reductions in defense expenditures, and budget process reform to assure that any bipartisan agreement is enforceable and that the deficit problem is brought under responsible control.[141]

One hundred House Republicans almost immediately signed a letter of complaint opposing the president's statement.[142] Nonetheless, Bush persisted in the negotiations, in the context of a worsening recession, and on September 30, 1990, revealed a budget proposal that resulted from the closed-door session. The agreed plan included a 12 cent per gallon gasoline tax increase, a new tax on home heating oil, and a $60 billion cut in Medicare spending. It also included a "pay-as-you-go" funding provision for new program initiatives, requiring the sponsors of new programs to find savings in other programs to pay for the new ones.[143] The negotiated package intended to:

- Reduce future debt by $500 billion,
- Eliminate Gramm-Rudman-Hollings amendment in favor of the discretionary caps, and change the congressional budget process,
- Increase taxes in violation of Bush's promise of "no new taxes."[144]

The negotiated budget deal was defeated in an October 1, 1990, House vote with 149 Democrats voting "no" (108 voting "yes") and 105 Republicans voting "no" (71 voting "yes").[145] In the next round of negotiations, Bush operated out of a weakened position with the Democrats, and even with a group of disgruntled Republicans led by Newt Gingrich of Georgia (who would become speaker of the house in 1995, during the Clinton administration). The president and Congress agreed to a series of "continuing resolutions" (a measure used to keep the government operating at the previous year's budgetary level when a new budget has not been passed), and Bush had to suspend non-essential

---

[140]Ibid., 28.

[141]George Bush, Public Papers, 1990, 11390.

[142]Windsor, 29.

[143]Ibid.

[144]James Thurber and Samantha L. Durst, "The 1990 Budget Enforcement Act: The Decline of Congressional Accountability," in Lawrence C. Dodd and Bruce I. Oppenheimer, eds., *Congress Reconsidered* (Washington, D.C.: CQ Press, 1993), 376.

[145]Windsor, 29.

services during the Columbus Day weekend.[146] Finally, Bush agreed to the previously described Omnibus Budget Reconciliation Act of 1990.

To many commentators, Bush's leadership during the 1990 budget crisis was badly flawed.[147] His failings included the absence of strong determination to balance the budget on his terms, a flaccid willingness to revoke his own strongly worded campaign promise of "no new taxes," and mostly an unwillingness to educate the American citizenry on why he was actually acting in their best interest. According to political scientist Dennis Ippolito, "The dramatic reversal on tax policy antagonized many Congressional Republicans, frayed relations with party conservatives, and raised questions about Bush's political credibility with the broader electorate."[148]

By the accounts of people who admire Bush, including Richard Darman, President Bush was, in fact, acting on the basis of an "inescapable strategic necessity." But what is clear is that the president did not create a sense of urgency about the deficit in the minds of American citizens. And his reliance on a closed back-door summit process was ill-suited to the persuasion task at hand.[149] James Cicconi, who served in the Bush administration, described the problem as follows:

> I think we also ignored the importance of popular political backing. If taxes are to be raised—again in defiance of a pledge not to do so— I think we never made . . . a compelling case for this sort of dramatic shift . . . I think we chose what I would call an "insider process" in place of a public process. We opted for private, behind closed-doors negotiations rather than a more public process of debate over these very important issues that were going to affect all Americans: whether taxes were increased, whether we passed the burden of debt on to our children, whether and how much we cut spending, and how to deal with entitlements. These were all questions that the public itself had not really been willing to confront, and rather than choose a course of public debate in a democratic process, we chose a behind closed-door process. And again, I think a public process would have made much better use of the president's high approval ratings with the public, his popularity, his ability to lead, and also would have exploited the Democrats' comparatively low ratings in these same categories.[150]

George Bush missed a significant educational opportunity, which is a central part of the presidential job portfolio. He refused to "go public" as other presidents have done to directly promote their programs to the American

---

[146]Ibid., 30.

[147]Mervin, 151.

[148]Dennis Ippolito, "Governance versus Politics: The Budget Policy Legacy of the Bush Administration," in Himelfarb and Perotti, *Principle over Politics?*, 3.

[149]Barilleaux and Rozell, 38.

[150]James Cicconi, "Discussant: James W. Cicconi," in Himelfarb and Perotti, *Principle over Politics?*, 50.

people and enhance their chances of success in Washington.[151] Writing from the perspective of the 2008 presidential race, journalist and former Carter speechwriter James Fallows underlined the importance of the rhetorical aspects of presidential leadership in an essay in the *Atlantic*:

> Rhetoric is only part of a president's power, but it's an important part. Building public enthusiasm for your program helps overcome legislative and administrative barriers, as in their different ways Franklin Roosevelt, John Kennedy, Ronald Reagan, and Bill Clinton showed.[152]

On the other hand, Bush displayed courage, leadership, and an ability to join Democrats when he actively supported the Americans with Disabilities Act, which he signed into law on July 26, 1990.[153] Bush viewed the legislation as a humanitarian gesture to protect the weak, but also as part of a long-term Republican strategy on disability to emphasize independence in the labor force over dependence on the welfare rolls. The law helped accomplish this goal through its major provisions:

- It prohibited discrimination in hiring and on the job against qualified individuals with disabilities.
- It required businesses of more than fifteen employees to provide "reasonable accommodation" to people with disabilities unless the accommodations created an "undue hardship" for business.
- It mandated that public accommodations, such as hotels, restaurants, theaters, and shops, be made accessible to people with disabilities.[154]

In international relations, Bush showed great dexterity and leadership acumen in the Persian Gulf War, for which he was handsomely rewarded by the public with one of the highest approval ratings ever achieved by an American president, 89 percent in March 1991.[155] His success in Operation Desert Storm, the U.S.-led coalition effort to oust Saddam Hussein from Kuwait, emanated from the strong personal relationships Bush had developed with foreign leaders, as well as those he nourished in his own administration, especially with Dick Cheney.[156] According to Cheney, "All of Bush's experiences came into play during the course of Operation Desert Storm. He made certain that the US government was given a clear mission and objective to achieve, but left the formulation of plans to the Defense Department and the US military."[157]

---

[151]Samuel Kernell, *Going Public: New Strategies of Presidential Leadership*, 3rd ed. (Washington, D.C.: CQ Press, 1997), Preface.

[152]James Fallows, "Rhetorical Questions," *Atlantic*, September 2008, http://www.theatlantic.com/doc/200809/fallows-debates/6, accessed June 22, 2009.

[153]Edward Berkowitz, "George Bush and the Americans with Disabilities Act," in Himelfarb and Perotti, *Principle over Politics?*, 143.

[154]Ibid., 144–145.

[155]Greenstein, 160.

[156]Cheney, 6.

[157]Ibid., 9.

Bush used the relationships he had developed over the years with Saudi officials to positive effect during the Gulf War. As vice president, Bush visited Saudi Arabia and bolstered his relationship with Saudi King Fahd. The two men often dined together and enjoyed after-dinner talks late into the night.[158] President Bush had ingeniously maintained that link, talking regularly with Fahd on the phone and sharing bits of gossip about the inside politics of the royal family.[159] During the first week of the Persian Gulf crisis, the president sent Cheney to Saudi Arabia to persuade King Fahd to allow U.S. forces into his kingdom, which was necessary for the defense of Saudi Arabia and also to help reverse Iraqi aggression.[160] Cheney met with King Fahd, along with General Norman Schwarzkopf (the commanding officer in Operation Desert Storm) and Paul Wolfowitz (undersecretary for defense policy). In the course of the two-hour meeting, the Americans explained why it was important for the Saudis to join in the effort to defend the kingdom and defeat Saddam Hussein. King Fahd, according to Cheney, conferred with his colleagues for five minutes and granted permission for the United States to undertake the mission. This occasion marked the first time that the Saudis had ever invited a significant contingent of foreign forces onto their soil. Fahd said he could trust the United States (including trusting them to withdraw the troops after hostilities), because he "trusted George Bush."[161]

In addition to sending Cheney to meet with the Saudis, Bush was also reaching out (through "rolodex diplomacy") to British Prime Minister Thatcher, President Mubarak of Egypt, and Soviet Premier Gorbachev.[162] "Bush's phone log during the Gulf Crisis looked like a roll call of world leaders, from Prime Minister Giulio Andreotti of Italy to Sheikh Zayid ibn Sultan Al Nuhayyan of the United Arab Emirates," according to Duffy and Goodgame.[163] They add, "It listed sixty-two calls to heads of state and government during the first thirty days after the invasion of Iraq."[164]

The president also conducted meetings with congressional leaders to address the concerns of Democrats who were resisting the military option. On October 30, 1990, Bush met with a bipartisan delegation of congressional leaders and the Democrats expressed deep reservations about a military attack. Bush made the strategic decision to withhold the details of the military operation until after the November 6 congressional elections.[165]

Concomitant with his negotiations with congressional leaders, Bush was intensifying U.S. efforts at the United Nations and achieved success with

---

[158]Duffy and Goodgame, 142.

[159]Ibid.

[160]Cheney, 10.

[161]Ibid., 127.

[162]Barilleaux and Rozell, 127.

[163]Duffy and Goodgame, 153.

[164]Ibid.

[165]Barilleaux and Rozell, 128.

passage of UN Security Council Resolution 678 on November 29, 1990. The resolution set a deadline of January 15, 1991, for the withdrawal of Iraqi troops from Kuwait or the anti-Iraqi coalition of UN states would be authorized to use "all necessary means" to "restore peace and security" to the area.[166]

Back in Washington, on December 5, fifty-four Democratic House members sought a federal court injunction that would have prevented Bush from embarking on offensive military action without first obtaining an explicit congressional authorization. The suit was dismissed by U.S. Federal District Court (District of Columbia) Judge Harold Greene on December 13 for insufficiency of evidence of an imminent clash between the legislative and executive branches.[167] Although never conceding the fact that Congress had a formal role in the ultimate decision to go to war, President Bush on January 8, 1991, requested a congressional resolution authorizing the use of force against Saddam Hussein's troops. The Senate approved the resolution on January 12 by a relatively close vote of 57–42, and the House voted 250–183. In both cases, the vote was to give President Bush the authority to use military force against Iraq to achieve the implementation of the various security council resolutions.[168]

Operation Desert Storm began on January 17, 1991, with aerial bombings, naval shellings, and cruise missile attacks. Meanwhile, Bush and the coalition proposed another deadline for the withdrawal of Iraqi troops to prevent the beginning of a ground war. Once again, Hussein balked, and the ground war was launched in late February 1991.[169] It ended quickly and decisively. According to Barilleaux and Rozell:

> The conclusion of the Persian Gulf War was both remarkable and controversial. It was remarkable for the speed with which it occurred and the relatively small loss of life by coalition forces that accompanied it. Barely a hundred hours after it had begun, the ground offensive was halted and President Bush declared victory. This abrupt closure made the war's conclusion controversial, for Bush was criticized then and later for not going all the way to Baghdad and completing the destruction of Saddam Hussein.[170]

Bush argued that the UN mandate did not authorize going all the way to Baghdad, but merely throwing the Iraqis out of the sovereign nation they had attacked. He was acting with circumspection, heeding the advice of his national security adviser, who admonished him of the dangers posed by "mission creep" in military operations.[171] Years later, Bush's son, George W. Bush, would take

---

[166]Ibid.

[167]Michael J. Glennon, "A Conveniently Unlawful War," *Policy Review*, no. 150 (August/September 2008).

[168]Mervin, 179.

[169]Barilleaux and Rozell, 129.

[170]Ibid., 130.

[171]Duffy and Goodgame, 150.

up the task of destroying Saddam Hussein and liberating Iraq itself; however, his actions led to a long, protracted, and ultimately unpopular war.

In summation, George Bush's political performance demonstrated both strengths and weaknesses. It is clear that his remarkable ability to build friendships and relationships assisted him in accomplishing his policy objectives. Relationship building helped George Bush in Congress, in the politics of his own administration, and in international relations. He was far more adept, in this way, at "retail politics" than Jimmy Carter was, and far more knowledgeable on policy details than Ronald Reagan was. Moreover, Bush's calm, unemotional style, augmented by a particularly strong national security team,[172] helped him effectively manage the dissolution of the Soviet Empire and the crumbling of the Soviet Union itself, as well as Operation Desert Storm. In these cases, the country needed a manager in chief who could methodically apply the resources at hand to the demands of the operation.

On the other hand, he may have over-emphasized the relationship aspects of politics and diplomacy, leading him to prefer closed-door negotiations and the art of the deal instead of a clear articulation of his objectives followed by outreach and persuasion to build popular support for his policies. It was almost as if Bush preferred the game of negotiations and bargaining to the conceptual tasks associated with identifying policy objectives in priority order and going after them.

Furthermore, the focus on relationships and "rolodex diplomacy" led Bush to minimize the public relations and educational aspects of the presidency. He did not adequately explain his volte-face on tax policy, or his loyalty to Senator John Tower, who was clearly an unpopular choice as a nominee for the secretary of defense, nor did he fully explain to American citizens the important changes occurring in the international arena. Bush's behavior seems to reflect a view that politics is an elite game for insiders, and that citizens need to be consulted from time to time, but not fully engaged in the process. This style of leadership almost relegates the citizenry to the role of spectators, which is how political scientist E. E. Schattschneider described the average citizen's role in the American polity several decades ago.[173]

Finally, Bush's tactical approach bespeaks incoherence or inarticulateness on core ideology or vision. It's hard to know where the tactician stands on important policy issues. A tactical orientation favors the micro over the macro issues as well. For instance, for Bush the moral question at the heart of the abortion debate—balancing the rights of a fetus versus those of its mother—is of less interest than the *number* of fetuses involved.[174] His dismissal of vision—when he mocked the "vision thing"—hurt his political performance and weakened his appeal to the American people and even to Congress.

---

[172]Ross.

[173]E. E. Schattschneider, *The Semi Sovereign People: A Realist's View of American Democracy* (New York: Holt, Rinehart, and Winston, 1967).

[174]Mervin, 92.

Bush's belief in friendships and loyalties as a basis of political leadership overestimates the importance of relationships in politics and undervalues the important insight of political scientist Hans Morgenthau: In international relations, there is no such thing as permanent friends, only permanent interests.[175]

STRUCTURE

President-elect Bush faced a difficult situation in the transition to his presidency. Although his campaign made it clear that he saw no need for a dramatic shift in direction from the Reagan presidency, he did not want to appear to be presiding over a third Reagan term.[176] Bush emphasized symbolic changes. During the transition and inauguration, the extended Bush family was highly visible, in contrast to the Reagan transition period. President Bush made a point of meeting publicly and visibly with African American leaders, which President Reagan had not done.[177]

Bush emphasized the importance of high ethical standards in setting up his administration; however, this issue would haunt him later with concerns raised about James Baker's financial holdings by White House Counsel Boyden Grey, by the revelations that came out in the Tower nomination, and by questionable behaviors by his chief of staff, John Sununu.[178]

Bush was clearly a more hands-on president than Reagan was. In contrast to Reagan's 9 to 5 schedule, Bush adopted a White House schedule of 7 to 6. Bush promised reporters that he would stay in touch and not allow himself to be isolated by White House staff.[179] He was not in favor of a heavily managed White House and attempted to downplay the pomp and circumstance of the office. The modest approach to leadership paralleled the modest policy objectives of the administration, and perhaps also reflects the fact that Bush had internalized his mother's disdain of self-importance.

Bush's initial White House staff was highly experienced: Twenty-four of the twenty-nine positions were held by people who had prior White House experience. Unlike Jimmy Carter, Bush did not hesitate to name a chief of staff. Craig Fuller had been his chief of staff in the vice presidency and was one of the main candidates to continue in this role when Bush assumed the presidency.[180] But after several weeks of contemplation, Bush chose John Sununu, governor of New Hampshire, who had been of tremendous assistance to Bush during the primaries, especially in New Hampshire.

Sununu was a powerful chief of staff and one of the first to have been a chief executive himself. His experience as governor of New Hampshire from

[175]Hans Morgenthau et al., *Politics among Nations* (New York: McGraw Hill, 2005).

[176]Pfiffner, 69.

[177]Ibid.

[178]Ibid.

[179]Ibid.

[180]Ibid., 68.

1983 to 1989 profoundly influenced his White House career. Andrew Card, who served as assistant to the president and deputy chief of staff from 1989 to 1992 (and would serve as chief of staff in the first administration of George W. Bush from 2000 to 2004), noted that "governors, in my opinion, always have a difficult time being staffers. Sununu, although a staffer, kept reverting to the role of executive decision maker."[181]

Sununu's role as Bush's chief of staff resembled Donald Regan's more than James Baker's during the Reagan years. He was abrupt, demanding, and not always patient with those who disagreed with him. Given Bush's own reluctance to confront people with whom he disagreed, but to seek compromises and patch over differences, he needed someone like Sununu who would be loyal to him and would take the heat for him when needed.[182]

Because personal ties rather than conviction drove Bush's political success, he needed someone to manage the ever-widening circle of allies who would place demands on the president's time. He needed someone with the heft to match the stature of James Baker, Brent Scowcroft, Robert Mosbacher, and Nicolas Brady, all of whom had strong personal relationships with Bush. Moreover, Bush, Baker, Cheney, Scowcroft, Darman, and Carla Hills (U.S. trade representative) had all worked for Gerald Ford. Bush needed someone who was outside of this group.[183]

Bush and Sununu made an interesting pair. According to Duffy and Goodgame:

> Like Arnold Schwarzenegger and Danny DeVito, George Bush and John Sununu were about to become the stars of a real life buddy film: one was tall, well built, and handsome; the other was short, pear-shaped, and homely. One was polite, graceful, and courteous, even when angry; the other was hostile, brash, and rude, even when perfectly happy. One dressed impeccably; the other couldn't keep his shirttail tucked in. One had been blessed with a fortune, a famous name, and a powerful father on a first-name basis with presidents, CEO's and other power brokers. The other was born in Havana, the son of a foreign film distributor, who bequeathed to his children a funny-sounding name and a polyglot Lebanese, Greek, and Salvadoran heritage.[184]

Nevertheless, the two men also had a great deal in common: big families located in New England, bright, well-trained politicians, a healthy sense of humor and an ability to laugh at themselves, political success by bringing together long-feuding wings of the Republican Party, and repeatedly underestimated throughout their political careers.[185]

---

[181]Andrew Card, "The Bush White House and His Presidency," in Thompson, *The Bush Presidency*, 45–61.

[182]Duffy and Goodgame, 112.

[183]Ibid.

[184]Ibid., 113.

[185]Ibid., 114.

Sununu proved to be a highly loyal chief of staff. Indeed, he took many arrows on behalf of his boss—from environmental groups who felt betrayed by Bush's public support for their goals that went unmatched by his actions, to teachers disappointed by his inadequate action on behalf of improving American education. Those who felt double-crossed rarely blamed Bush—they blamed Sununu.[186] Bush always maintained the pleasant demeanor—mastered the art of disagreeing without being disagreeable[187]—and left the nay-saying to his trusted chief of staff. According to Duffy and Goodgame:

> Sununu ran interference when Bush needed to shuffle to the right on such issues as judicial appointments or abortion, absorbing the blame of Bush's latest pander to his party's extremist wing. But because his ties to conservatives were so strong, Sununu could mollify the powerful GOP faction when the President needed to veer back to the middle on taxes and judicial questions.[188]

On the other hand, Sununu created problems for some of Bush's other appointees and advisers. For example, during the drafting of the Clean Air Act of 1990, Sununu out-muscled some principals who had an equal or greater interest in the subject than he did. The act had not been successfully amended since 1977, and it was a strong priority for William Riley, head of the Environmental Protection Agency, and James Watkins, secretary of energy. Roger Porter also worked on it, but Sununu forced his way in and took control of the legislation, which provided the government with regulatory power to reduce urban smog, toxic air pollutants, and acid rain.[189]

Ultimately, Sununu was dismissed from his position for running afoul of White House travel rules by taking taxpayer-financed and free Gulfstream jets on ninety-nine official political and personal trips, including visits to his dentist in Boston and ski resorts in the West.[190] Instead of simply apologizing and reimbursing the treasury, he displayed his typical arrogance and designated all but a few of the trips as official business. As the president's popularity began to sag under the pressure of a looming recession, he could no longer afford the added burden of an irascible chief of staff, and sent his son—the future president—to deliver a note to notify Sununu that his services would no longer be needed at the White House.[191]

In short, Bush was a seasoned political professional in charge of a network of similarly credentialed professionals. Those who worked for him were competent managers and experienced public servants; however, they were not

---

[186]Ibid., 115.

[187]Parmet, 35.

[188]Duffy and Goodgame, 115.

[189]John W. Sloan, "The Burden of the Reagan Legacy in the Bush Presidency," in Himelfarb and Perotti, *Principle over Politics?*, 115; Card, 53–54.

[190]Duffy and Goodgame, 124.

[191]Ibid., 129.

particularly animated by a sense of purpose or a guiding vision. They proved to be loyal to the president and his executive team. But the team had important elements of dysfunction and conflict that Bush failed to confront. Problems were particularly evident in the domestic policy arena.

PROCESS

As mentioned earlier, Bush promised to be a more hands-on chief executive than Reagan and that he would not allow himself to be isolated and dominated by his White House staff. In fact, Bush undervalued the importance of the public relations aspects of his presidency because he was well-informed and competent, obviating, in his mind, the need to promote himself to the American citizenry. In many respects, this focus on substance over style meant that Bush would resemble Carter more than Reagan. Like Carter, Bush believed that appearing well informed about issues and the policy process would serve his administration's goals far better than any public relations gimmickry.

On the other hand, Bush's administrative style did not provide him with the political cover that Reagan's "hands-off" method did. When Reagan compromised, the political heat was dissipated among his presidential staff; when Bush compromised—as he did on the budget agreement discussed above—he frequently became the focus of conservative outrage.[192]

Bush was certainly an active president who fulfilled his job with energy and enthusiasm. But the range of his contacts was limited to the circle of professional men and women with whom Bush could communicate freely and effectively. The discussions of the professional politicians and federal officials were based on many years of accumulated wisdom and the status of insider conservation (*insiders* means people who are in positions of power, or those who have the necessary connections to comprehend the details of political negotiations or policy formulations). When times were good and the status quo was guaranteed, the focus on incrementalism, insider exchanges, and proceduralism seemed to work fine. But when confronted with a need to change and shift policy direction, proceduralism did not work as well. Its service and prospects weren't overly innovative, its outreach necessarily limited.[193] Bush's "procedural" presidency was perfectly matched with his philosophy of stewardship and incrementalism and proved functional to guide the nation in the first few years of Bush's administration. But proceduralism is no match for times that call for fundamental change and innovation.

And things did change on the economic front during the run-up to the 1992 presidential election, when Bush would run for a second term against Arkansas Governor Bill Clinton. The economy remained lethargic accompanied by a rising chorus of Democratic accusations that the "aristocratic" Bush did not understand or care about the plight of the unemployed (for

---

[192]Sloan, 112.
[193]Mullins and Wildavsky.

almost a year Bush opposed the extension of unemployment benefits from twenty-six to thirty-nine weeks) and the increasingly nervous middle class.[194] In June 1992, the unemployment rate was 7.7 percent, and a *New York Times*/CBS poll found that only 16 percent of the public approved of how the President was managing the economy.[195] The inaction fed the belief that Bush was primarily interested in foreign policy and had no "vision" for domestic policy. During the campaign, Clinton stated that no president since Herbert Hoover (1929–1933) had a poorer record than did Bush in promoting economic growth and new jobs.[196]

Furthermore, although there is little doubt about the level of energy Bush invested in the presidency, he never seemed animated by a central purpose the way Reagan was. According to political scientist Collin Campbell, the Bush presidency presents us with an enigma: "On the one hand he pursued the job with great energy and apparent enthusiasm. On the other hand, he seemed to lack a game plan."[197]

SUMMING UP

What can one say about the presidency of George H. W. Bush in light of the four-part leadership framework? There is no doubt that President Bush brought to the White House a highly impressive résumé and a series of significant previous political appointments. He was the ultimate insider and did not, like many presidential candidates, campaign against Washington. He asked the American people to elect him because he was a competent, knowledgeable executive who understood the issues of the day and knew many of the domestic and international players on a personal basis. Bush promised to parlay his experience and contacts into meaningful political accomplishments.

In many respects, the promise worked in the foreign policy arena where Bush was able to manage the American reaction to the transformation of the Soviet-dominated Eastern Europe with dignity, calm, and grace. He was also able to perceive a significant threat to world stability from Saddam Hussein's invasion of Kuwait and to organize an impressive international coalition to address the menace with speed and efficiency. He was rewarded handsomely for these efforts with unusual levels of popular support, making the unprecedented level of 90 percent approval from a usually skeptical American public.

On the other hand, President Bush lacked a vision of domestic policy and his pragmatic, incremental, and "guardian" approach came up short when the economic and budgetary imperatives and challenges called for action. His foreign successes, in fact, served to accentuate his relative weakness in the domestic agenda. According to political scientist Stephen Skowronek, "If there is

---

[194]Sloan, 116.

[195]Ibid., 196.

[196]R. W. Apple, "The Economy's Casualty," *New York Times*, November 4, 1992, A1.

[197]Campbell, 185.

an irony in Bush's performance in the war with Iraq, it may be that this stirring demonstration of how effective he could be made all the more irritating his apparent inattentiveness to domestic affairs and the disarray of his domestic commitments."[198] There was no "Domestic Storm" equivalent to "Desert Storm."[199]

The public relations gaps in this presidency were also particularly glaring: because Bush needed to appear tough, he promised in the "Read My Lips" pledge that he would never raise taxes, in spite of strong admonitions from his budget director Richard Darman not to do so. When he was unable to deliver on the promise (largely through no fault of his own), Bush looked duplicitous and weak. Moreover, as discussed earlier, he was inattentive to the need to educate American citizens on serious policy issues facing the nation, especially regarding the budget deficit. He eschewed the public aspects of the presidency to such a great extent that he would not use the bully pulpit aspect of power that Teddy Roosevelt assigned to the White House when he was president. But his strongest weaknesses were in the vision area. By mocking the need for a vision, Bush failed to appreciate the importance of vision to effective leadership. His pragmatic incrementalism in the end was insufficient to motivate citizens to stand by his side, especially as economic times worsened, and they needed reassurance, or some measure of vision to help. Historian Forest McDonald put it this way:

> He was, in the parlance of people inside the beltway, a pragmatic, meaning a person who had no guiding philosophy but who had to manage the machinery of government well. But, to shift the metaphor, merely being competent at steering the ship of state became meaningless, for the passengers felt that the skipper knew not his destination.[200]

Or, perhaps the real problem was that Bush's vision was limited by his own aristocratic background. He never had to experience poverty, or unemployment, or face the monthly nightmare of American families who gather at the kitchen table in search of a way to pay all the bills and have a little cash left for entertainment. His offer of "a thousand points of light" as a solution to poverty and economic distress in America was certainly insufficient to address America's daunting economic problems. According to Duffy and Goodgame:

> Bush's "points of light" program, soon ensconced in a suite of White House offices and bolstered by a private foundation, could claim success in encouraging volunteerism, removing liability insurance hurdles to it, and publicizing nonprofit programs that worked. More Americans were visiting elderly shut-ins and coaching Little League baseball. But the

---

[198]Stephen Skowronek, *The Politics Presidents Make: Leadership from John Adams to Bill Clinton* (Cambridge, MA: The Belknap Press of Harvard University Press, 2003), 439.

[199]Sloan, 114.

[200]Barilleaux and Rozell, 11.

"points of light" did not, and could not, cast much light on the inner city and the underclass. Middle-class volunteers might be willing to dish out stew to the homeless at a well-staffed downtown soup kitchen, but they would not venture into the inner-city neighborhoods terrorized by gun-toting drug gangs. They could not provide ghetto children with equal opportunity to health care, to decent schools, to money for college, to job training. And on these issues Bush had no coherent approach.[201]

Some of Bush's own aides began to realize that he saw the "points of light" not as an adjunct to domestic policy strategy, but as a substitute for one.[202] In the end, the portrayal of George Bush as a spoiled "preppy," surrounded by Ralph Lauren artifacts, resonated as true in the minds of many Americans. He proved to be no match for the compassionate, articulate, and charismatic governor of Arkansas, Bill Clinton.

[201]Duffy and Goodgame, 210.
[202]Ibid., 211.

The Presidency of William Jefferson Clinton

Bill Clinton's political aspirations began early in life. In his autobiography, *My Life*, he described his political awakening at the age of sixteen:

> Sometime in my sixteenth year I decided that I wanted to be in public life as an elected official . . . I knew I could be great in public service. I was fascinated by people, politics, and policy, and I thought I would make it without family wealth, or connections, or establishment southern positions on race and other issues. Of course, it was improbable, but isn't that what America is all about?[1]

It certainly was improbable for Clinton to achieve his dream and ascend all the way to the White House. Clinton's attainment of the highest office in the nation could be accomplished only with an intense determination to overcome his notably inauspicious personal circumstances for political success. The story of Bill Clinton's political career is filled with instances of defying the odds, bouncing back from adversity, and using his considerable talents to surprise and outmaneuver his political opponents. According to David Gergen, who served in the Clinton White House from 1993 to 1994, "No one can grow up in a relatively poor state, survive a difficult childhood, rise to the White House—and then win re-election—unless he has formidable strengths."[2] His formidable strengths, however, were offset by significant faults and weaknesses. Throughout his life, and especially in the White House, Bill Clinton exhibited "striking strengths and glaring failures," according to *New York Times* reporter Todd Purdum.[3]

EARLY LIFE

William Jefferson Blythe was born on August 14, 1946, to a recently widowed registered nurse, Virginia Cassidy, and a recently deceased military veteran, William Blythe, who had married Virginia in 1943 while still technically married to his fourth wife.[4] Billy Blythe was born at the Julia Chester Hospital in Hope, a town of 6,000 mostly poor people in southwestern Arkansas, three months after his father died in a car accident.[5]

In June 1950, Virginia married Roger Clinton, a Hot Springs Buick dealer known as a "fast-talking, hard drinking gambling man"; however, the marriage was not a happy one, as Roger Clinton's gambling problems, addiction to alcohol, and psychological instability created many pressures for the young

---

[1]Bill Clinton, *My Life* (New York: Alfred A. Knopf, 2004), 63.

[2]David Gergen, *Eyewitness to Power: The Essence of Leadership, Nixon to Clinton* (New York: Simon and Schuster, 2000), 317.

[3]Todd S. Purdum, "Striking Strengths, Glaring Failures," *New York Times*, December 24, 2000, 1.

[4]Nigel Hamilton, *Bill Clinton: An American Journey, Great Expectations* (New York: Random House, 2003), 27.

[5]Clinton, 2004, 4.

family.[6] He repeatedly abused Virginia, and young Billy often played the role of peacemaker at home.[7] According to biographer Nigel Hamilton, Billy Blythe also applied his peacemaking skills at school, St. John's Academy, to break up fights and to endear himself to students and teachers alike. Indeed, Hamilton identifies the peacemaking skills that Billy used as a survival technique in a hostile world, and also as a harbinger of his need to be liked and his inability to admit wrongdoing later in life.[8]

The hostile world imploded in 1960, when Roger Clinton came home one evening after drinking heavily and began screaming at Virginia. He forced her into their bedroom and locked the door. Billy, concerned about his mother's well-being, broke into the room with a golf club, only to find Roger Clinton slouched in a chair. He made Clinton stand up, looked him in the eye and told him never to touch his mother again.[9] Finally, in April 1962, Virginia left her husband and took Bill and his younger brother Roger to live in the Cumberland Manor Apartments in Hot Springs, Arkansas.[10] She divorced and remarried Roger Clinton, and when she remarried him, Billy went to the Garland County Court and changed his name from Blythe to Clinton.[11] He worked hard to develop a cordial and almost warm relationship with the man he came to call *daddy*.

In July 1963, Bill Clinton went on a Boys Nations–sponsored trip to Washington, D.C. Clinton had been chosen as a "senator" for the civic exercise the group would rehearse, and his cause was civil rights protection for minorities. (A few years earlier, in 1957, Bill and his mother were severely disillusioned when Arkansas Governor Orval Faubus used the Arkansas National Guard to prevent nine African American students from attending all-white Little Rock's Central High School.)[12] In Washington, on July 24, 1963, the students had lunch with Arkansas Senator J. William Fulbright, the Democratic chairman of the Senate Foreign Relations Committee. On the same day, the group was invited to the White House Rose Garden for an audience with President John F. Kennedy, who had just returned from Berlin where he gave his famous "Ich bin ein Berliner" speech.[13] Kennedy complimented the Arkansas students for their condemnation of racial prejudice, and then walked toward them and extended his hand to the boys at the front of the line. The tall boy from Hope, William Jefferson Clinton, had assured himself a place near the front of the line and got a handshake from President Kennedy, which was captured

---

[6]Ibid., 51.
[7]Ibid., 18.
[8]Hamilton, 95 or 99.
[9]Clinton, 2004, 49.
[10]Ibid., 50.
[11]Ibid., 52.
[12]Hamilton, 80.
[13]Ibid., 119.

in a now well-known photograph. In his autobiography, Clinton described the moment, "It was an amazing moment for me, meeting the President whom I had supported in my ninth-grade debates, and about whom I felt even more strongly after his first two years in office."[14]

Shaking hands with President Kennedy helped convince Bill Clinton that he was destined to spend time in Washington, D.C. In fact, he applied to only one college, the Georgetown University School of Foreign Service.[15] At Georgetown, where he was accepted with a modicum of skepticism, as a Southern Baptist in an Eastern Catholic School, Clinton became the East Campus Freshman President in 1968.[16] He was gregarious and ambitious, well liked by school administrators and many faculty members, but to some of his contemporaries, Clinton was a "student government goody goody," a sycophant to the administrators.[17]

With the help of Raymond Clinton (Roger Clinton's more responsible brother with whom Bill had developed a good relationship), Clinton landed a summer job in 1966 as a volunteer and aide to the gubernatorial campaign of Judge Frank Holt, an Arkansas Supreme Court justice who was the Democrats' challenger to Governor Orval Faubus.[18] In campaigning for Holt, Clinton visited almost every hamlet in the state and observed the lingering racial prejudice. One country schoolhouse in the Mississippi Delta still had "white" and "colored" designations on the doors of the restrooms.[19]

The judge lost the Democratic nomination race to a judicial colleague, James Johnson, who in turn lost the general election to the Republican candidate, Winthrop Rockefeller.[20] Nevertheless, Bill Clinton used his connections to arrange an appointment with Senator Fulbright's administrative assistant, Lee Williams, who hired him to work in the documents room of the Senate Foreign Relations Committee.[21]

Working for Fulbright allowed Bill Clinton to learn from a powerful political mentor. According to biographer David Maraniss, "at age sixty-one, James William Fulbright, a Rhodes Scholar, former president of the University of Arkansas, and scion of a wealthy Fayetteville family, was seen as a dignified statesman of superior intellect whose presence in Washington countered the mocking stereotypes of unsophisticated Arkansas."[22] Clinton's apprenticeship in Fulbright's office also helped him become well versed on the

---

[14]Clinton, 2004, 62.

[15]Ibid., 66.

[16]Hamilton, 132.

[17]Ibid., 135.

[18]Ibid., 136.

[19]Clinton, 2004, 86.

[20]David Maraniss, *First in His Class: A Biography of Bill Clinton* (New York: Simon and Schuster, 1995), 81.

[21]Martin Walker, *The President We Deserve* (New York: Crown, 1996), 56.

[22]Maraniss, 84.

senator's negative assessment of the Vietnam War. Fulbright was particularly incensed over President Johnson's pressure on Congress to authorize him to deploy increased military power against the government of North Vietnam, as specified in the 1964 Gulf of Tonkin Resolution. The president's request was based on the need for an immediate reaction to two reported attacks on American destroyers patrolling the Gulf of Tonkin. Fulbright hastened to support President Johnson, as did ninety-five of his Senate colleagues, but later came to doubt the veracity of the second attack.[23] Clinton's research on the Gulf of Tonkin Resolution and on the Vietnam War led him to take a dim view of the Johnson administration's strategy toward the war, and laid the foundation for the deeply personal agony he would experience a few years later when called to serve his nation in that war.

Clinton worked hard on his congressional assignments, and also achieved considerable academic success at Georgetown University. From there, he decided to follow Fulbright's example in yet another way—he won a Rhodes Scholarship to study at Oxford University, the first student from Georgetown University ever to receive this award.[24] He enjoyed studying at Oxford and living in England, but his idyllic existence was interrupted rather abruptly in April 1969 when he received a letter informing him of his draft induction. According to Hamilton, "For the first time in his life he had no idea what to do."[25]

Clinton considered his options, as he did not wish to be drafted or to fight in Vietnam. Nor did he wish to be a draft resister like his Oxford friend Frank Aller, a troubled young man who would ultimately commit suicide.[26] When he arrived home from England at the end of June, he determined that there were no available slots open in the National Guard or the reserves. He was unable to enlist in the Air Force because he couldn't pass the vision test, and he was rejected as a naval officer candidate because of a slight hearing problem.[27] Clinton's best option was to find a way to void the induction notice in exchange for enlistment in a military alternative that would allow him to continue his education. He decided to join the Reserve Officers' Training Corps (ROTC) at the University of Arkansas Law School.

In discussing the matter with his friend, Cliff Jackson, an Oxford University classmate now working for the Republican Party in Arkansas, Clinton realized that the only way he could enroll in the ROTC program was with the approval of the state Selective Service director in Little Rock, Colonel William Hawkins, an appointee of Governor Winthrop Rockefeller.[28] Meanwhile Lee Williams,

---

[23]Merideth Oakley, *On the Make: The Rise of Bill Clinton* (Washington, D.C.: Regency Publishing, 1994), 52.

[24]Hamilton, 165.

[25]Ibid., 195.

[26]Maraniss, 167.

[27]Clinton, 2004, 154.

[28]Maraniss, 168.

Fulbright's aide and a graduate of the University of Arkansas Law School, contacted the director of the ROTC program, Colonel Eugene Holmes, to discuss Clinton's enrollment.[29]

Holmes agreed to enroll Clinton in the University of Arkansas Law School and to nullify the induction notice. By his own account, Clinton suggests that Holmes admitted him because he thought Bill Clinton would be of greater service to his nation as an officer than as an enlisted soldier.[30] The participation in ROTC would be followed, presumably, by active military service.

Having accomplished his goal of nullifying his draft induction and achieving an academic deferment status, 1-D, Clinton continued to agonize about his condition. In a letter to his friend Rick Stearns on September 9, 1969, he said, "Nothing could be worse than this torment, and I just hope I have made the right decision, if there is such a thing. I know one of the worst side effects of this whole thing is the way it's ravaged my own image of myself, taken my mind off the higher things, restricted my ability to become involved in good causes with other people."[31]

But he did not enroll in the University of Arkansas Law School in the fall of 1969. Instead he returned to Oxford to continue his studies. As Maraniss suggests, "the series of events that led Clinton back to Oxford are in dispute."[32] According to Hamilton, who is generally tough on Clinton overall, Bill Clinton never had any intention of going to the University of Arkansas Law School and couldn't imagine himself enrolled as a student there or participating in ROTC. He simply manipulated the system to achieve his draft deferment, used his friends, notably Cliff Jackson and Lee Williams, and ultimately betrayed a promise to Colonel Holmes. Many people had gone out of their way for Bill Clinton and he deliberately misled them.[33] According to Clinton's own account, he talked to Colonel Homes and gained permission to return to Oxford for a second year, considering the basic training for ROTC did not begin until the following summer.[34] Colonel Holmes remembered having had a conversation with Clinton, but expected him to return to Arkansas after a month or two to enroll in the University of Arkansas Law School.[35] Holmes approved the plan, but apparently never informed his subordinates of his decision.[36]

Shortly after his return to Oxford, Clinton wrote the Selective Service officer in Arkansas asking that he or she rescind his draft deferment (1-D) and subjected himself to the draft again, regaining the 1-A status. But there were increasing signs that he would not get drafted, because on October 1, 1969,

---

[29]Ibid., 173.

[30]Clinton, 2004, 185.

[31]Maraniss, 180.

[32]Ibid.

[33]Hamilton, 199.

[34]Clinton, 2004, 155.

[35]Maraniss, 180.

[36]Ibid.

President Nixon instructed the Selective Service system to change its policy toward draft deferments for graduate students; they would now be allowed to complete their entire graduate education without fear of being drafted. Nixon also began publicly discussing the idea of withdrawing 35,000 American troops from Vietnam.[37] In December 1969, the Selective Service introduced a draft lottery system where young men would draw numbers that corresponded to their birthday, and the numbers would determine their chances of being drafted. Bill Clinton drew number 311, which made it highly unlikely he would be drafted.

According to Maraniss, Clinton ended up in a good place. He did not resist the draft, which would have endangered his political future; he did not have to spend three years in ROTC, nor attend the University of Arkansas Law School; and perhaps most importantly he did not have to fight in Vietnam.[38] As summarized by Maraniss:

> What happened to Clinton during that fateful year did not happen by accident. He fretted and planned every move, he got help from others when needed, he resorted to some deception and manipulation when necessary, and he was ultimately lucky. In the end, by not serving in the military, he did what 16 million other young American men did during this troublesome era.[39]

On December 3, Clinton wrote a letter explaining his actions to Colonel Holmes, which would become the most famous essay he would ever write. In considerable detail, Clinton thanked Holmes for the help he had given him, explained how his work on the Senate Foreign Relations Committee had led him to oppose the Vietnam War, described why he considered the draft system to be illegitimate (drawing a distinction to war, between a just war—World War II—and an unjust one—the Vietnam War), and expressed his sympathy to those who opposed and even resisted the war.[40]

Holmes was not pleased when he received the letter, and in response he and his colleagues opened a Bill Clinton file in the dissidents section at ROTC headquarters in Little Rock.[41] Early in the 1992 presidential campaign, Holmes told the *Wall Street Journal* that he felt he had been manipulated by Clinton, followed by a September 1992 statement that questioned Clinton's "patriotism and integrity" and said he came to believe that Clinton used him to avoid the draft.[42]

The same week that Bill Clinton wrote his famous essay to Colonel Holmes, he also sent in his application for Yale Law School. He was accepted,

---

[37]Ibid., 197.

[38]Ibid., 198.

[39]Ibid., 199.

[40]See ibid., 199–204, for a paragraph-by-paragraph analysis of the letter to Holmes.

[41]Maraniss, 204.

[42]Ibid., 205.

and during his years at Yale two profoundly important experiences occurred that would influence the future course of his life: He met Hillary Rodham, and he participated in the U.S. Senate campaign (in Connecticut) of Joseph Duffey, a thirty-eight-year-old peace and civil rights activist and ethics professor at Hartford Seminary.[43]

Bill and Hillary's relationship would prove to be a long, complicated but lasting one. Its beginning was in a civil rights law class, where she confronted the tall young man and said, "Look, if you're going to stare at me, I'm going to keep looking back, and I think we ought to know each other's names. I'm Hillary Rodham."[44] They dated throughout law school, occasionally living together, and grew closer intellectually and emotionally. And each one saw the other as critical in their own envisioned arc of ambition. The couple married on October 11, 1975.[45]

Duffey's campaign did not succeed. Connecticut voters elected a moderate Republican, Lowell Weicker. But by participating in this campaign, Bill Clinton significantly expanded his political education, particularly on the need to reform the Democratic Party. He also participated in the 1972 McGovern for president campaign and took charge of its operation in Texas. These experiences helped plant the seeds for Clinton to take on a leading role in reshaping and reinvigorating the Democratic Party.

In the summer of 1973, Bill Clinton was appointed to the law faculty at the University of Arkansas and proved to be a brilliant teacher who was popular among students.[46] But the political clock was ticking, and several months later Clinton asked the university for a leave of absence to enter the local congressional race.

POLITICAL CAREER

In November 1974, Professor William Clinton became the Democratic Party candidate for the U.S. House of Representatives Third Congressional District of Arkansas facing the incumbent, Representative John Paul Hammerschmidt, a four-term Republican member of Congress who had learned how to appeal to both parties.[47] Hammerschmidt had a solidly conservative voting record and was a strong defender of President Nixon; he also had a friendly, low-key manner and was effective at helping the little towns of Arkansas as well as protecting the interests of the timber and poultry industries in the state.[48] But he had never seen the likes of Bill Clinton, a young

---

[43]Ibid., 234.

[44]Hamilton, 235.

[45]Lewis Gould, "William Jefferson Clinton: Prosperity and Turmoil," in Michael Beschloss, ed., *American Heritage Illustrated History of the Presidents* (New York: Crown Publishers, 2000), 501.

[46]Hamilton, 283.

[47]Ibid., 288.

[48]Clinton, 2004, 212.

man of the age of twenty-seven who seemed to have an inexhaustible energy for "retail politics."[49]

In January 1974, the Senate Judiciary Committee by a vote of 27–4 voted for the commencement of impeachment proceedings against President Nixon. Nixon's subsequent resignation took some of the wind out of Bill Clinton's congressional campaign, but he came within two percentage points of beating John Hammerschmidt.[50] During Bill's congressional campaign, Hillary, who was temporarily stationed in Washington, D.C., to work on the Watergate impeachment proceedings, dispatched her brother and father to Little Rock, ostensibly to assist in Bill's campaign, but actually to keep an eye on him, as talk of his "extracurricular" affairs with young female campaign aides mounted.[51]

According to Maraniss, "Losing the congressional election did not hurt Clinton's political status in Arkansas, and enhanced his image as an emerging star of the Democratic Party."[52] He decided to run for attorney general and took an unpaid leave of absence from the law school for the 1976 campaign.[53] In his campaign for attorney general, Clinton showed a willingness to depart from traditional Democratic values and constituents, refusing, for example, to support a repeal of the right to work law in Arkansas.[54] He would continue to show a willingness to defy traditional Democratic values throughout his political career. At age thirty, Bill Clinton became the attorney general of Arkansas.

After consulting with New York political consultant Dick Morris, who would be an important part of Clinton's political destiny, Clinton decided that his next political step would be to run for governor.[55] He swept the state with 63 percent of the vote in the general election and at age thirty-two became the youngest governor in Arkansas in four decades.[56]

The young governor arrived with an ambitious agenda, having made fifty-three specific promises before he took office, but lacking an effective plan to fulfill them.[57] Moreover, the governor's three executive assistants—Steve Smith, John Danner, and Rudy Moore—were young, liberal, and hirsute, causing them to be named "the Three Beards." They were not an ideal group to help manage Clinton's policy objectives in Arkansas.[58] As governor, Bill Clinton displayed a loose, free-ranging management style that reflected his non-disciplined personality. As well, he brought in many people from outside Arkansas to run the state agencies, including the departments of education

---

[49]Hamilton, 288.

[50]Ibid., 298.

[51]Ibid., 289.

[52]Maraniss, 340.

[53]Ibid., 346.

[54]Ibid., 348.

[55]Ibid., 352.

[56]Clinton, 2004, 258.

[57]Maraniss, 360.

[58]Hamilton, 338.

and energy.[59] Governor Clinton's top policy objective was roads; his inspiration was a legislative report that had declared the state highway system a disaster in need of $3.3 billion in improvements.[60] Clinton's revenue specialists told him that the quickest way to raise large sums was to increase the annual car license fees, and his political advisers opined that the largest burden of the road improvements should be placed on eighteen-wheel trucks that were causing the most damage. Dick Morris' polls indicated 53 percent of the people would support an increase in car license fees.[61]

Accordingly, the administration drafted a proposal placing most of the tax burden on heavy trucks, and raising car license fees based on the value of each car.[62] The plan immediately encountered intense resistance from two powerful lobbies: the trucking industry and the poultry industry, a major user of trucks and highways. Both groups were already angry at Clinton for abandoning a campaign promise to increase the allowable weight from 73,000 pounds to 80,000 pounds for trucks driving in Arkansas. The poultry industry killed the bill in committee, forcing Clinton to sign off on a compromise shifting the main tax burden from trucks to cars and pickups, which still did not satisfy the trucking and poultry industries. And the car license increase was altered to account for the weight of a vehicle rather than the value. Unfortunately, in Arkansas, a rural state, many people drove heavy old clunkers, and they were faced with steep increases in fees.[63]

Clinton also antagonized the giant timber industries, especially Weyerhauser, when he took a strong stand against clear-cutting (acres of timberland bulldozed at one time). Clinton, along with environmental activists, claimed that clear-cutting harmed the wildlife and created pollution and run-off problems.[64] He established a timber management task force and conducted hearings throughout the state. The political pressure, however, was intense, and Clinton ordered several changes, including softening the criticisms of the timber industry and removing the threat of mandatory state action against clear-cutting, calling instead for voluntary changes in industry practice.[65] Nevertheless, the timber industry was not totally mollified.

But perhaps the most troubling political experience that Governor Clinton faced was the one involving thousands of Cuban refugees who were sent to Fort Chaffee, Arkansas. In the spring of 1980, Fidel Castro deported 120,000 political prisoners and other "undesirables," many with criminal records or mental problems, to the United States. They sailed to Florida, seeking political asylum, and created a serious drain on the political resources of President

---

[59]Clinton, 2004, 267.

[60]Maraniss, 361.

[61]Ibid.

[62]Ibid.

[63]Ibid.

[64]Ibid., 365.

[65]Ibid., 367.

Jimmy Carter.[66] When Carter proposed sending several thousand refugees to Arkansas, Clinton suggested to Carter White House staffer Gene Eidenberg that the administration conduct screenings of the refugees to be sure they weren't criminals or lunatics, but Eidenberg demurred saying there would be no place to send the Cubans who were rejected in the screening.[67]

By May 20, there were nearly 20,000 Cubans at Fort Chaffee, and some of them engaged in disturbances spilling out to the highly conservative environment of Fort Smith. On May 26, a couple of hundred refugees charged the barricades and ran out of the fort through an opened gate.[68] Clinton asked President Carter for federal troops to help quell the disturbances, and Carter said he would comply. On June 1, 1980, 1,000 Cubans ran out of the fort, right past the federal troops, and onto Highway 22. The troops did not lift a finger to stop them. Clinton activated the Arkansas National Guard, who fired warning shots over the Cubans' heads, causing a retreat to the fort.[69] But the damage had been done.

Frank White, Clinton's Republican challenger for the governor's seat in 1980, effectively exploited the Cuban issue with a television advertisement showing rioting Cubans, with a voice-over telling viewers that the governors of Pennsylvania and Wisconsin cared more about their people and got rid of the Cubans, but Bill Clinton cared more about Jimmy Carter than the people of Arkansas.[70] Winning only 48 percent of the vote, Clinton lost his bid for re-election as governor, largely due to the car tax and Cuban refugee issues.

In the political wilderness at age thirty-four, Bill Clinton's political comeback was effectuated with the help of two telephone calls. Hillary called Dick Morris and asked him to return to Little Rock.[71] She also decided to change her name and to be known from that point forward as Hillary Clinton. Bill called Betsy Wright, a powerful political ally whom he had met on the McGovern campaign in Texas, and asked that she assist in the preparation for a political campaign and a return to power.[72]

Governor Frank White's style of governance paved the way for Clinton's re-election in 1982. White acknowledged the help of television evangelicals and fundamentalists in his victory and boasted that his election was a "victory for the Lord." In his first legislative session, he signed the Creation Science Act, which required all Arkansas public schools to give equal time to teaching the biblical assertion that God created the world (along with Darwin's theory of evolution).[73]

Clinton, encouraged by a Morris poll showing White was beatable, began actively campaigning again, enlisting friends and making speeches. In

---

[66]Clinton, 274.

[67]Ibid., 275.

[68]Ibid.

[69]Ibid., 276.

[70]Ibid., 282.

[71]Ibid., 391.

[72]Ibid., 195.

[73]Walker, 94.

February 1982, he went on television and offered a statement of apology for trying too hard in his first term. Dick Morris wanted him to offer a firm apology; however, Clinton revised the script overnight and never quite apologized. Instead, he used the homely Arkansas phrase: "My Daddy never had to whip me twice for the same thing," explaining that he had failed his constituents, especially on the car tax issue.[74] He regained the governor's office, beating White with 55 percent of the vote.[75]

This time, he knew he would have to scale back his ambition from reform on all fronts and take on tasks one at a time. He had learned to deal gently with the likes of Tyson and the state's corporate giants, and backed the bill that raised the truck weight limit, just as Tyson wanted.[76] Morris' polling told him that voters would not recall any of his achievements in office, and he would have to pin his governorship to some grand pursuit that was popular and memorable. And if possible it should be something that would help reconcile Arkansas to Hillary.[77] "The choice almost chose itself: education," according to professor Martin Walker.[78]

Clinton demonstrated his strong interest in education in his inaugural address in Little Rock in 1983:

> Over the long run education is the key to our economic survival and our personal quest for prosperity. We must dedicate more of our limited resources to paying teachers better, expanding educational opportunities in poor and small districts, inspiring and diversifying vocational and high technology pursuits, and perhaps more importantly strengthening basic education.[79]

Testing schemes introduced in Clinton's first term provided hard evidence that Arkansas school children ranked far below the national average in basic skills such as reading and mathematics.[80] The improvement of the Education Act of 1983 authorized the state's board of education to draft minimum standards of achievement for each grade and approved an education standards committee to produce the draft.[81] In 1983, Governor Clinton appointed Hillary to head the fifteen-person Arkansas Educational Standards Committee to draft new standards for Arkansas' ailing educational system.[82]

Hillary took a leave of absence from the Rose Law Firm and organized a series of seventy-five hearings across the state. Her colleagues were awed by

---

[74]Ibid., 96.

[75]Ibid., 98.

[76]Ibid.

[77]Ibid.

[78]Ibid.

[79]Clinton, "Hard Times and the Promise of Our Tomorrows," in Stephen Smith, ed., *Preface to the Presidency: Selected Speeches of Bill Clinton 1974–1992* (Fayetteville: University of Arkansas Press, 1996), 29.

[80]Walker, 98.

[81]Ibid.

[82]Hamilton, 409.

"her clarity in analyzing public school problems, her behaviors in setting out the cure, and her resolve to administer the medicine."[83] Meanwhile, Governor Clinton and Betsy Wright started the Blue Ribbon Education Committee and urged friends and supporters to join and wear a small blue lapel ribbon, and recruit others to do the same. Clinton raised money from Tyson Foods and the TCBY Yogurt Corporation, based in Little Rock, to support the cause of educational reform.[84]

Clinton's education package amounted to $180 million, including provisions for smaller class sizes, a longer school year, and a basic state curriculum.[85] The standards that Hillary's committee came up with included required kindergarten; a maximum class size of twenty through third grade; counselors in all elementary schools; uniform testing of students in third, sixth, and eighth grade; and more mathematics and science.[86] Normally, the strongest lobby in support of reform would have been the teachers. But Clinton added the requirement, not recommended by Hillary's committee, that Arkansas teachers would also have to pass a test of competence.[87] According to Walker:

> There was political calculation here. The Dick Morris polls found this had 75 percent support among Arkansas voters, many of whom suspected that in his first term Clinton had been too close to special interests like the teachers' lobby. The Arkansas Education Association, the 17,000 strong teachers union, had made the mistake of supporting Clinton's opponent in the primary. And Clinton insisted, relating the old story about one who taught "World War Eleven" from ignorance of the Roman numerals of World War II, some teachers were scandalously bad.[88]

Clinton engaged in every form of retail politics to secure passage of his education reform package, which would be funded by a sales tax. He stood at the door of the legislative chamber yelling to his aides to "run up and down the aisles" to keep legislators in their seats. He brought in the Razorbacks football coach to help him lobby.[89]

When the tests were first given to teachers and administrators in 1984, 10 percent failed. In the end, 1,215 teachers, about 3.5 percent, had to leave the classroom because they failed the test.[90] It was a victory for Clinton because he had taken on his friends in the unions, orchestrated an intense lobbying effort, and squeezed out the incompetent teachers. Afterward he would have an achievement to trumpet and a lapel to sport, "The Education Governor."[91]

---

[83]Ibid.
[84]Walker, 99.
[85]Ibid.
[86]Clinton, 2004, 309.
[87]Walker, 99.
[88]Ibid., 100.
[89]Ibid., 102.
[90]Clinton, 2004, 312.
[91]Walker, 102.

He sailed back to victory in 1984, elected governor again with 63 percent of the vote.[92]

During the 1980s, Bill Clinton was noticed by the national Democratic Party, and several job offices were dangled before him, including a chance to become chief of staff to Governor Jerry Brown of California.[93] In 1980, he accepted an offer to become a fund-raiser for PamPAC, a political action committee founded by Pamela Harriman, wife of the former ambassador and New York governor (and multimillionaire) Averill Harriman.[94] She inherited a great deal of wealth when her husband died in 1986, and used the money to revive the Democratic Party. She also showed interest in Al Gore of Tennessee, Bob Kerry of Nebraska, Jay Rockefeller of West Virginia, and Chuck Robb of Virginia.[95]

Harriman's goal was to use the money she raised to bypass a bureaucratic Democratic National Committee,[96] and start a new interest group with the party to push it back to the electable center. In the wake of Reagan's re-election landslide in 1984, in which he won forty-nine states against Walter Mondale, the Democratic Leadership Council (DLC) was founded.[97] Its executive director was Al Fromm, who began as a staffer in President Johnson's war on poverty and then served in Jimmy Carter's White House. Other DLC founders, including southern senators Sam Nunn, Chuck Robb, and John Breaux, argued that the Democrats had shifted to the left since 1972, and had become captured by organized labor, the urban poor, and ethnic minorities. Clinton was attracted to the DLC and became its chairman in 1990. He served as the chairman of the National Governors Association, which helped him establish relationships that would be important to him in the future.

Clinton was easily re-elected governor of Arkansas in 1986, beating back a primary challenge from Orval Faubus and defeating Frank White in their third encounter with 64 percent of the vote.[98] Several of his supporters urged him to run for the 1988 presidential nomination, and he seemed to be gearing up for an effort in the early summer of 1987. Between January and July 1987, Clinton made thirty-four trips to twenty states.[99]

His opportunity seemed to open up when Colorado Senator Gary Hart withdrew from the presidential race because of revelations of his marital infidelity by Miami newspapers. But Betsy Wright, Clinton's political aide, sat him down and suggested he could have the same problem as Hart. Clinton decided for the sake of his family, and especially for his now seven-year-old daughter Chelsea, that he would not run. On July 15, 1987, at the Excelsior

---

[92]Ibid.
[93]Ibid., 105.
[94]Ibid., 106.
[95]Ibid.
[96]Ibid., 107.
[97]Ibid.
[98]Ibid., 109.
[99]Hamilton, 458.

Hotel in Little Rock, he said, "I hope I will have another opportunity to seek the presidency when I can do that and still be faithful to my family."[100]

Through his activities in the DLC and National Governors Association, Clinton maintained his national presence, participated in redefining the Democratic Party, and helped convince others that the party needed a new approach to take back the White House. He announced his intentions to run for the presidency in Little Rock on October 3, 1991. Those who watched and listened considered the speech to be one of the best speeches of his political career.[101] The sentiments he expressed resonated with a new generation that looked forward to a future filled with change.

> All of you, in different ways, have brought me here today, to step beyond a life and a job I love, to make a commitment to a larger cause: pursuing the American dream, restoring the hopes of a forgotten middle class, reclaiming the future for our children. . .
>
> I refuse to be part of the generation that celebrates the death of communism abroad with death of the American dream at home. I refuse to be part of a generation that fails to compete in a global economy and so condemns hardworking Americans to a life of struggle without reward or success. That's why I stand here today, because I refuse to stand by and let our children become part of the first generation of Americans to do worse than their parents.[102]

The competition Clinton faced in the Democratic field consisted mostly of "second-tier" candidates, including Senator Paul Tsongas of Massachusetts, Governor Doug Wilder of Virginia, Senator Tom Harkin of Iowa, Senator Bob Kerrey of Nebraska, and California Governor Jerry Brown.[103]

The true test of Bill Clinton's candidacy came in the New Hampshire primary, which proved to be an extraordinary event for him. During this primary, Clinton's campaign was "torpedoed twice," according to Walker, once by a taped phone conversation about his twelve-year extramarital affair with Gennifer Flowers, and once by the *Wall Street Journal*'s revelation of his equivocations over the military draft.[104] In particular, the journal highlighted two phrases that Clinton used in his letter to Colonel Holmes: Clinton describing himself as part of a generation that "loved the country but loathed the military," and also admitted to Holmes that his motives in trying to avoid the draft by joining ROTC were to "maintain my political viability within the system."[105]

According to Walker, had there been a strong and well-funded Democratic alternative to Clinton, his campaign would have ended in New

---

[100]Ibid., 480.

[101]Ibid., 586.

[102]Bill Clinton, "A Campaign for the Future," in Smith, *Preface to the Presidency*.

[103]Hamilton, 591.

[104]Walker, 124.

[105]Ibid.

Hampshire.[106] The only serious challenger to Clinton in New Hampshire was Paul Tsongas, a former senator who had resigned to fight cancer and who made a virtue out of belt-tightening and sacrifice as an economic program. Tsongas hammered away at the need for a balanced budget and the inadvisability of tax credits for couples having children and middle-class tax cuts. He also advocated a sharp increase in gasoline taxes.[107]

Clinton stayed in the game in New Hampshire through his own grit and determination and through the impressive discipline and aggressiveness of his campaign team, headed by James Carville, Paul Begala, and George Stephanopoulos (all of whom were heavily involved Clinton's campaign and Stephanopoulos and Begala would end up serving in his administration).[108] They were determined not to allow the Republican attack machine to destroy another credible Democratic candidate with a smear story the way the "Willie Horton" advertisement had destroyed the Dukakis campaign in 1988.[109] Clinton himself "never stopped campaigning, never ceased to fight back, and it was later calculated that he had personally met every fifth voter, over 20,000 New Hampshire citizens."[110] He found a resonance for his message of economic renewal among New Hampshire voters, as the state had the fastest growing welfare and food stamp rolls during the 1980s and the highest number of bankruptcies.[111] Clinton came in second in New Hampshire, winning 25 percent of the vote to Tsongas's 36 percent, and earning the title "the Comeback Kid."

The comeback, however, would not have been complete, or even possible, without Hillary and her unflinching support for her husband on a *60 Minutes* episode right after the Superbowl, the most watched event of the year. In Bedford, two days after the alleged affair surfaced, she was "cheered to the rafters" when she said, "Is anything about our marriage as important to the people of New Hampshire as whether or not they will have a chance to keep their own families together?"[112] According to Walker:

> The synergistic stories of draft and womanizing were still covered thoroughly, were still the prime question that the reporters fanned out to ask of the departing rally crowds. But another story was beginning to emerge, of a candidate and, more interestingly, of a husband and wife team whose marriage had been terribly strained, keeping their nerve and fighting back under an intense bombardment. It was this that enabled Clinton's cool effrontery, in claiming that coming in a poor second in New Hampshire made him the "Comeback Kid" to prevail and to the final reporting of the election result.[113]

---

[106]Ibid.

[107]Ibid., 125.

[108]R. Cutler and A. Pennebaker, *The War Room* (Cyclone Films, 1993).

[109]Hamilton, 622.

[110]Walker, 126.

[111]Clinton, 2004, 378.

[112]Walker, 127.

[113]Ibid.

Clinton's campaign ruthlessly attacked Tsongas as a watered-down Republican who espoused a trickle-down economics of the Reagan-Bush variety and who proposed a corporate gains tax for the rich. Clinton's campaign machine hit Tsongas hardest in Florida with leaflets that asserted that Tsongas would cut Social Security checks, and claimed, unfairly, that Tsongas was not a friend of Israel.[114]

The campaign became more interesting when Texas billionaire Ross Perot entered the race. Perot had made his fortune with Electronic Data Systems (EDS), a technology company that did a good deal of business with government, and he became nationally known when he financed and engineered the rescue of EDS employees from Iran after the fall of the shah. Perot appealed to middle- and upper-class white people who were tired of the status quo; he was offering to apply a businessman's perspective to the demands of social and economic reform in America. Perot was especially hostile toward George H. W. Bush and his inability to respond to the economic maelstrom that was affecting people in places such as New Hampshire.

Clinton won primaries in Illinois (52 percent), Michigan (42 percent), Georgia (57 percent), and Texas (66 percent).[115] He went on to win thirty-two races, assuring himself the 1992 presidential nomination for the Democratic Party.[116] Shortly before the important New York primary, Clinton selected Tennessee Senator Al Gore as his running mate. In choosing Al Gore, Clinton defied the advice of several political pundits who suggested the need to balance his ticket. Instead, Clinton chose another young man from the south of moderate political persuasion. But Gore brought a great deal to the ticket and proved to be a shrewd choice. He had sixteen years of congressional experience, eight of them in the U.S. Senate, with service on the Armed Services Committee. Clinton also admired the fact that Gore was one of only ten Democratic senators to support President George H. W. Bush in the first Gulf War.[117] If Clinton lacked foreign policy acumen, Gore could certainly supply it. Gore also brought "family values" and a passionate belief in environmental protection. Soon to be the author of a widely acclaimed book, *Earth in the Balance*, Gore had travelled to Antarctica to study the hole in the ozone layer, to the Aral Sea in the old Soviet Union to study desertification, and to the Amazon to witness the destruction of the rain forest.

At the nominating convention in New York City, Texas Governor Ann Richards introduced Bill Clinton as a "real human being, a son, a father, a husband and a friend."[118] Convention organizers played a film that had been made about their candidate entitled, "The Man from Hope," and Clinton's own words and voice provided commentary to moving scenes of his background and significant accomplishments: "I was born in a little town called Hope,

---

[114]Ibid.

[115]Clinton, 2004, 354.

[116]Walker, 136.

[117]Clinton, 414.

[118]Hamilton, 656.

Arkansas, three months after my father died. It was small town, you know, where it seemed everyone knew everyone else."[119] Hamilton describes the film as powerful and poignant, "the critical moments of his life—the confrontation with his abusive stepfather, the meeting with President Kennedy, the import of the civil rights struggle, his relationship with Hillary, his presence at the birth of his daughter."[120] The film was astonishing and helped transform peoples' image of Bill Clinton from the adulterous draft dodger, marijuana smoker who claimed he "never inhaled" into a proud son of Arkansas who overcame serious obstacles and political defeats to emerge as a champion of change for America. According to Hamilton, the film was a masterpiece of political advertising, which would have communication professors talking for years to come.[121]

Clinton delivered a moving and powerful acceptance speech headlined by the following introduction:

> In the name of all those who do the work and pay the taxes, raise the kids and play by the rules, in the name of the hardworking Americans who make up our forgotten middle class, I proudly accept your nomination for the President of the United States. I am a product of that middle class, and when I am President you will be forgotten no more.[122]

From Madison Square Garden, the Clinton team fanned out across the nation in eight buses. Bill Clinton chose to meet voters and to display his special talents of retail politics. According to Hamilton, "Something of JFK's youthful vigor, energy and sheer attractiveness was on local and national display as the young man from Hope, buoyed up by his nomination for the presidency met, embraced and talked to Americans in bars, coffee shops, and fast food restaurants."[123] The candidate and running mate, both in their mid-forties with attractive young wives, proved formidable as they took the campaign on the road.

George H. W. Bush, running behind in the polls, allowed the conservative wing of the Republican Party to take a prominent role at the Houston convention. He permitted arch-conservative Patrick Buchanan to address the convention on opening night. Buchanan's severe language and angry tone expressed a disdain for everything that was not Republican, white-washed, ultra-conservative, and Christian. He characterized Clinton as a liberal politician who would permit abortion on demand, a litmus test for Supreme Court nominees, discrimination against religious schools, and women in combat units.[124] Bush also gave his support to a new alliance with the Christian Coalition, and accepted the Republican Party's endorsement of a platform that called for a constitutional right to ban abortion.[125] In short,

---

[119]Ibid.

[120]Ibid.

[121]Ibid., 656–657.

[122]Clinton, 2004, 419.

[123]Hamilton, 663.

[124]Ibid., 667.

[125]Walker, 151.

the Republican Party, under the leadership of George Bush, abandoned the center ground to Clinton. Bush refused to go for the jugular—given some of his vulnerabilities—by personally squashing plans for a thirty-second television advertisement using extracts from Clinton's taped conversations with Gennifer Flowers.[126]

Clinton's victory may have been sealed in the second presidential debate, in a format he chose—a single moderator roaming a large studio audience offering a microphone to people to pose questions. The audience seemed impatient with Bush's character attacks on Clinton, and they were not overly impressed with his foreign policy credentials. They wanted to discuss health care, education reform, and crime.[127] Clinton was the clear winner of the debate, according to 53 percent of those who viewed it. He appeared more relaxed, sometimes perching on a stool and then strolling down toward the audience. Toward the end of the debate, a young African American woman asked the following question: "How has the national debt affected each of your lives? And if it hasn't, how do honestly find a cure for the economic problems of the common people if you have no experience in what's ailing them?"[128]

Ross Perot replied that his concern about the national debt had caused him to disrupt his private life and business and get involved in the campaign—because he cared so much. Bush began by saying that the national debt affects everybody and had a strong bearing on interest rates. He fumbled to find a personal connection with the question, and said, "I'm sure it has. I love my grandchildren."[129] The questioner, not quite satisfied with Bush's response, began to talk about the people she knew who had been laid off. At that point, Bush replied, "You ought to be in the White House for a day and hear what I hear and see what I see." And then, he added, "I don't think it's fair to say if you haven't had cancer you don't know what it is like."[130]

Clinton rose from his stool, and approached the woman, established direct eye contact with her, and spoke to her as follows:

> I've been governor of a small state for 12 years. I'll tell you how it's affected me. In my state, when people lose their jobs, there's a good chance I'll know them by their names. When a factory closes, I'll know people who ran it . . . And I've been out here for 13 months meeting in meetings just like this ever since October, with people like you all over America, people that have lost their jobs, lost their livelihood, lost their health insurance. What I want you to understand is the national debt is not the only cause for that. It is because America has not invested in its people . . . It's because we've had 12 years of trickle-down economics.[131]

---

[126]Ibid., 152.

[127]Ibid., 156.

[128]Ibid.

[129]Ibid.

[130]Ibid., 157.

[131]Ibid., 158.

Bush suffered another disappointment on the Friday before the election when the Iran-Contra special prosecutor, Lawrence Walsh, indicted President Reagan's defense secretary, Casper Weinberger, and five others. A note in the indictment indicated that President Bush had played a greater role in and had more knowledge about the illegal sales of arms authorized by the Reagan White House than he had previously admitted.[132]

Clinton went on to win the election with 43 percent of the popular vote; Bush got 37.4 percent, and Perot 19 percent. Clinton accumulated 370 electoral votes, wining thirty-two states and the District of Columbia. Bush won 168 electoral votes, achieving victory in eighteen states.[133] Bush became the second Republican president to lose a bid for re-election since Herbert Hoover did so in 1932.

POLICY

Perhaps the inspiration for Bill Clinton to present himself as a "New Democrat" in the 1992 presidential election can be traced to the failure of Joe Duffey to win the Connecticut Senate seat for the Democratic Party in 1980. Clinton had worked hard in Duffey's campaign, and he was one of many Duffey supporters who received a letter from the candidate explaining his failure to win the election. Duffey's commentary illustrates the eventual direction of Clinton's political vision, as well as foreshadowing the future revitalization of the Democratic Party.[134] Duffey summed up the reasoning for his defeat as follows:

> Many of our policies have been formulated as if the nation were composed of only two major groups, the affluent and the welfare poor. But somewhere between affluence and grinding poverty stand the majority of American families, being on the margins of social and economic insecurity. The new politics has thus far not spoken to the needs and interests of those Americans.[135]

Like Duffey, Clinton came to believe that the Democratic Party could no longer gather a coalition of votes large enough to win the White House and needed a new direction. He, and his DLC colleagues, averred that the Democratic Party of Franklin Roosevelt and Lyndon Johnson was effective for its day, but that the party was floundering and suffering consistent defeat by the likes of Ronald Reagan and had lost its ability to address the hopes and dreams of middle-class Americans.

Clinton's claim to be a New Democrat was not based on empty rhetoric, but reflected the evolution of his thinking about the Democratic Party. Clinton had expressed his nascent ideas about his vision of leadership in a 1986 speech

---

[132]Clinton, 2004, 441.

[133]Ibid., 444.

[134]Walker, 71.

[135]Ibid.

to the year-end management meeting of Gannett, the newspaper chain that had recently purchased the *Arkansas Gazette*.[136]

(1) Change may be the only constant in today's economy.

(2) Human capital is probably more important than physical capital now.

(3) A more constructive partnership between business and government is far more important than the dominance of either.

(4) As we try to solve problems of the internationalization of American life and the changes in our population, cooperation is more important than conflict . . . We have to share responsibilities and opportunities—we are going up or down together.

(5) Waste is going to be punished . . . it appears to me that we are spending billions of dollars of investment capital increasing the debt of corporations without increasing the productivity.

(6) A strong America requires a resurgent sense of community, a strong sense of mutual obligations, and a conviction that we cannot pursue our individual interests independent of the needs of our fellow citizens.[137]

Embedded in these principles are several aspects of Clinton's vision as a New Democrat: the Democratic Party must embrace change and be willing to find a new direction consistent with the advances of technology; the Democrats need not be perceived as antithetical to businesses, but as a party that could cooperate and collaborate with businesses and develop innovative policy initiatives and market-based solutions; human capital is vital to human progress, and the Democrats need to "put people first"[138] in a progressive political party; the United States has entered a globalized environment and the distinction between domestic and international progress may well be obliterated; the Democrats share a responsibility to protect the environment. Some of these ideas found their way into the more prosaic expression of the 1992 Clinton presidential campaign themes, which were posted in the campaign headquarters by James Carville and described as a political haiku by George Stephanopoulos:

Change versus more of the same.
It's the economy stupid!
Don't forget about health care.[139]

There was another aspect of Clinton's vision that he exhibited when he was governor of Arkansas and that would help define him as a New Democrat: personal responsibility. As governor, Clinton had asked the Arkansas

---

[136]Clinton, 2004, 326.

[137]Ibid., 326–327.

[138]Bill Clinton and Al Gore, *Putting People First: How We Can All Change America* (New York: Three Rivers Press, 1992).

[139]George Stephanopoulos, *All Too Human: A Political Education* (Boston: Little, Brown & Co, 1999), 88.

legislature to require welfare recipients with children three years or older to sign a contract, committing them to a course of independence through literacy, job training, and work.[140] He went to Washington with other governors to testify before the House Ways and Means Committee on welfare prevention and reforms. He and his colleagues asked Congress to give the state tools to "promote work, not welfare; independence, not dependence." They argued for programs that would keep people off welfare in the first place, including adult literacy, teen pregnancy, and drug and alcohol abuse programs.[141]

In Clinton's New Democrat formulation, government is not a source of gifts to be parceled out, but a sector in a constant social contract. Government delivers services in return for civic responsibility; a college grant in return for two years of public service; a welfare stipend in return for training for future employment.[142] Clinton used terms such as the "New Covenant" to signal his expectation that government would not be in the business of giveaway, but in the business of investment. Indeed, in his second inaugural address, which he described as the "last Presidential Inauguration of the 20th Century," he called for a "New Government for a New Century," one that was "humble enough not to try to solve all our problems for us," and one that is "smaller, lives within its means, and does more with less."[143]

But if the era of "big government" was over, the era of better government was possible. As mentioned earlier, Clinton possessed a deep faith in the power of technology to make government more efficient and more accessible. In March 1993, he designated Vice President Al Gore to lead an effort to reinvent the federal government. In announcing the program, President Clinton displayed a good grasp of the vision. He said:

> Our goal is to make the entire federal government both less expensive and more efficient and to change the climate of our national bureaucracy away from complacency and entitlement toward innovative and improvement. We intend to redesign, to reinvent, to reinvigorate the entire national government.[144]

Unlike past efforts of this kind, the National Performance Review (NPR; later renamed the National Partnership to Reinvent Government) was staffed primarily by experienced federal managers and employees from all parts of the government and not by outsiders.[145] Gore organized experienced government

---

[140]Clinton, 2004, 329.

[141]Ibid.

[142]Walker, 13–14.

[143]William Jefferson Clinton, "Inaugural Address, January 20, 1997," in *Public Papers of the Presidents of the United States. Book I: January 1 to June 30, 1997* (Washington, D.C.: Government Printing Office, 1997), 44.

[144]Ibid.

[145]Al Gore, *Creating a Government That Works Better and Costs Less* (New York: Plume, 1993), Introduction.

managers into teams to analyze problems and invent solutions in budgetary, procurement, information technology, and personnel. The NPR recommendation promised to develop a government that "costs less and works better," specifically cutting red tape, perfecting customer service in government, empowering federal employees to innovate for results, and cutting wasteful practices and programs.[146]

Previously in December 1991, Clinton helped launch the DLC in Texas. In a speech in Austin, he argued that DLC members were good Democrats, who believed in keeping the American dream alive for all people. He said that DLC members believed in government, but not in the status quo, and they believed that government was spending too much on yesterday and today—interest on debt, defense, more money for the same health care—and too little on tomorrow—education, research and development, the infrastructure. Clinton said the DLC stood for a modern, mainstream agenda: the expansion of opportunity, not bureaucracy; choice in public school and child care; responsibility and empowerment for poor people; and reinventing government, away from the top-down bureaucracy of the industrial era, to a leaner, more flexible, more innovative model appropriate for the modern global economy.[147]

And he delivered the keynote address at the DLC in Cleveland in May 1991, characterizing the speech as "the most effective and important I ever made."[148] He told his colleagues in Cleveland that America needed to change course and that the DLC could and should lead the way. He rebuked the leadership of the Republicans and noted that the Democrats had not been able to win elections "because too many people that used to vote for us, the very burdened middle class we are talking about, have not trusted us in national elections to defend our national interests abroad, to put their values into our social policy at home, or to take their tax money and spend it with discipline."[149] There is a strong echo of the Joseph Duffey memo in these words.

Clinton helped write and deeply believed in the DLC's five core beliefs. He explained them this way:

> Andrew Jackson's credo of opportunity for all and special privilege for none; the basic American values of work and family, freedom and responsibility, faith, tolerance and inclusion; Kennedy's show of mutual responsibility, asking citizens to give something back to the country; the advancement of democracy and humanitarian values around the world, and property and upward mobility at home; and Franklin Roosevelt's commitment to innovation, to redesigning government for the information age and ensuring people by giving them the tools to make the most of themselves.[150]

---

[146]Ibid.

[147]Clinton, 2004, 361.

[148]Ibid., 366.

[149]Ibid., 365.

[150]Ibid., 381.

Martin Walker sums up Bill Clinton's vision in this manner:

An embrace of free markets and free enterprise comes with a commitment to activist government that sees its mission in providing the lifelong education and job training that can equip people to compete in an entirely global economy. That competition is welcome throughout active diplomacy to achieve a global free trading system.[151]

This highlights Clinton's dominant vision in the area of foreign policy: globalization. According to Zbigniew Brzezinski, professor of international relations at Columbia University and national security adviser under President Carter, President Clinton had a truly global vision.[152] Clinton perceived, says Brzezinski, that the disappearance of the Soviet Union and the bipolar world created three important opportunities for the United States:

- More comprehensive American and Russian initiatives to limit the arms race.
- The possibility of an even wider global system of security.
- A larger, viable Europe, linked closely to the United States.[153]

Clinton's global vision led him to lobby successfully for the expansion of the number of countries associated with NATO (North Atlantic Treaty Organization). In May 1997, the NATO-Russia Founding Act was signed, its intent being to reassure Russia that NATO was now a security partner.[154] He reiterated America's interest in friendship with Yelstin's Russia. In July, Poland, the Czech Republic, and Hungary were officially invited to join NATO, followed soon thereafter by invitations to Romania and Bulgaria.[155]

President Clinton also backed the establishment of the World Trade Organization (WTO), which was founded on January 1, 1995, and marked a significant step in the emergence of a global economic order.[156] The WTO included an institutionalized mechanism for the resolution of conflicting interests, allowing the agency to address the inequalities in economic conditions between countries.

As will be discussed in the "Politics" section, Clinton embraced the North American Free Trade Agreement (NAFTA), which was intended to ease trade restrictions from the north of Canada to the southern tip of Mexico, "allowing some 400 million people to enrich each other economically and culturally."[157] To obtain a legislative victory for NAFTA, Clinton had to

---

[151]Walker, 13.

[152]Zbigniew Brzezinski, *Second Chance: Three Presidents and the Crises of American Superpower* (New York: Basic Books, 2007).

[153]Ibid., 93–94.

[154]Ibid., 106.

[155]Ibid.

[156]Ibid., 109.

[157]Gergen, 280.

fight strong union opposition, but he believed it was the right thing to do in a global environment.

On the other hand, Clinton's belief in globalization and its positive attributes may have caused him to underestimate the growing dangers inherent in the North Korean refusal to allow inspections of its nuclear program by the International Atomic Energy Agency (IAEA). Not only did the North Koreans refuse inspection, but they bluntly announced their intent to withdraw from the Nonproliferation Treaty (NPT), citing Article 10, which allows withdrawal on grounds of national security.[158] Brzezinski faults Clinton for not taking a more aggressive stand in reaction to many levels of North Korean defiance.[159] But as Clinton added in his autobiography, "In October 1994, we reached an agreement with North Korea to end their threat of nuclear proliferation on the Korean peninsula." The agreed framework, signed by U.S. negotiator Bob Gallucci and the North Koreans in 1994, committed North Korea to freeze all activity of existing nuclear reactions and allow inspectors to continue. In return, the United States offered improved trade conditions for North Korea.[160]

As well, Clinton's belief in globalization led him to support the Bush administration's policy of providing humanitarian aid through military means to Somalia. The situation in that country deteriorated, however, when Somali warlord Mohammed Aidid killed fifteen Pakistani peacekeepers and extended his control over a significant portion of the capital city, Mogadishu. In consultation with the chairman of the joint chiefs of staff, General Colin Powell (who was near the end of his tenure in that position), President Clinton decided to launch a military operation to take down Aidid. Clinton and Powell assumed the operation would occur during the dead of night; however, the operation commander decided to act in the light of day, with disastrous consequences. Somali insurgents downed an army Black Hawk helicopter, killed nineteen Special Forces troops, and humiliated Captain Mike Durant by dragging his wounded body through the streets of Mogadishu.[161] Clinton seemed slightly inept in figuring out an appropriate response. In this situation, and in an equally vexing problem in Haiti, where the question was how to react to Haitian boat people seeking refuge in the United States, the challenge for Clinton as an internationalist was that the United States could not do everything, but it would be unacceptable to do nothing. His instinct was to turn to the United Nations, but that institution did not possess unlimited resources either. Clinton launched a major policy review on peacekeeping that was charged with coming up with standards to guide U.S. involvement overseas. The process was led by Richard Clarke, who served as national coordinator for national security and counterterrorism under presidents Clinton and

---

[158]Brzezinski, 97.

[159]Ibid., 100.

[160]Clinton, 2004, 624–625.

[161]Ibid., 551.

George W. Bush. Clarke drafted Presidential Directive (PD) 25 that codified new limits on humanitarian military aid. It also imposed several tests on future peacekeeping operations: They needed to be in America's interests, have clear objectives, and have a defined exit date.[162] In many ways, PD 25 paralleled similar principles enunciated earlier by Powell, which became known as the Powell Doctrine.[163] In short, Clinton's belief in globalization was modified by his experiences.

Finally, although Clinton claimed legitimacy as a New Democrat, and a change agent, his embrace of a complex, bureaucratic, and government-managed health care proposal cast doubt on his authenticity in the minds of Republicans and Democrats alike. When this disastrous policy was unveiled in 1993–1994, many were quick to allege that Clinton was an "old-line Democrat" in New Democrat's clothing.[164] *Washington Post* reporters Haynes Johnson and David S. Broder thought it made no sense for Clinton to sign on to the most liberal of the Democratic policy alternatives in health care. In their words:

> The whole premise of his campaign was that he was a "New Democrat,"
> unenamored of big, bureaucratic government and fully aware of the
> need for spending discipline. His political base lay in the Democratic
> Leadership Council, a group of moderate to conservative office holders
> with no ties to organized labor, the chief proponent of the Canadian
> plan. His allies were the governors who had bitter experience with the
> government-financed Medicaid program.[165]

Nevertheless, Clinton's approach to political leadership as a New Democrat, which others characterized as a third way between liberalism and conservatism, found an international resonance in the 1997 election of Tony Blair as prime minister of Great Britain. Blair developed an effective formulation between the left-leaning Labor Party and the right-leaning Tories. At an early meeting with Clinton, Blair saluted his American friend with these words, "This is the generation that prefers reason to doctrine, that is strong in ideals but not to ideology, whose instinct to judge government not on grand design but by practical results."[166]

To sum up, Bill Clinton was a visionary in the sense of redefining the Democratic Party and imagining a third way of governing America,

---

[162]John F. Harris, *The Survivor: Bill Clinton in the White House* (New York: Random House, 2006).

[163]Walter Le Feber, "The Rise and Fall of Collin Powell and the Powell Doctrine," *Political Science Quarterly*, 129, no. 1 (Spring 2009).

[164]Joe Klein, *The Natural: The Misunderstood Presidency of Bill Clinton* (New York: Broadway, 2002), 119.

[165]Haynes Johnson and David S. Broder, *The System: The American Way of Politics at the Breaking Point* (Boston: Little, Brown & Co, 1996), 77.

[166]Harris, 286.

capitalizing on technological advances to make government more efficient, borrowing progressive social policy ideas from other people and other nations (e.g., Germany—during the 1980s and 1990s, the Germans established a reputation for innovation and progressive government politics such as encouraging individuals to open up "training accounts" to save funds for education during periods of job change), abandoning the sclerotic practices and adages of the moribund Roosevelt-Johnson Democratic coalition, and embracing a clear and vibrant collaboration between business and government. According to his speechwriter, Michael Waldman, "this will most likely be his lasting legacy: redefining the role of government and then successfully convincing the public to share that vision."[167] He was clearly a global thinker who believed the United States could act in the concert of nations to find viable solutions to transnational problems such as global warming, poverty, and AIDS. Rising way above his modest and parochial Arkansas roots, this New Democrat pumped life into a party that had lost its connection to the middle class and been captured by the labor movement and racial minorities. And yet, although his aim was grand, the sum of his capabilities to carry out an agenda ebbed and flowed. The arc of his ambition surpassed the capabilities of him and his staff at times, and ran into the realities of Washington, D.C.

POLITICS

A *New York Times*/CBS poll taken just before Bill Clinton's inauguration suggested that Americans were awaiting his presidency with "renewed optimism about the nation and its economy" and a "burst of confidence in him as an effective leader who cares about them."[168] As well, there was great hope among Democrats in particular for the presidency of Bill Clinton. The party had been out of power in the White House for twelve years and had been "playing defense," according to Clinton's aide George Stephanopoulos.[169] According to Stephanopoulos:

> We could seek a capital gains tax but not enact a tax cut for working poor. We could stop cuts in Head Start or Medicaid but not expand student loans or pass national health care. We could piece together a bare majority to pass a gun control bill, but not get enough votes to override the inevitable veto. We could make a lot of noise about a Supreme Court appointment—maybe even block the president's top choice—but conservative judges would control the federal courts for another generation. We could win moral victories on Capitol Hill, but we couldn't make history.[170]

---

[167]Michael Waldman, *POTUS SPEAKS: Finding the Words That Defined the Clinton Presidency* (New York: Simon and Schuster, 2000), 16.

[168]Adam Clymer, "Americans Have High Hopes for Clinton, Poll Finds," *New York Times*, January 19, 1993, A13.

[169]Stephanopoulos, 23.

[170]Ibid.

Nevertheless, Clinton's early days in the White House were problematic. He came into office with barely 43 percent of the popular vote, 37 percent having gone to George Bush, and an astounding 19 percent to third-party candidate Ross Perot.[171] According to David Gergen, who served for one year in the Clinton White House, only two other presidents had entered the office with such slim plurality: Woodrow Wilson in 1912 with 42 percent and Richard Nixon in 1968 with 43 percent.[172] But in the cases of Wilson and Nixon, their parties picked up seats in Congress, giving them a needed source of leverage. In Clinton's case, on the other hand, Democrats lost ten seats in the House in 1992 and one in the Senate (in a special election a short time later).[173] As cognately expressed by Gergen, "Clinton had neither a mandate nor coattails. He had won office but not power."[174] In addition, in Clinton's highly personalized campaign, he had distanced himself from Democratic regulars. The press, for its part, was poised to pounce on the "character" issue that followed him everywhere.

Given these challenges, Gergen suggests, one would have thought Clinton would buckle down immediately to plot out a serious sustaining strategy for governing—the way Reagan did. Instead, he let time slip away from him. In the eleven weeks between his election and the inauguration, he failed to "hit the ground running."[175]

According to Gergen, who worked for several presidents, a newly elected president "must seize upon these intervening weeks to appoint his new team, map out policy and communicate plans, build bridges to constituencies, and— whenever he can—get some rest."[176] But Clinton was still in campaign, and not yet in governing, mode.

Gergen identifies principle shortfalls of the Clinton presidential transition process:

> He failed to create a team that could govern. Staffing a new administration means making more than 9,000 appointments, including roughly 600 Senate confirmed cabinet and sub-cabinet members.[177]

Clinton began effectively, by designating experienced people to take charge of transition operations. Leading the transition effort were Warren Christopher, who had served as deputy attorney general under Johnson and deputy secretary of state for Carter, and Vernon Jordan, who had been CEO of National Urban League. They met regularly with Al Gore to ensure the Clinton goal of choosing a team that would "look like America." But Clinton's

---

[171]Gergen, 256.

[172]Ibid.

[173]Ibid.

[174]Ibid.

[175]Ibid.

[176]Ibid., 257.

[177]Ibid., 258.

obsessive demands for balance and agonizing over choices prolonged the process and prevented the filling of other important jobs.

Furthermore, according to Gergen, Clinton inexplicably chose his top staff almost entirely from his campaign team.[178] Unlike Reagan, who blended campaign loyalists with Washington veterans, Clinton seemed to purposely avoid the selection of Washington professionals such as Stuart Eizenstat, who had been Jimmy Carter's domestic policy adviser and was under serious consideration by the transition team as deputy chief of staff to Clinton's long-time friend Mack McLarty (Eizenstat eventually took a post in the diplomatic circuit).[179] Gergen believes that "had Clinton reached out for veteran players in his White House as he had for his campaign he would not have floundered in those early weeks in office."[180] The people Clinton selected for White House staff—George Stephanopoulos, Dee Dee Myers, Rahm Emanuel (who served as senior adviser to President Clinton), and Gene Sperling (who served as deputy director of the National Economic Council in the first Clinton administration)—were talented people who had provided the backbone of the first successful Democratic campaign for the White House in sixteen years. "But they were also young and inexperienced in governing."[181]

The selection of Mack McLarty as chief of staff was emblematic of the president's over-reliance on friends and under-reliance on D.C. insiders. McLarty, who was a CEO of a Fortune 500 natural gas company, offered himself as a potential liaison to businesses. But President Clinton insisted that he take the chief of staff position and he proved to be generally weak in that position, though he did help the president score some legislative victories.[182]

Clinton failed to use the transition to make strategic plans for his first weeks in office and to rally congressional support behind him.[183] He had not articulated an attainable, actionable vision in the same way Reagan had. According to Gergen, "It's the economy stupid" was a winning campaign slogan but an insufficient guide to policy development. His economics team was split into groups of budget deficit leaders such as Robert Rubin and Senator Lloyd Bentsen, his treasury secretary, and more traditional pro-government–spending liberals, such as Stephanopoulos and Begala.[184]

Trying to avoid the Carter problems in congressional relations, Clinton invited Democratic congressional leaders for an early get-together, but even that went awry, according to Gergen.[185] In December, a delegation headed by Senate Majority Leader George Mitchell and House Speaker Thomas Foley traveled

---

[178]Ibid., 259.

[179]Ibid.

[180]Ibid.

[181]Ibid.

[182]Ibid., 260.

[183]Ibid.

[184]Ibid.

[185]Ibid.

to Little Rock for a private dinner with Bill and Hillary. Clinton asked for support in reducing the deficit, overhauling health care, and enacting family and medical leave. The members agreed, but in exchange asked for the president to fulfill campaign promises on campaign finance reform, the line-item veto, and significant reduction in congressional staff. Clinton, assuming he had no choice, agreed to these demands. Clinton felt he had won friends on Capitol Hill; however, the congressional leaders came away thinking, "This is a man who can be willed." He had given in too easily, in their estimation.[186]

> He did little to prepare himself physically for the road ahead. He habitually stayed up till all hours of the night and never seemed well-rested. He seemed "worn-out" and "hyper," according to David Gergen.[187] His attention span was short, to the point that it seemed difficult to have a lengthy conversation with him. The state of physical exhaustion that Clinton was in when he came to Washington did not prepare him for the grisly schedule that would face him as president. According to Gergen, "History and research have repeatedly shown that fitness and stamina are the hidden ingredients of leadership."[188]

On the other hand, it is clear that Clinton effectively accomplished one aspect of the transition with high impact; he assembled a first-rate economic team, established a personal bond with Federal Reserve Chairman Alan Greenspan, and moved in a courageous manner to bring down budget deficits.[189] Clinton had taken the economy more seriously than any other issue in the campaign and stacked the economic team in favor of deficit hawks who believed if the deficit of the Reagan/Bush era—estimated to be over $300 billion in Clinton's first year in office—could be brought under control, interest rates would be reduced, and the economy would begin to grow.[190] Clinton chose deficit hawks to lead his economic team: Texas Senator Lloyd Bentsen, as his treasury secretary; Congressman Leon Panetta, chairman of the House Budget Committee, to head the Office of Management and Budget; and Robert Rubin, former co-chairman of Goldman-Sachs, to head the National Economic Council (NEC).[191] Created in 1993 by executive order, the NEC's functions are to "coordinate policy making for domestic and international economic issues, to coordinate economic advice for the president, and to ensure that policy decisions and programs are consistent with the president's economic goals."[192]

---

[186]Ibid., 261.

[187]Ibid.

[188]Ibid., 262.

[189]Ibid.

[190]Ibid.

[191]Clinton, 452.

[192]Description of NEC at http://www.whitehouse.gov/nec.

Clinton also named one of the most diverse administrations in history by appointing University of Wisconsin chancellor, Donna Shalala, of Lebanese ancestry, as secretary of health and human services; Carol Browner, Florida's environmental director, as head of the Environmental Protection Agency; Henry Cisneros, the dynamic and popular Hispanic mayor of San Antonio, as secretary of housing and urban development; and Ron Brown, a prominent African American, to head the Department of Commerce. He appointed Dee Dee Myers as the first female White House press secretary, and Hazel O'Leary, an African American, as energy secretary.[193]

But the missteps of the transition gradually began to manifest themselves in the early months of Clinton's presidency. His first two choices for attorney general were forced to withdraw due to a "Nanny" problem (nominees Zoe Baird and Kimba Wood had not been paying social security taxes for domestic workers whom they employed at their homes). The president tried to redeem a campaign promise to allow gays to freely enlist in the military, but during the first week of his young administration it became clear that this was not going to happen. On January 25, Clinton called a meeting at the Roosevelt Room

▅ THE FIRST CLINTON ADMINISTRATION

INAUGURATION: January 20, 1993, the Capitol, Washington, D.C.

VICE PRESIDENT: Albert "Al" Gore Jr.

SECRETARY OF STATE: Warren M. Christopher

SECRETARY OF THE TREASURY: Lloyd M. Bentsen Jr.; Robert E. Rubin (from January 11, 1995)

SECRETARY OF DEFENSE: Les Aspin; William J. Perry (from February 7, 1994)

ATTORNEY GENERAL: Janet Reno

SECRETARY OF THE INTERIOR: Bruce Babbitt

SECRETARY OF AGRICULTURE: Mike Espy; Daniel R. Glickman (from March 30, 1995)

SECRETARY OF COMMERCE: Ronald H. Brown; Mickey Kantor (from April 12, 1996)

SECRETARY OF LABOR: Robert B. Reich

SECRETARY OF HEALTH AND HUMAN SERVICES: Donna E. Shalala

SECRETARY OF HOUSING AND URBAN DEVELOPMENT: Henry G. Cisneros

SECRETARY OF TRANSPORTATION: Frederico F. Peña

SECRETARY OF ENERGY: Hazel R. O'Leary

SECRETARY OF EDUCATION: Richard W. Riley

SECRETARY OF VETERANS AFFAIRS: Jesse Brown

---

[193]Clinton, 454.

with all four service commanders—army, navy, air force, and marines—who arrived in full uniform, along with chairman Powell. The chiefs congratulated Clinton on his victory, and quickly indicated that they were not going to allow the new president, who had been elected with only 43 percent of the vote, never served in the military, and been accused of dodging the draft, to allow gays in the military.[194] The military leaders knew they had backup on the Hill, especially in the presence of Senator Sam Nunn, chairman of the Senate Armed Services Committee. Powell added emphasis to the argument against enlisting gays when he stated that the American military was in exquisite shape and should not be changed. Powell offered an alternative, saying they should "stop asking and stop pursuing,"[195] which provided the basis for the eventual policy choice of "don't ask, don't tell."

The problem of gays in the military, the failed cabinet nominations, the firing of the head of the White House travel office, and Clinton's dropping in popularity led him to call David Gergen in early 1993 to say "I'm in trouble. I need your help."[196] Gergen joined the Clinton White House staff as a counselor and to assist in the administration's communications effort.

Over the next several months, Bill Clinton staged a spectacular comeback, according to Gergen.[197] His public opinion approval rating moved from 38 percent in May 1993, to 58 percent by December.[198] The increase in popularity reflected several substantial accomplishments of his presidency: congressional passage of his budget plan; NAFTA; national service; the Brady Bill (regulating handgun sales and registration); the signing of a peace agreement between the Israelis and Palestinians on the White House lawn; and the launch of Vice President Gore's effort to reinvent the federal government.[199]

According to Gergen, the budget victory was the "most important legislative achievement of his presidency."[200] It established his credentials as a budget deficit hawk, much to the delight of Wall Street. Clinton had promised a middle-class tax cut; however, an early analysis of the deficit situation by his economic team indicated that the deficit was deeper than previously believed and could be closed only by tight fiscal discipline.[201] By Panetta's calculation, the budget deficit would reach $360 billion a year by the end of fiscal year 1997.[202]

Accordingly Clinton, in consultation with Bentsen, Rubin, and Panetta, proposed a budget plan that purposed, above all, to increase the top income tax rate from 31 to 36 percent on incomes over $180,000, with a 10 percent

---

[194]Stephanopoulos, 123.

[195]Ibid., 126.

[196]Gergen, 265.

[197]Ibid., 274.

[198]Ibid.

[199]Ibid.

[200]Ibid., 279.

[201]Stephanopoulos, 176.

[202]Walker, 172.

surcharge on incomes over $250,000, and to raise the corporate income tax from 34 to 36 percent on incomes over $10 million.[203] Clinton's plan sought to reduce the deficit by raising taxes on the wealthiest Americans (top 5 percent income bracket) while cutting taxes for the poor and middle class.[204] The president introduced the budget plan on national television and undertook an active lobbying campaign—with a great deal of retail politics included—to get it adopted.

The chief lobbyist in the battle of the budget was Clinton himself. He "called, cajoled, begged, pressured, and promised—whatever it took."[205] He told wavering Democrat members that he was the first Democrat in the White House in twelve years, and they could not let him fail. Clinton was assisted in the persuasion effort by his congressional liaison, Howard Paster, and by staff member George Stephanopoulos, who had strong relationships in the House based on his years working with members and staff.[206] The Clinton team developed printouts for each of the members, showing how many people in their congressional districts would get a tax cut under EITC (Earned Income Tax Credit; for people making less than $30,000) compared to those who would get an increase.[207] Meanwhile, the Republicans mounted a vehement campaign in opposition to the Clinton budget plan, characterizing it as the "biggest tax increase in the history of the universe."[208]

The Clinton lobbying team achieved the slimmest of victories, gaining passage of the president's budget bill by a vote of 218–216 in the House (with no Republican support) and a 50–50 tie in the Senate, with Vice President Gore casting the deciding vote.[209] Nevertheless, the budget victory proved to be a substantial one for Bill Clinton. When he surprised Wall Street by moving in a more fiscally conservative direction, there was a very good reaction. With the budget deficit heavily diminished, Alan Greenspan's Federal Reserve board felt it safe to lower interest rates. The economy grew more rapidly, inflation fell, unemployment fell, and the stock market rose.[210] Budget deficits, which stood at around $300 billion when Clinton took office, shrunk to $22 billion by 1997 and were totally gone by 1998.[211] Clinton was emphatic in explaining that his economic program was not only aimed at deficit reduction, but also included investing in the nation's health. He said:

> In addition to deficit reduction, my economic plan would provide
> incentives to business to create new jobs; a short-term stimulus to add

---

[203]Clinton, 2004, 496.

[204]Ibid.

[205]Gergen, 279.

[206]Stephanopoulos, 177.

[207]Clinton, 2004, 535.

[208]Stephanopoulos, 177.

[209]Gergen, 279.

[210]Ibid.

[211]Harris, 262.

50,000 jobs right away, investments in education and training, and special programs to help displaced defense workers, welfare reform and a big increase in the Earned Income Tax Credit (tax cuts for those making less than $30,000); a Head Start appropriations and vaccinations for all children who need them.[212]

The NAFTA was the next Clinton legislative victory, and this time the win would be accompanied by considerable Republican support. The agreement, which had been partly negotiated by Clinton's predecessor, George H. W. Bush, was intended to ease trade barriers from the north of Canada to the southern tip of Mexico, allowing some 400 million people to share the economic and social benefits of free trade.[213] Clinton had warily supported NAFTA during his campaign, because it represented good government, but organized labor and many environmentalists adamantly opposed it.[214] The Clinton team was split, with solid support coming from Treasury Secretary Lloyd Bentsen, who advocated the economic benefits, and Secretary of State Warren Christopher, who stressed the importance of NAFTA to America's position as a global leader.[215] The political advisers, including Stephanopoulos, Carville, Begala, and Hillary, lined up against it. They thought NAFTA was a disaster and could not win passage, and even if it did, Clinton would antagonize the unions and health care reform, among other interests, would suffer.[216]

Clinton stood his ground and enlisted lobbying assistance from Bill Daley, an executive in Chicago and brother of its mayor; Mickey Kantor, Clinton's trade representative; and Bill Frenzel, a former Republican Congressman.[217] Clinton spoke forcefully for passage and worked the Hill tirelessly, adjusting details of the bill—making a side agreement on citrus for Florida delegates and one on sugar for Louisiana—to secure passage. Kantor managed to obtain concessions for the Mexicans, and even Chief of Staff McLarty participated in the lobbying.[218] In the words of Gergen, "It takes presidential leadership to bring the public around, and Clinton provided plenty of it."[219]

One additional challenge to the NAFTA bill emerged when Ross Perot joined the debate and alerted the public to the "giant sucking sound" of jobs leaving the country that would be caused by NAFTA. The Clinton team persuaded Vice President Gore to debate Perot on television, and he turned out a masterful performance. With the assistance of 132 Republicans in

---

[212]Clinton, 2004, 495.

[213]Gergen, 280.

[214]Ibid.

[215]Ibid.

[216]Ibid.

[217]Ibid., 281.

[218]Ibid., 282.

[219]Ibid.

the House, and the support of House Speaker Newt Gingrich, NAFTA was adopted.[220] Only 102 Democrats in the House voted for NAFTA, whereas 156 opposed it.

The positive political momentum continued in the foreign policy realm. Capitalizing on the evolving peace process between the Israelis and Palestinians that took place during the early 1990s, primarily in Oslo, Norway, President Clinton had the unusual opportunity of hosting a historic event on the White House lawn in September 1993: the signing of a Declaration of Principles by Prime Minister Yitzhak Rabin of Israel and Yasser Arafat of the Palestine Liberation Organization (PLO).[221] The Declaration of Principles committed the PLO to recognizing the state of Israel, and the state of Israel to recognizing the PLO (and later the Palestine Authority) as the legitimate representative of the Palestinian people. It also created a process in which Israel would gradually relinquish its control over some aspects of Palestinian lives by establishing a timetable for the creation of a Palestine Authority, beginning in Gaza and Jericho.[222] Clinton and his secretary of state, Warren Christopher, arranged for the declaration to be signed at the White House, and with the assistance of Middle East envoy Dennis Ross, overcame last-minute problems, such as Arafat's attempt to appear at the ceremony in military uniform and the refusal of the Israelis to include a specific reference to the PLO in the documents. The mood of the day was, perhaps, most eloquently expressed by Rabin who said, "Enough of blood and tears."[223]

But the positive political momentum was interrupted by the health care reform movement, an episode that proved to be nearly fatal to Clinton's continued effectiveness as a leader. During the campaign, Clinton and his advisers had decided to focus on health care because of the success of Harris Wofford in defeating Richard Thornburgh in a 1991 off-year U.S. Senate election in Pennsylvania. Just months before the election, Wofford had been appointed to the Senate by Governor Robert Casey following the untimely death of the Republican incumbent, Senator John Heinz. Wofford was not very well known, and his Republican opponent, Dick Thornburgh, had been a member of President George H. W. Bush's cabinet.[224] Wofford's campaign strategists, including James Carville and Paul Begala, believed that by focusing on health care reform, Wofford, clearly the underdog, could defeat Thornburgh. Wofford won Pennsylvania's Senate race with an astounding 55 percent of the vote—a landslide by Pennsylvania standards. Past election polls indicated that for half of Pennsylvania's voters "national health insurance" was among

---

[220]Ibid., 284.

[221]Dennis Ross, *The Missing Peace: The Inside Story of the Fight for Middle East Peace* (New York: Farrar, Straus and Giroux, 2004), 120–121.

[222]Ibid., 116.

[223]Ibid., 122.

[224]Jacob S. Haches, *The Road to Nowhere: The Genesis of President Clinton's Plan for Heath Security* (Princeton, NJ: Princeton University Press, 1997), 10.

the top two concerns in their voting decision; for almost a quarter of voters, it was the top concern.[225]

The Pennsylvania Senate race was particularly meaningful due to its timing. It was the only off-year Senate race in 1991, and it occurred in the year prior to a presidential election. President Bush, who had seemed invincible because of the impressive military victory in Iraq, suddenly looked more vulnerable. Moreover, Bush and Thornburgh were closely identified with each other. Thornburgh had stepped down from the Bush cabinet to run, had made his service in the administration a major campaign theme, and had requested personal appearances on his behalf from Bush and Vice President Quayle.[226] Even President Bush joined in the post-election analysis, indicating in a news conference the day after the election that the vote bore a message for him and his administration. "When the economy is slow, people are concerned. They're hurting out there. They're concerned about their livelihood. One of the messages in Pennsylvania: Try to help people with health care."[227]

In short, Harris Wofford's surprise win in Pennsylvania brought to light the depth of middle class angst about the rising cost of health care and the insecurity of health insurance coverage, issues voters also found in Clinton's 1992 presidential campaign. Added to these concerns was the fact that some 37 million Americans lacked any health care coverage.[228] Now that he was in the White House, the president, strongly influenced by Hillary, would try to deliver on a promise to reform health care in America. Indeed, the first lady was hugely frustrated by the repeated postponement of a health care proposal, due to the administration's choice to focus on the budget, NAFTA, and even the vice president's project of reinventing government. "We've been waiting in line," she complained at one meeting.[229]

And so on January 25, 1994, Clinton went to the podium of the House of Representatives to deliver his State of the Union address and presented a proposal that the first lady had crafted to overhaul the nation's health insurance and delivery system. He told the assembled legislators that he was willing to compromise on the particulars of reform, but that he would not negotiate on one goal: universal coverage—every American would have coverage.[230] And in a dramatic gesture, the president brandished a pen and announced, "If you send me legislation that does not guarantee every American private health insurance that can never be taken away, you will force me to take this pen into the legislation, and we'll come right back here and start all over again."[231]

---

[225]Ibid., 11.

[226]Ibid., 32.

[227]Ibid., 39.

[228]Harris, 112.

[229]Ibid., 96.

[230]Ibid., 110.

[231]Ibid., 111.

Hillary Clinton, who had been designated by the president to head the reform effort, and her deputy, Ira Magaziner, had operated with great dispatch and in an environment of relative secrecy to concoct a proposal that became the Clinton health care initiative. The Clintons sought but never really achieved a middle ground. They assured, for instance, that private insurance, not government, should continue to finance health care for most Americans, albeit under closer federal supervision.[232] They also assumed that employers, from whom most Americans already received health insurance, should remain the stop of first resort. They wanted an employer mandate, not an individual one favored by many Republicans.[233]

But the Clintons added two more concepts, the first one known as "managed competition," which described a system where insurance companies would compete for customers under rules strictly enforced by the government. The government would guarantee customers a minimum level of benefits; the insurance companies would be guaranteed a fixed amount of money for each participant in their plan. Competing companies would try and attract more customers and force hospitals and physicians to find efficiencies, thereby holding down costs and improving their own profits. Market incentives would bring health care costs down for government and business alike, and the savings could be captured to provide subsidies and leave the would-be uninsured to zero. "Thus," according to John Harris, "the two most pressing problems in health care—rising costs and inadequate access—would be solved in one swoop."[234]

The second pillar of managed care competition was a concept known as "community rating." This meant that every person would be insured at the same cost. Companies would have to stop the traditional practice of charging people according to individual risk factors such as age or preexisting conditions. Under this concept, the young and healthy would subsidize the costs of society's older and sicker population.[235]

The ideas were certainly innovative, but they became enormously complicated once given programmatic expression. Clinton's health care bill, once presented to Congress, was 1,342 pages long. To implement managed competition, the president proposed a series of regional cooperatives that would raise money from employers, negotiate benefit packages with insurers, and regulate the quality of care.[236] For many, this plan looked highly complex and bureaucratic. The opposition had a predictable field day. Chris Cox, a California Republican, remarked, "We're going to do to health care in America what Stalin did to agriculture in the Soviet Union!"[237]

232Ibid., 113.
233Ibid.
234Ibid.
235Ibid., 114.
236Ibid.
237Ibid.

Lobbyists sprung into action, and the insurance industry prepared a series of television advertisements featuring "Harry and Louise," a young couple at home trying to comprehend the Clinton health care plan, but growing increasingly alarmed as they pored over the details at their kitchen table.[238]

Nonetheless, according to Gergen, there was still a chance that significant reform could be rescued if the White House compromised and supported a more modest, bipartisan plan. Early in 1994, Senate Minority Leader Bob Dole was genuinely interested in striking a bargain, as was the Democratic chairman of the Senate Finance Committee, New York Senator Daniel Patrick Moynihan.[239] But Hillary was in no compromising mood. Ralph Larsen, chief executive of Johnson & Johnson and a member of the Business Roundtable lobbying group, once observed calmly in a meeting that the regional alliances in Clinton's plan sounded more like serious regulatory bodies and less like benign "purchasing corporations" to negotiate better insurance rates. Hillary slammed the table and said, "I said they were purchasing corporations and that's what they're going to be."[240] In another instance, in a speech before the American Academy of Pediatrics, the first lady became so angry about the Harry and Louise advertisements that she threw out prepared remarks and offered vitriol to the audience. "Insurance companies," she said, "like being able to exclude people from coverage, because the more they can exclude the more money they can make."[241]

By June, Daniel Patrick Moynihan, in an appearance on *Meet the Press*, suggested there was no chance of enacting Clinton's goal of universal coverage in one year; it could take a decade to achieve. Why not, he argued, immediately pass some more-modest reforms? Moynihan's alternative of insurance reforms and subsidies could achieve 91 percent coverage for Americans, a considerable improvement over the existing 85 percent.[242] He argued that 91 percent is not failure, it's progress and added, "Government is about increments by which you move towards the goals you desire."[243]

Moynihan's compromising language was actually consistent with President Clinton's governing style, but Hillary again warned publicly that the president would veto anything that fell short of universal coverage. When the president himself alluded to his willingness to accept 95 percent coverage, in a speech to the National Governors Association in Boston, and intimated flexibility specifically on the nature of employee mandates, Hillary ordered him to back off, which he quickly did.[244] The next day, he issued a humiliating retraction for his remarks to the governors, professing that he was still committed to universal coverage.[245]

---

[238]Ibid.

[239]Gergen, 301.

[240]Harris, 116.

[241]Ibid.

[242]Ibid., 117.

[243]Ibid.

[244]Ibid., 118.

[245]Ibid.

David Gergen, who participated in many White House discussions on health care, opined that if the president had paid more attention to the interests of Moynihan, augmented by those of Secretary of Health and Human Services Shalala and Treasury Secretary Bentsen, a compromise could have been reached with Dole and the Republicans.[246] But it was not to be. Health care reform never came to a vote in the House and the Senate. "The biggest initiative of Clinton's presidency," reflected Gergen, "died in committee."[247]

Summing up the Clinton health care experience, Gergen first commends the intentions of the Clintons:

> In trying to overhaul the troubled health care industry, the Clintons were tackling one of the toughest challenges in public policy; they were walking down a path littered with the skeletons of past reformers stretching back six decades. And they were willing to stake their reputations on the fight. For that alone, they deserve credit for political courage.[248]

On the other hand, they made several errors in judgment, according to Gergen.[249]

- They misjudged the values of the country and proposed a health care plan that smacked of government control.
- They misjudged the president's potential strength. Clinton had too slender a majority to offer one of the most sweeping legislative reforms of the century. His slim margin of electoral victory and early missteps in the White House had eroded his power. There was an unrealistic belief in the White House that Clinton could "sell" anything. But even a powerful orator cannot always sell an idea his audience perceives to be poor.
- They misjudged Congress. Clinton arguably attempted to bypass traditional committee hearings (and a potential Senate filibuster) by including health reform in a budget reconciliation bill in 1993. But Senator Robert Byrd, invoking the Byrd rule where non-generic bills were not allowed, put the kibosh on the means but left bad feelings on Capitol Hill. The Clinton team never accepted Republican moderates, as they had on NAFTA, for instance.
- They misjudged the interest groups. The AFL-CIO and AARP did not prove as effective as expected, and the Health Insurance Associates of America and the National Federation of Independent Business were adamantly opposed to the Clinton plan. The authors of the plan were not really hearing their opponents.
- They let the excellent become the enemy of the good. Gergen believes that a compromise plan that Lloyd Bentsen had developed could have formed the basis for a deal across party aisles. Incremental in outcome,

---

[246]Gergen, 303.

[247]Ibid.

[248]Ibid., 309.

[249]Ibid., 304–306.

Bentsen's plan would have addressed at least parts of the problem. But the Clintons could not scrutinize their own plan with a critical eye.

Gergen further speculated that the president was not fully himself in the fight for health care. "He was not as engaged, politically and intellectually, as I saw him in the budget and NAFTA struggles."[250] Although he worked hard to promote the plan, he did not "exercise his own independent judgment in the formation, presentation or final resolution of the plan."[251] According to Gergen, the matter gets back to the nature of the partnership he had with Hillary and how that partnership was influenced by his own past. To involve Hillary in a national crusade for health care reform would have been a wise idea but to assign her primary responsibility for designing the program and guiding its passage through Congress was "to place on her more of a burden than any First Lady could bear, even Mrs. Clinton."[252] That responsibility should have been assigned to Donna Shalala, according to Gergen.

The political consequences of the health care debacle appeared quickly. In the 1994 congressional elections, the Democrats were handily defeated at the polls, losing eight seats in the Senate and fifty-four in the House. Moreover, the center of gravity for the Republican Party shifted notably rightward. The Republicans elected Newt Gingrich of Georgia as the speaker of the house. Gingrich and his Republican colleagues proposed a "Contract with America," promising to achieve a balanced budget amendment, a limitation on "unfunded mandates," a congressional accountability act, and the return of prayer to the schools, all within the first 100 days. In the words of *Washington Post* journalist, John Harris, "a new era was at hand in Washington."[253]

At this point in his presidency, Bill Clinton was despondent, but found new hope in the "triangulation" strategy proposed by his political adviser, Dick Morris.[254] Clinton's curiosity was piqued when Morris mentioned the word *triangulation* and then illustrated the concept by shaping his fingers into a triangle and explaining, "triangulation, create a third position, not just in between the old position of the two parties, but above them as well. Identify a new cause that accommodates the needs of Republicans and Democrats but does it in a way that is uniquely yours."[255] Morris did not equivocate, as some of Clinton's aides were wont to do, and as Clinton himself did. He issued emphatic certitudes like "you must endorse a balanced budget. You must SIGN a welfare reform bill. If you do your second term is GUARANTEED."[256]

As if under the Dick Morris spell, Clinton proceeded to implement the triangulation strategy. He took up welfare reform with the zeal of a missionary.

[250]Ibid., 307.

[251]Ibid.

[252]Ibid.

[253]Harris, 153.

[254]Ibid., 164.

[255]Ibid.

[256]Ibid., 165. Emphasis in original.

On August 22, 1995, Clinton signed a landmark welfare reform bill, which had passed with bipartisan majority of more than 70 percent in both houses. The legislation retained the federal guarantee of medical care and food aid and increased federal child care assistances by 40 percent; however, it also ended the federal guarantee of a fixed monthly benefit to welfare recipients, placed a five-year limit on welfare benefits, and cut overall spending in the food stamp program.[257] Liberal Democrats strongly objected, and when Clinton signed the bill, two prominent officials in the Department of Health and Human Services, Mary Jo Bane and Peter Edelman, resigned in protest.[258]

By the spring of 1995, Clinton was poised to recapture the political momentum from the speaker. The president's strategy, influenced by the Morris notion of triangulation, changed from a focus on grandiose political innovation, such as the reform of health care, to one of incremental policy advances. His acceptance of the strongly Republican influenced welfare reform bill, angered many die-hard Democrats, but reinforced belief in personal responsibility for Americans.

In the spring and summer of 1995, Clinton deepened the U.S. involvement in the conflict in Bosnia, where the Serbs had been conducting a brutal campaign against Muslims, resorting to genocide and ethnic cleansing. Clinton, along with national security adviser, Tony Lake, and Richard Holbrooke, serving as assistant secretary of state for European affairs, drafted an ultimatum to the Serbs and the Muslims demanding that the two sides come to an agreement or NATO would begin dropping bombs.[259] But on August 28, a mortar shell landed in a crowded Sarajevo marketplace killing thirty-eight Croatians. Clinton and Lake quickly mobilized the European community to authorize NATO to unleash its largest military operation in its history. Operation Deliberate Force began on August 30, with airplanes flying from American air bases in Italy and off the *USS Theodore Roosevelt* in the Adriatic. The bombs fell on Bosnian Serbs surrounding Sarajevo.[260] The tough actions encouraged the parties to come to the negotiating table and resulted in the Dayton Peace Accords moderated by Richard Holbrooke.

During the fall of 1995, Clinton fought a fierce battle with Speaker Gingrich over the federal budget, a battle that he would decisively win. The Republican budget called for significant cuts in Medicare, Medicaid, education, and environmental protection, and Clinton promised to protect these appropriations. Although the Republicans expressed a willingness to compromise on Medicare, Clinton feared that an accommodation would endanger other social programs, and he refused.[261] Unable to find a viable compromise by the night of November 13, the White House and the Republican leadership

---

[257]Clinton, 2004, 720.

[258]Ibid., 700.

[259]Harris, 200.

[260]Ibid.

[261]Ibid., 215.

were still at odds, and the government was scheduled to shut down at midnight. In final discussions, Clinton took a strong negotiating position with Speaker Gingrich and Senate Leader Bob Dole. "I do not care what happens," he said, "I don't care if I go to five percent in the polls, I am not going to sign your budget. It is wrong for the country."[262]

The next morning, everything except emergency services shut down across the federal government. Commerce Secretary Ron Brown reported that some services under his department, including the National Weather Service, were being curtailed. Clinton instructed every other cabinet secretary to compile a list of the most admired government functions under their jurisdiction that were not in operation. The president could recite the list at his appearances. Clinton understood that people might not like government in the abstract, but they liked it in the particulars that touch their lives.[263] In the end, most citizens blamed Gingrich and the Republicans for the shutdown, and Clinton's standing improved.

By the fall of 1995, with the triumphs of the Bosnia peace talks and the budget negotiations under his belt, President Clinton emerged as a "more self-confident and commanding leader," according to biographer John Harris.[264] It is ironic that on the first night of the government shutdown on November 14, 1995, Clinton encountered Monica Lewinsky, a young intern working in the chief of staff's office, roaming the halls of the White House because offices were operating on a skeleton basis with most people home on furlough. The two began an affair that night in the Oval Office that would endanger Clinton's marriage as well as lead to impeachment hearings against him.[265]

What can one say of his politics overall? According to political scientist Fred I. Greenstein, there were actually two Bill Clintons in the White House:

- One who took a no-holds barred style of striving for policy outcomes with little attention to establishing priorities or accommodating to political realities.
- A second who evidenced a more measured, pragmatic style of focusing on a limited number of goals and attending closely to the politics of executing his program.[266]

Greenstein's notion of an oscillatory leadership style can be observed in some events and decisions described earlier. The first leadership style is evident in the health care episode and in the persistent attempts to integrate gays into the military, whereas the second is apparent in the addition of Gergen and the streamlining of White House operations in 1993, and with the embrace of

---

[262]Ibid., 216.

[263]Ibid.

[264]Ibid., 221.

[265]Ibid., 223.

[266]Fred I. Greenstein, "The Two Leadership Styles of William Jefferson Clinton," *Political Psychology*, 15, no. 2 (June 1999), 351–352.

Morris' triangulation strategy, bringing with it the support of welfare reform during 1994–1995.

There is, of course, a tendency to wonder which Clinton leadership style was the real one? It is a difficult question to answer, but there is little doubt of Clinton's mastery of political skills. When used to achieve specific policy goals—budget reform, NAFTA, welfare reform—Clinton's abilities were impressive. He was willing to use retail politics to the fullest extent, develop strong outreach to the opposition and with his own party, and extend the energy needed to seal the deal. He was resolute, but open to compromise, visionary but rarely dogmatic.

On the other hand, he often lost focus, over-promised, sought too many objectives simultaneously, and showed himself too willing to compromise on some issues and unwilling on others. In some ways, his oscillatory style made people wonder who the real Bill Clinton was. Nonetheless, in his first term in office, he accomplished important goals, including driving down the budget deficit and establishing the nation's status as a global power.

STRUCTURE

Based on his observation of the early days of the Clinton presidency, Fred Greenstein observed that Clinton seemed "insensitive to organization."[267] According to Greenstein, Clinton tended to take on a large number of personal responsibilities and delegate little, or avail himself of overall strategic advice. In fact, Greenstein added that Clinton himself acknowledged entering the White House without a plan for White House organization and staffing major White House positions with aides who had little Washington experience.[268]

Indeed, Clinton and his transition chief, Warren Christopher, paid far greater attention to staffing the cabinet than to choosing White House staff. Christopher himself became part of the cabinet, which "looked like America," as suggested earlier, but did not necessarily "think like America."[269] According to Michael Waldman, the cabinet included citizens of Cambridge, Berkeley, and Madison, Wisconsin, but none from swing states of Illinois, Ohio, Michigan, or Pennsylvania.[270] And Clinton did not even bother to name his White House staff, or determine its structure, until days before his inauguration.

The structure that Clinton developed for his White House was unusual. Unlike previous presidents, Clinton installed his wife and his vice president in the West Wing of the White House. No other first lady had been there before.[271] The physical arrangement reflected the unusually large influence of the

---

[267]Ibid., 356.

[268]Ibid.

[269]Waldman, 25.

[270]Ibid.

[271]Gergen, 293.

first lady and vice president in the Clinton administration. When David Gergen joined the White House in 1993, he asked Chief of Staff McLarty to summarize the White House organization. "Every White House has its own personality," reflected McLarty, "In this White House, as you will find, we usually have three people in the top box: the President, the Vice-President, and the First Lady. All of them sign off on big decisions. You'll just have to get used to that."[272]

Hillary's influence was so pervasive that Gergen mused about a co-presidency. Gergen believed that the Clintons worked effectively as a team when they were "in balance." According to Gergen, "She was the anchor, he the sail. He was the dreamer, she the realist. She was the strategist, he the tactician . . . She helped him gain office, he helped her gain power. He leaned to the center politically, she leaned to the left. She was composed, he flew off the handle. He liked to laugh, she was serious."[273] On the other hand, Gergen expressed serious concern about the way they structured the relationship. It was problematic, because, "no matter how talented, two people cannot occupy the space jointly making decisions."[274]

Hillary's influence was obvious long before the health care debacle. It surfaced in December 1993, when *Washington Post* reporter Bob Kaiser sent a letter to Clinton White House aide Bruce Lindsay requesting information about the couples' financial dealings before they came to Washington.[275] The request stemmed from questions about a land development deal the Clintons had entered in 1978 when Bill was attorney general of Arkansas. Whitewater was the name of a development of vacation homes along Arkansas' White River. In 1978, Bill and Hillary borrowed money for an investment in this property. Their partner, who arranged a highly attractive deal, was Jim McDougal, a financial and political impresario whom Bill had met when both men worked for Senator J. William Fulbright. But Whitewater turned out to be a bad investment. The project languished unprofitability from the beginning, and McDougal proved to be a questionable connection for the politically ambitious couple. During the flush 1980s, McDougal became involved in finance and headed an institution called Madison Guaranty Savings and Loan. McDougal used Madison's assets as a source of ready loans for politicians such as Bill Clinton. As well, Hillary Clinton, while employed at the Rose Law Firm, performed legal work for Madison. When boom went bust, crushing both Madison and McDougal, taxpayers bailed out the failed savings and loan at a cost of $50 million. (This was part of a much larger savings and loan scandal that was discussed in Chapter 5.) Subsequently, McDougal suffered a nervous breakdown and was put on trial for fraud before being acquitted in 1990. There was a suspicion that in return for campaign contributions and other favors, Governor Clinton and his wife had used their influence to curb the regulatory scrutiny that would have exposed Madison's malfeasance

---

[272]Ibid., 292.

[273]Ibid.

[274]Ibid., 293.

[275]Ibid., 247.

before taxpayers bailed them out.[276] Government regulators cleaning up the S & L mess in 1993 recommended prosecution of Madison for transactions in which the Clintons had a tangential role. The questions prosecutors were asking were, Where did the money go when taxpayers were forced to pick up the tab for the failure of Madison? Were these institutions run as piggy banks for a small group of Little Rock politicians and elites? Did some of the money fund Bill Clinton's campaign?

These were the questions that Robert Kaiser was asking on behalf of the *Washington Post*. David Gergen made the argument that if Watergate had taught us anything, surely it was that a president must come clean up front and take his lumps, rather than hiding the facts, letting them be dragged out piece by piece, and stimulating his opponents to initiate a criminal investigation.[277] In addition, he argued that the *Post* had legitimate questions and had been generally fair in its coverage of President Clinton.[278] Bill Clinton agreed to turn over the documents, but said he could not make the decision alone because Hillary had been a partner in the Whitewater transaction. Hillary said "No!"

The Clintons' decision not to disclose their documents precipitated a growing call by other news organizations—including *Newsweek* and the *New York Times*—for disclosure. Within a few months, a drumbeat started for the appointment of an independent counsel by Attorney General Reno. On January 20, 1994, she named Edward Fiske, a former federal prosecutor.[279] Clinton characterized the decision to call for a special prosecutor to be "the worst presidential decision" he made.[280] A year later, Fiske was succeeded by Kenneth Starr who used his role as special prosecutor to become Bill Clinton's major nemesis. According to David Gergen:

> If they had turned over the Whitewater documents to the *Washington Post* in December 1993, their seven-year-old land deal would have soon disappeared as an issue and the history of the next seven years would have been entirely different. Yes, disclosure would have brought embarrassments. Among other items, Mrs. Clinton's investments in commodity futures apparently would have come to light. But we know today that nothing in those documents constituted a case for criminal prosecution of either one of the Clintons in their Whitewater land dealings . . . More to the point by disclosing the documents, we would have punctured the growing pressure for an independent counsel. Edward Fiske and Kenneth Starr would have never arrived on the scene, we might never have heard of Monica Lewinsky (who had nothing to do with the original Whitewater matter) and there would have been no impeachment.[281]

---

[276]Ibid., 290.

[277]Ibid., 288.

[278]Ibid., 289.

[279]Ibid., 290.

[280]Clinton, 2004, 574.

[281]Gergen, 290–291.

PROCESS

The early Clinton White House was not a hospitable environment for orderly or rapid decision making. Clinton was highly knowledgeable about the details of policy and could easily see the complexity of any issue that came to his desk. In many respects, his approach to decision making was one of constructing decisions rather than making them.[282] In contrast to President George W. Bush who prided himself on being a "decider," president Clinton could probably be characterized as the "contemplator" or the "procrastinator." His White House meetings had the appearance of college seminars more than executive business sessions.

There was an absence of discipline in the Clinton White House deliberations, paralleling an absence of that quality in the president. When advising the president in preparation for the 1996 presidential election campaign against Republican Senator Bob Dole, Vice President Gore suggested that Clinton would have to elevate self-discipline as the hallmark of his strategy—in his remarks, ideas, and behavior.[283] Gore was giving expression to a widely held view that Clinton's lack of self-discipline had contributed to the chaotic, inconsistent White House decision making that produced numerous gaffs, scandals, and political failures in the early years of his presidency. Many saw the Clinton White House as the embodiment of indecision, uncertainty, and delay.[284] Clinton became increasingly aware of the problem, and added more experienced managers, such as David Gergen, to his White House.

Clinton had grown in office and realized that in the first term he presided over a dysfunctional operation. In 1994, shortly after the mid-term elections, the president replaced the affable, but somewhat ineffective chief of staff, Mack McLarty, with the more driven Lean Panetta. He also hired banker Erskine Bowles as White House deputy chief of staff. Bowles had headed the Small Business Administration during the first part of the Clinton administration. He was a buttoned-down, calm forty-nine-year-old North Carolinian who had done a time management study on Clinton and was being added to bring more order to Clinton's decision making. "When there is no front door to give way for doing things," Bowles quipped, "everybody uses the backdoor." He wanted to eliminate the backdoor options.[285] Bowles served as chief of staff during the second Clinton administration.

The president showed a capacity to learn and to grow as a decision maker. For instance, he became more comfortable with the decisional aspect of the

---

[282]This distinction was offered to the author by an IBM executive who completed a Washington, D.C.,–based seminar sponsored by the American University and led by the author in December 1984 on "Decision Making in Washington."

[283]Bob Woodward, *The Choice* (New York: Simon and Schuster, 1996), 14.

[284]Bert Rockman, "Leadership Styles and the Clinton Presidency," in Colin Campbell and Burt A. Rockman, eds., *The Clinton Presidency: First Appraisals* (Chatham, NJ: Chatham House, 1995), 352–362.

[285]Woodward, 128.

commander in chief role. On September 2, 1996, when Tony Lake made a secret trip to Little Rock to brief the president on options for a cruise missile attack on Iraq, Clinton appeared confident and animated as he peppered Lake with technical questions about "target sites" and "BDAs" (bomb damage assessments). By contrast, in the summer of 1993 when he had to order a missile strike against Iraq for the first time, Clinton seemed tense and wobbly. He had asked Lake up to the last minute, "are you sure this is the right thing to do?"[286] "By 1996," according to political scientists Paul Quirk and Sean Matheson, "Clinton had leaned a great deal from his mistakes. He had strengthened the White House staff and submitted himself to orderly process for decision-making."[287]

In short, Clinton began with an ill-considered and overly flexible decision-making style that incorporated many points of view, but was plodding and slow. Moreover, the decisions made by the administration seemed to evolve out of responses to emerging conditions and crisis, and not out of grand strategy for reform. Where Reagan's decision-making style seemed to maximize his chances to implement his vision, Clinton's did not. When Clinton settled on a policy decision—such as cutting the deficit or introducing NAFTA—he could be more decisive than usual. If the policy overlapped with his New Democrat focus, it was an effective combination. But he seemed unable to maintain the discipline of deliberation and discussion in all policy areas.

1996 PRESIDENTIAL ELECTION

In the 1996 presidential election, Clinton and Gore ran against Republicans— Kansas Senator Bob Dole and former New York Senator Jack Kemp. Dole presented voters with an impressive résumé for a potential president. He had served twenty-eight years as a senator, two as the Republican National Committee chair, and twelve as leader of the Senate, in both the majority and minority capacities. He had also been chair of the Senate Finance Committee. According to Quirk and Matheson, "In these capacities, he had been continually involved in the major issues facing the nation, especially the budget and taxes, and had worked closely with several presidents. Dole was widely praised as a responsible and effective Senate leader."[288]

Dole presented himself as a steady hand, a man of considerable expertise, who would know how to get things done, such as cutting taxes. He overcame challenges for the Republican nomination from journalist Pat Buchanan and from Steve Forbes, a publishing mogul who embraced the notion of a flat tax. Surprisingly, Dole made little use of his extensive governmental experiences in

[286]Karen Breslau, Debra Rosenberg, Leslie Kaufman, Andrew Murr, and Evan Thomas, *Back from the Dead: How Clinton Survived the Republican Revolution* (New York: Atlantic Monthly Press, 1997), 1.

[287]Paul J. Quirk and Sean Matheson, "The Presidency: Elections and Presidential Governance," in Michael Nelson, ed., The Elections of 1996 (Washington, D.C.: CQ Press, 1997), 127.

[288]Ibid., 126.

the campaign, and, in fact, decided to resign his seat in the Senate, hoping to sever his connections to Washington in the minds of voters.[289] Dole oriented his campaign around attacking Clinton's character and portraying his opponent as a big-spending liberal.

Perhaps the central policy proposed by the Dole campaign was his promise, announced in his 1996 Republican National Convention acceptance speech, to "reduce taxes 15 percent across the board for every taxpayer in America."[290] He also promised to balance the budget by 2000 without touching Social Security or Medicare, and without cutting defense.[291] Many economists were skeptical about Dole's economic plans, suggesting that they would reverse the trend of decreases in the deficit in the preceding years.[292] As well, Americans were expressing greater levels of confidence in the health of the economy than they had in several years. In August 1996, the Consumer Confidence Index was higher than it was during the Reagan recovery of 1984, and by two-to-one Americans said they were better off in 1996 than they had been in 1992.[293]

For his part, Clinton presented himself as a moderate who had cut the deficit and reformed welfare, and characterized Dole and the Republicans as radicals who wanted to cut Social Security and Medicare, force people into poverty, cut Head Start, and allow toxic pollution. He repeatedly linked Dole to Gingrich, who was unpopular at the time.[294]

Clinton chose the campaign theme of "A Bridge to the 21st Century," which subtly emphasized the differences in age of the candidates and also cast Clinton as a man of many ideas for the future. On the age issue, Dole was seventy-three years old and, if elected, would be the oldest president to assume office in history. Clinton was more than twenty years younger. On the issue of future thinking, Clinton highlighted the positive things that government could do to affect people's lives—pointing to his leadership in securing passage of the Family and Medical Leave Act and the ban on assault weapons, both of which Dole had opposed.[295] In illustrating his themes, Clinton made a series of proposals aimed at improving schools, extending family leave provisions, protecting the environment, and expanding the Internet.[296]

---

[289]Ibid., 128.

[290]Bob Dole, Acceptance Speech, Republican National Convention, August 15, 1996, reprinted in *Congressional Quarterly Weekly Report*, August 17, 1996, 2346–2350.

[291]Quirk and Matheson, 130–131.

[292]Allison Mitchell, "Clinton Hails Drop in Deficit, Declaring 'America's Awake,' " *New York Times*, October 29, 1996, A1.

[293]Richard Morin and John M. Berry, "A Nation That Poor Mouths Its Good Times," *Washington Post*, October 13, 1996, A1.

[294]Paul Herrnson and Clyde Wilcox, "The 1996 Presidential Election: A Take of a Campaign That Didn't Seem to Matter," in Larry J. Sabato ed., *Toward the Millennium: The Elections of 1996* (Boston: Allyn & Bacon, 1997), 129.

[295]Ibid., 134.

[296]Ibid.

Clinton began the campaign with a 15 percent lead in the polls, and Dole was unable to close the gap, mainly because of his own weaknesses as a candidate. According to *Washington Post* reporter John Harris, Dole was a "brave man and commendable senator, but was a miserable presidential candidate."[297] He chose as his campaign theme of "A Better Man for a Better America," suggesting that he would exploit Clinton's character vulnerability. But he was often inarticulate on the campaign trail and often relied on cryptic "inside the Beltway" language to refer to complex issues of which the public had little awareness. He tended to depart from prepared speeches and made off the cuff comments that he was later forced to defend. For instance, early in the campaign, Dole told an audience in tobacco country that tobacco was not addictive, and then spent a week trying to answer reporters' questions about this assertion.[298]

Clinton won the election with 49.2 percent of the popular vote, compared to Dole's 40.8 percent and Perot's 8.5 percent.[299] Clinton accumulated 379 electoral votes (compared to 370 in 1992), and Dole received 159 electoral votes. Clinton became the first Democratic president since Franklin Delano Roosevelt to be re-elected, and also the only Democratic president of the twentieth century to win alongside a GOP legislature.[300] In an election where only 48.8 percent of voters turned out, Clinton won 59 percent of the female vote, when Dole won the male vote by a narrow 44 to 43 percent.[301]

The party composition in Congress would play a significant role in Clinton's second term, as it had in his first. In 1993 and 1994, when he enjoyed Democratic majorities in both the House and the Senate, Clinton achieved success more than 85 percent of the time in each house on roll-call votes when he took a position. After the loss of both houses to the Republicans in the 1994 mid-term elections, his success rate dropped precipitously. In 1995, Clinton won only 26 percent of the roll calls in the House, the lowest success rate on record, and 41 percent in the Senate.[302] As both Clinton and congressional Republicans moved toward the center in 1996, Clinton had greater success, winning 53 percent of the important votes in the House and 58 percent in the Senate.[303]

THE SECOND TERM

Although he did not win 50 percent of the popular vote in the 1996 presidential election, Bill Clinton determined he could win a claim on the public imagination by articulating compelling national goals for the next four years.

---

[297]Harris, 241.

[298]Ibid., 132.

[299]Larry J. Sabato, "The November Vote: A Status Quo Election," in Sabato, *Toward the Millennium*, 144.

[300]Ibid., 132.

[301]Ibid., 148.

[302]Quirk and Matheson, 133.

[303]Ibid.

According to John Harris, "He was going to have a second chance at making history."[304]

Clinton had a lot to be proud of. The economy was strong, unemployment and crime were down, and Americans were relatively confident about the future. The president had addressed some of the management problems of his early White House days; by 1997, he had developed a more routinized schedule, and there were fewer pitched battles to deform this ideological identity of his presidency.[305] There was a significant amount of turnover in White House staff, and in the cabinet. Some of those who left included Warren Christopher, secretary of state; William Perry, secretary of defense; John Deutch, CIA director; Robert Reich, secretary of labor; Hazel O'Leary, secretary of energy; and Henry Cisneros, secretary of housing and urban development. Clinton built a new national security team featuring Madeline Albright at state, William Cohen (former Republican senator from Maine) at defense, George Tenet as CIA director, and Sandy Berger as national security adviser.[306]

But on May 27, 1997, the U.S. Supreme Court dealt President Clinton a significant blow by rejecting his argument that sitting presidents should be immune from civil lawsuits. In a unanimous decision in the case of *Clinton v. Jones*, the Court ruled that neither the separation of powers nor the need for confidentiality of high-level information can justify president immunity from the judicial process.[307]

The facts of the case dated back to May 8, 1991, when then Governor Bill Clinton spoke at an official state conference at the Excelsior Hotel in Little Rock. Shortly after his talk, the governor allegedly dispatched a state trooper to personally escort Paula Corbin Jones, a state employee staffing the registration desk, to the governor's suite in the hotel. The governor allegedly proceeded to make "abhorrent" sexual advances that Jones vehemently rejected. Jones claimed that because of her rejection of the governor, her superiors at work dealt with her in a hostile and rude manner and changed her duties. She brought a civil lawsuit to the U.S. District Court Arkansas East in May 1994, suing for damages of $750,000 and punitive damages of $100,000.[308] Clinton filed a motion to dismiss the case claiming presidential immunity and requested that all other pleadings and motions be deferred until the immunity issue was resolved. The district judge—Susan Webber Wright, who had been Bill Clinton's law student—denied dismissal on immunity grounds and ruled that discovery could go forward, but ordered any trial stayed until Clinton's presidency ended. The Eighth Circuit Court of Appeals affirmed the dismissal denial but reversed the trial postponement as the "functional equivalent" of a

---

[304]Harris, 253.

[305]Peter Baker, *The Breach: Inside the Impeachment and Trial of William Jefferson Clinton* (New York: Berkley Publishing Group, 2000), 37.

[306]Clinton, 737.

[307]*Clinton v. Jones*, 520 U.S. 681 (1997); available through the Oyez Project at http://oyez.org/cases/1990-1999/1996_95_1853.

[308]Justice Stevens, opinion for the court.

grant of temporary immunity to which Clinton was not constitutionally entitled. The court explained that the president, like other officials, is subject to the same laws that apply to all citizens and that no case had been found in which an official was granted immunity from suit for his unofficial acts.[309] The Supreme Court basically affirmed the Eighth Circuit, deciding that deferral of the litigation until the end of Clinton's term was not necessary. Justice Stevens opined for the court that "The Court rejects petitioner's contention that this case—as well as the potential additional litigation that an affirmance of the Eighth Circuit's judgment might spawn—may place unacceptable burdens on the President that will hamper the performance of his official duties."[310]

It was not immediately apparent that the *Clinton v. Jones* decision would precipitate a series of events that would lead to the impeachment trial of a president. Paula Jones' legal team almost immediately used the judicial process to pry open the president's sexual history.[311] On December 6, 1997, the prosecutors unveiled that one of the women on Paula Jones' witness list was Monica Lewinsky.[312]

The president and his advisers were unaware that Lewinsky had been telling the story of her affair with Clinton to a personal confidante, Linda Tripp, and that Tripp had been taping the conversations. Nor did they know that Lewinsky had shared her recollections with a New York literary agent, Lucianne Goldberg, in hopes of a book contract. Nor did they know that Goldberg had shared the information about Lewinsky with Jones' attorney. And they clearly did not know that there would be an intersection between the Jones case and Kenneth Star's criminal prosecution that still went by the name Whitewater.[313]

In a January 17, 1998, deposition Clinton denied the accusations that he had had an improper relationship with Monica Lewinsky and then made a public statement saying, "I want you to listen to me, I'm going to say this again: I did not have sexual relations with that woman, Miss Lewinsky. I never told anybody to lie, not a single time, never. These allegations are false."[314]

By August, Monica Lewinsky reached an agreement with Kenneth Starr to provide the details of her experiences with the president under oath in exchange for immunity from prosecution for any wrongdoings. She revealed the story in great detail, including mentioning incriminating evidence such as a stain on her dress that had been made by Bill Clinton's semen. When the prosecutors tested a blood sample from Clinton and proved a DNA match, the stage was set for a full-scale attack by Kenneth Starr and his team of prosecutors.

On August 17, 1998, President Clinton confronted Independent Counsel Kenneth Starr in the Map Room of the White House and testified via closed

---

[309]*Clinton v. Jones.*

[310]Ibid.; Stevens.

[311]Harris, 293.

[312]Ibid., 295.

[313]Ibid.

[314]Jim Lehrer, "The Big Speech," *The Newshour with Jim Lehrer*, Public Broadcasting System, January 26, 1998, http://www.pbs.org/newshour/bb/white_house/jan-june98/historians_1-26.html.

circuit television to the federal grand jury about his relationship with Monica Samille Lewinsky.[315] Clinton had been forced by incontrovertible DNA evidence to admit that he had, in fact, an improper relationship with Lewinsky, after seven months of adamant denials. He read the following statement to the prosecution:

> When I was alone with Ms. Lewinsky on certain occasions in early 1996 and once in 1997, I engaged in conduct that was wrong. These encounters did not consist of sexual intercourse. They did not constitute sexual relations, as I understood that term to be defined at my January 17, 1998 deposition. But they did include involve inappropriate intimate contact. These inappropriate encounters ended at my insistences, in early 1997.[316]

Clinton jousted with Starr lawyers for hours, insisting there was no legal inconsistency between his post statements and his current admission, asserting that he had been technically accurate and had not committed perjury. He even went to split hairs over the meaning of the word *is*, when asked by a prosecutor about his previous statement stating that "is absolutely no sex of any kind in any shape or form" between him and Lewinsky.[317] But he could not talk himself out of the problem.

The 453-page report that Kenneth Starr issued to Congress recommended the commencement of impeachment hearings against the president based on eleven counts against him—four alleging that he committed perjury in his January 17 deposition in the Paula Jones case, one alleging perjury in his August 17 grand jury appearance, five alleging obstruction of justice, and one asserting abuse of office.[318]

The Republican leadership was determined to bring down the president, pursuant to the findings of Kenneth Starr. Texas Republican Tom DeLay, majority whip, called on Clinton to resign to spare the nation the turmoil of an impeachment hearing.[319]

But Clinton made it clear that he had no intention of resigning and showed an equally strong determination to continue to discharge his presidential responsibilities. He was, perhaps, encouraged by the results of the 1998 mid-term elections, as the Democrats gained five seats in the House, narrowing the Republican margin to 223–211. Newt Gingrich, sensing the implication of the election, resigned his position in November. Also, one of Clinton's most aggressive opponents, Senator Alfonse D'Amato, was defeated in his Senate race.[320]

In his January 27, 1998, State of the Union address, Clinton proudly celebrated the accomplishments of his administration and cited the creation of

---

[315]Baker, 23.

[316]Ibid., 28.

[317]Ibid., 29.

[318]Ibid., 80.

[319]Ibid., 44.

[320]Ibid.

14 million jobs, the lowest unemployment rate in twenty-four years, the lowest core inflation in thirty years, decreases in crime rates for five years in a row, and the lowest welfare rates in twenty-seven years.[321] He added a reference to the achievement of a significant decrease in budget deficits during his watch and proclaimed that for 1999, he would submit the first balanced budget to Congress in thirty years. The president noted that the budgetary tide would soon turn, and the nation would start to enjoy budget surpluses for "as far as the eye can see." And what did he recommend doing with the surpluses? Saving social security! Clinton recommended using 100 percent of the surplus to take all necessary measure to strengthen the Social Security system for the twenty-first century.[322]

The president also prevailed in tough budget negotiation with the Republican leadership and achieved an impressive victory of rolling eight spending bills with a mammoth 4,000-page package that busted spending caps to achieve many of his goals. Clinton obtained money for the International Monetary Fund and seed money for a program to hire 100,000 school teachers.[323]

Meanwhile, as the House Judiciary Committee, under the leadership of Congressman Henry Hyde (R-IL), began preparing for a formal inquiry to consider impeachment hearings, House Minority Leader Dick Gephardt (D-MO), sought an alternative course of action. Gephardt proposed to introduce a resolution that would condemn Clinton by issuing a finding that "the President engaged in misconduct unbecoming the stature and high responsibility of the office the President holds." Citing the Starr report, the resolution concluded that Clinton "engaged in an improper relationship with an individual in the employ of the President of the United States" and sidestepping the legislation, Gephardt's resolution asserted merely that Clinton failed to provide completely truthful and forthcoming testimony in the Paula Jones case, and that in his subsequent appearance before the grand jury, "relied instead on evasive and technical formulation in answering certain inquiries of the Independent Council."[324] The proposal would strip Clinton of his government pension for five years after leaving office in January 2001, but would allow him to retain Secret Service protection and allotments for office space, staff, and expenses.[325]

But DeLay and his Republican colleagues were fiercely determined to proceed with impeachment, and the House voted 258–176 for a formal impeachment inquiry.[326] House Judiciary Committee chairman Henry Hyde attempted to conduct all phases of the impeachment process with evenhandedness; but

---

[321]William Jefferson Clinton, "Address Before a Joint Session of Congress on the State of the Union," in *Public Papers of the Presidents of the United States. Book I: January 1 to June 20, 1998* (Washington, D.C.: U.S. Government Printing Office, 1999), 112.

[322]Ibid., 113.

[323]Baker, 133.

[324]Ibid., 112–113.

[325]Ibid., 113.

[326]Ibid., 129.

John Conyers (D-MI), the ranking democrat on the Judiciary Committee, came out swinging. The real enemy, Conyers argued, was Starr, not Clinton. He opined that even worse than an extramarital relationship was the use of federal prosecutors and federal agents to expose that relationship.[327] The 1998 election results seemed to confer some legitimacy to Conyers' point of view. Nevertheless, on December 11 and 12, 1998, the House finalized four articles of impeachment as follows:

- Article I accused Clinton of perjury before the grand jury on August 17, 1998, by lying about the "nature and details of his relationship with a subordinate Government employee," about the truthfulness of his earlier testimony in the Jones deposition, about the untrue statement he had allowed his attorney to make during the deposition, and about his "corrupt efforts" to influence testimony and hide evidence.
- Article II accused Clinton of perjury in the Jones case, in his answers to written interrogation on December 23, 1997, when he denied having sexual relations with any subordinate federal employee.
- Article III accused him of obstruction of justice, citing seven examples, including his encouragement of Lewinsky to file a false affidavit, his efforts to find her a job to keep her quiet about the affair, his coaching of Betty Currie (Clinton's personal secretary), and his efforts at hiding gifts.
- Article IV accused him of abusing the power of his office by lying to the American public, lying to aides and cabinet secretaries who would respect the statements publicly, and "frivolously" asserting executive privilege to impede Starr's investigation.[328]

On December 19, 1998, the full House approved Article I and Article III, and rejected Article II and Article IV.[329] As prescribed by Article I, Section 2, of the U.S. Constitution, the next phase of the impeachment process would occur in the U.S. Senate, which would serve as an impeachment court with the chief justice of the United States presiding. Two-thirds of the senators, serving essentially as jurors, would have to vote to convict President Clinton and remove him from office.

The prosecution of the case against President Clinton was led by several House "managers," including Henry Hyde; Arkansas Republican Asa Hutchinson, who ironically was Bill Clinton's past political opponent; and a team of lawyers headed by David P. Schippers.[330] Hyde opened the case by citing the Ten Commandments, Roman Law, and the Magna Carta and framed the choice before the Senate as a question of patriotism. He said, "We must never tolerate one law for the ruler and another for the ruled. If we do,

---

[327]Ibid., 120.

[328]For a verbatim transcription of the four articles of impeachment, see ibid., 445–449.

[329]Baker, 449, gives the votes as follows: Article I: 228–206; Article II: 205–229; Article III: 221–212; Article IV: 198–285.

[330]Baker, 67.

we break faith with our ancestors from Bunker Hill, Lexington, Concord, to Flanders Fields, Normandy, Hiroshima and Dessert Storm."[331]

The Democrats recruited Dale Bumpers, another Arkansan who had served in the U.S. Senate for twenty-four years, to lead the defense effort for President Clinton. The Democrats also included D.C. attorneys Abe Lowell and Charles Ruff on their team. Ruff attacked the managers case for conviction as the product of "nothing more than a rush to judgment," and a "witches brew of charges."[332] And he paced the issue in personal terms for the senators to consider:

> We are not here to defend William Jefferson Clinton the man. He, like all of us, will find his judges elsewhere. We are here to defend William Jefferson Clinton, the president, for whom you are the only judges. You are free to criticize him, to find his personal conduct distasteful. But ask whether there is the moment when, for the first time in our history, the actions of a president have so put at risk the government the framers created that there is only one solution. You must find that removal is an acceptable option, that we will be okay the day after you vote.[333]

Throughout the six-week Senate trial, several attempts were made to dispose of the matter without forcing a vote. Senator Robert Byrd (D/WVA), the dean of the Senate and defender of its rituals and prestige, introduced a motion to dismiss the case, which was defeated by a vote of 56 "nays" and 44 "ayes."[334] Republican Senator Susan Collins of Maine suggested a "findings of fault" that would allow the Senate to conclude by a mere majority vote that Clinton had lied under oath and impeded the discovery of evidence even if it failed to convict him by the two-thirds majority vote required by the constitution.[335] Senator Diane Feinstein (D-CA) labored hard to move the idea of a censure as a reasonable outcome of the trial.[336]

All the alternative ideas for disposing of the problem were abandoned, and the six-week process moved toward the predictable conclusion of a vote against impeachment. During the waning days, key Republicans, such as Susan Collins of Maine, verbalized their opposition to removing the president from office. She made a particularly eloquent statement on the floor of the U.S. Senate:

> In voting to acquit the president, I do so with grave misgivings for I do not mean in any way to exonerate this man. He lied under oath; he sought to interfere with the evidence; he tried to influence the testimony of key witnesses. And while it may not be a crime, he exploited a very young star struck employee whom he then proceeded to smear in an attempt to destroy her credibility. . .

---

[331]Ibid., 312.

[332]Ibid., 315.

[333]Ibid., 314–315.

[334]Ibid., 360.

[335]Ibid., 380.

[336]Ibid., 386.

As much as it troubles me to acquit the president, I cannot do otherwise and remain true to my role as a Senator. To remove a popularly elected president for the first time in our nation's history is an extraordinary action that should be undertaken only when the President's misconduct so injures the fabric of democracy that the Senate is left with no option but to oust the offender from the office the people have entrusted to him.[337]

The senators rejected Article I of impeachment by a vote of 45–55, including all forty-five Democrats and ten Republicans, and rejected Article II by a vote of 50–50, with only five Republicans joining the acquittal forces.[338] Clinton had survived. Ironically on the same day that Bill Clinton's trial ended, Hillary decided to enter the race for Senator of New York, to replace retiring Senator Daniel Patrick Moynihan.[339]

SUMMING UP

As we analyze Clinton's two terms, it seems apparent that Clinton evidenced strong leadership in the areas of *policy*, or *vision*. He took a courageous position to refocus the Democratic Party and position it to achieve greater electoral success in the future. According to *New York Times* reporter Robin Toner, "it is easy to forget how beleaguered the Democratic Party was at the dawn of the 1990's. A generation had come of age with only the dimmest memories of a successful presidential campaign."[340]

Reagan's extraordinary popularity had placed the Democrats on the defensive as a candidate, and later as the president. Clinton provided solutions to Democratic vulnerabilities: perceptions that the party was soft on crime; Democrats were big taxers and spenders; they are addicted to giveaway programs; they were overly sensitive to the needs of minorities and tone deaf to the issues of the white middle class; and they were more interested in redistributing the wealth than in fostering economic growth.[341]

Clinton's belief in a third way provided a new definition to the party and a more attractive set of propositions to appeal to voters; he showed a strong belief in fiscal responsibility and taming deficit spending; he insisted on a culture of responsibility where beneficiaries of government succor would have to earn their right to those benefits and recognize that their benefits would not last forever; he appreciated the importance of the quickly evolving technologies to improve the performance of government, and even reduce

---

[337]Congressional Record, 145, no. 26 (Friday, February 12, 1999), Senate, S1462–S1637, from the Congressional Record Online through the Government Printing Office, http://www.gpo.gov.
[338]Ibid., 409–411.
[339]Ibid., 415.
[340]Robin Toner, "A Revival and a Party Transformed," *New York Times*, December 27, 2000, 1.
[341]Ibid.

its size; and he embrace the notions of globalism in trade policies emanating from Washington.

When aligned closely to his *vision*, Clinton's politics were impressive. He took great interest, and demonstrated considerable skill, in retail politics and in selling his programs. These traits were strongly apparent in the early legislative victory on his budget and, later on, with NAFTA, and even welfare reform. But he lost his bearing on core beliefs from time to time, and caved in to personal and political forces that intruded on his plans. At times he seemed to lack the courage of his convictions and seemed to become more "consumed with winning than leading," in the estimation of Lani Guinier, a Harvard law professor and onetime friend whom Clinton nominated to be assistant attorney general for civil rights (but then withdrew the nomination because of controversy over her writings).[342]

President Clinton's *structure*, his White House management, was somewhat peculiar. He gave unusual influence to the first lady and vice president, going so far as to place the first lady's office in the West Wing for the first time in history. In many instances, Bill Clinton benefitted from Hillary's advice and considerable policy expertise, but at times seemed to give too much room to her wishes and decisions. He seems to have realized his "shop" was in need of repair when he reached out to management inputs, said David Gergen and Erskine Bowles. Finally, Clinton's early days in the White House were characterized as disorganized in terms of process, or decision-making style.

In practical terms, Clinton left office having helped more Americans escape poverty than any other president since Johnson. During an earlier period of economic expansion, President Reagan lifted 290,000 Americans from poverty. Clinton multiplied that number twenty-four times, reducing the number of Americans in poverty by 7 million.[343] Under Clinton's watch, crime rates dropped to a three-decade low, whereas wages for unskilled workers reversed a fifteen-year decline. Finally, Clinton's push for welfare reform lowered the number of people on welfare rolls by 50 percent.[344]

Overall, Clinton helped the Democratic Party achieve a revitalized sense of purpose and helped the nation achieve sustained economic prosperity and respected global leadership in times of great transformation. With regard to the office of the presidency itself:

> Mr. Clinton managed to shape a new kind of executive activism that kept the presidency in the thick of things, whether in modest domestic initiatives or efforts to promote peace or trade around the world. Without ever winning a majority of the popular vote, and despite the huge failure of his effort to overhaul the nation's health care system,

---

[342]Purdum, 3.

[343]Jason DeParle and Steve A. Holmes, "A War on Poverty Subtly Linked to Race," *New York Times*, December 26, 2000, A1.

[344]Ibid.

he still helped bring the federal budget into balance for the first time in a generation and signed a major restructuring of the welfare laws. . . . He used surpassing gifts of innate sympathy to find a new presidential style of relating to the public and to forge an extraordinary connection with ordinary Americans, especially minorities.[345]

Sharing a view of Fred Greenstein, Clinton's chief of staff, and budget director Leon Panetta, Clinton's presidency is a tale of two presidencies. One was "obliviously brilliant and extremely capable with the ability to help produce the greatest economy in the history of this country and to focus on major domestic priority and, in effect, protect peace in the world." And the other, added Panetta, "is the darker side, the one that made a terrible human mistake that will forever shadow that other presidency."[346]

---

[345]Purdum, 3.
[346]Ibid.

The Presidency of George W. Bush

Geoge W. Bush decided to run for president because of his triumphs and accomplishments, not because he was the son of a former president and grandson of a deceased senator. Bush gained the confidence to run because he had started at the bottom of the oil business and became a millionaire, distinguished himself as a dynamic and somewhat innovative co-owner of a baseball team, waged a successful underdog campaign against a popular Texas governor, and emerged as a bold and popular governor in his own right.[1] These accomplishments, augmented by a desire to implement big ideas, animated Bush's successful presidential campaign and his assumption of power in January 2001.

EARLY LIFE

George Walker Bush was born on July 6, 1946, in New Haven, Connecticut, the home of his father's alma mater, Yale University, and the state that his grandfather had represented as a U.S. senator.[2] When he was two years old, his parents, George and Barbara Bush, moved to Midland, Texas, to make it in the oil business.[3] Later, he would emphasize Texas and its culture as self-defining, perpetually fending off criticism that he was not authentically Texan. As critics dismissed his formation of an exploratory committee to run for president, Bush countered, "I went to Sam Houston Elementary School in Midland, Texas, and he [Bush Sr.] went to Greenwich Country Day in Connecticut . . . There's a difference between my dad and how he was raised and how I was raised. In Midland, they don't ask, 'What's your pedigree?' they ask, 'Can you hit a baseball?' "[4]

At the age of fifteen, George W. was sent to boarding school at Phillips Academy Andover in Andover, Massachusetts, where his father had attended high school. Though Bush and other students not educated in northeastern schools were heavily challenged by the school's demanding curriculum and harsh discipline, Bush excelled by his senior year; he served as head cheerleader and high commissioner of the intramural stickball league, and is still remembered as a popular member of the class, a somewhat restless young man with a decidedly frivolous orientation to life.[5] But he was also strongly influenced by a gifted history teacher who helped Bush develop a passion for the subject that would continue throughout his academic career and adult years.[6]

---

[1]Robert Draper, *Dead Certain: The Presidency of George W. Bush* (New York: Free Press, 2007), 58.

[2]Michael Kranish, "For George W. Bush, Early Life a Wrangle between East, West," *Boston Globe,* March 28, 1999.

[3]"Frontline: The Choice 2004: George W. Bush: Chronology," http://www.pbs.org/wgbh/pages/ frontline/shows/choice2004/bush/cron.html, accessed June 23, 2009.

[4]Kranish.

[5]Bill Minutaglio, *First Son: George Bush and the Bush Family Dynasty* (New York: Crown, 1999), 66.

[6]George W. Bush, *A Charge to Keep* (New York: William Morrow and Co., 1999), 20.

He continued in his father's footsteps when he chose to matriculate at Yale in 1964.[7] At Yale, Bush struggled to emerge from his father's shadow, and felt intellectually overwhelmed and patronized by the elite culture. He also complained about the heaviness he perceived in the growing anti-war movement and left-leaning tendencies of the Yale student body and faculty.[8] As a result, he put most of his energy into his fraternity, Delta Kappa Epsilon, serving as its president. Indeed, Bush's list of extracurricular activities could have been a copy of his father's—at Yale, he too played baseball and was tapped into the exclusive Skull and Bones secret society as a senior.[9] As Bush's classmate and *New York Times* reporter Steven Weisman notes, "Bush did all the same things as his father—Andover, Yale, baseball, Skull and Bones—but only half as well, a trend that would continue. And knowing he [his father] was a legacy in all things probably ate away at his self-esteem."[10]

Upon graduating from Yale in 1968, Bush immediately enlisted in the Texas Air National Guard. His draft deferment would expire with his college enrollment, and he could avoid being deployed to Vietnam by serving at home. After receiving an early discharge in late 1973, Bush enrolled at the Harvard Business School, and graduated with an MBA in 1975.[11] Harvard Business School helped Bush develop a sense of discipline, which he previously lacked. He thrived in courses that were practical and based on a "case-study approach."[12] Bush enjoyed working with colleagues to solve cases built around questions of marketing, production, and financing.[13] He was particularly fond of a course titled "Human Organizations and Behavior" and fascinated with course content on organizational design, managerial decision making, and corporate–government relations.[14]

Another benefit of the Harvard "case study" method for George W. was its emphasis on the idea that managers could not know everything, and that expertise was dispersed throughout organizations. A leader who tapped into the knowledge of his or her employees, and built a strong team would be a strong leader.[15]

POLITICAL CAREER

After graduating from Harvard, Bush returned to his home of Midland, hoping to make his fortune in the oil business—again, like his father. During this period, his earlier habits caught up with him. He lived a somewhat

---

[7]Minutaglio, 71–72.

[8]Ibid., 80–82.

[9]Zeke Miller, "Bush Shaped by Family Legacy," *Yale Daily News*, January 22, 2009.

[10]Ibid.

[11]Ibid.

[12]Minutaglio, 157.

[13]Ibid.

[14]Ibid.

[15]Donald F. Kettle, *Team Bush: Leadership Lessons from the Bush White House* (New York: McGraw-Hill, 2003), 17.

irresponsible lifestyle, frequently drinking to excess and even facing alcohol-related scrapes with the law.[16] To some, he was well on his way to earning the reputation of a "callow, spoiled, intellectually incurious" brat.[17] Gradually, his life came together; within a few years, he had started his own oil and gas company in Midland and courted teacher and librarian Laura Welch. They married in 1977, when Bush was in the middle of his first congressional campaign.[18] Bush decided to run for Congress to represent the nineteenth congressional district, including Midland and Lubbock, Texas, when incumbent member George H. Mahon decided not to run for re-election. Mahon had been elected to the U.S. House of Representatives in the second year of the New Deal. He was seventy-seven years old, the longest serving house member on Capitol Hill.[19] In his campaign against Jim Reese and Joe Hickox for the GOP nomination, Bush made few specific promises, but called himself a conservative who would work to get the energy industry deregulated and "battle the bureaucratic spread of the federal government that is invading more and more of our lives."[20] Reese had won 45 percent of the vote against Mahon in 1976, and was a strong ally of Ronald Reagan.[21] Nevertheless, Bush won more votes than Reese and prepared himself to face the Democratic candidate, state senator Kent Hance, a fifty-five-year-old graduate of Dimmitt High School, Texas Technological University, and University of Texas Law School.[22] Hance taught law at Texas Tech and related easily to the farmers in his constituency. He played a strong contrast to George Bush, emphasizing his service as a state lawmaker, and his attendance at Texas public schools. He was *not* an elite outsider parading into Texas on nothing more than his dad's name and family connections.[23] Bush lost to Hance by a margin of 53,917–47,497.[24]

After his unsuccessful congressional bid, Bush, unlike Bill Clinton, decided to steer clear of politics for quite some time. He focused on his oil company throughout the 1980s before changing professions in 1989, when he purchased, along with a team of investors, the Texas Rangers baseball team. Contemporaries recount that Bush led admirably during his time at the helm of the Rangers—his childhood passion for the sport translated to an effective management style as the team's owner: "As an owner, Mr. Bush proved himself an outstanding manager, still remembered fondly by players who pitched and

---

[16]Fred Greenstein, *The Presidential Difference: Leadership Styles from FDR to George W. Bush* (Princeton, NJ: Princeton University Press, 2004), 194.

[17]Lou Cannon and Carl M. Cannon, *Reagan's Disciple: George W. Bush's Troubled Quest for a Presidential Legacy* (New York: Public Affairs, 2008), 6.

[18]Biography.com, "George W. Bush Biography," http://www.biography.com/articles/George-W.-Bush-9232768?part=0, accessed June 23, 2009.

[19]Cannon and Cannon, 9.

[20]Minutaglio, 180.

[21]Ibid., 186.

[22]Ibid., 188.

[23]Ibid., 189.

[24]Ibid., 191.

batted for him, by fans he wooed, even by executives he fired."[25] This success prompted him to consider a run in 1994 for Texas governor; as Democratic incumbent Ann Richards' popularity took a downturn in the face of education and budget woes, he became convinced.

Bush's political education had been considerably enhanced when he assumed the role of senior adviser to his dad's successful 1987–1988 presidential race. George W. served as a "loyalty monitor" for the senior Bush and as a bridge to the gathering political force that his dad feared the most and understood the least, the far right wing of the Republican Party, particularly the Christian right.[26] During the race, George W. took an office adjacent to political consultant Lee Atwater. He worked hard to balance team Bush moderate conservatives with hard-right commanders and he prompted some semblance of vision, understandable ideals, and phrases in his father to make him more acceptable to ordinary Americans.[27] George W. enjoyed the role, which also included serving as an emissary for his dad to the southern states and diffusing negative allegations about the senior Bush.[28] Once George H. W. Bush was elected, his son was named head of the "Scrub Team," a secret group that decided who deserved jobs in the White House.[29]

Bush's newfound thirst to succeed in the political arena was quenched as he fought and won a successful gubernatorial campaign against Ann Richards, who apparently underestimated the threat posed to her by the Rangers' owner. Bush adopted "message discipline" as the mantra of his gubernatorial campaign, and his "message" focused on four issues: tort reform, crime, education, and welfare reform. His stands centered on giving local control of education back to school districts, reducing frivolous lawsuits, cutting crime by refusing parole to sex offenders and imposing harsher penalties on juvenile offenders, and slashing welfare rosters.[30] His campaign refused to be thrown off its central messages by Richards' consistent attacks. Although Bush's campaign was forced to contend with allegations of insider trading, concerning an $835,000 sale of Harken Energy Corporation stock he had made in 1990 (two months before Harken announced a loss), nothing came of a Securities and Exchange Commission investigation.[31] Bush won the 1994 race for Texas governor with 53 percent of the vote, coinciding with the 1994 takeover of the

---

[25]Nicholas Kristof, in Lee Banville, "Vote 2004: George W. Bush—Baseball Owner to Governor," Online NewsHour (PBS), http://www.pbs.org/newshour/vote2004/candidates/can_bush-baseball. html, accessed June 24, 2009.

[26]Minutaglio, 210–211.

[27]Ibid., 217.

[28]Ibid., 219.

[29]Ibid., 232.

[30]Ibid., 288.

[31]Brooks Jackson, "Bush as Businessman: How the Texas Governor Made His Millions," CNN. com, May 13, 1999, http://www.cnn.com/ALLPOLITICS/stories/1999/05/13/president.2000/ jackson.bush/, accessed June 30, 2009.

U.S. House of Representatives by the Republican Party under the leadership of Representative Newt Gingrich of Georgia.[32]

Because Bush only focused on a small number of issues in his campaign platform, he was able to follow through on pursuing those initiatives during his tenure as governor. He fulfilled promises for tort reform by narrowing the legal definition of "gross negligence," toughened Texas's juvenile justice laws, such that children as young as fourteen could be tried as adults in Texas courts, and pushed through "concealed carry laws to allow everyone to carry a gun."[33]

Moreover, Bush refused to submit to the apparent shortfalls of his position, as Texas is known for its so-called weak governorship. The state's governor is not allowed to appoint top officials; has little control over agencies (most of which are run by appointed boards whose members' terms last longer than the governor's); and exerts little influence with the lieutenant governor, who is elected independently, can belong to a different political party, and has strong control over the Texas legislature. Bush's remarkable feat, as a result, was shepherding legislation through this system without having much official power to do so. As Chris Suellentrop of *Slate* magazine put it, Bush was "the most powerful politician in Texas. Personal charisma, a hefty electoral mandate, and the cooperation of the legislature can augment the power of any governor. Bush had all three, and he has used them to persuade the legislature to enact incremental portions of his agenda."[34] Even some Texas Democrats praised Bush for his willingness to reach across party lines on issues such as education reform.[35] In particular, he developed an effective working relationship with the lieutenant governor, Bob Bullock, a Democrat who was a nonconventional and somewhat colorful political powerhouse in Austin.[36]

Some, however, call Bush's Texas record misleading; Texas journalist Wayne Slater notes that "in fact, Bush's biggest defeat as governor was on education . . . he failed, and he failed in part because the plan that he pushed . . . failed with his own Republicans in the House and Senate."[37] Slater also notes that it was Bush's intense determination that allowed him to be perceived as successful in an area where he failed. "Spend the political capital that I'd gained in order to do something that's truly meaningful. That is to lower property taxes dramatically and put real money and change the education

---

[32]Draper, 136.

[33]Biography.com; and Grover Norquist, "Bush as Governor," *Frontline: The Choice 2004,* http://www.pbs.org/wgbh/pages/frontline/shows/choice2004/bush/governor.html, accessed July 2, 2009.

[34]Chris Suellentrop, "Is George W. Bush a 'Weak' Governor?" *Slate,* January 5, 2000, http://www.slate.com/id/1004307/, accessed July 2, 2009.

[35]Alison Mitchell, "Bush's Bipartisanship Would Face Tough Test," *New York Times,* April 28, 2000.

[36]Minutaglio, 295.

[37]Wayne Slater, "Bush as Governor," *Frontline: The Choice 2004,* http://www.pbs.org/wgbh/pages/frontline/shows/choice2004/bush/governor.html, accessed July 1, 2009.

system of Texas," Slater recounts Bush as saying.[38] Because he had such a strong vision, Bush was respected even in the face of his major defeats. In fact, though Bush did present the Texas legislature with bills lowering property tax rates and reforming education, he allowed them to be so altered by legislative opponents that the passed bills only subtly resembled the proposals Bush had originally put forth. In its highly altered form, his property tax bill amounted to only "modest relief."[39] His education bill, which advocated for some level of teacher and student accountability based on success or failure, was nevertheless changed in intent.[40] Yet, Bush still claimed responsibility for what happened in the Texas education system as a result of the bill—its system of punishment and reward for schools that lowered or raised their students' test scores helped raise scores in general and narrow the performance gap between white and minority students. State officials dubbed the reform the "Texas miracle." In an ironic parallel to Clinton, Bush became the "education governor" in his eyes and those of his constituents because of his passion for the topic. He carried this passion into the White House, passing a major education reform bill called No Child Left Behind.

Like his father, Bush relied on personal connections and relationships to lead; however, those human elements were backed up by his determined efforts to fulfill his vision. His firm, even idealistic beliefs on issues such as education and immigration reform shored up political support and made him seem more proactive. Unlike his father, who dismissed the "vision thing," George W. embraced the notion of visionary leadership in governance. He was very much persuaded by messages of personal responsibility and attacks on the welfare state embedded in the works of academics such as David Horowitz and Myron Magnet, authors whom Karl Rove acquainted him with.[41]

His leadership style proved popular in Texas, and Bush was re-elected to the governorship in 1998, easily defeating the Democratic candidate, Gary Mauro. Mauro had served as the Texas land commissioner for sixteen years, and had chaired President Clinton's campaign in Texas.[42] By 1999, Bush was widely considered as a possible Republican nominee for the 2000 presidential election cycle. Major publications such as *Time*, the *Christian Science Monitor*, and the *Boston Globe* took note of him, not so much for the scope of his ideological vision as the blossoming bipartisan approach he seemed to embrace. Nevertheless, some swooning Democrats, baby boomers, and moderate Republicans began to worry when Governor Bush defended large health maintenance organizations, said that Texas might consider requiring children to pay their parents' nursing home bills currently covered by Medicaid, opposed environmental regulations, and blasted proposals to help minority

---

[38]Ibid.
[39]Ibid.
[40]Ibid.
[41]Minutaglio, 289–290.
[42]Karen Hughes, *Ten Minutes from Normal* (New York: Viking Press, 2008), 102.

firms earn state contracts.[43] But the momentum toward his nomination was strong. Even before Bush officially formed a presidential exploratory committee in mid-1999, a tremendous groundswell of Republican support catapulted Bush into the presidential limelight almost without any action on his part; even by February 1999, he maintained that family considerations might prevent him from being involved in the 2000 race. In early 1999, over half of the country's Republican governors mobilized in support of Bush without his making any sort of official plans. The *Washington Post* called the mobilization "completely unprecedented."[44] Sensing his chances, Bush began meeting with advisers on domestic and foreign policy—including Stanford University academic heavyweights Condoleezza Rice and Michael Boskin—in Austin in 1998, months before officially announcing his candidacy. He announced his intention to form a presidential exploratory committee in early March 1999, and his solid phalanx of Republican supporters only continued to grow. Within weeks, Bush's fund-raising had soared above that of his Republican opponents; by April, he had raised more than $7.6 million.[45] Within months, GOP house leaders were so assured of a Bush victory in the Republican primary that they set up meetings with him to discuss a common agenda for the 2000 campaign season.[46] Contemporary political analysts cite Bush's pedigree and strong Texan record as a self-styled "compassionate conservative"—combining "country-club Republican" agendas such as tax cuts with social concern for the downtrodden—as reasons for the great deal of enthusiasm that accompanied his rise to fame.[47]

Yet as Bush's campaign became almost inevitable, his positions remained vague. Bush refused to answer any questions about his positions on domestic policy until after the Texas legislature finished its summer session. On the issues he would speak about, mostly related to initiatives he had championed while working in Texas, Bush seemed to represent the compassionate conservative. Though he had embraced the traditionally Republican goal of lowering taxes, Bush also had a record of spending large amounts of government money on education reform, a decidedly liberal pursuit. As he put it at the Republican debate in Des Moines, Iowa, in December 1999:

> My policies and my programs have been conservative with compassionate results, and that's the kind of president I'm going to be. I want to keep our economy growing by cutting the taxes. I want to be a free trade

[43]Minutaglio, 304.

[44]Dan Balz and David S. Broder, "Many GOP Governors Early to Back Bush; Early Support Could Be Critical for the Race," *Washington Post,* February 23, 1999.

[45]Don Van Natta Jr., "Bush, with $7.6 Million in Donations, Eclipses Rivals for G.O.P. Nomination," *New York Times,* April 16, 1999.

[46]Richard L. Berke, "House GOP Backs Bush and Pursues a Common Agenda," *New York Times,* May 7, 1999.

[47]Editorial Board, "The Fight in George Bush's Future," *New York Times,* March 3, 1999; and see Marvin Olasky, *Compassionate Conservatism: What It Is, What It Does, and How It Can Change America* (New York: Free Press, 2000).

president so that Iowa farmers can sell their products all across the world. I want to strengthen and save Social security. I want every child to be educated and not one single child be left behind in this great country.[48]

This winning combination pushed Bush's fund-raising efforts as high as they could go; in late 1999, having raised $37 million and the support of a large majority of the elected officials in his party, Bush chose to forego receiving public funds (and the spending limits they carried with them).[49] The momentum of his position as the Republican favorite helped him win the Iowa caucuses with 41 percent of the vote. Bush's favored status, however, began to falter in the New Hampshire primary where Senator John McCain of Arizona staged an upset, beating Bush by almost twenty points. McCain, who had a strong reputation as a maverick, supplied always-independent New Hampshire voters with an even more balanced and moderate shade of Bush's compassionate tint of Republican values. He differed from Bush on issues such as campaign finance reform, arguing for more limits on donations and spending. McCain labeled Bush's passion for slashing taxes across the board as illogical, calling instead for smaller, targeted tax cuts. In addition, McCain was a celebrated war hero who had been imprisoned for several years during the Vietnam War and had written popular books about courage.[50]

Political journalists theorize that Bush's loss in New Hampshire was just the kind of slap in the face Bush needed to jolt him out of complacency and give him the drive he needed to wage a successful campaign for the next nine months. The Bush campaign worked night and day to soundly defeat McCain in their next direct contest: the South Carolina primary. Here, the campaign's tactics became harsher, in part due to one of Bush's most trusted political advisers, Karl Rove, whom Bush had met during the 1970s. By that time, Rove had established a reputation as a "political wizard" inside Texas political circles and was particularly known for his tough but effective campaign tactics.[51]

Journalists Wayne Slater and James Moore argue that Rove, who had been working with Bush since the early 1990s, engineered Bush's entire political career. Even at that early date Rove claimed he saw the White House in the baseball club–owner's future. It was Rove who felt he had been personally beaten in New Hampshire, and it was Rove who encouraged Bush's two-pronged campaign strategy in South Carolina: the first, tamer tactic painted McCain as a Washington insider and Bush as the reforming cowboy, galloping a white horse to clean up the city; the second was somewhat more

---

[48]John T. Woolley and Gerhard Peters, *The American Presidency Project* [online], University of California (hosted), Gerhard Peters (database), Santa Barbara, http://www.presidency.ucsb.edu/ws/?pid=76120 July 9, 2009.

[49]Robert V. Friedenberg, *Notable Speeches by Contemporary Presidential Campaigns* (Westport, CT: Praeger Publications, 2002), 230.

[50]See John McCain, *Worth the Fighting For: The Education of an American Maverick, and the Heroes Who Inspired Him* (New York: Random House, 2003).

[51]Minutaglio, 167.

underhanded.[52] Bush's polling company initiated a series of so-called push polls, a series of questions designed to implicate McCain in embarrassing (and false) scenarios. Richard H. Davis, McCain's campaign manager, noted a particularly invidious poll that McCain's opponents used to imply that McCain's adopted Bangladeshi daughter was in fact an illegitimate child he had fathered with a black woman.[53] Others claimed that McCain's wife, Cindy, was a drug addict.[54] Though nobody ever claimed that Bush was involved with that particular poll, there is no denying that his campaign was heavily on the offensive in South Carolina. He flouted his credentials as a southern social conservative and employed the services of his supporter organizations such as the National Rifle Association to supplement his strategies.[55] When a group of Vietnam veterans decided to attack McCain on the issue of withholding financial support for veterans, Bush did nothing to distance himself or his campaign from the attacks. It was more than ironic that McCain, who was captured and tortured in Vietnam, would be the object of attacks by disgruntled war veterans.[56] Bush's intense campaign focus paid off, and he beat McCain by eleven points in the South Carolina primary; though later losses in Michigan, among other states, would continue to remind the Bush campaign that McCain was not the easiest competition to sweep under the rug, a decisive nationwide win on Super Tuesday in March 2000 assured Bush of the Republican nomination. McCain called him to concede the Republican nomination a few days later.

Echoes of Bush's priorities and campaign strategies are evident in his August 2000 speech accepting the nomination at the Republican National Convention. Bush helped design the look of the convention to reflect a more diverse, compassionate Republican Party, and included several ethnic and racial minorities on the podium, and even an AIDS activist addressed the convention. As he had in Texas governors' races, Bush chose his policy issues for the general election carefully, not wanting to veer into areas of discussion where he might be perceived as weaker than his opponent. The speech drew attention to what Bush perceived as weakness in American military forces, excessively high tax rates, and the "soft bigotry of low expectations" of a poor system of public education.[57] Bush largely withheld criticism of the Clinton-Gore record; such a criticism would have been futile in the context of the era's strong economy. In fact, all the initiatives that Bush's speech proposed employed the use of surplus funds generated by the Clinton administration: "the surplus," he proclaimed, "is not the government's money. The surplus is the people's money."[58]

---

[52]James Moore and Wayne Slater, *Bush's Brain* (Hoboken, NJ: John Wiley and Sons, 2003), 256.

[53]Richard H. Davis, "The Anatomy of a Smear Campaign," *Boston Globe*, March 21, 2004.

[54]Moore and Slater, 257.

[55]Friedenberg, 233.

[56]Draper, 72–78.

[57]Woolley and Peters.

[58]Ibid.

Bush and Rove realized the challenges ahead of them: The Clinton-Gore team had presided over one of the most widespread and sustained periods of economic growth in the twentieth century. In fact, the growth rate of the economy, the general prosperity Americans were enjoying, and the continued popularity of President Clinton (in spite of scandal) all pointed toward an easy Gore victory.[59] Every single political model in existence predicted that Gore had all advantages over any Republican incumbent regardless of pedigree, likability, or compassion.[60] As a result, the Bush campaign steered clear of focusing on major policy issues such as the economy, and attempted to make the campaign about character. Bush and Rove again used their push polling techniques to degrade national opinions of Gore, and the campaign became quite heated.[61] Sticking to his guns, Bush temporarily dodged questions of policy, repeatedly implying that voters simply ought to trust his personal abilities to achieve the right results. In response to a question about his experience with foreign policy and how effective he would be as president, Bush said "that voters should simply trust him . . . 'Until I'm the president, it's going to be hard for me to verify that I think I'll be more effective.' "[62] Though the strategy seems simplistic, it was effective given the fact that popular sentiment on policy was so in line with the Clinton-Gore record of success: personality was the only weakness of the Clinton record in voters' minds, both because of Clinton's recent sex scandals and because of Al Gore's oft-derided robotic personality. Bush hinted that he would replicate the leadership strategies of his father, who had built a leadership career based on the development of strong personal relationships. He also suggested that the former president himself would be an asset to a George W. Bush administration. As Bush attempted to defend his claim that he could raise the American oil supply, the *New York Times* wrote, "implicit was that as the son of the president who built the coalition that drove the Iraqis out of Kuwait, Mr. Bush would be able to establish ties on a personal level that would persuade oil-producing nations that they owed the United States something in return."[63]

Yet, as the *Washington Post* noted in an October 2000 article about Bush's leadership style, it remained unclear whether Bush's successes in navigating Texan politics could translate to the national stage: "In Texas, where the legislature meets only once every two years and the governorship is a constitutionally weak office, focusing on a few big issues makes sense. A president doesn't often have that luxury."[64] But Bush only focused on a few big issues in the general

---

[59]James E. Campbell, "The 2000 Presidential Election of George W. Bush: The Difficult Birth of a Presidency," in John Kraus, Kevin J. McMahon, and David M. Rankin, eds., *Transformed by Crisis: The Presidency of George W. Bush and American Politics* (New York: Palgrave Macmillan, 2004).

[60]Moore and Slater, 261–262.

[61]Ibid., 263.

[62]Katharine Q. Seelye, "The 2000 Campaign: The Texas Governor; Bush Would Use Power of Persuasion to Raise Oil Supply," *New York Times*, June 28, 2000.

[63]Ibid.

[64]Dan Balz and Terry M. Neal, "Questions, Clues, and Contradiction; Bush and White House: How Do They Match Up?" *New York Times*, October 22, 2000.

election, attempting to diminish their importance in comparison to the character argument he was painting. In addition to championing education reform, tax cuts, and military spending, Bush advocated for new Social Security rules and nuclear arms policies. Wrote the *Times*, "In contrast to Clinton, who loved the give-and-take of policy debate but who often agonized over decisions, Bush may be less knowledgeable, less interested and less committed to the details of his own proposals. But when he puts his mind to it, he might also be a far crisper decision maker."[65] This stood in sharp contrast to the view of his opponent: Al Gore. Whereas Bush seemed content to deflect in-depth policy inquiries with reassurances and reiterations of his campaign's basic message, Gore "appear[ed] overly eager to impress voters with his breadth of knowledge."[66] As a result, Bush pulled ahead of Gore in the polls. In addition, Gore chose to orient his election around a prospective (future-oriented) theme, and not on a retrospective strategy. Instead of celebrating the accomplishment of the Clinton-Gore administration, including a robust economy and a decline in unemployment and crime, Gore chose to look forward and promised a fairer, better America. This proved to be a strategic error on his part.[67]

Indeed, it was Gore's attention to detail that turned the first debate between the two candidates into a game of numbers. Perhaps trying to chastise Bush for his vague policy positions, Gore initiated the debate by going into a detailed description of his tax cut plan and prompted Bush to do the same. When Bush was able to do so, the entire debate evolved into a mathematical jousting match, with each candidate trying to explain exactly why the particulars of his plan were better for the American people. As Bush and Gore shouted about differences in tax plans, health care, and Social Security (Gore's insistence that he would put Social Security funds in a "lockbox" became fodder for late-night talk shows), the idea that Bush would falter in debate with Gore began to lose credence. In fact, although a *Washington Post* article that came out immediately after the first debate argued that its lack of serious gaffes by either candidate changed the election little, poll numbers indicated the opposite.[68] Gallup, CNN, and ABC News polls all conducted in late September and early October before the debate showed Gore with a slight-to-moderate lead over Bush. After the debate, however, Bush regained the lead he had held since January.[69] He had been able to cultivate an advantage over Gore by playing to his conservative stance on wedge issues in certain instances: guns, abortion, and the environment.[70] According to Moore and Slater, Rove reasoned that

---

[65]Campbell, 20.

[66]Ibid.

[67]Ibid., 21.

[68]Dan Balz, "Debate Changes Little; Both Sides Agree Flaws Emerged," *Washington Post,* October 5, 2000.

[69]"White House 2000: Trial Heats," PollingReport.com, http://www.pollingreport.com/wh2gen1.htm, accessed July 22, 2009.

[70]Moore and Slater, 265.

these topics would serve Bush well in key battleground states such as Michigan and Pennsylvania, and even in usually Democratic enclaves such as West Virginia.[71]

In addition, Bush's generalist strategy seemed to play well with many Americans, who viewed Gore's presentation of detailed plans for Social Security and foreign policy as stuffy and arrogant. Though Gore may have outscored Bush on policy issues in the debates, many considered him to have performed badly in the first two of three debates. In the first, he was criticized for his overly aggressive and condescending attitude toward Bush's answers, often sighing audibly in the middle of his opponent's responses; in the second, he retreated into a shy shell of quiescence.[72] Yet, Gore's performance in the third debate helped him rebound to some extent. Said one California Democrat, "[The third debate] was the first night that I felt Gore's tendency to be more specific helped him and Bush's tendency to speak in generalities did not work. For example, when someone asked what you would [do] about the Mideast crisis, that seemed to stump Bush."[73] Thus Bush's character-centric strategy—which had gotten him through the first two debates—finally started to crack. Nevertheless, many believed that Bush came out of the debates having gained more than Gore. "I think Bush gained the most of them just by surviving," noted Democratic strategist David Axelrod, "There was an unrealistic expectation among some Democrats that Gore would just grind him in the dust and that Bush would be tongue-tied and tearful."[74]

The race remained a dead heat. An October 20 article in the *New York Times* noted that Democratic leaders continued to ridicule Bush both for his performance in the debates and for his frequent verbal gaffes. But the public wasn't buying it. As Election Day approached, Bush maintained his narrow lead over Gore, but in most instances the difference between the two candidates remained within the margin of error.[75]

Unfortunately—both for the candidates and for the country—the tight battle between the two candidates was not resolved on election night. The race had been too close to call when most Americans went to bed on Tuesday night, November 7. When they woke up the next morning, nothing had changed. The election results controversy centered on the state of Florida and its twenty-five Electoral College votes. Major television networks, using their accepted exit polling techniques and algorithms, declared Florida as going to Vice President Gore shortly after the polls closed, at 8 PM. Later that night, however, the networks retracted their predictions before eventually declaring

---

[71]Ibid.

[72]Naftali Bendavid and Bob Kempner, "Candidates Combative in Final Matchup; More Relaxed Format Stimulates Clash over Spending, Health Care," *Chicago Tribune,* October 18, 2000.

[73]Rusty Cundieff, "The Presidential Debate; What They Liked, What They Didn't; a Sampling of Viewpoints from Informed Voters," *Los Angeles Times,* October 18, 2000.

[74]Richard L. Berke, "Debates Put in Focus Images and Reality," *New York Times,* October 19, 2000.

[75]http://www.pollingreport.com/wh2gen1.htm.

Bush the winner of Florida—and, therefore, the presidency—early the next morning. Though Gore called Bush to concede, Bush's lead in Florida began to narrow as more votes were counted; the final tally was so close that an existing Florida state law forced an automatic statewide recount. Gore reversed his concession, and when the second recount also did not go in his favor, he initiated a thirty-five-day legal battle to determine the true winner of the state's electoral votes.[76]

For more than a month, the identity of the forty-third president remained a mystery as both candidates lacked the 270 electoral votes necessary to secure the position—Bush had 246, Gore had 266. The state of Florida became a media circus. After the automatic machine recount ended on November 9, Bush's lead had narrowed to under 350 votes. Vice President Gore, sensing that continued appeals could turn the election in his favor, called attention to voting irregularities in several Democratic counties. In Palm Beach County, a confusing ballot layout may have caused thousands of voters intending to vote for Gore to mistakenly vote for conservative Pat Buchanan; in primarily African American precincts, reports emerged that some were denied the right to vote due to incorrect voter registration lists. On November 9, Gore requested manual hand recounts of all ballots in four Florida counties, and Bush's lawsuit to block the recounts was thrown out by a Florida court. Nevertheless, Florida's secretary of state, Katherine Harris, elected to officially certify the vote tally that did not include any results that had been part of the hand recount. The Florida Supreme Court ordered Harris, a Bush supporter, to extend the certification deadline to November 20 so that all hand recounts could be completed; however, when they were slightly late in arriving, Harris certified the original machine recount voting results.[77]

Gore sued. Meanwhile, Bush's suit contesting the Florida Supreme Court's decision to allow many manual recounts had arrived at the U.S. Supreme Court. In *Bush v. Palm Beach County Canvassing Board, et al.,* the high court ruled that the Florida Supreme Court had not adequately justified its decision to extend the vote certification deadline and allow time for hand recounts in the first place: essentially, the court asked the Floridians to explain their ruling.[78] Gore's options were dwindling, despite the many suspected voting irregularities. As manual recounts proceeded, vote-counters were held to varying, inconsistent standards of what constituted a vote; Florida's punch card ballots, which sometimes had not been completely perforated by voters, became a nationwide dinner-table discussion as Americans considered whether a vote was legal if a piece of paper, or chad, was hanging off the ballot, or merely dimpled by a voting stylus. Nevertheless, Gore, who aimed to continue recounting contested votes in Miami-Dade and Palm Beach counties, still had

---

[76]For a blow-by-blow summary of the events in Florida, see Correspondents of *The New York Times, 36 Days: The Complete Chronicle of the 2000 Presidential Election Crisis* (New York: Henry Holt, 2001).

[77]Ibid.

[78]*Bush v. Palm Beach County Canvassing Board, et al.,* 531 U.S. 70 (2000).

an appeal progressing through the judicial system. The Florida Supreme Court again ruled in Gore's favor, ordering a statewide recount of 14,000 "under-vote" ballots that had not been acknowledged in the machine recount.[79]

Bush again appealed, and the U.S. Supreme Court agreed with him. In their 5–4 ruling in *Bush v. Gore*, the majority wrote that the manual recount process was too onerous to complete before the December 12 national deadline for states to appoint their slate of electors. They also noted that voters' rights under the Equal Protection Clause were being violated because not all counties or precincts statewide received the same close scrutiny as the ballots in Miami-Dade and Palm Beach counties would under this recount. "The idea that one group can be granted greater voting strength than another is hostile to the one man, one vote basis of our representative government," they cited.[80] All recounts in the state of Florida were halted. Yet, dissenters were bitter. Noted Justice John Paul Stevens, "One thing . . . is certain. Although we may never know with complete certainty the identity of the winner of this year's Presidential election, the identity of the loser is perfectly clear. It is the Nation's confidence in the judge as an impartial guardian of the rule of law."[81] The majority, however, disagreed:

> None are more conscious of the vital limits on judicial authority than are the members of this Court, and none stand more in admiration of the Constitution's design to leave the selection of the President to the people, through their legislatures, and to the political sphere. When contending parties invoke the process of the courts, however, it becomes our unsought responsibility to resolve the federal and constitutional issues the judicial system has been forced to confront.[82]

The Supreme Court therefore effectively gave George Bush Florida's twenty-five electoral votes, and the presidency.

The election of 2000 was the first in which the winner of the electoral vote failed to win a plurality of the popular vote.Although George W. Bush received 271 electoral votes to Gore's 266, Gore received 50.26 percent of the national popular vote to 49.73 percent.[83]

POLICY

Though hardly an intellectual in orientation, and frequently skeptical about "heavy" ideas and philosophical musings, George W. Bush embraced the idea of visionary leadership. Although his experience in politics during his younger days was primarily mechanical—getting people elected, imposing discipline on

---

[79]Correspondents of *The New York Times*.

[80]*Moore v. Ogilvy*, 394 U.S. 814 (1969) in *Bush v. Gore*, 531 U.S. 98 (2000).

[81]John Paul Stevens, dissenting in *Bush v. Gore*, 531 U.S. 98 (2000).

[82]*Bush v. Gore*, 531 U.S. 98 (2000).

[83]Campbell, 9.

campaigns, building personal relationships—he developed an attraction to numerous core political beliefs and to reflect a leadership vision.

On domestic policy, his core belief was compassionate conservatism, an expression he used frequently and an identity he pursued avidly. According to Bush adviser Marvin Olasky, "compassionate conservatism is neither an easy slogan nor one immune from vehement attack. It is a full-fledged program with a carefully considered philosophy."[84] Olasky explained that the word *compassion* literally means *suffering with*, reflecting the close personal tie of a caring individual and a person in distress.[85] Conservatives believe that compassion is not the monopoly of government institutions, but resides in the hearts and actions of private, frequently religious people and groups. Indeed, in Olasky's previous publication, *The Tragedy of American Compassion*, he showed how, long before the federal government's involvement, thousands of local, faith-based charitable agencies and churches around the country waged a war on poverty more successful than the government's later attempts.

To Olasky, faith-based groups helped millions out of poverty with the detailed knowledge and flexibility needed to administer a combination of loving compassion and rigorous discipline needed to improve peoples' lives.[86] The approach of government welfare programs, on the other hand, was to provide assistance without compassion. Government assistance, according to Olasky, is stingy, because it allows Americans to salve U.S. consciences even as they scrimp on what the destitute need the most—love, time, and challenge.[87]

The Tragedy of American Compassion did not achieve best-seller status, but George W. Bush became aware of the book while preparing to run for governor of Texas. In 1993, Bush and Rove met with Olasky to discuss the policy implications of the book. Bush showed a good understanding of the history of poverty fighting, according to Olasky, and asked questions that went to the heart of issues.[88]

Other conservative leaders, including former U.S. Secretary of Education Bill Bennett and John Fund of the *Wall Street Journal*, also became aware of *The Tragedy of American Compassion*, at the same time the Republicans captured the U.S. House of Representatives for the first time in forty years under the leadership of Georgia congressman Newt Gingrich.[89] Former professor Gingrich recommended Olasky's book as assigned reading to members of Congress. That same year, George W. Bush became governor of Texas.

In Bush's first year as governor, a state agency had to shut down a Christian anti-drug organization that was effective because of its refusal to obey state requirements that counselors have extensive training in

---

[84]Olasky, 1.

[85]Ibid., 2.

[86]Ibid., 4.

[87]Ibid.

[88]Ibid., 5.

[89]Ibid.

anti-addiction techniques. Three hundred of the group's drug-free alumni demonstrated "with great Texas resonance" at the Alamo, and the *Wall Street Journal* covered the event. Letters poured out of Governor Bush's office asking him to call off the regulatory "dogs." He did so, and subsequently proposed (and in 1997 succeeded in passing) legislation to pen them up permanently.[90] Moreover, Bush issued an executive order making Texas the first state to establish the option of using private and religious charities to distribute welfare services.[91] He set up an equal competition for religious and non-religious groups to bid on Texas social services contracts, abstinence education grants, and poverty-fighting initiatives. He made Texas the first state to permit a state prison to be run by a ministry. And he recommended and signed a law requiring government agencies to develop welfare-to-work partnerships with faith-based groups in a way that respects those groups' religious characters.[92]

When Governor George W. Bush ran for re-election in 1998, he spoke in a conservative manner about how some Americans had replaced responsibility for self with blame of others.[93] He noted that Washington was only too happy to take up responsibility that people sought to shed, and to exact massive, bureaucratic programs of national assistance, which caused further erosion of the civic institutions that had once given assistance to promote moral accountability.[94] Bush opined that a minimizing of personal responsibility had pushed America toward a moral and spiritual crisis with familiar symptoms: broken families, teen drug abuse and pregnancy, crime, and civic disengagement.[95]

Bush offered his understanding of compassionate conservatism shortly after his successful 1998 race for governor: "It is conservative to cut taxes," he said, "and it is compassionate to help people save and grow and build."[96] He continued, "conservative to reform welfare, compassionate to encourage charity. Conservative to set challenging educational standards, compassionate to make sure no child is left behind."[97]

On February 26, 1999, Governor Bush invited some of the country's best thinkers on the subject of compassionate conservatism—Bob Woodson from Washington, James Q. Wilson from California, John Diuilo from Princeton, and Indianapolis mayor Steve Goldsmith—to Austin for a three-hour meeting dedicated to considering the policy implications of compassionate conservatism.[98] On the basis of these discussions, Bush made an announcement on July 22, 1999, "in every instance where my administration sees a responsibility

---

[90]Ibid., 8.
[91]Ibid.
[92]Ibid., 9.
[93]Ibid., 11.
[94]Ibid.
[95]Ibid.
[96]Ibid., 13.
[97]Ibid.
[98]Ibid., 13–14.

to help people, we will look first to faith-based organizations, charities, and community groups that have shown this belief to save and change lives."[99] He praised the work of religious groups and promised to never "ask an organization to compromise its core values and spiritual mission to get the help it needs."[100]Governor Bush pledged specific institutional innovations, including a "compassion capital fund" to identify grand ideas for transforming neighborhoods and seed money for helping them.[101]

Bush carried these ideas with him to the White House. In an early presidential initiative, he established a White House Office of Faith-Based and Community Initiatives (OFBCI) to facilitate the use of federal funds for social purposes to be administered by faith-based organizations.[102] The initial focus of the office was the promotion of H.R. 7, a legislative proposal to ease government restrictions on religious organizations so that faith-based groups could more easily provide government services, such as day care and alcohol-abuse rehabilitation. Republicans and Democrats deliberated constitutional questions about financial assistance to religious institutions that provide government services; nonetheless, the House passed the president's initiative. On the other hand, the Senate version differed substantially from H.R. 7, and the OFBCI was forced to shift its focus to a less controversial legislative goal—tax incentives for charitable giving.[103]

Closely tied to his belief in compassionate conservatism was Bush's rejection of many of the tenants of the Great Society and the welfare state. Like Reagan, Bush strongly embraced lower taxation and less government regulation. He was strongly influenced by the negative view of the 1960s expressed by Professor David Horowitz in his book, *Destructive Generation: Second Thoughts about the 60's*. Karl Rove introduced Bush to the book, and he quickly identified with its messages.[104]

It was not surprising, therefore, that President Bush's first and largest legislative initiative was to propose an enormous tax cut—$1.6 trillion over ten years that included reducing top brackets, eliminating the estate tax, reducing the marriage penalty, and increasing child credits. Although Democrats objected to the proposal, arguing most benefits would go to the relatively well-off and that the considerable reduction in revenues would shrink the projected surpluses, the House passed Bush's plan. After negotiation, the Senate went along with the House and voted for an only slightly smaller $1.35 trillion cut.[105]

---

[99]Ibid., 14.

[100]Ibid., 15.

[101]Ibid.

[102]James P. Pfiffner, "Introduction: Assessing the Bush Presidency," in Gary L. Gregg II and Mark J. Rozell, eds., *Considering the Bush Presidency* (New York: Oxford University Press, 2004), 4.

[103]CARE Act, S. 1924. Kathryn Dunn Tenpas and Stephen Hess, "Organizing the Bush Presidency," in Gregg and Rozell, 41.

[104]Minutaglio, 108.

[105]Pfiffner, 2004, 4.

A final aspect of President George W. Bush's domestic vision was his belief in market solutions and business principles in government programs; he was, after all, the nation's first MBA president.[106] Perhaps the strongest expression of this belief occurred in his unsuccessful attempt to privatize Social Security by setting aside a portion of contributions to the surplus for private investment in personal retirement accounts, allowing Americans to make their own investment decisions. But the business perspective is also seen in his successful legislative effort to reform American education, known as the No Child Left Behind act, which mandated testing students in grades 3 and 8 in reading and mathematics and making schools accountable for the results—well-performing schools would be rewarded while poor ones were penalized.

In foreign policy, Bush did not express a particularly strong vision during the campaign, other than suggest we ought to have a humble approach and to dismiss the alleged obsession of the Democratic party with "nation-building." Perhaps an early view of Bush's foreign policy inclinations can be found in a 1999 speech he gave at the Reagan Presidential Library while running for president. The themes he expressed in the speech presaged some of the principles of his subsequent leadership in the national security area. In the 1999 speech, Bush used the following phrases: "The empire [Soviet Union] has passed but evil remains"; "America has determined enemies who hate our values"; "we must protect our homeland and our allies against missiles and terror"; "in defense of our nation, a president must be a clear-eyed realist."[107]

Bush's inclinations were transformed into strong policy directives and preferences on September 11, 2001, the day radical Islamic terrorists attacked the World Trade Center and the Pentagon. Almost 3,000 people died in the attacks, and according to political scientist James Pfiffner, "thus were world history, international relations, American politics, and the Bush presidency transformed within minutes."[108]

Bush took strong control of events and planned the American response with confidence and effectiveness. He conducted a largely successful military operation in Afghanistan where the radical Taliban regime was harboring al Qaeda terrorists and the group's leader, Osama bin Laden; provided swift and generous relief to New York City; initiated several legislative proposals to keep Americans safe; and presented himself with eloquence and passion to a nation that had been dubious about his leadership skills.[109] The public rewarded Bush handsomely for his impressive performance after 9/11. His public approval rating rose from 51 percent on September 7–10 to 86 percent on

---

[106]James P. Pfiffner, "The First MBA President: George Bush as Public Administrator," *Public Administration Review*, January/February 2007, 67.

[107]Stanley A. Renshon, "The Bush Doctrine Considered," in Stanley A. Renshon and Peter Suedfeld, eds., *Understanding the Bush Doctrine: Psychology and Strategy in an Age of Terrorism* (New York: Routledge, 2007), 12–13.

[108]Pfiffner, 2007, 5.

[109]Gary L. Gregg II, "Dignified Authenticity: George W. Bush and the Symbolic Presidency," in Gregg and Rozell.

September 14–15.[110] An October 9, 2001, ABC News poll put the president's approval rating at 92 percent, the highest level recorded since polling on the subject began in 1938.[111]

Along with his display of strong leadership skills, Bush's vision was quickly developing in these trying and troubling days. Encouraged by a group of military hawks surrounding him—notably Vice President Dick Cheney, Secretary of Defense Donald Rumsfeld, and Deputy Secretary of Defense Paul Wolfowitz, who were known as "the Vulcans"[112]—Bush conceptualized a broader security threat to the United States than the one represented by the al Qaeda terrorists. In his January 29, 2002, State of the Union address before a joint session of Congress, Bush stated that due to the valiant efforts of the American military and the proud spirit of the American people, "we are winning the war on terror."[113] But he cautioned that the war on terror was "only beginning . . . thousands of dangerous killers, schooled in the methods of murder, often supported by outlaw regimes, are now spread throughout the world like ticking time-bombs, set to go off without warning."[114] The president outlined two specific goals: (1) "to shut down terrorist camps, disrupt terrorist plans, and bring terrorists to justice" and (2) "to prevent regions that sponsor terror from threatening America or our friends and allies with weapons of mass destruction." He went on:

> Some of these regimes have been pretty quiet since September the 11th, but we know their true nature. North Korea is a regime arming with missiles and weapons of mass destruction, while starving its citizens. Iran aggressively pursues these weapons and exports terror, while an unelected few repress the Iranian people's hope for freedom. Iraq continues to flaunt its hostility toward America and to support terror. The Iraqi regime has plotted to develop anthrax and nerve gas and nuclear weapons for over a decade. This is a regime that has already used poison gas to murder thousands of its own citizens . . . This is a regime that agreed to international inspections, then kicked out the inspectors . . . . States like these and their terrorist allies constitute an axis of evil, arming to threaten the peace of the world. By seeking weapons of mass destruction, these regimes pose a grave and growing danger . . . The price of indifference would be catastrophic.[115]

In identifying the three nations as part of an "axis of evil," Bush was trying to persuade the American people, and Congress, that they would have

---

[110]Pfiffner, 2007, 5.

[111]Kettle, 67.

[112]See James Mann, *The Rise of the Vulcans: The History of Bush's War Cabinet* (New York: Viking, 2004).

[113]George W. Bush, "Address before a Joint Session of the Congress in the State of the Union," in *Public Papers of the Presidents of the United States, January 29, 2002, George Bush. Book I: January 1–June 30, 2002* (Washington, D.C.: Government Printing Office, 2004), 130.

[114]Ibid.

[115]Ibid., 131.

to take action to *prevent* rogue nations from doing harm to the United States. Foreshadowing an imminent re-alignment of American foreign policy, Bush made his point in clear terms: "We'll be deliberate; yet, time is not on our side. I will not wait on events while dangers gather. I will not stand by as peril draws closer and closer. The United States of America will not permit the world's most dangerous regimes to threaten us with the world's most destructive weapons."[116] It was almost inevitable, then, that President Bush would lay the groundwork for an attack on Iraq, part of the axis of evil.[117] Bush and his advisers convinced themselves that there was a strong case against Iraqi leader Saddam Hussein. After all, they argued, he fought a long and bloody war with Iran, invaded Kuwait, and threatened Saudi Arabia in 1991; brutally oppressed his people and used poison gas against the Kurds in Northern Iraq; launched scud missiles into Israeli cities during the Gulf war; and stockpiled and developed chemical and biological weapons and conceived the development of nuclear weapons. Moreover, the administration was convinced of a connection between the Iraqi government and the terrorists after an alleged meeting in Prague in April 2001 between an Iraqi diplomat and Muhammad Atta, one of the al Qaeda jihadists who crashed planes into the World Trade Center on 9/11.[118] This Iraq-al Qaeda connection was later dismissed as baseless by the 9/11 commission.[119]

The administration pushed hard to galvanize public opinion and won congressional support for a war to topple Saddam Hussein. But the major innovation in terms of Bush's vision was that the United States would undertake this action in a preemptive attack. The notion of initiating an attack on a sovereign nation before that nation had attacked the United States, or even threatened such an attack, represented a significant paradigm shift in U.S. foreign policy. According to political scientists Raymond Tanter and Stephen Kerstig, writing in 2002, "George W Bush has instigated the broadest reformulation of US grand strategy since the presidency of Franklin D. Roosevelt, again based on the shock of a surprise attack."[120] Bush and his advisers believed that the sense of urgency spawned by the 9/11 attacks, augmented by the existence of rogue states that could harbor terrorists or even share nuclear technology with them, demanded a re-formulation of U.S. national security policy. To prevent a second attack, the Bush national security team crafted a new strategy,

---

[116]Ibid.

[117]The "axis of evil" phrase was developed by Bush's speechwriter, Michael Gerson, who modified the original construct "axis of hatred" developed by Bush adviser David Frum. See Bob Woodward, *Plan of Attack: The Definitive Account of the Decision to Invade Iraq* (New York: Simon and Schuster, 2004), 86.

[118]Pfiffner, 2007, 10.

[119]*9/11 Commission Report: Final Report of the National Commission on Terrorist Attacks on the United States*, authorized ed. (New York: W.W. Norton and Company, 2004), 66.

[120]Raymond Tanter and Stephen Kerstig, "Grand Strategy and National Security Policy: Politics, Rhetoric, and the Bush Legacy," in Colin Campbell, Bert A. Rockman, and Andrew Rudalevige, eds., *The George W. Bush Legacy* (Washington, D.C.: Congressional Quarterly Press, 2008), 216.

the *2002 National Security Strategy of the United States of America*, which, again, emphasized preemption and featured the following themes:

■ Allows for preemptive military action.
■ Calls for American military primacy to be maintained.
■ Acknowledges multilateralism, but cautions that the United States will act unilaterally if circumstances warrant.
■ Declares America's goal of promoting democracy and human rights.[121]

But Bush's conception of preemption exceeded responding to an imminent danger of attack. Bush advocated preventative wars of regime change.[122] The United States claimed the right, under this formulation, to oust leaders it disliked long before they would threaten American security.[123]

The resulting Bush Doctrine provoked a series of questions and attacks from supposed political allies, including Representative Dick Armey (R-TX), who made the following statement in August 2002, "I don't believe that America will justifiably make an unprovoked attack on another nation. It would not be consistent with what we have been as a nation or what we should be as a nation."[124] Henry Kissinger, former Secretary of State to Richard Nixon, supported the administration's goal of regime change in Iraq, but noted that a preemptory U.S. attack would undermine conventions of international law that were centuries old. In a *Washington Post* op-ed, Kissinger stated that the Treaty of Westphalia of 1648 "established the principle 'that nations are not justified in intruding in the national affairs of other nations.' " Contemporary international law, he added, justifies war in response to an attack, "but does not provide for preemptive wars in many circumstances."[125]

In a speech in Cincinnati on October 7, 2002, in anticipation of a congressional vote on a resolution authorizing war in Iraq (which Bush would achieve), the president spoke again of the need for a preemptive attack:

> Some citizens wonder, "After 11 years of living with this problem, why do we need to confront it now?" And there's a reason. We have experienced the horror of September the 11th. We have seen that those who hate America are willing to crash airplanes into buildings full of innocent people. Our enemies would be no less willing; in fact they would be eager, to use biological or chemical or a nuclear weapon. Knowing these realities, America must not ignore the threat gathering against us. Facing clear evidence of peril, we cannot wait for the final

---

[121]Ibid., 221; see also "The National Security Strategy of the United States," September 17, 2002, National Defense University, http://merln.ndu.edu/whitepapers/USnss2002.pdf.

[122]Ivo H. Dadler and James M. Lindsay, "The Preemptive War Doctrine Has Met an Early Death in Iraq," *Los Angeles Times*, May 30, 2004.

[123]Ibid.

[124]Eric Schmitt, "House GOP Leader Warns against Iraq Attacks," *New York Times*, August 9, 2002.

[125]Henry Kissinger, "Our Future in Iraq," *Washington Post*, August 12, 2002.

proof, the smoking gun that could come in the form of a mushroom cloud.[126]

Deeply influenced by the events of 9/11, George W. Bush had introduced a fundamental transformation in American foreign policy. In a July 2002 commencement speech at the U.S. Military Academy at West Point, he explained himself:

> For much of the last century, America's defense relied on the cold war doctrines of deterrence and containment. In some cases, those strategies still apply, but new threats also require new thinking. Deterrence—the promise of massive retaliation against nations—means nothing against shadowy terrorist networks with no nation or citizens to defend. Containment is not possible when unbalanced dictators with weapons of mass destruction can deliver those weapons on missiles or secretly provide them to terrorist allies. We cannot defend America and our friends by hoping for the best. We cannot put our faith in the word of tyrants who solemnly sign nonproliferation treaties and then systemically break them. If we wait for threats to fully materialize, we will have waited too long . . . [T]he war on terror will not be won on the defensive. We must take the battle to the enemy, disrupt his plans, and confront the worst threats before they emerge. In the world we have entered, the only path to safety is the path of action, and this Nation will act.[127]

Along with the doctrinal shift to preemption, President Bush also argued that in fighting a new type of "asymmetrical warfare"—where a superpower could be directly attacked by shadowy cells of non-state actors—the rules by which the United States had historically operated needed to change.[128] Military commanders would require more leverage, executive authority would need to be expanded, and protections afforded to "enemy combatants" would decrease. The president claimed that he needed more freedom to get tough with enemies who were ruthless. In consultation with White House counsel Alberto Gonzalez, Bush decided that the Geneva Conventions had to be set aside for the war on terror.[129] In a January 25, 2002, memo, Gonzalez (who had worked with Bush in Texas) recommended that the Geneva Conventions on the treatment of prisoners of war did not apply to al Qaeda and Taliban prisoners. He reasoned that the war on terrorism was "a new kind of war" and a "new paradigm renders obsolete Geneva's strict limitations on questioning of enemy prisoners."[130]

In summation, George W. Bush was determined that his administration pursue big ideas, and not become mired in playing "small ball." In a 2007 interview he expressed his views to journalist Robert Draper as follows, "The job of

---

[126]George W. Bush, "Saddam Hussein Is a Threat to Peace," *Washington Post,* October 8, 2002.

[127]George W. Bush, "Commencement Address at the United States Military Academy in West Point, New York," in *Public Papers of the President of the United States,* 919.

[128]Pfiffner, 2007, 11.

[129]Ibid.

[130]Ibid.

the president is to think strategically so that you can accomplish big objectives, as opposed to playing mini-ball. You can't play mini-ball with the influence we have and expect them to be more. You've gotta think, think BIG. The Iranian issue is *the* strategic threat facing . . . Americans."[131] Shortly after Bush's re-election to the White House in 2004, Pete Wehner, Rove's new Strategic Initiatives director, circulated a memo assessing what he termed "The Most Important Election in Our Lifetime." Wehner described Bush as "one of history's consequential presidents," adding that in foreign policy the president would be known as one of history's Great Liberators and in domestic policy one of the Great Reformers.[132] Bush clearly showed an instinct to seize the moment and to shape history in both domains.

President Bush developed a strong vision for America's role in the world. Alarmed by the incalculable tragedy of 9/11 and the ongoing threat posed by jihadist activity, along with the extended threats he perceived from rogue nations, Bush evolved a role for himself as a war-time president with a strong mission.

But he became nearly obsessed with this vision and applied it in dubious ways to places where the vision was a poor fit, notably Iraq. Bush and his advisers, especially Vice President Cheney and Secretary of Defense Rumsfeld, worked hard to convince Americans that Iraq was the next logical place to confront the international terrorist threat. On January 20, 2005, in his second inaugural address, dubbed "The Freedom Speech," Bush waxed eloquently, albeit dangerously, on America's purpose in the world:

> There is only one force of history that can break the reign of hatred and resentment and expose the pretensions of tyrants and reward the hopes of the decent and tolerant, and that is the force of human freedom . . .
> So it is the policy of the United States to seek and support the growth of democratic movements and institutions in every nation and culture, with the ultimate goal of ending tyranny in our world.[133]

But the public did not truly accept the argument about the universality of the jihadist threat, nor, ultimately, did many members of Congress. The president's vision led to the fighting of a largely unpopular war, the diversion from the real source of international terrorism—al Qaeda, which literally means "the base"—and of course to a massive spilling of American blood and treasure. Bush fought the war without an adequate number of troops to accomplish the goal of liberating Iraq (as opposed to merely deposing Saddam), and without a competent plan of action to transform that nation into a stable democracy.[134]

---

[131]Draper, Foreword, vii. Emphasis in the original.

[132]Ibid., 279.

[133]George W. Bush, "Inaugural Address. January 20, 2005," in Public Papers of the Presidents of the United States, 2005. Book I: January 1 to June 30, 2005 (Washington D.C.: Government Printing Office, 2005), 66.

[134]Pfiffner, 2007, 8–11; and Thomas E. Ricks, *Fiasco: The American Military Adventure in Italy* (New York: Penguin Books, 2007).

Domestically, Bush enumerated the views of a compassionate conservative and pursued policies to go along with those beliefs. He actively built faith-based initiatives into his welfare approach and developed new institutions to reflect this view. As well, he showed great interest in market-based strategies to public policy, undertaking a major education reform effort that rewarded successful schools and penalized failing ones. He tested the limits of market-based solutions by proposing privatization of part of the Social Security system, but also had the savvy to back down when he recognized it would not work politically.

On the other hand, his deeds did not always match the philosophy. He certainly did not appear compassionate when Hurricane Katrina decimated the city of New Orleans and a significant part of the Mississippi Gulf Coast. He seemed increasingly uncaring about the growing gaps between rich and poor Americans, exacerbated by his deep tax cuts. And he never quite overcame the perception that he lacked the gravitas of a serious leader. Although he showed a brief period of eloquence after 9/11, he frequently displayed a passive, casual style and impatience with policy deliberations and debate.

Another gap widely noted on the dimension of Bush's vision was the one between the "clarity of the stakes laid out in presidential rhetoric and the administrative effort devoted to achieving them."[135] The boldness of vision (invade Iraq and create a democratic nation in the Middle East) was not adequately supported by an execution strategy, and consequently did not deliver concrete, positive results.

Finally, he evidenced a clear preference for strong decisions, eschewed the need for "nuance," and seemed to be frequently captured by the appeal of "dualistic" thinking—"you're either with us or against us," being perhaps the ultimate expression of that tendency. The complexity of international affairs, and even the intricate matters of domestic politics, call for leaders who are comfortable with ambiguity or "multiplicity," as summarized in a popular book, *Leadership without Easy Answers*.[136]

POLITICS

The transition process for the Bush presidency was challenged by the ongoing dispute in Florida over the vote count. The Supreme Court's decision in *Bush v. Gore* was handed down on December 12, 2000, giving the Bush team less than fifty days to prepare for the presidency.[137] Fortunately, Bush and his colleagues had started planning for the transition in the spring of 1999, when Bush asked his friend from his Yale days, Clay Johnson, to start the process.

---

[135]Colin Campbell, Bert A. Rockman, and Andrew Rudalevige, "Introduction: Legacies and Leadership in Context," in Campbell et al., *The George W. Bush Legacy*.

[136]Ronald Heifetz, *Leadership without Easy Answers* (Cambridge, MA: Harvard University Press, 1998).

[137]Tenpas and Hess, 38.

Johnson acted quickly and reached out to James A. Baker and George Schultz, who provided excellent advice.[138] Also, Bush's running mate, Dick Cheney, was heavily involved in the transition process, including "crafting his future role as the most powerful vice president in history."[139]

In June 2000, Johnson expressed the components of a successful transition effort:

- Picking a chief of staff early.
- Identifying cabinet secretaries by mid-December, and senior staff earlier.
- Hiring based on the new administration's policy priorities.
- Developing a clear set of policy goals.
- Recognizing that Congress and career executives pay attention to how a new administration reaches out to and communicates with them.[140]

Johnson's ideas were implemented with near precision. Andrew Card, who had served as a deputy chief of staff in the George H. W. Bush administration, was selected as chief of staff for the George W. Bush administration before Election Day.[141] Card used the period from Election Day through mid-December profitably and by December 17, with strong input from Cheney,[142] announced the first set of appointments: Condoleezza Rice as National Security Council assistant; Alberto Gonzalez as White House legal counsel; Karen Hughes as counselor to the president; Mitch Daniels as Office of Management and Budget (OMB) director; Ari Fleischer as press secretary; Joshua Bolton and Joe Hagin as deputy chief of staff; Nick Calio as legislative affairs director; and Margaret LaMontagne Spellings as assistant to the president for domestic policy.[143]

In short, unlike Clinton, Bush "hit the ground running." By January 4, Bush had chosen almost his entire team.[144] Furthermore, according the *National Journal*, a prestigious Washington political journal, the Bush team was "one of the most experienced senior staff[s] in modern memory."[145]

Bush rolled out his cabinet posts in three weeks from the time of the official transition on December 13, instead of taking eight to ten weeks like presidents since Carter.[146] His cabinet selections were surprisingly diverse. He chose four women (Elaine Chao at labor, Ann Veneman at agriculture, Gale Norton at interior, and Christine Whitman at Environmental Protection

---

[138]John P. Burke, "The Bush Transition," in Gregg and Rozell, *Considering the Bush Presidency*, 22.

[139]Shirley Anne Warshaw, *The Co-presidency of Bush and Cheney* (Stanford, CA: Stanford University Press, 2009), 1.

[140]Tenpas and Hess, 39.

[141]Ibid.

[142]See Barton Gellman, *Angler: The Cheney Vice Presidency* (New York: Penguin Press, 2008), 33–40.

[143]Ibid., 28.

[144]Tenpas and Hess, 38.

[145]Alexis Simendinger, "Stepping into Power," *National Journal*, January 4, 2001, 246.

[146]Burke, 27.

Agency [EPA]); two African Americans (Colin Powell at state and Roderick Page at education); one Arab American (Spencer Abraham at energy); one Hispanic (Mel Martinez at Housing and Urban Development [HUD]); and two Asian Americans (Chao and Norman Minetta at transportation—who was also a Democrat). Only six of fifteen cabinet appointments were white males.[147] In terms of staffing the fifteen cabinet departments, Clay Johnson took responsibility for most of the subcabinet political positions, whereas Cheney focused on recruiting the executive-level cabinet positions.[148]

The original Bush cabinet appointments were lauded for their experience and gravitas. This was particularly true for foreign affairs where Vice President Cheney, a former defense secretary, was joined by Colin Powell (a retired four-star general and former national security adviser) and Donald Rumsfeld (former defense secretary and White House chief of staff).[149] The domestic

◥ THE FIRST ADMINISTRATION OF GEORGE W. BUSH

INAUGURATION: January 20, 2001, the Capitol, Washington, D.C.

VICE PRESIDENT: Richard B. Cheney.

SECRETARY OF STATE: Colin L. Powell

SECRETARY OF THE TREASURY: Paul H. O'Neill (2001–2002); John W. Snow (2003–2006)

SECRETARY OF DEFENSE: Donald H. Rumsfeld

ATTORNEY GENERAL: John Ashcroft

SECRETARY OF THE INTERIOR: Gale Norton

SECRETARY OF AGRICULTURE: Ann M. Veneman

SECRETARY OF COMMERCE: Don Evans

SECRETARY OF LABOR: Elaine Chao

SECRETARY OF HEALTH AND HUMAN SERVICES: Tommy G. Thompson

SECRETARY OF HOUSING AND URBAN DEVELOPMENT: Melquiades Martinez (2001–2003); Alphonso Jackson (2004–2008)

SECRETARY OF TRANSPORTATION: Norman Y. Mineta

SECRETARY OF ENERGY: Spencer Abraham

SECRETARY OF EDUCATION: Rod Paige

SECRETARY OF VETERANS' AFFAIRS: Anthony Principi

SECRETARY OF HOMELAND SECURITY: Tom Ridge (2003–2005)

107TH CONGRESS (January 3, 2001 to January 3, 2003):

SENATE: 50 Republicans; 50 Democrats

HOUSE: 222 Republicans; 211 Democrats; 2 Independents

108TH CONGRESS (January 3, 2003 to January 3, 2005):

SENATE: 51 Republicans; 48 Democrats; 1 Independent

HOUSE: 229 Republicans; 205 Democrats; 1 Independent

---

[147]Pfiffner, 2004, 3.

[148]Warshaw, 2009, 50.

[149]Andrew Rudalevige, "The Decider," in Campbell et al., *The George W. Bush Legacy*, 141.

cabinet choices were also impressive. Bush selected Paul O'Neill as secretary of the treasury. O'Neill had been CEO of Alcoa and a widely respected government manager who served in the OMB during the 1970s. Other notables in the cabinet included Wisconsin Governor Tommy Thompson as secretary of health and human services, and Governor Christine Whitman.[150] The Bush cabinet was relatively stable during first term, with the exception of O'Neill and Whitman, who resigned late in 2002 and in spring of 2003, respectively.[151] In both cases, the Bush appointees had become disgruntled with the Bush approach to decision making and governance.

There were a few distinguishing features of the Bush administration: first, the unusually large portfolio of Cheney, which reflected in his central role in staffing the Bush presidency and in the integration of his personal staff with that of the president.[152] According to political scientist Shirley Anne Warshaw:

> Vice presidents had never before been significantly integrated in the White House or given wide-ranging policy-making authority. Cheney, with the full support of the president created what he called a "single-executive office." Cheney had domestic and national security policy staffs and a press secretary, legislative staff, legal counsel, and a chief of staff, as well as other extensive staff support in essence, an organization that paralleled the President's. Cheney's staff was present at all meetings and included on the circulation list for all interoffice memoranda within the White House. As a result, Cheney and his staff became omnipresent in White House meetings, with the full encouragement of President Bush.[153]

Cheney's outsized role as vice president invited a great deal of commentary. *Washington Post* journalist Barton Gellman, in his Pulitzer Prize winning book, *Angler*, characterized the situation as follows: "Vice presidents traditionally joined the president at 'policy time,' if the president so desired. Cheney intended to get involved sooner, long before the moment of decision. Cheney would exert a quiet dominance over meeting in which advisors framed their goals, narrowed options, and decided when or whether to bring them to the president. Cheney's presence unavoidably changed this tone, and often the outcome."[154]

Other unique features of the Bush administration were the inclusion of an Office of Strategic Initiatives (OSI), which came under the dominion of Karl Rove, and, as already mentioned, the development of an OFBCI.[155] Neither office had existed in previous presidential administrations.

---

[150]Ibid.

[151]Ibid.

[152]Gellman, 48–49.

[153]Warshaw, 2009, 5.

[154]Gellman, 55.

[155]Tenpas and Hess, 40–41.

George Bush had promoted himself as a "uniter" and not a "divider" in the presidential campaign and he intended to "change the tone in Washington."[156] When Al Gore conceded the presidential election to Bush on the evening of December 13, 2000, Bush decided to make his victory speech from the chamber of the Texas House of Representatives to symbolize the idea of bipartisan cooperation, which had been on display in Texas during his tenure as governor. Bush stated that the "spirit of cooperation we have seen in this hall is what is needed in Washington, DC."[157] On January 22, 2001—his first day in office—the president invited six pillars of the Democratic Party—former Democratic National Committee (DNC) Chair Robert Strauss, former Carter press secretary Judy Powell, former senators Paul Simon and John Culver, former Vice President Mondale's chief of staff Richard Moe—to the White House and expressed his interest in reaching out to Democrats. "In my administration," he said, "I hope to create bipartisanship. In Texas, I was able to do that. I recognize there'll be times when we have partisan battles. But what I'd like is to ask your opinion on issues where we might find common ground."[158]

Bush was attuned to the political realities of his administration. While the Republican Party held a slim margin of seats in the House of Representatives (222–211, with two Independents), they were exactly even in the Senate (50–50) and could secure certain legislation there only with the tie-breaking vote of the vice president.[159] His choice of early policy initiatives reflected his intent on working with the Democrats.

As it had been in Texas, education was prominent on the agenda. The president's first appeal for national education reform centered on members of his party. For instance, he reached out to Senate Education Committee second-ranking Senator Judd Gregg (R-NH), who had little interest in education reform if it omitted vouchers. House Education and the Workforce Committee chairman (and future speaker of the house) John Boehner (R-OH) had lobbied to eliminate the Department of Education. Bush built on personal relationships with both men to win their support for education reform.[160]

On January 23, 2001, he welcomed his first four congressional visitors to the White House to discuss education reform: Boehner, Gregg, Senate Education Committee chairman Jim Jeffords, and the committee's ranking Democrat, Senator Edward Kennedy.[161] Kennedy told Bush, "I want to help you do this," and Bush responded, "I'll pledge to you that we'll work together . . . and we're going to resolve our differences."[162] Once Kennedy's commitment had been

---

[156]Gary C. Jacobson, *A Divider Not a Uniter: George W. Bush and the American People* (New York: Pearson Longman, 2007).

[157]Greenstein, 198.

[158]Draper, 111.

[159]Pfiffner, 2007, 4.

[160]Draper, 111.

[161]Ibid.

[162]Ibid., 116.

secured, there was little doubt that Bush would achieve passage of the No Child Left Behind act, which he signed into law on January 8, 2002.[163] The House passed the bill 384–45, with 34 of the "no" votes cast by Republicans. The Senate passed a slightly different version of the bill by an overwhelming majority of 91–8, and both chambers easily approved a final version negotiated in conference committee.[164] The bill included more funding than Bush had originally requested and excluded vouchers that he wanted included.[165]

On the other hand, Bush's relationship with Vermont Republican Senator Jeffords soured when the White House refused to even consider inserting a $200 billion commitment to special education. On top of this, Jeffords considered the $1.6 trillion tax cut proposal of the administration to be alarmingly high, and felt slighted when the Bush staff neglected to invite him to the White House ceremony honoring a Vermont educator as teacher of the year. Three weeks later, on May 24, Jeffords bolted from the Republican Party, throwing control of the Senate back to the Democrats.[166] Some Republican leaders, notably Majority Leader Senator Trent Lott (MS), counseled compromise with Jeffords; however, Cheney convinced the president to refuse to cave in on basic principles.[167]

The first legislative accomplishment of the young administration came earlier, on June 7, 2001, when Bush signed a major tax cut. Bush worked effectively with Congress to achieve his goal, although he was forced to compromise on the *size* of the tax cut—he proposed a cut of $1.6 trillion over ten years and accepted a figure, after negotiations, of $1.35 trillion.[168] The victory on the tax cut was secured with a relatively close vote of 230–198 in the House and 53–47 in the Senate.[169]

The Jeffords defection changed the political landscape for Bush. But events did not provide him with time to think about it. The terrorist attacks of September 11, 2001, dominated the agenda for the next several months.

On the evening of September 10, Bush stayed at the Colony Beach and Tennis Resort in Sarasota, Florida, where he shared dinner with his brother, Florida Governor Jeb Bush.[170] The next day he had scheduled a visit to a second-grade classroom at the mostly African American Emma Booker Elementary School, to be followed by a speech on education funding.

Early that morning, Bush had received a telephone call from his national security adviser, Condoleezza Rice, about some sort of plane crash into the

---

[163]Dana Milbank, "With Fanfare, Bush Signs Education Bill: President, Lawmakers Hit 3 States in 12 Hours to Tout Biggest School Change Since 65," *Washington Post,* January 9, 2002.

[164]Barbara Sinclair, "Living and (and Dying?) by the Sword: George W. Bush as Legislative Leader," in Campbell et al., *The George W. Bush Legacy,* 172–173.

[165]Ibid., 173.

[166]Draper, 117.

[167]Gellman, 78–79.

[168]Pfiffner, 2007, 4.

[169]Ibid., 170–171.

[170]Draper, 134.

North Tower of Manhattan's World Trade Center.[171] Rice described the most likely cause of the crash to have been "pilot error," and Bush proceeded to read to the eager second graders. Several minutes later, however, chief of staff Andy Card entered the room and whispered into the president's ear, "a second plane hit the second tower. America is under attack."[172]

Bush finished reading to the kids, arguing later that he did not want to appear panicked, and then, in a holding room outside the school auditorium, Bush spoke by phone to Vice President Cheney, to New York Governor George Pataki, and to FBI Director Robert Mueller.[173] The president returned to the auditorium, escorted by Secret Service agents and nodded to the applause of teachers and students, and issued this statement, "Ladies and gentlemen, this is a difficult moment for America. I unfortunately will be going back to Washington after my remarks . . . Today we've had a national tragedy. Two airplanes have crashed into the World Trade Center in an apparent terrorist attack on our country." He said that he had spoken to Cheney, Pataki, and Mueller, and that the federal government would render immediate assistance to New York.[174] He also vowed to "hunt down and find the folks who committed this act," and added in an ironic echo of his dad's 1991 speech about Saddam Hussein's march into Kuwait, "Terrorism against our nation will not stand."[175]

Bush wanted to return to Washington, but Vice President Cheney and the Secret Service convinced him not to do so. Instead, he landed at Barksdale Air Force Base in Louisiana, and issued a brief statement to the nation.[176] He addressed the nation from the Oval Office at eight-thirty that night, his first address from that spot as president.

In the days, weeks, and months following the terrorist attacks, George Bush "seemed to have met his place in history, and the public was rallying to his side," according to political scientist Gary L. Gregg II.[177] Bush demonstrated several aspects of effective leadership in a crisis situation.

He projected reassurance

As mentioned earlier, upon hearing of the attacks, Bush did not panic. He continued to listen to the second graders reading their lessons for him. Only when they were finished—which must have seemed like an eternity—did he calmly get up and leave the room. In his first public words, delivered from the elementary school auditorium, Bush pledged the full resources of the federal

---

[171]Ibid., 135.

[172]Ibid.

[173]Ibid., 137.

[174]Ibid.

[175]Ibid.

[176]Ibid., 141.

[177]Gary L. Gregg II, "George W. Bush and the Symbolic Presidency," in Gregg and Rozell, *Considering the Bush Presidency*, 88.

government to help the victims, promised to "hunt down and find the perpetrators," and asked for a moment of silent prayer.[178]

Three hours later, when he landed at Barksdale Air Force Base, when he would take another message to the American people, he explained his intent to his aides, as follows, "I think it's important for people to see the government is functioning. The government is not chaotic. It's functioning smoothly."[179] And in his speech he tried to reassure the public of the continuity of government operations, of the high-alert status of the American military, and that the nation would pass the test.[180]

In a "symbolic gesture," Bush also insisted that when he returned to Washington, he would land on the South Lawn of the White House, and *not* at Andrews Air Force Base in Maryland, as recommended by the Secret Service.[181] According to Gregg, "Bush seemed to understand the need for a traumatized public to see its leader safe, unharmed, and in charge."[182]

He reflected the public mind

A critical part of Bush's transformed relationship with the American public after September 11 was his ability to project the extent to which he shared their pain and their demand for justice. By characterizing September 11 as a "difficult moment for America," and then asking for a moment of silence, Bush symbolized the "prayerful" questioning of people glued to the terrifying drama on television sets all over the nation."[183]

But the public was also angry and in a mood to seek revenge. Bush showed the anger and reflected the interest in finding justice. In his initial statement he, again, vowed to "hunt down and find those folks who committed this act" and later described the enemy as "faceless cowards."[184]

From the Oval Office in the evening of September 11, he expressed his "disbelief, terrible sadness, and a quiet, unyielding anger" that he sensed among the public. This aspect of Bush's post–September 11 leadership culminated a few days later, with the president standing among the rubble of the collapsed World Trade Center, arm draped around an aged firefighter, and speaking through a bull horn to assembled iron workers and firefighters who were having trouble hearing him, declaring, "I can hear you. The rest of the world hears you, and the people who knocked down these buildings will hear all of us soon."[185] This unscripted moment was

---

[178]Ibid., 95.

[179]Bill Sammon, *Fighting Back: The War on Terrorism—from inside the Bush White House* (Washington, D.C.: Regency Publishing, 2002), 113.

[180]Woolley and Peters.

[181]Sammon, 120, 127.

[182]Gregg II, 95.

[183]Ibid., 96.

[184]Ibid.

[185]Ibid., 97; Draper, 135.

followed by firefighters' chants of "USA! USA! USA!" and proved to be a "defining" one for George Bush, as "millions across the nation now knew the president shared their emotions, including anger and an unbending determination that justice would be served."[186]

He instructed the public mind

A president must do more than reflect the public mind; he must also educate the public. Bush performed the role admirably in several ways.

First, *he defined the enemy*. Bush made it clear that the United States was at war with an "evil" enemy, but was emphatic in noting that it was at war with terrorists, not with Islam. According to White House aides, Bush was determined not to allow history to repeat itself with regard to the treatment of Japanese Americans during World War II.[187] Representative David Bonier from Michigan had informed Bush of the large number of Islamic constituents he represented.[188] Bush included an Islamic cleric as part of the National Prayer Service, and visited Washington's largest Islamic Center where, with shoes off, the president declared "the face of terror is not the face of Islam."[189]

In his nationally televised address to a joint session of Congress on September 20, which journalist Robert Draper described as the best speech of his presidency,[190] Bush separated the terrorists from Islam by saying the terrorists practiced a fringe form of Islamic extremism that has been rejected by Muslim scholars and the vast majority of Muslim clerics.[191] He appealed directly to the Muslim world:

> We respect your faith. It's practiced freely by many millions of Americans and by millions more in countries that America counts as friends. Its teachings are good and peaceful, and those who commit evil in the name of Allah blaspheme the name of Allah. The terrorists are traitors to their own faith, trying, in effect, to hijack Islam itself. The enemy of America is not our many Muslim friends; it is not our many Arab friends. Our enemy is a radical network of terrorists and every government that supports them.[192]

The president and the administration made some missteps in their efforts to define the enemy; for instance, at one point Bush referred to the war on

---

[186]Ibid.

[187]Gregg II, 98.

[188]Draper, 146.

[189]Gregg II, 98.

[190]Draper, 140.

[191]Gregg II, 98.

[192]George W. Bush, "Address before a Joint Session of the Congress of the United States – Response to the Terrorist Attacks of September 11, 20 September 2001," in *Public Papers of the Presidents of the United States, George Bush 2001, Book II: July 1 – December 31, 2001* (Washington, D.C.: US Government Printing Office, 2006), 1141.

terror as a "crusade," and the Defense Department named the military operation in Afghanistan "Infinite Justice," which offended some Muslims because they believe only Allah could achieve infinite justice.[193] But the president persisted in his attempts to clearly identify the enemy and to protect the innocent, stating in his national address: "No one should be singled out for unfair treatment or unkind words, because of their ethnic background or religious faith."[194]

In another educational effort, President Bush counseled patience. Although he was willing to clearly express his anger at the murder of thousands of innocent Americans, he took great pains to remind Americans that this new kind of war would be unconventional, would be frequently unpublicized, and would require patience and persistence. "Over and over again," according to political scientist Gary Gregg, "he would use the bully pulpit of the presidency to convince the American people that justice delayed would not be justice denied. He was not willing to settle for a quick strike that would be immediately popular but would not be effective."[195]

In his vaunted September 20 address to a joint session of Congress, Bush meticulously laid out how the current battle differed from past wars and warned that "Americans should not expect one battle, but a lengthy campaign, unlike any other we have ever seen." He continued by asking for citizens' patience "with the delay and inconvenience that may accompany tighter security."[196]

He balanced the realities of war with the hope for peace

Among his vows to achieve justice and to "smoke out" the terrorists, Bush would also strike a gentler chord of humanitarianism and compassion. In his speech, he outlined non-negotiable demands on the government of Afghanistan, but also noted that the United States "respects the people of Afghanistan" and was that nation's largest source of humanitarian aid.[197] According to Gregg, "The balance the president sought to hit would even influence the war itself, as the United States Military began using planes to provide humanitarian supplies to the citizens of Afghanistan while other planes were focusing on bombing targets."[198] Furthermore, on November 17, 2001, Laura Bush became the first first lady to deliver an entire weekly radio address, focused on the plight of women and children under the severe rulership of the Taliban in Afghanistan.[199]

---

[193]Gregg II, 99.

[194]Ibid., http://www.whitehouse.gov/news/releases/2001/09/20010920-8.html.

[195]Ibid., 99–100.

[196]Bush, 2006, 1142.

[197]Ibid., 1141.

[198]Gregg II, 101.

[199]Ibid.

A new George W. Bush had emerged. According to reporter Robert Draper, "after 9/11 George W. Bush filled the arena. All the man's undersized, self-conscious ways—the smirk, the reedy defensiveness, the exaggerated imperiousness of his executive stroll—had collapsed into the new persona . . . . He was a war president and perfectly at ease with the role."[200]

And Congress was at his beck and call. Whatever he asked for, Congress now gave him by wide margins. Bush's position won eleven of the twelve votes in the House and thirty of the thirty-one votes in the Senate immediately following the attack.[201] He immediately won approval for a $40 billion aid package for New York City, a massive bailout for the nation's crippled airlines, and another $42 billion in tax cuts. He also won authorization for the incipient military intervention in Afghanistan. In the Senate, the bill was sponsored by a Democrat, Tom Daschle of South Dakota, and passed with all ninety-eight votes casted; in the House, the corresponding bill merited 420 supporting votes and only one detractor.[202]

Nevertheless, the bipartisanship that Bush championed, and that was evident in the early days of his administration and in the immediate aftermath of 9/11, began to recede. In the 2002 budget cycle, Bush slashed funding for No Child Left Behind by $90 million, prompting Senator Kennedy and Representative George Miller (D-CA) to hold a February 12 press conference to call Bush a liar.[203] Reporters noted that at weekly breakfasts with congressional leaders Bush was doing more talking and less listening.[204]

And the administration went on the attack with regard to the war on terror and the need for a preemptive strike against Iraq. According to Scott McClellan, "In January 2002, the first cracks appeared in the façade of bipartisan comity. During an open press Republican National Committee meeting in Austin, Texas, Karl Rove stated that the GOP would make the President's leadership in the war on terror the top issue for retaining control of the House and winning back the Senate in the midterms."[205] As the administration geared up to convince the public and members of Congress to support a war in Iraq, it resorted to what congressional scholar Louis Fisher described as a "frenzied mode." [206] In an August 27, 2002, address, Vice President Cheney warned that Saddam Hussein would "fairly soon" have nuclear weapons and that it would be useless to seek a Security Council requiring Iraq to submit to weapons inspectors. Cheney declared that the threat posed by Saddam made

---

[200]Draper, 165–166.

[201]Colinv C. Campbell and Robert P. Watson, "Changing the Tone? Congressional-Presidential Relations in the Second Bush Administrations," in Kraus et al.

[202]THOMAS Legislative Database, The Library of Congress, http://thomas.loc.gov/cgi-bin/bdquery/z?d107:SJ00023:@@@X, accessed August 26, 2009.

[203]Draper, 169.

[204]Ibid.

[205]Scott McClellan, *What Happened: Inside the Bush White House and Washington's Culture of Deception* (New York: Public Affairs, 2008), 112.

[206]Louis Fisher, "The Way We Go to War," in Gregg and Rozell, 109.

preemptive attacks against Iraq imperative.[207] Two *Washington Post* reporters noted the abrupt change in the administration's posture regarding Iraq, from serious concern to palpable alarm, remarking, "This week's frenzy of attention to Iraq was entirely generated by a White House whose occupants returned from the August recess anxious and ready to push the debate to a new level."[208]

Although increasingly convinced that the United States would have to go to war with Iraq, the Bush administration announced its intention to "consult with Congress, and to seek authorization from Congress for its intended actions."[209] But the administration was expecting Congress to act quickly, and not to slow down the war planning through lengthy deliberations and debate.[210] Bush wanted Congress to complete action on an authorizing resolution prior to the lawmakers adjourning for the 2002 elections. Senator Robert Byrd (D-W. VA) raised the reasonable question of why the administration seemed to be in such a hurry and remarked that "this war hysteria has blown in like a hurricane."[211]

There was political calculation by the Bush administration, according to Louis Fisher.[212] Republican nominees in the 2002 congressional contests made a political weapon out of Iraq. They compared their "strong stand" on Iraq to "weak" positions of Democratic competitors. Several key congressional races appeared to turn on the positions candidates articulated in the war issue.[213] At this point, Democrats were unable to redirect the political agenda to issues such as corporate crime, the state of the stock market, or the struggling economy.[214]

In a strong partisan statement, President Bush in a speech in Trenton, New Jersey, on September 23, accused the Senate of being "more interested in special interests in Washington" than they were with the "security of the American people."[215] Bush and other top officials invited members of Congress to special sessions in which they received confidential information from Iraq; however, the members were largely unimpressed with the quality of the information. After one briefing, Senator Bob Graham (D-FL), chairman of the Senate Intelligence Committee, remarked, "I did not receive any new information."[216] House Minority Whip (and future speaker) Nancy Pelosi (D-CA), the ranking Democrat on the House Intelligence Committee, remarked that

---

[207]Ibid .

[208]Dan Balz and Dana Milabank, "Iraq Policy Shift Follows Patter," *Washington Post*, September 6, 2002, A19.

[209]Fisher, 112.

[210]Ibid., 113.

[211]Ibid.

[212]Ibid.

[213]Ibid.

[214]Ibid.

[215]Ibid., 114.

[216]Mike Allen and Karen D. Young, "Bush to Seek Hill Approval on Iraq War," *Washington Post*, September 5, 2002, A1.

she knew of "no information that the threat is so imminent from Iraq that Congress could not wait until January to vote on an authorizing resolution."[217]

Prominent military officials shared the skepticism of some members of Congress. According to *Washington Post* reporter Thomas E. Ricks, "there were profound doubts about invading Iraq and about a policy of preemption."[218] Several generals expressed specific concerns about invading Iraq: the possibility that an invasion would cause Saddam to use weapons of mass destruction (WMDs; assuming he had them), the dangers of being immersed in urban warfare, and the worry that a post-war occupation would be costly.[219] General Eric Shinseki, U.S. army chief of staff, raised serious questions about the adequacy of the invasion/ reoccupation troop levels being contemplated by Secretary of Defense Rumsfeld.[220]

The administration, however, kept a steady drumbeat for war, according to Fisher, releasing numerous accounts to demonstrate the seriousness of the threat emanating from Baghdad. On September 7, President Bush cited an International Atomic Energy Agency report, indicating that the Iraqis were "Six months away from developing a weapon," adding "I don't know what more evidence we need."[221] On September 27, Rumsfeld announced that the administration had "bulletproof evidence of Iraq's links to Al Qaeda."[222] But Rumsfeld repeatedly failed to substantiate the claim.

According to journalist Thomas Ricks, the Bush administration pursued two contradictory "delusions" in building its case for war in the summer of 2002. To make the case for war, administration spokespersons focused on the worst-case scenarios for WMDs, dismissing contrary evidence. They asserted that Saddam Hussein possessed WMDs and was on the road to acquiring nuclear weapons and could share them with terrorists. On the other hand, the administration's consideration of post-war issues took a leap of faith in the other direction, positing that the Iraqis would greet the United States warmly, that a post-Saddam regime could be built quickly, and that U.S. troops could be deployed and easily withdrawn.[223]

The Democrats, including those considering a run in the 2004 presidential race, folded their tents and joined the chorus in favor of war. House Minority Leader Dick Gephardt (D-MO), Senator John Edwards (D-NC), and Senator Joseph Lieberman (D-CT) all came out in support of an authorizing resolution. Massachusetts Senator John Kerry, who would become the Democratic Party's presidential nominee in 2004, expressed considerable doubt, but eventually voted for the resolution.[224]

---

[217]Jim VanDer Hein and Juliet Eilperin, "Democrats Uncommitted on Iraq War," *Washington Post,* September 11, 2002.

[218]Ricks, 40.

[219]Ibid.

[220]Woodward, 2004, 119.

[221]Fisher, 115.

[222]Ibid.

[223]Ricks, 58–59.

[224]Fisher, 117.

Students of history, according to Louis Fisher, might wonder why Democrats were supportive of President Bush when there was scant evidence that the public supported a war in Iraq. Another question is why very few of the Democrats (or members of Congress in general) read the Central Intelligence Agency's September 2002 National Intelligence Estimates (NIE). This ninety-two-page classified report contained many doubts, caveats, and disagreements with Bush's assertions.[225]

It is hard to deny the fact that the vote on the resolution was inseparably a political decision. Karl Rove, George Bush, and their allies created an atmosphere of fear in the country, and the vote took place only a month before the November 2002 congressional elections. Senator Kerry, who had previously raised substantial questions about going to war in Iraq, now accepted presidential superiority over Congress. He stated, "We are affirming a president's right and responsibility to keep the American people safe, and the president must take that grant of responsibility seriously."[226] According to Fisher, however, trust in the president and a call for bipartisanship do not adequately substitute for an analysis by Congress of the justification for using military force against another nation.[227] He continued:

> with that kind of reasoning, Congress had little reason to participate in the debate other than to offer words of encouragement and support to a president who already seemed to possess all the constitutional authority he needed to act single-handedly. Congress was no longer an authorizing body. It merely endorsed what the president had already decided.[228]

The outcome of the vote (taken on October 10–11, 2002) was foreordained. It was not surprising that Bush received a convincing margin of support; the exact numbers in favor of authorizing the president to use military force in Iraq were as follows: House: 296–133; Senate: 77–23.[229]

In the 2002 mid-term elections, the Republicans gained two Senate seats, giving them a narrow (51–49) majority, and, defying historical trends, picked up six House seats to expand their narrow majority (229–205).[230]

In December 2002—after Congress passed the authorizing resolution—seventy national security experts and Mideast scholars met for two days at the National Defense University, a premier military education institution located in Washington, D.C., to discuss, "Iraq: Looking Beyond Saddam's Role." They concluded that occupying Iraq "will be the most daunting and complex task the U.S. and the international community will have undertaken since

---

[225]Ricks, 61.

[226]Fisher, 119.

[227]Ibid.

[228]Ibid.

[229]Draper, 184.

[230]Donald Beachler, "Ordinary and Extraordinary Times: The 2002 Congressional Elections," in Kraus et al., 30.

the end of World War II."[231] The group also raised a strong cautionary note about an abrupt, uncoordinated dissolution of the Iraqi military, and said, "There should be a phased downsizing to avoid dumping 1.4 million men into a shattered economy."[232] This advice was subsequently ignored by the Bush administration and the Coalition Provisional Authority.

Although the United States scored a quick military victory, taking control of Baghdad within a month of the beginning of hostilities, the military was unable to establish control or unify the country in a common purpose. By the fall of 2003, the tragedy in Iraq was beginning to appear: Saddam's legendary WMDs had not been discovered, and Hamid Karzai–like unifying presence had emerged in the fractured country.[233] The Coalition Provisional Authority had disbanded the entire Iraqi military, and the Americans were in for a long, bloody, and costly war whose outcome was uncertain. The Iraq study group, co-chaired by former Secretary of State James Baker and former Indiana congressman Lee Hamilton, described the situation as "grave and deteriorating."[234] Nevertheless, before all these problems were apparent, the Republicans achieved a significant electoral victory in the 2002 congressional races, and Bush felt vindicated in the pursuit of his policies.

In summing up the politics of George W. Bush, it is tempting to agree with Professor Pfiffner's assessment:

> The first two years of George W. Bush's term were remarkable. He quickly overcame the deficit of having 500,000 fewer votes than Al Gore in the 2000 election and set out on a concerted conservative agenda. Though not successful in all policy objectives, he was able to achieve a $1.35 trillion tax cut over 10 years through a closely split Republican-controlled congress. He also won approval for a large new federal role in education, with funding linked to student performance. After the attacks on New York and Washington, he reassured the nation and won significant power to pursue terror suspects in the U.S. Though he did not capture Osama Bin Laden he led an effective war in Afghanistan that overthrew the Taliban, scattered Al Qaeda, and undermined its infrastructure.[235]

On the other hand, in the subsequent two years of his administration, Bush took the country into an unpopular, costly war without a true sense of strategy; reflected increasingly vitriolic and adversarial relationships with the Democratic leadership; damaged his trust levels and popularity with the American people with false assertions of WMDs in Iraq; and displayed

---

[231]Ricks, 72.

[232]Ibid.

[233]Draper, 202.

[234]*The Iraq Study Group Report,* http://media.usip.org/reports/iraq_study_group_report.pdf, accessed September 18, 2009.

[235]Pfiffner, 2004, 17.

increasing indifference to or incompetence in the details of public administration and management. Although he continued to display acumen in winning elections, his performance in leadership terms threatened the importance of the electoral victories.

According to estranged press secretary Scott McClellan, the "permanent campaign" mentality had overcome George Bush. As president he became determined to win above all else, and governing became a subset of campaigning.[236] According to journalists Lou and Carl Cannon, "winning at all costs—the accusation leveled by McCain in South Carolina—came to be a hallmark of George W. Bush's administration as well."[237] Bush's leadership credibility had been seriously eroded as citizens pondered the following questions: Had the president and his team exaggerated or distorted the intelligence on WMDs to deliberately mislead the nation to war? How was the war in Iraq part of the war on terror when Iraq had no connection to 9/11 or relationship with al Qaeda? Why did Bush rush to war with no adequate plan to win the peace? How did the administration underestimate the strength of the insurgency or the number of American troops needed to deal with it?[238]

STRUCTURE

As previously mentioned, Bush was the nation's first MBA president, and therefore he preferred to set a bold direction, within a clearly limited agenda, and delegate administrative matters to his executive team, led by his chief operating officer Vice President Cheney.[239] As an MBA, Bush's management style was characterized by speed, secrecy, and top-down control.[240] Bush conceived his role as chief executive as mirroring that of an executive officer of a corporation: tough-minded and making decisions easily, while leaving the details of implementation to his capable team. He also stressed tight message discipline and evinced a particular disdain for unauthorized leaks.[241]

The Bush management style was also notably influenced by the president's strong reliance on a highly capable team.[242] The team was led by Cheney, who wielded an unusual amount of power. The other important members of his team included a triumvirate:

> **Andrew H. Card Jr., chief of staff:** Card had served in George H. W. Bush's administration as secretary of transportation and deputy chief of staff. He was President Reagan's liaison to the nation's governors and mayors.

---

[236]McClellan, especially ch. 5.

[237]Cannon and Cannon, 88.

[238]McClellan, 191.

[239]Pfiffner, 2007, 6; Kettle, 31.

[240]Pfiffner, 2007, 6.

[241]Ibid., 7.

[242]Kettle, 39.

Karen Hughes, counselor to the president: Hughes had been a member of Bush's staff while he served as governor of Texas. Previously, she had been a television reporter and executive director of the Texas Republican Party. She was particularly close to Bush, and ranked with Karl Rove as one of the president's closest advisers. As counselor to the president, Hughes supervised the Communications Office, the Office of the Press Secretary, the Office of Media Affairs, and the Office of Speechwriting.[243]

Karl Rove, senior White House adviser: Close observers described Rove as "Bush's brain" for his uncanny political instincts and his influence on Bush's strategy. He had headed an Austin-based public affairs company and had masterminded Bush's gubernatorial wins.[244] As noted by Scott McClellan, who served as Bush's press secretary and resigned after becoming disillusioned with administration policy, Rove was given an enormous center of influence within the White House from the start. This was only strengthened by Rove's force of personality and closeness to the president.[245] Rove supervised several offices, including the OSI; the Office of Political Affairs; the Office of Public Liaison; and the Office of Instrumental Affairs.[246]

While informal in his personal demeanor, Bush also instituted a tough, disciplined approach for his staff. Chief of staff Andrew Card spelled out the following rules for White House staffers:

- *Attire:* Suit and tie were required for men and equivalent business attire for women. The casual dress code of the Clinton years was over.
- *Brevity is vital:* Bush demanded that briefing papers be limited to one or two pages.
- *Punctuality:* Bush was ruthless in starting and ending meeting on time, another dramatic contrast to Clinton.
- *Treat everyone with respect:* The president demanded that staffers return each other's phone calls promptly.
- *Develop healthy work habits:* Bush stressed the importance of life balance and encouraged his staff to spend time with their families. Like Reagan, and unlike Clinton, Bush expected most work to be completed during the normal workday.[247]

Bush also introduced institutional and managerial innovations into his administration. In terms of the institutional changes, he added the following offices:

Office of Strategic Initiatives: The OSI headed by Karl Rove was designed to think ahead and devise long-term political strategy. Clinton had

---

[243]McClellan, 82–83.

[244]Kettle, 43–45.

[245]McClellan, 73.

[246]Ibid., 77–78.

[247]Kettle, 29–31.

relied on an informal network of advisers—including James Carville, Stanley Greenberg, and Dick Morris—to help him get ahead of the day-to-day White House crises and focus on the big picture. Bush wished to accomplish the same goal through a more formal process, and thoroughly integrated Rove into the chain of command. From this office, Rove was also instrumental in generating campaign advice for the president, along with Ken Mehlman.[248]

Office of Faith-Based and Community Initiatives: The OFBCI was established by executive order. It was meant to demonstrate the president's commitment to compassionate conservatism by reaching out to faith-based and community organizations to help the needy.[249]

In terms of management, from the beginning of his presidency, President George W. Bush demanded better management and performance for the federal government.[250] The first significant Bush management initiative was the President's Management Agenda (PMA), which was released by the OMB in August 2001. The PMA established five priorities for all federal departments and agencies: (1) strategic management of human capital, (2) competitive sourcing, (3) improved financial performance, (4) expanded use of e-government, and (5) budget and performance integration.[251] The administration assigned four political appointees in the OMB and one in the Office of Personnel Management (OPM) as government-wide "owners" for each initiative, holding them personally responsible for implementation of change. Agencies were expected to develop plans, identify responsible officials, and apply resources to achieve those improvement goals with the organization.[252]

The administration developed an Executive Branch Management Scorecard to track the implementation of the PMA. The scorecard was a "traffic light" grading system to assess progress of each department and agency: a "green" score meant the agency had met all the elements of the standard for success; "yellow" meant the agency had succeeded at intermediate level of achievement; and "red" meant the agency had one or more serious flaws.[253] When the PMA was launched, 110 of the 130 scores (based on twenty-six agencies working on five separate initiatives) were red. Almost none of the agencies scored were satisfactorily managing their people, programs, costs, or investments in information technology. As of June 30, 2006, the U.S. Department of Labor was judged to be the most successful in utilizing management disciplines and habits that comprised the PMA, with five green scores.[254]

---

[248]Tenpas and Hess, 40.

[249]Ibid., 41.

[250]Jonathan D. Bruel, "Three Bush Management Reform Initiatives; the President's Management Agenda, Freedom to Manage Legislative Proposals, and the Program Assessment Rating System," *Public Administrative Review*, January/February, 2007, 21.

[251]Ibid., 22.

[252]Ibid.

[253]Ibid.

[254]Ibid.

Bush also introduced legislative proposals to improve management effectiveness; however, he was unable to secure congressional passage of the bills. One proposal was the Freedom to Manage Act of 2001, which was the first bill President Bush transmitted to congress.[255] The proposed bill established a procedure whereby heads of department and agencies could indentify statutory barriers to good management, and recommend that Congress remove them. The Managerial Flexibility Act of 2001 would have provided federal managers with tools and flexibility in areas such as personnel, budgeting, and property management and disposal.[256] But members of both parties in Congress had concerns about ceding any legislative power to the White House. In addition, the proposals met with stiff opposition from the American Foundation of Government Employees. Nevertheless, a number of ideas contained in those failed pieces of legislation found their way into subsequent legislative proposals, notably the administration's legislation proposal to create the U.S. Department of Homeland Security.[257]

A third management reform initiative developed by the Bush administration was the Program Assessment Rating Tool (PART) to bring performance information into the budgeting process. The PART centered around twenty-five diagnostic questions focused on (1) program purpose and design, (2) strategic planning, (3) program management, and (4) program results.[258] The PART developed "scores" for agencies based on their performance on the aforementioned four areas.

Although the PART ratings did not automatically translate into funding decisions, they did help surface ideas and recommendations for improved program design, planning, and management.[259] As of February 2002, the administration assessed 794 programs, representing 80 percent of the federal budget, with the use of PART.[260] According to Jonathan Bruel, over time, there was a "substantial increase" in the number of programs rated "effective," "moderately effective," or "adequate." In the first year, 45 percent of programs received such scores. By 2006, the percentage had increased to 72.[261]

In 2005, PART won the Prestigious Innovations in American Government Award, a joint program of the Ash Institute at Harvard University, John F. Kennedy School of Government, and the Council for Excellence in Government.[262] According to Bruel, "taken together, the Bush management reforms represent a highly disciplined, diplomatic, transparent, and sustained approach to reforming the inner workings of government."[263]

---

[255]Ibid., 23.

[256]Ibid.

[257]Ibid., 23–24.

[258]Ibid., 24.

[259]Ibid.

[260]Ibid., 25.

[261]Ibid.

[262]Ibid.

[263]Ibid.

Another Bush initiative in the area of structure was the creation of the Department of Homeland Security. In the previously discussed January 29, 2002, State of the Union address, President Bush named Pennsylvania Republican Governor Tom Ridge as the director of a new federal effort in homeland security. At the time, however, Bush did not contemplate elevating Ridge to cabinet level status or creating an entirely new (and large) government agency to effectuate his vision of protecting the American homeland from terrorist attacks, or other potential threats.

That vision actually belonged to Connecticut Democratic Senator Joseph Lieberman, who advocated for the creation of a cabinet agency for homeland security. Bush originally opposed Lieberman's idea, but yielded to the entreaties of Andrew Card and others, while also calculating the political advantage of supporting the proposal, and endorsed the creation of a new cabinet agency. In fact, Bush and Rove used the creation of the Department of Homeland Security as a political weapon in the 2002 mid-term election.[264] Advertisements charged Senator Max Cleland (D-GA), Vietnam veteran army captain and triple amputee running for re-election in Georgia, with, in essence, a lack of patriotism because Cleland challenged the weakening of worker rights in the Bush proposal. Cleland lost to Republican Saxby Chambliss, and Democrats were infuriated.[265]

On November 25, 2002, President Bush signed legislation that merged twenty-two federal agencies with more than 170,000 employees to create the Department of Homeland Security.[266] A few days earlier in a November 19 statement, President Bush commended Congress for passing legislation creating the department "to help our nation meet the emerging threat of terrorism in the 21st century."[267] The following agencies, among others, constituted the new department.[268]

Although it seems clear the nation needed a consolidated approach to homeland security, the department was developed rapidly and without adequate planning for melding disparate organizational cultures and visions into a new organization amalgam called Department of Homeland Security. Federal Emergency Management Agency's (FEMA) placement within this vast bureaucratic network reduced its visibility and may have deteriorated its effectiveness in dealing with high-voltage issues such as Hurricane Katrina.

In short, Bush was serious about applying business principles to government, drawing on his MBA training and the insights he gained from the

---

[264]Draper.

[265]Sinclair, 175.

[266]Homeland Security Act of November 25, 2002, PL 107-296.

[267]George W. Bush, "Statement on Congressional Action on Homeland Security Legislation. November 19, 2002," in *Public Paper of the Presidents of the United States. George W. Bush 2002. Book II: July 1 –December 31, 2002* (Washington, D.C.: U.S. Government Printing Office, 2006), 2095.

[268]Taken from DHS website, http://www.dhs.gov/xabout/history/editorial_0133.shtm.

Original Agency (department)	Current Agency/Office
The U.S. Customs Service (treasury)	U.S. Customs and Border Protection (inspection, border and ports of entry responsibilities)
	U.S. Immigration and Custom Enforcement (customs, law enforcement responsibilities)
The Immigration and Naturalization Service (justice)	U.S. Customs and Border Protection (inspection functions and the U.S. Border Patrol)
	U.S. Immigration and Customs Enforcement (immigration law enforcement, detention and removal, intelligence and investigation)
The Federal Protective Service	U.S. Immigration and Customs Enforcement
The Federal Law Enforcement Training Center (treasury)	Federal Law Enforcements Training Center
U.S. Coast Guard	U.S. Coast Guard
U.S. Secret Service	U.S. Secret Service
National Infrastructure Protection Center	Dispersed throughout the department, including Office of Operations Coordination and Office of Infrastructure Protection

administration of government programs in Texas. He introduced several innovative offices in the White House and program management techniques throughout the executive branch of government. He dramatically modified the executive branch of government by adding new bureaucracy, the Department of Homeland Security, melding several parts of existing agencies.

But Bush was not a purist around scientific management. His administration was deeply infused with politics. Bush was adept, as Reagan had been, in populating the subcabinet names with conservative ideologues,[269] and he used the creation of the Department of Homeland Security in a decidedly political fashion. He relied heavily on the advice of Vice President Cheney,

---

[269]Shirley Cume Warshaw, "Mastering Presidential Government," in Kraus et al.

whose influence reached far down the bureaucracy that he knew so well, from years of government service.[270] Cheney's principal strategy was to advance his business-friendly agenda in the appointment process to staff the government and in the operation of the administration. Using his hiring power during the transition, Cheney filled executive agencies with appointees who shared his (and the president's) views. When he needed someone to manage surface mines, he turned to the mining industry. When he needed someone to manage the national parks, he selected someone from the logging industry. And when he needed someone to manage environmental policy, he drew from the energy industry.[271]

Although he professed allegiance to the MBA style of professional management, Bush's true allegiance was to his conservative principles and his political success. Program outcomes were subordinated to political calculations. This tendency was dramatically exhibited in the Bush administration's replacement of several U.S. attorneys because they were not ardent Bush loyalists.[272]

Finally, Bush and Cheney believed there was a management imperative of restoring the presidency to the dominant force in American government. As far back as when he served as chief of staff to President Gerald Ford in the mid-1970s, Cheney was concerned with the post-Watergate shrinkage of the presidency and the concomitant power grabs by Congress and the courts that, in his perception, intruded on the dominion of the executive.[273] Cheney wanted the president's authority to be as close to absolute as is constitutionally allowed, and advocated for a "unitary" executive. In Cheney's mind, the president's inherent functions—command of the army and navy, director of the cabinet, executor of the law—were indivisible.[274] Given Bush's narrow view of his responsibilities as president, modified of course after 9/11, Cheney's schemes and plans proceeded with great ease. According to Shirley Anne Warshaw:

> The narrow lens through which Bush saw his presidency allowed Cheney wide latitude to implement his own agenda. Since the Bush staff had a limited agenda, Cheney moved into areas that were of little interest to them such as energy, environmental policy, and regulatory issues. He had the information; he knew Bush's goals. Cheney stayed away from issues of greatest importance to Bush and his staff, such as faith-based policies and programs with a moral component.[275]

---

[270]Gellman, 195–213.

[271]Warshaw, 2009, 103.

[272]Dan Eggen and Paul Kane, "Gonzales: Mistakes Were Made," *Washington Post*, March 14, 2007, A01.

[273]Gellman, 82.

[274]Ibid., 96.

[275]Warshaw, 2009, 75–76.

PROCESS

Bush liked to refer to himself as the "the Decider"; he believed in making firm and unambiguous decisions. The president favored the "business" approach to managing and leading and felt his job was to listen carefully to advisers, permit a free flow of information, but ultimately declare a clear and concise verdict. Secretary of State Rice described how Bush frowned on statements that begin with the words, "this is complicated."

There were signs that Bush was open to hearing a variety of opinions on urgent policy matters. He extended "walk-in" access to a greater number of presidential aides than Reagan had, and certainly more than Nixon had.[276] And, as indicated earlier, Bush invited a notably diverse group of professionals to join his administration. Furthermore, Bush expressed an awareness of the dangers of group-think in policy making in a 2002 interview with *Washington Post* reporter Bob Woodward: "If everybody had the same opinion and the same prejudices and same belief structure, I would not get the best advice."[277] And as late as 2005, he commented about meeting with his staff as follows, "They walk in here and they get just overwhelmed by the Oval Office, and they say. 'Man you're looking good, Mr. President.' So I need people walking in here saying, 'You're not looking so good.' "[278]

But as the Bush administration progressed, the "open mind" approach changed. Bush's Treasury Secretary O'Neill described cabinet meetings as entirely "scripted," with the participants assigned the order and substance of their comments in advance.[279] Dissenting opinions expressed publicly were quickly rebuked. For instance, when National Economic Council Chairman Lawrence Lindsay suggested that the cost of the Iraq war might approach $200 billion (it ended up surpassing $500 billion), he was dismissed. When General Eric Shinseki told congress that several hundred thousand soldiers would be needed to provide post-war security in Iraq, he was publicly chided by deputy Secretary of Defense Paul Wolfowitz, and his replacement as army chief of staff was amended a year before his planned retirement.[280]

In the lead-up to the Iraqi invasion, dissenters from the small footprint, "shock and awe" battle plan prepared by Rumsfeld and Cheney, and drawn to specifications by General Tommy Franks, were not warmly received. Cheney put heavy pressure to bring questioning public figures into line with administration policy. He worked particularly hard on House Majority Leader Dick Armey (R-TX), who had expressed doubts about the incipient military intervention. In a private meeting in the vice president's borrowed Capitol hideaway, Cheney presented maps, and blood chilling graphics displaying Saddam's aluminum tubes (allegedly being used to enrich uranium for a bomb) and even

---

[276]Draper.

[277]Bob Woodward, "A Course of Confident Action," *Washington Post*, November 19, 2002, A1.

[278]Rudalevige, 152.

[279]Ibid.

[280]Ibid.

adding the unproved assertion that Iraq had developed the ability to miniaturize WMDs.[281] Armey felt like he was being manipulated by his old friend, but eventually he could not resist Cheney's pressure and cast his vote in favor of the resolution for war.[282]

Another aspect of Bush's decision making was a seeming reluctance to examine the consequences of his decision. Once he made a decision, the Decider was unlikely to doubt himself and even less likely to change course, even in the face of the availability of data indicating an absence of the desired results. During the first presidential debate in the 2004 election between George W. Bush and his Democratic challenger Senator John Kerry (D-MA), Kerry explained, "It's one thing to be certain, but you can be certain and wrong."[283] Treasury Secretary O'Neill experienced the obstinacy of the Bush decisional style when he attempted to convince the president on a less ambitious tax cut. O'Neill reminded Bush that he and Greenspan had backed the Bush tax plan but insisted that it be introduced gradually and in the context of its effects on the economy. In a private meeting, the president told O'Neill, "I don't negotiate with myself."[284] According to Scott McClellan "Bush was not one to look back once a decision was made. Rather than suffer any sense of guilt and anguish, Bush chose not to go down the road of self-doubt or take on the difficult task of honest evaluation and assessment."[285]

THE 2004 ELECTION

George W. Bush anticipated the 2004 presidential election with great confidence, thinking he would be easily re-elected and that his popularity would help Republicans increase their margins in both houses of Congress. His assumptions turned out to be accurate, but his victory over Senator John Kerry was, perhaps, less decisive than he had hoped.

The big advantage that President Bush held, in addition to his incumbency, was his ability to set the agenda for the election. According to political scientist Gerald Pomper, "The election of 2004 was fought primarily on Bush's agenda: foreign policy and terrorism. The Republican campaign focused on those questions, both as substantive policy questions and as choices about which candidate would be the better commander in chief."[286]

---

[281]Gellman, 216–217.

[282]Ibid.

[283]Commission on Presidential Debates, "Debate Transcripts: The First Bush-Kerry Presidential Debate," September 30, 2004, http://www.debates.org/pages/trans2004a.html, accessed September 30, 2009.

[284]Ron Suskind, *The Price of Loyalty: George W. Bush, the White House, and the Education of Paul O'Neil* (New York: Simon and Schuster, 2004), 117.

[285]McClellan, 208.

[286]Gerald Pomper, "The Presidential Election: The Ills of American Politics," in Michael Nelson, ed., *The Election of 2004* (Washington, D.C.: Congressional Quarterly Press, 2004), 58.

In fact, Bush's power in defining the agenda helped narrow the robust field of Democratic contenders for their party's nomination and, in some aspects, made the choice of Massachusetts Senator John Kerry almost inevitable. Ten Democrats announced their intention to capture the party's nomination, including six members of Congress (Senator John Edwards [NC], Senator Bob Graham [FL], Senator John Kerry [MA], Senator Joe Lieberman [CT], Congressman Richard Gephardt [MO], and Congressman Dennis Kucinich [OH]); a former governor (Howard Dean from Vermont); a former senator (Carol Moseley Braun from Illinois); a former army general (Wesley Clark); and an activist minister (Al Sharpton). The field quickly narrowed to Dean, Edwards, and Kerry. The advantages that Dean possessed were that he, unlike Kerry or Edwards, had not been in the Senate to authorize the use of force against Iraq, and that he proved particularly adept at using the Internet to organize support and raise money.[287] But after losing to Kerry in the Iowa caucuses, Dean delivered an overly dramatic and impassioned speech to his supporters, at an unusually high decibel level, screaming that he would "Take back the White House," followed by "Yeeaah!" The speech was dubbed the "I Have a Scream Speech" by journalists and proved to be an important, though not exclusive factor in the demise of Dean's campaign.[288]

John Kerry emerged as the clear winner of the Democratic primaries and as the party's candidate for the presidency. He had a long career in the Senate, but in the particular milieu of the 2004 election, Kerry chose to emphasize his military credentials and his experience as a decorated war hero in Vietnam. Kerry had captained a navy "Swift Boat" on the rivers of South Vietnam during 1968–1969. He received the Bronze Star and Silver Star for heroism and three Purple Hearts for wounds suffered in combat.[289] Nevertheless, Kerry had become a serious critic of the Vietnam War when he returned to Massachusetts.

During the 2004 campaign, a group of his political opponents tied to the Bush campaign, and calling themselves "Swift Vets and POW's for Truth," spent $13.8 million on advertisements attacking Kerry's record and questioning his fitness to be commander in chief. The attacks made several allegations: Kerry had exaggerated his wounds to escape further service; he did not save crew members under fire (the basis for the Bronze Star); he had committed a wartime atrocity (shooting a wounded enemy soldier in the back); and he had undermined the morale of U.S. troops and may have lengthened the war by criticizing it.[290] Investigation by major newspapers and by the Political Fact Check project at the University of Pennsylvania proved that the charges were

---

[287]Barry C. Burden, "The Nomination: Technology, Money, and Transferable Momentum," in Nelson, 27.

[288]Ibid., 30.

[289]Paul J. Quirk and Sean C. Matheson, "The Presidency: The 2004 Elections and the Prospects for Leadership," in Nelson, 138.

[290]Ibid.

fallacious; nonetheless, they had hurt Senator Kerry's standing in the polls. In addition, it took Kerry three weeks to respond to the attacks, far too long in a world of instantaneous communication.[291]

Kerry had another problem. In October 2002, he had joined seventy-six other senators in voting for the use of force against Saddam Hussein. A year later, with Howard Dean's campaign gaining great momentum, Senator Kerry joined only eleven other senators in voting against a supplemental defense appropriation to fund the wars in Iraq and Afghanistan.[292] Before the vote on the defense appropriation, Kerry co-sponsored an unsuccessful amendment to the bill that would have offset the costs of the wars by repealing the Bush tax cuts for the highest income brackets. Kerry was caught in a peculiar political situation of supporting a war but failing to approve funding. The Bush campaign focused heavily on Kerry's ambivalence and tied it to his character as a "flip-flopper."[293]

For his part, George W. Bush ran a highly disciplined campaign. The president stayed relentlessly on message, as he had done in previous campaigns, and conveyed personal warmth through appearances with family members.[294] Even the staging of the Republican National Convention in New York City, a few miles from Ground Zero, added to the urgency that the Bush team associated with re-electing the president and not changing leaders in the middle of a crisis. According to political scientist Roger H. Davidson:

> President Bush . . . won the image contest about keeping the nation safe from terrorism. Whatever the facts of his performance—critics held, for example, that the Iraq venture was a needless and even harmful division from the campaign against terrorism—a majority of voters regarded Bush as a strong leader who had the nation's safety at heart. Conversely, Senator Kerry failed to convince a majority that he would be a steady, conservative leader—the very crux of his campaign task.[295]

Bush prevailed in the November election gaining 62 million votes (50.7 percent) to Kerry's 59 million (48.3 percent), and accumulating 286 electoral votes to Kerry's 251.[296] Moreover, the Republican Party gained seven seats in the House and four in the Senate.[297] Bush explained that the election results were meaningful: "I earned capital in the campaign, political capital . . . and

---

[291]Pomper, 56–57.

[292]Quirk and Matheson, 140.

[293]Pomper, 57.

[294]Ibid.

[295]Roger H. Davidson, "Public Opinion, Presidential Campaigns, and Presidential Governance," in Robert Maranto, Douglas M. Brattebo, and Tom Lansford, eds., *The Second Term of George W. Bush: Prospects and Perils* (New York: Palgrave McMillan, 2006), 36–37.

[296]Nelson, 1.

[297]Jeremy Johnson, Doug Brattebo, Robert Maranto, and Tom Lansford, "Are Second Terms Second Best? Why George W. Bush Might (or might not) Beat the Expectations," in Maranto et al., 4.

now I intend to spend it . . . I've got the will of the people at my back . . . and that's what I intend to tell Congress."[298]

THE SECOND TERM

Bush and his supporters pronounced an electoral mandate for a bold second term agenda to include privatizing social security accounts, further lowering income taxes (and simplifying the tax code itself), filling the federal courts with conservative judges, initiating tort reform, changing bankruptcy procedures, and installing democratic regimes in largely inhospitable environments.[299] But the realities of politics caught up with the president, and he was able to realize only a few of his grand ambitions for change in the second term, as his popularity declined.

Bush hoped for continued legislative and political success and took steps to ensure that his loyal partners dominate the government. Bush placed several high-level White House staff from the first administration into cabinet positions in the second.[300] He had ample opportunity to replace cabinet secretaries, as nine of fifteen who served in the first term resigned. Bush nominated Alberto Gonzalez, previously the White House counsel, to become attorney general; Condoleezza Rice, previously the national security adviser, to become secretary of state; and Margaret Spellings, previously head of the domestic policy council, to become secretary of education. Bush attempted to strategically place his loyalists in executive agencies; however, what they found once they arrived in their new positions was a different political topography than the one they had grown accustomed to in the White House. The new cabinet secretaries would now have to work with large bureaucracies in some cases filled with career civil servants who did not share the administration's vision, and with jealous congressional oversight committees.[301] As well, Bush experienced a significant setback when his first nominee for secretary of homeland security, former New York City Police Commissioner Bernard Kerik, was forced to withdraw his nomination due to press revelations about ethical lapses in previous public positions.[302]

Personnel and administrative issues would not be his only challenges, however. The war in Iraq continued to be unpopular among Americans, Bush's proposal for the reform of social security—featuring individually managed private accounts—went down in flames in Congress, and the president's staff appeared overwhelmed and incompetent when an unprecedented

---

[298]Mike Allen, "Confident Bush Vows to Move Aggressively," *Washington Post*, November 5, 2004, A1.

[299]Davidson, 39.

[300]Bradley H. Patterson, "The Bush White House Staff in the Second Term: New Structures? New Face?" in Maranto et al.

[301]Ibid., 52.

[302]McClellan, 245–246.

hurricane, Katrina, decimated the city of New Orleans and the surrounding Gulf Coast in August 2005.

In terms of Hurricane Katrina, the "chain of failure"[303] started with President Bush and included his secretary of homeland security—Michael Chertoff—and his director of the FEMA—Michael Brown.

On August 26, 2005, when experts described the hurricane approaching Louisiana and Mississippi as unprecedented in nature, it would have behooved Secretary Chertoff and Director Brown, not to mention President Bush, to move into a rapid response mode. Instead, they responded with a sense of calm and bureaucratic routine. Chertoff never left Washington, D.C., staying at his home and office for the crucial forty-eight hours before landfall.[304] As Katrina ravaged nearly 29,000 square miles of Louisiana and Mississippi on Monday, August 29, Chertoff did not even speak to Brown until 8 PM. When CNN, Fox News, and ABC started reporting horrific flooding in New Orleans, due to the levee breaks, Chertoff was dismissive of the media reports.[305] He insisted that Brown and FEMA were doing an excellent job, an assessment shared by President Bush, who proclaimed, "You're doing a heck of a job, Brownie!"

For his part, Michael Brown had received a briefing on Saturday, August 27, from the National Hurricane Center on the severity of Katrina and the likelihood that it would make a direct hit on New Orleans. Brown responded by "letting the day pass."[306] He failed to send emergency response management teams to the South Gulf region, a routine action for a FEMA director in the face of potential problems.

President Bush was on a western vacation as Katrina approached the Gulf Coast, and according to his secretary Scott McClellan, the president should have cancelled the remainder of his trip and returned to Washington before Katrina unleashed its full fury.[307] "Instead," said McClellan, "We delayed and temporized and partially continued with business as usual."[308] In the meantime thousands of people were stranded in attics and on rooftops or elsewhere in New Orleans, waiting for help. Hospitals, filled with gravely ill patients, were losing power, and makeshift shelters, such as the New Orleans Superdome, were filling with tens of thousands of displaced people, "hungry, sick, and scared."[309]

Bush finally took charge of the situation on August 30, when he interrupted his vacation and established a Joint Task Force on Katrina, based at Camp Shelby Mississippi and led by General Russell Honore. He delegated power to Defense Secretary Rumsfeld and Navy Admiral Keating who

---

[303]Douglas Brinkley, *The Great Deluge: Hurricane Katrina, New Orleans and the Mississippi Gulf Coast* (New York: Harper-Perennia 2006), 39.

[304]Ibid., 270.

[305]Ibid.

[306]Ibid., 37.

[307]McClellan, 279.

[308]Ibid.

[309]Ibid., 280.

outlined assets being deployed, including several navy ships, nearly 200 helicopters, and a growing number of National Guard troops.[310]

But for many American citizens, the president's response was too late, and he was having trouble convincing people he truly cared about the people of the Gulf Coast. According to McClellan, Katrina left an "indelible stain" on the Bush presidency, and "one of the worst disasters in our nation's history became one of the biggest disasters in the Bush presidency."[311]

The problems facing Bush seemed to grow daily during the second term. The continuing violence in Iraq—suicide bombings, improvised explosive devices, sniper fire, and the daily killing of American solders—was causing many Americans to view the war as a "quagmire" from which there was no obvious escape. The president's proposal to reform social security by introducing voluntary personal retirement accounts failed in Congress, and proved to be unpopular among ordinary Americans, as revealed in Gallup polls.[312] His proposal to add prescription drug coverage for Medicare recipients passed; however, the price tag was estimated to be $400 billion over ten years.[313] Finally, several highly visible political scandals involving Republican lobbyist Jack Abramoff and Republican House leader Tom DeLay, among others, also sapped some of the strength from the Republican Party. In the 2006 congressional elections, the GOP, and its leader, George W. Bush, took a serious beating by the Democrats. When the dust settled, the nation elected thirty new Democrats to the House and six to the Senate, and the Democrats made California Congresswoman Nancy Pelosi the first female speaker of the house in U.S. history. Remarkably, Democrats did not lose a single seat in either body, the first election in U.S. history where a party retained all its congressional seats.[314] Research by political scientist Gary Jacobsen clearly showed that the war in Iraq, Republican scandals, and the leadership deficits of President Bush all contributed to this outcome.[315]

FINANCIAL CRISIS AID: BUSH ADMINISTRATIVE RESPONSE

In August 2006, President Bush met with his economic team at Camp David under generally favorable economic conditions. Although the dollar had shown some weakness, especially against the euro, the U.S. economy was generally sound. The nation's gross domestic product (GDP) had risen by nearly

---

[310]Ibid., 287.

[311]Ibid., 290.

[312]http://www.gallup.com/poll/1693/Social-Security.aspx#.

[313]Robin Toner and Robert Pear, "Compromise Seen as Harder to Find on Medicare Drugs," *New York Times,* July 13, 2002, A1.

[314]Gary C. Jacobson, "Referendum: The 2006 Midterm Elections," *Political Science Quarterly* (Spring 2007), 1.

[315]Ibid., 13–20.

5 percent in the first quarter and just under 3 percent in the second.[316] Nevertheless, recently appointed Treasury Secretary Henry Paulson expressed some uneasiness to his colleagues. He indicated that the United States was conducting two wars (Iraq and Afghanistan), expenses for hurricanes Katrina and Rita were mounting, and entitlement spending was on the increase.[317] In addition, Paulson noted that to support unprecedented consumer spending and to compensate for its low savings rate, the United States was borrowing heavily from abroad, while export-driven countries—notably China and oil producers—were shipping capital to the United States and inadvertently fueling its spendthrift ways. Their recycled dollars enriched Wall Street and inflated tax receipts in the short term, but undermined long-term economic strategy.[318] Paulson added that markets in general rarely went many years without a severe disruption and that we had not had a major financial dislocation since 1998. He did not include the housing market in particular in his listing of the underlying threats to continued economic prosperity; that was a significant oversight. The financial crisis of 2007–2008, which was caused largely by the housing market, arrived in full force on August 9, 2007, and according to Paulson, "the damage was deeper and more long lasting than any of us could have imagined."[319]

The crisis that began in August 2007 had been building for several years. The problem was created by an unprecedented boom in the housing industry, fueled in part by low interest rates that helped Americans recover from the downturn following the end of the dot-com influenced prosperity. The housing bubble was driven by a significant increase in loans to less credit worthy individuals who were called "subprime borrowers."[320]

Subprime lending and associated practices helped lift homeownership to historic levels; 69 percent of U.S. households owned their own home by July 2006. Subprime loans had soared from 5 percent of total mortgage obligations in 1994 to 20 percent in July 2006.[321] In short, the issue was that too many homes had been purchased with little or no money down, often for speculative purposes, on the hope that property values would go up. According to Paulson, "Predatory lenders and unscrupulous brokers pushed increasingly complex mortgages on unsuspecting buyers."[322]

By the fourth quarter of 2006, the housing market was in a rapid decline, as delinquencies on subprime mortgages escalated, leading to a wave of foreclosures and huge financial losses at subprime lending institutions. In

---

[316]Henry Paulson Jr., *On the Brink: Inside the Race to Stop the Collapse of the Financial System* (New York: Busuirs Plus, 2010), 43.

[317]Ibid., 43–44.

[318]Ibid., 44.

[319]Ibid., 61.

[320]Ibid., 64.

[321]Ibid.

[322]Ibid., 65.

February 2007, London-based HSBC Holdings, the world's third largest bank, announced it was setting aside $10.6 billion to cover bad debts on U.S. subprime lending portfolios. In the same month, New Century Financial Corporation, the second biggest subprime lender, said it would show serious losses for 2006, and by April 2007 it was bankrupt.[323]

Secretary Paulson and his staff organized a series of meetings across the government to assess the situation. He also reinvigorated the President's Working Group on Financial Markets (PWG) that had been formed after the October 1987 stock market crash. The PWG brought together senior officials from the treasury department, the Fed (Federal Reserve Board), the SEC (Securities and Exchange Commission), and the CFTC (Commodity Future Trading Commission) to discuss financial and economic developments and potential problems.[324] Paulson developed particularly close working relationships with Timothy Geithner, chairman of the New York Federal Reserve Bank, and Ben Bernanke, chairman of the U.S. Federal Reserve Board.

The housing decline would have been a problem in its own right. But the changes in the way mortgages were made and sold, combined with a reshaped financial system, amplified the potential damages to banks and non-bank financial institutions.[325]

One of the biggest problems requiring the attention of Paulson and his colleagues was the fate of Fannie Mae and Freddie Mac, which had been chartered by Congress years earlier to stabilize U.S. mortgage markets and promote affordable housing for American families. These institutions did not lend directly to homeowners, but sold insurance guaranteeing timely payment of mortgages, which were packaged into securities and sold by bankers to investors. The congressional charter protected Fannie and Freddie from state and local taxes and gave them emergency lines of credit at treasury, which backed up their assets. Both agencies had prospered in this environment, and by 2005 they jointly guaranteed nearly one-half of residual mortgages in the United States, equivalent to $4.4 trillion at the time.[326] According to Paulson, with weak oversight and dual regulators (the U.S. Department of HUD oversaw the housing mission, whereas the Office of Federal Housing Enterprise Oversight, OFHEO, the finances), Fannie and Freddie were "disasters ready to happen."[327]

Paulson detailed how central Fannie Mae and Freddie Mac were to U.S. markets. Between them they owned or guaranteed more than $5 trillion in residential mortgages and mortgage-based securities—almost half of all those in the country. To finance operations, they were among the biggest issuers of

---

[323]Ibid.

[324]Philip Swagel, *The Financial Crisis: An Inside View*, Brooking's Paper on Economic Activity, Conference Draft, Spring 2009, 4.

[325]Paulson, 67.

[326]Ibid., 56.

[327]Ibid., 57.

debt in the world, a total of about $1.7 trillion for the pair. They were perpetually in the markets, borrowing more than $20 billion a week at times.[328]

But investors were losing faith in these institutions; combined they already had $5.5 billion in net losses for the year 2008. Their common share value had plunged, and Standard & Poor's had twice downgraded both companies. The ripple effects on the financial system of a Fannie–Freddie failure would be enormous, and Paulson proposed that the government put $100 billion of capital behind each with more to come. The plans amounted to a "conservatorship" for Fannie and Freddie.

Concern mounted in the White House about the long-term implications of Paulson's bold plan, and President Bush insisted that the action be properly explained to the public. "We have to make clear," said President Bush, "that what we are doing now is transitory, because otherwise it looks like nationalization."[329]

Working with White House staff and gaining the support of Congress, while overcoming strong resistance from Senator Richard Shelby (R-AL), Paulson helped achieve passage of the Housing and Economic Recovery Act (HERA) of 2008, which set the foundation for the government rescue of Fannie Mae and Freddie Mac.[330] The bill passed in the House by a vote of 272–152 and in the Senate by 72–13.[331] President Bush signed the bill on July 30 in the Oval Office.[332] Secretary Paulson summarized the rescue of Fannie and Freddie as follows:

- The Federal Housing Finances Agency (FHFA) would place the companies into conservatorship.
- The government would provide up to $100 billion to each company to backstop any capital shortfalls.
- Treasury would establish a new secure lending credit faculty for Fannie and Freddie and would begin a temporary program to buy mortgage-backed securities they guaranteed, to boost the housing market.[333]

Another feature of the HERA legislation was the HOPE Now Alliance, a joint effort by the U.S. departments of Treasury and HUD to reach out to struggling borrowers and encourage them to work with counselors and their mortgage servicers.[334] HOPE was criticized by conservatives, who claimed that the government was bailing out homeowners (in spite of the fact that HOPE gave out no public money), and from liberals who complained that

---

[328]Ibid., 3.

[329]Ibid., 5.

[330]H.R. 3221, Housing and Economic Recovery Act of 2008, Congressional Research Service Summary, http://thomas.loc.gov/cgi-bio, accessed on 12/15/1`0.

[331]Paulson, 155.

[332]Ibid., 156.

[333]Ibid., 17.

[334]Ibid., 75.

the government was not doing enough. Nevertheless, according to Paulson, HOPE helped about 700,000 homeowners obtain loan modifications during the last three months of 2008.[335]

The financial crisis, however, had spread into other areas, including conventional and investment banks. On November 15, 2007, the Federal Reserve Board pumped $47.25 billion in temporary reserves into the banking system—its biggest injection since 9/11.[336] The White House began to consider a tax stimulus, and on January 2, 2008, Paulson met with President Bush to lay the groundwork for a stimulus plan. On January 18, 2008, President Bush called for a spending package of 1 percent of GDP, or about $150 billion designed to give the economy a "shot in the arm" with onetime tax rebates and tax breaks to encourage businesses to purchase equipment.[337] Paulson worked with the Speaker of the House Nancy Pelosi (D-CA) and Minority Leader John Boehner (R-OH) to craft a $150 billion stimulus plan centered on a $100 billion in tax rebates for an estimated 117 million American families. The stimulus would give as much as $1,200 to certain households, with an additional $300 for each child.[338] According to Paulson, the stimulus represented a huge political and legislative accomplishment and President Bush signed it into law on February 13, after a remarkable two-week passage through the House and Senate.[339]

But the markets continued to slip, troubled by oil prices, a weakening dollar, and ongoing concern about credit. During the week of March 3–7, the Dow lost almost 373 points.[340] Investment firms showed great vulnerability and Bear Stearns, one of the giants of Wall Street that had a long reputation as one of the most astute risk managers, was under the most intense pressure. Its portfolio featured a large mortgage business, but also had a less diverse mix of other businesses than did its investment banking rivals, such as Goldman Sachs and Morgan Stanley.[341] The reliance on mortgages meant that Bear was especially vulnerable during the accelerating housing crisis, and it was becoming clear that the firm could not withstand a significant retreat by worried customers—in effect, a run on the bank.[342] There was great concern about a Bear Stearns bankruptcy, and Paulson brokered a deal whereby the federal government through the Federal Reserve would lend money to JP Morgan which in turn would lend money to Bear Stearns and prevent a bankruptcy. The deal was set specifying that JP Morgan would buy Bear for

---

[335]Ibid., 77.

[336]Ibid., 83.

[337]Ibid., 85.

[338]Ibid., 86.

[339]Ibid.

[340]Ibid., 87.

[341]Kate Kelly, Greg Ip, and Robin Sidel, "Fed Races to Rescue Bear Stearns in Bid to Steady Financial Crisis," *Wall Street Journal*, March 15, 2008, A1.

[342]Ibid.

$2 per share; however, the offer had to be raised to $10 a share to get the approval of Bear Stearns stockholders, which they gave on May 29, 2008.[343]

Lehman Brothers was also in trouble. Paulson and his colleagues literally searched the world for a buyer for the beleaguered company. But the country, Congress, and both parties were fed up with bailouts.[344] In addition, research conducted by major banks and federal officials revealed that Lehman Brothers was actually in worse shape than Bear Stearns had been, due to a gaping hole in its balance sheet.[345] The White House, through Chief of Staff Josh Bolten, delivered the verdict that no federal resources were to be committed to save Lehman, and Bush cautioned Paulson on the need to educate the public on the differences between Bear Stearns and Lehman Brothers.[346] With no buyer, no legal authority, and no injection of capital, Lehman Brothers eventually went bankrupt, the biggest bankruptcy in U.S. history.

After the fall of Lehman Brothers, Paulson admonished his staff that they would need a broader approach to save the financial system than that of the "one-off firefights" that they had been pursuing. He also escalated his rhetoric in conversation with colleagues such as Fed Chairman Ben Bernanke, exclaiming, "This is the economic equivalent of war. The market is ready to collapse."[347] Reflecting on the situation in his memoir, Paulson quipped, "We couldn't keep using duct tape and bailing wire to try to hold the system together. This was a national crisis and both the executive and legislative branches of government needed to be involved."[348]

On September 18, 2008, Paulson explained to President Bush and Deputy Chief of Staff Joel Kaplan that the crisis had reached a "tipping" point and more dramatic action was needed. He counseled Bush and Kaplan that the administration would have to go to Congress and seek "sweeping" fiscal authority.[349] Bush promised full White House support.

Paulson consulted with congressional leaders and economists, and reached the conclusion that the government would have to buy the troubled assets of some of the nation's largest banks and corporate entities, and President Bush agreed to the plan. Treasury staff would take the lead, and would work closely with the House and Senate financial service committees to outline what would become the Troubled Assets Relief Program (TARP).[350] The cost was set at $700 billion. Paulson summarized the administration's plan in a three-page proposal asking Congress for broad power to spend up to $700 billion to buy troubled assets, including mortgages and mortgage-backed securities, under

---

[343]Paulson, 120.

[344]Ibid., 181.

[345]Ibid., 208.

[346]Ibid., 216.

[347]Ibid., 254.

[348]Ibid.

[349]Ibid., 251.

[350]Ibid., 265.

the terms that the administration saw fit to use. The proposal went to the Hill on September 19, 2008.[351]

The release of the TARP proposal coincided with the most intense period of the 2008 presidential race; GOP candidate John McCain (R-AZ) decided to suspend his presidential campaign and fly to Washington, D.C., to consult with his Republican colleagues. Meanwhile, President Bush went on national television on September 24, 2008, and explained to American citizens the urgency of the financial crisis and the need for dramatic action.[352] The president subsequently met with congressional leaders and treasury staff, and the three-page TARP outline morphed into a forty-page bill sponsored by Senator Christopher Dodd (D-CT), chairman of the Senate Banking Committee, and Representative Barney Frank (D-MA), chairman of the House Committee on Financial Services. The proposed legislation featured a compromise on the release of the TARP funds: Congress would release an initial $250 billion that would be increased if the president certified to Congress that it was necessary to release the additional $350 billion. The U.S. Treasury Department would have to submit a report to Congress with detailed plans for the use of the funds.[353] The bill also contained restrictions on compensation for executives participating in TARP, as well as multiple levels of oversight.[354] But on September, 29, 2008, TARP was defeated in the House of Representatives by a vote of 228–205. Many Republicans refused to support what they considered to be a "bailout."[355]

Shortly after the House defeat of TARP, the White House Chief of Staff Josh Bolten approached Secretary Paulson and said, "Hank, you've done what you can do. Give me the ball for a few days and let me see if we can corral the votes."[356] The elevated activity of the White House helped move the proposal toward a more successful outcome. Also helpful was Congressman Rahm Emanuel's (D-IL) strategy in collaboration with Senate Minority Leader Harry Reid (D-NV) to push the legislation through the Senate first. The calculation was that Senate Republicans were more secure in their seats than were their House counterparts and more sympathetic to a bold government action such as TARP,[357] and to gain increased Republican support in the House, Paulson and his colleagues added the inducement of combining TARP with energy-related tax credits that were set to expire. Another sweetener was raising the Federal Deposit Insurance Company (FDIC) deposit insurance limit.[358]

---

[351]Ibid., 268.
[352]Ibid., 290.
[353]Ibid., 310.
[354]Ibid., 314.
[355]Ibid., 319.
[356]Ibid., 321.
[357]Ibid., 322.
[358]Ibid., 323.

With significant assistance from Reid, the administration obtained passage of TARP by the U.S. Senate on October 1, 2008, by a vote of 74–25.[359] And on October 3, the House passed TARP in the Emergency Economic Stabilization Act of 2008, by a margin of 263–171, with ninety-one Republicans voting for the bill.[360]

In spite of the passage of TARP legislation, the financial situation continued to deteriorate. Paulson and his colleagues determined that the asset-buying strategy would have to be augmented by the infusion of cash into struggling financial institutions and corporations. Accordingly, Paulson devised the Term Asset-Backed Securities Loan Facility (TALF) as an adjunct to TARP, allowing the Fed to loan $125 billion to the nine largest U.S. banks, and $40 billion to the struggling insurance giant AIG.[361]

The cash infusion strategy would replace asset buying as the government's main weapon to save the economy during the waning days of the Bush administration. Paulson also determined that he would need to convince Congress to release the second half of the TARP funds, and this action would require the close collaboration between the outgoing Bush administration and the incoming Obama administration. It would also free up money that could be used to help the struggling automobile companies that had appealed to Congress for billions of dollars in assistance. According to Paulson:

> For President Bush, an auto bailout was a bitter pill to swallow, especially as the last major decision of his administration. He disliked bailouts and he disdained Detroit for not making cars people wanted to buy. But we were in the midst of a financial crisis and a deepening economic recession, and he recognized that if these giant companies were to declare bankruptcy, they would be doing so without advance planning or adequate financing for an orderly restructuring. The consequence for the economy would be devastating.[362]

President Bush decided that the government would loan Chrysler $4 billion and General Motors (GM) a total of $13.4 billion from TARP.[363] Paulson also realized that the auto companies had spun off their own financial industries, and that these were also in trouble. On December 29, 2008, the treasury announced a $5 billion infusion of capital from TARP into GMAC Financial Services, along with an additional $1 billion for GM to invest in GMAC. And on January 16, 2009, the treasury committed $1.5 billion of TARP funds to Chrysler Financial, to make new loans to car buyers.[364] Finally, on January

---

[359]Ibid., 326.

[360]Ibid., 328.

[361]Ibid., 351, 369.

[362]Ibid., 424.

[363]David E. Sanger, David M. Herszenhorn, and Bill Vlasic, "Bush Aids Detroit, but Hard Choices Wait for Obama," *New York Times*, December 20, 2008, B1.

[364]Paulson, 431.

12, 2009, President Bush formally requested the second $350 billion from Congress. On January 15, 2009, the Senate voted to give the President-elect Obama these funds.[365]

In the end, the Bush administration had helped the nation avert a major financial disaster. According to Paulson, "We had been on the brink, but we had not fallen."[366]

And in his moving words, Paulson summed it all up as follows:

> The crises that began in 2007 was far more severe, and the risks to the economy and the American people much greater. Between March and September 2008, eight major U.S. financial institutions failed—Bear Stearns, Indy Mac, Fannie Mae, Freddie Mac, Lehman Brothers, AIG, Washington Mutual, and Wachovia—six of them in September alone. And the damage was not limited to the U.S. More than 20 European banks, across 10 countries, were rescued from July 2007 through February 2009. This, the most wrenching financial crisis since the Great Depression, caused a terrible recession in the U.S. and severe harm around the world. Yet it could have been so much worse. Had it not been for unprecedented interventions by the U.S. and other governments, many more financial institutions would have gone under—and the economic damage would have been far greater and longer lasting.[367]

In dealing with the financial crisis, President Bush was able to suspend his strong ideological convictions and take the necessary measures to restore the health of the nation's financial system and economy. He empowered his staff, including Secretary Paulson and Chairman Bernanke, to manage the crisis with the tools that they believed were needed. He provided the political cover and support for congressional passage of bailout measures, gaining several Republican votes along the way. But neither the president nor his close associates ever admitted that the administration's tax policies, antipathy to regulations, and their strong belief in the wonders of unfettered capitalism could have contributed to the crisis in the first place.

SUMMING UP

George W. Bush was a visionary president who embraced the philosophical tenets of compassionate conservatism and demonstrated programmatic expression of its ideals in his White House structure and domestic policy initiatives. In foreign policy, he became convinced of the strategy of preemption and the need to reorient American foreign policy, for 9/11 had opened the door to a new, more dangerous world for America and her ideals.

---

[365]Ibid.

[366]Ibid., 434.

[367]Ibid., 436.

In both cases, he displayed strong convictions and a willingness to fight for his beliefs, as well as a preference to surround himself with people who shared them. And yet, in both instances he also displayed the "instincts of an absolutist."[368] To the absolutist, according to *Washington Post* reporter John Harris, adherence to principle is the supreme virtue. "In the Iraq context," continued Harris, "this led him—with little self doubt or agonizing—on a path of confrontation with Saddam Hussein within weeks of the September 11th attacks."[369] In the domestic arena, Bush's belief in the conservative philosophy of tax cuts led him to push for them at all costs and without much regard to consequences. His deep religious convictions influenced his unyielding support of faith-based initiatives, opposition to stem-cell research, opposition to same-sex marriage, and insouciance to the dangers of church–state overlap.[370] His visionary leadership, then, was flawed in the sense that it was fundamentally unchallenged, especially by the president. Focusing on decisiveness as his defining attribute, Bush pursued his vision with the tenacity of a fanatic.

In terms of politics, Bush promised to change the tone in Washington and to be a "uniter, not a divider." A great deal of his political history—especially as governor of Texas—suggested that he would stay true to those goals, and his early days in the White House Bush seemed to be consistent with that message. As noted by Jerome Ciulla, professor of leadership studies at the University of Richmond, what made Bush popular in the days after 9/11 was his resolve, but also his willingness to reach out to Democrats, to foreign leaders, and to peace-loving Muslims.[371] He achieved early legislative success in the passage of No Child Left Behind and a massive tax cut. He performed admirably as a leader in the aftermath of 9/11 and was rewarded handsomely, with the highest public approval rating ever known to be received by a sitting president.

But the bipartisanship did not last long, as the permanent campaign style of governance set in. According to Scott McClellan, "The permanent campaign approach we publicly denounced and distanced ourselves from in the 2000 campaign was vigorously embraced . . . The massive Bush campaign machine was integrally woven into his White House governance, without adequate controls or corresponding checks and balances."[372]

Once Bush decided to attack Saddam Hussein, the administration moved into a marketing campaign. According to McClellan, "Selling war through a political marketing campaign rather than openly and forthrightly discussing the need for war with the American people is fraught with danger."[373] Bush

---

[368]John F. Harris, "George W. Bush and William J. Clinton: The Hedgehog and the Fox," in Steven E. Schier, ed., *High Risk and Big Ambition: The Presidency of George W. Bush* (Pittsburg: University of Pittsburg Press, 2004), 114.

[369]Ibid.

[370]See "God and George W. Bush," in Warshaw, 2009, 77–101.

[371]Cannon and Cannon, 94.

[372]McClellan, 311.

[373]Ibid., 312.

integrated his political operation into the White House, primarily through Karl Rove, and he allowed Rove to influence the politics of his administration toward the right. Rove's insistence on appeasing "the base," conservative and evangelical Republicans who came out in great force for Bush in both presidential elections, precluded Bush from governing from the center. Indeed Rove was convinced that Bush could help establish a realignment of politics favoring the Republican Party, just as Franklin Roosevelt had done for the Democrats. In addition, the unprecedented freedom of action that Bush granted to Vice President Cheney, and Cheney's integration of his staff with that of the president, gave Cheney an unparalleled amount of power. His influence was clear in Bush's failure to accommodate Senator Jim Jeffords; in the administration's repudiation of almost any environmental legislation and pulling out of international treaties on the subject; in the tendency of the president to continue to influence laws that survived the legislative process, through presidential "signing statements"; in the assertion of presidential prerogatives and actions reinforcing the notion of a "unitary executive"; and in countless other ways. It may be an exaggeration to characterize the presidency as a co-presidency (as Professor Warshaw does), but it is no exaggeration to suggest that Cheney's power as vice president was unprecedented.

Bush proved particularly adept at cultivating an image as a strong, decisive leader with the courage to defeat the terrorists. He was more than willing to take on elevated executive powers to guarantee success and he was effective in portraying his political opponents as lacking courage. This strategy helped Bush and his party attain electoral success in the congressional elections of 2002, as well as the presidential and congressional elections of 2004. Nonetheless, by 2006, the magic had worn thin, and Democrats trounced the Republicans and George W. Bush at the polls.

In the structure of his presidency, Bush emphasized his MBA degree and business credentials. He sought to achieve better management of the executive branch and to instill a culture of accountability in the federal government. In several respects, he succeeded in these endeavors. In addition, President Bush eventually bought in the idea of adding a new, large federal agency to the panoply of executive departments with the specific task of protecting the homeland from attacks. The tragic events of 9/11 helped convince Bush that a focused and high-level approach was needed to help Americans stay one or two steps ahead of terrorists. But he allowed his campaign to use the Department of Homeland Security as a political weapon by creating huge political problems for senatorial candidates who questioned specific provisions of the enabling legislation. His goal was not merely to fashion the new department to his image, but as Lou and Carl Cannon point out, to get the Senate back into Republican hands.[374] In short, Bush's proclamation of business acumen notwithstanding, he was fundamentally a political animal whose instincts for getting re-elected trumped his belief in administrative excellence.

---

[374]Cannon and Cannon, 90.

Finally, as a decision maker, the president gave himself the moniker of the Decider. He was proud of his ability to make clear, unambiguous decisions. But he was particularly inept on the matter of honestly assessing the impact of his decisions and evaluating the results. He exhibited self-confidence that bordered on hubris when it came to his actions. An egregious example of this dynamic occurred at a press conference in April 2004 when the president called on John Dickerson, a White House correspondent for *Time* magazine. Dickerson had an easy-going, down-to-earth manner, not unlike Bush's own, which made Bush partial to him, according to Scott McClellan. Dickerson had asked Bush to talk about the biggest mistake he had made after 9/11 and the lessons he had drawn from it. McClellan described what happened next:

> The president began with a lighthearted quip: "I wish you would have given this written question ahead of time, so I could plan for it." The assembled reporters chuckled. "John, I'm sure historians will look back and say, gosh, he could have done it better this way, or that way. You know, I just—I'm sure something will pop into my head in the midst of this press conference, with all the pressure, of trying to come up with an answer, but it hasn't yet." His response was followed by an agonizingly long pause.[375]

---

[375]McClellan, 204–205.

Conclusion

The following quote from boxer Muhammad Ali's manager/
coach, Angelo Dundee, is on display in the Muhammad Ali Center in
Louisville, Kentucky:

> If you take the endurance of a tennis player, the courage of a racing driver,
> the sensibility of an actor, the continued discipline of a long-distance runner,
> and mix them together, you are on your way to knowing what it takes to be a
> professional boxer.[1]

This formulation can be used to concoct the skill set of an ideal U.S. president: Someone who has the experience and networks of George H. W. Bush,
the courage and strength of purpose of Ronald Reagan, the intellectual power
and political insight of Bill Clinton, the moral integrity of Jimmy Carter, and
the clarity of vision and perseverance of George W. Bush.

Of course it will be hard to find a president who possesses all those skills,
and the search for that person would be highly frustrating. The book has set
out a more modest, though still formidable, skill set for effectiveness in the
White House: A president who as a leader develops and enunciates a clear and
compelling vision or purpose for his administration; one who can persuade influential people and opinion leaders, including Congress and interest groups,
to support his vision, while simultaneously staying open to modifying it before
final implementation; one who designs the White House staff and executive
office of the president in ways that will help attain the president's goals, while
also assuring appropriate policy implementation through huge executive agencies; and finally, one who exhibits a solid approach to decision making, one
who tolerates and even encourages diverse views but ends up with clear and
unambiguous decisions and options.

How have the five presidents covered in this book performed?

Of course they all have significant achievements attached to their names:
Carter, the Camp David Accords between Israel and Egypt; Reagan, the revitalization of the conservative movement in the United States, substantial economic reform, and the achievement of substantial arms control agreements

---

[1]Muhammad Ali Center, Louisville, Kentucky, www.alicenter.org.

with the Soviet Union; George H. W. Bush, the competent management of the end of the Cold War, along with the substantial political-military victory in the Persian Gulf War; Clinton, the revitalization of the Democratic Party, along with substantial reduction in the nation's deficits, unemployment, and crime; and George W. Bush, the achievement of the first meaningful education reform law in decades, along with an effective, if only temporary, management of the post-9/11 political and strategic response of the United States to terror.

At the same time, each president also has a lugubrious legacy, a failure, that attaches to his name: Carter's inability to achieve a substantial energy policy, in addition to his lackluster performance in dealing with Congress; Reagan's seeming insouciance to growing levels of budgetary deficits and glaring disregard of constitutional boundaries in Iran-Contra; George H. W. Bush's highly visible and poorly explained about-face on his very public promise of "no new taxes"; Clinton's poor judgment in having an inappropriate sexual relationship with a White House intern, and then lying about it; and George W. Bush's ultimate obsession with a policy of preempting terrorists that drove the country deep into military commitments in Iraq at exorbitant expense.

The purpose of the book has not been to thoroughly analyze any one, or even several policy successes or failures, but to search for the deeper structures of leadership effectiveness that U.S. presidents are called upon to exercise. With the exceptions of the excellent work of Fred Greenstein and David Gergen along with the pioneering work of James David Barber and Stephen Skowronek, very few scholarly texts have addressed this issue.

So let us now examine the leadership performance of five presidents who have inhabited the Oval Office since Watergate, along the four leadership dimensions used throughout the book: policy (vision), politics (strategy), structure (management), and process (decision making).

POLICY: VISION/PURPOSE

Carter's vision was not entirely clear. He was forceful in his critique of the status quo, and fierce in his denunciation of Nixon's imperial presidency. He was comfortable with the identity of an outsider who could govern in a purer fashion than almost all conventional politicians. Carter was not beholden to strong interest groups or even the strictures imposed upon him by his political party. He was a man of honesty and ethics who could attack problems with an engineer's objectivity and a scientist's rigor. He mastered the details of governance as he had in Georgia and simply implement the correct policies for the nation on energy, health care, foreign policy, education, and the environment.

Above all, Carter's vision focused on his personal story. Carter's emphasis was more on who he *was* and less on what he would *do*. He was a good, honest, decent man who had strong religious values and believed in racial and social equality. He believed in the power of moral suasion and in the pursuit of peaceful solutions to daunting problems, such as Middle East peace.

Ronald Reagan was a truly visionary president. He was also an outsider clearly not wedded to conventional wisdom, and he successfully challenged the prevailing paradigms in both domestic and foreign policy arenas. Essentially, Reagan believed that government had become too big and bloated and that it was sapping the vitality and energy from the economic system by taxing its citizens at inordinately high levels and using their tax dollars to support overly generous public welfare programs, which had become entitlements in the eyes of the recipients. Government leaders had created a system of dependencies and lost sight of the true engine of economic progress: the market. Reagan believed in supply-side economics, holding the view that the money citizens saved by not paying high taxes would be invested in productive enterprises, and everyone would benefit. (In fact, Reagan quoted John F. Kennedy, who famously said, "A rising tide lifts all boats.") He fought hard to make substantial changes in federal budget and tax policy, and through the clarity of his vision and the dexterity of his lobbying efforts, succeeded in getting a good deal accomplished. David Gergen, who served in Reagan's White House, summarized the president's vision as follows:

> Reagan believed that government was creeping into too many areas of domestic life, smothering other forces in civil society. He wanted to restore the central role of the family, church and other mediating institutions. By reducing tax rates and lifting regulations, he thought he would do more than revive the economy. People would also reclaim personal freedom and self-reliance. And, over time, they would rebuild confidence in themselves. Reagan was an evangelist for a new civil religion. In the 1960s and 1970s, he was a voice in the wilderness; in the early 1990s, he was still seen as a reactionary; by the late 1990s his ideas were ascendant. When a Democratic president, Bill Clinton, declared in his 1996 State of the Union address that "the era of big government is over," it was clear that Reagan had introduced a new political regime.[2]

Alongside his non-conventional approach to domestic policy, Reagan developed a wholly different orientation to American foreign policy. Reagan's ultimate goal was a more peaceful world, with lower numbers of nuclear weapons; however, the means he chose to achieve these mostly peaceful goals were considerably more confrontational and assertive than the foreign policy thrusts of the Carter administration. Referring to the Soviet Union as the evil empire and demanding significant increases in U.S. military expenditures, Reagan projected the image of the ultimate cold warrior. His antipathy to communism was well developed, not only because of his negative estimation of a state-controlled economy, but perhaps most cogently because of the communist state's disdain for religion and oppression of religious minorities. And yet, toward the end of his years as president, in his second administration,

---

[2]David Gergen, *Eyewitness to Power: The Essence of Leadership, Nixon to Clinton* (New York: Simon and Schuster, 2000), 157.

Reagan's views became more conciliatory, more oriented toward arms control negotiation, and more attuned to diplomatic overtures from Gorbachev and other Soviet leaders.[3] He expressed very strong doubts about the effectiveness of mutual assured destruction (MAD), which had animated American and Soviet foreign policy for many years, and pointed to a more hopeful situation where both nations were in possession of fewer nuclear weapons.

George H. W. Bush expressed a discomfort, and in fact a cynicism with having a vision for the presidency, which he referred to as the "vision thing." Success in politics for him depended on building and sustaining important relationships and friendships. Bush had held almost every important position there was to hold in American government, and among all the presidents considered here, he's the only one who chose to—or even could—campaign as an insider. Based on the depth of his political experience and on the amazing extent of personal and professional networks he developed, George H. W. Bush could offer the nation a sense of trusted competence and a reservoir of impressive experience, particularly in the foreign policy realm.

Bush believed that leadership is not always grandiose and does not always occur in broad strategic leaps into the future, but that it lurches forward in small steps "as history unfolds one page at a time." As the world was undergoing profound transformation during his time as president, the role required of an American president, in his view, was a *manager* who could help maintain international stability as the massive changes unleashed by the dissolution of the Soviet Empire promised a more hopeful political future for millions of people in the Soviet bloc; but, if not properly managed, the changes could have also caused a stern and unpleasant reaction by the Soviet leadership. Conservative internationalism would be the best way to typify the Bush vision for international relations, though he might bristle at fancy words to characterize his practical actions.

Domestically, on the other hand, Bush displayed meager attempts at a vision, and in some cases his interest and capability in the whole enterprise could be questioned. He shared the basic conservative view of laissez-faire economics, translated into tax cuts, but believed there could be a great surge of volunteerism—a "thousand points of light"—to help America's most disadvantaged people. He thought that government was not always the answer, because it was not always capable and it was running up a huge deficit ("our will is bigger than our wallet"). So Bush did his best in a slow deliberate way, relying on the continued success of the Reagan Revolution, but introduced new programs reluctantly and slowly. Unsurprisingly, his domestic policy vision is characterized by journalists and political scientists as disjointed incrementalism.

Bill Clinton identified himself as a New Democrat and truly indicated a willingness to depart from the prevailing orthodoxy of the Democratic

---

[3]James Mann, *Reagan's Revolution. The Rebellion of Ronald Reagan: A History of the End of the Cold War* (New York: Viking Adult, 2009).

Party. Through his long and mostly successful involvement in political campaigns and through his active leadership of the Democratic Leadership Council, Clinton came to believe that the Democratic Party needed to revitalize itself. (Ironically, when third-party candidate Ross Perot temporarily pulled out of the 1988 presidential campaign, he said that he was doing so because Clinton and Gore had revitalized the Democratic Party.) Clinton encouraged his colleagues to develop a more positive embrace of business interests, global consciousness, a passion for education reform, and a belief in a culture of "personal responsibility." He fought hard to maintain budgetary discipline and brought down the deficit, fending off the supplications of his liberal allies inside and outside the administration. At the same time, when he veered off course, and retreated into the more familiar liberalism expressed in his (and his wife's) health care reform proposals, he was quick to acknowledge the error and the need to find his way back to the center.

In foreign policy, Clinton displayed an embrace of globalism and an interest in evolving trade and business policies that would enhance America's position as a global leader. He was, perhaps, slow to act in situations such as Bosnia, and inept in others, such as Somalia, but he displayed an acumen for grasping the nuances of foreign affairs and the details of diplomacy as he did with the Middle East, particularly when he turned his attention to the Israeli-Palestinian conflict.

George W. Bush did not want to repeat his father's cynicism toward vision and defined himself domestically as a compassionate conservative from his days as a Texas governor to his time in the Oval Office. Schooled by philosophers such as Marvin Olasky and others, Bush believed that private agencies and voluntary faith-based groups were more effective and had more experience administering social welfare programs than federal and even state governments did. Bush wanted to release the restrictions on faith-based groups from full participation in social welfare programs and in helping the poor. It was not a surprise that one of his first actions as president was to introduce an Office of Faith-Based Initiatives into the White House.

Domestically, Bush, like Reagan, was opposed to taxes and would doggedly pursue tax cuts throughout his presidency, usually with great success. An additional somewhat unique aspect to Bush's domestic vision was his application of MBA principles to government programs and projects. He believed government agencies should embrace managerial efficiencies and that they should be held accountable for their actions. The philosophy was put into practice in Bush's reform initiatives for education, expressed most prominently in No Child Left Behind.

In foreign policy, Bush campaigned against the Democrats' proclivity for nation building and suggested the United States should be modest in its approach to foreign policy. He seemed particularly ignorant of many foreign policy issues, and especially of the names of foreign leaders. But when America was attacked by Islamic terrorists on September 11, 2001, Bush developed a rather strong vision of American responsibility in a globalized world threatened by terrorists and the proliferation of weapons of mass destruction. He quickly evolved a strategy of preemption rejecting the now useless (in his mind) doctrines of deterrence and containment. Like Reagan's rejection of MAD, Bush's rejection of containment and deterrence surprised many conservatives and delighted the "Vulcans" who surrounded the president in Washington. The vision of preemption, however, led to a militaristic foreign policy and to an incredibly lofty (ultimately unattainable) goal of ridding the world of tyranny.

In sum, it is important for a president to have a vision, or what *New York Times* columnist Thomas Friedman calls a narrative for his presidency.[4] Without a vision, a sense of purpose or meaning, the administration will lose direction and focus and become the victim of the power of the strongest lobbyists or most skilled bureaucratic warriors. A president needs a vision to define his administration. Otherwise a president's daring but discrete policies "start to feel like a work plan that we have to slog through, and endlessly compromise over, just to finish for finishing's sake—not because they are building blocks of a great national project."[5] People are inspired by visionary leadership, as management gurus Jim Kouzes and Barry Posner have documented.[6]

On the other hand, a president's vision must never overshadow the realities of existence for the majority of Americans, or even for the citizens of the world. President Franklin Delano Roosevelt was a visionary, but his vision of an activist government, especially in what the British call the "commanding heights of the economy," was always tempered by his political sagacity and the excellent strategic advice from the "brain trust" he had assembled in the White House. Lincoln, who was also a visionary, recognized, nonetheless, that he had to pay particular attention to the sequence with which he pursued his goals, and that his supreme vision of saving the union had to take priority over the important goal of ending slavery. According to historian Garry Wills, "Lincoln trimmed and hedged on slavery in order to make people take small steps in the direction of facing the problem."[7] When a president becomes overly invested in his vision and gets to far ahead of his followers—as George W. Bush did with preemption and with fighting terrorism—he may lose his objectivity and balance. Sometimes, it is tempting to share the view of former German Chancellor Helmut Schmidt, who once quipped, "People with vision should go see a doctor."[8]

---

[4]Thomas L. Freidman, "More Poetry Please," *New York Times*, November 1, 2009.

[5]Ibid.

[6]James M. Kouzes and Barry Z. Posner, *The Leadership Challenge*, 4th ed. (San Francisco, CA: Jossey-Bass, 2007), 5–7.

[7]Garry Wills, *Certain Trumpets: The Call of Leaders* (New York: Simon and Schuster, 1994), 16.

[8]Joseph S. Nye Jr., *The Powers to Lead* (New York: Oxford University Press, 2008), 75.

POLITICS: STRATEGY/EXECUTION

Jimmy Carter disdained many aspects of retail politics. He believed that people needed to do the right things and the president ought to be the one to persuade them, but he need not play the insider's game of relationship building, influence pedaling, and logrolling. As a Democrat, Carter had an unusual political opportunity, because the House was still controlled by the Democrats. Nevertheless, Carter refused to accede to playing politics with the powerful but somewhat cooperative Speaker of the House Tip O'Neill. He sought a higher level of discussion than that provided by routine political exchange, and in this regard perhaps anticipated being a transformational rather than transactional leader.[9] The problem is that Washington, D.C., is very much a land of transactions and influence trading, and most political activists work to achieve progress on the basis of reciprocity.

Moreover, Carter did not truly prioritize his legislative goals and offered so many proposals that he overloaded the system set up to manage legislative proposals. Carter never spelled out his true bottom-line issues, those for which he had the most passion, and his aides were left in the difficult position of pushing forward on multiple fronts without clear direction or focus.

Finally, from a Washington perspective, Carter surrounded himself with mostly political amateurs. His closest aides were primarily from Georgia and they anticipated running Congress the way they ran the Georgia legislature when Carter was governor. They didn't anticipate that Congress is a unique and prideful institution that has its own schedule and unique rhythm, and certainly wishes to be treated as a co-equal branch of government, especially after Watergate. Because Carter never explained his legislative priorities to his staff, and because they were largely inexperienced in the ways of Washington, the administration frequently floundered and accomplished less than it should have with a Democratic Congress.

Ronald Reagan, by contrast, seemed particularly deft in the world of politics. He was a great communicator and had an effective and easy-going manner paired with a sunny, upbeat personality to drive his message home to anyone who would listen. Reagan moved expeditiously to build a highly effective White House staff that combined California ideologues with Washington practitioners, resulting in what David Gergen termed, "one of the strongest teams in the past forty years."[10]

> Reagan could count on the conservatives on staff to keep the
> administration heading in the right direction; he could count on the
> moderates to help chart the path and to strike compromises when
> necessary. The conservatives liked to ensure that Reagan carried
> bold colors into battle, the moderates said fine, but let's make sure
> that when the smoke clears he still has a victory. The conservatives

---

[9]James MagGregor Burns, *Leadership* (New York: Harper Torchbooks, 1978).
[10]Gergen, 169.

believed Reagan's strength lay in the heartland, which was true; the moderates said it was also true that to govern he had to make the inside Washington.[11]

Reagan's legislative strategy was developed in a team effort that focused on giving wide berth to the policy experts who really knew the issues, and saving Reagan for what he did best—making speeches and persuading legislators one-on-one. The negotiations carried out with a Democratic Congress, at least in the House, were led by highly competent people who had an amplitude of previous experience in politics. And their priorities were clear. Reagan had a limited agenda, compared to Carter's expansive one. All his effort was directed at the attainment of three main goals: tax cuts, social welfare spending cuts, and military expenditure increases. All other issues were temporarily shelved or minimized with decisive damage control.

Reagan's effectiveness, however, declined in his second term, due, in part, to the extremities of his macro-management approach and because he easily approved a switch between first-term Chief of Staff James Baker and first-term Treasury Secretary Donald Regan. Reagan lost a "courageous follower"[12] as his chief of staff and inherited a sycophant instead.

George H. W. Bush achieved great political success by mastering the art of relationship building and insider dealing. He was a pleasant, competent, and capable negotiator. He leveraged his valuable relationships into political and policy achievements and had played in the big field of national politics and international relations. Facing a Democratic Congress and a growing deficit, Bush moved with great caution domestically and operated out of a tactical, not strategic perspective. He campaigned and governed as an insider, and understood how to get things accomplished in government.

His most successful use of relationships as a form of political discourse and leadership played out in the international arena where he competently helped to manage the dissolution of the Soviet Empire and encouraged the emergence of democratic-capitalist societies in former Soviet bloc countries. He displayed impressive political and leadership roles in leading an international coalition to oust Iraqi dictator Saddam Hussein from Kuwait, a sovereign state Hussein invaded.

But Bush's political skills were seriously tested, and found wanting, in his failure to uphold a campaign promise, "Read my lips, no new taxes." Forced by circumstance to raise taxes, Bush proved inept at explaining his behavior to a disappointed public. He settled for the insider's game of compromise and negotiation, but failed to educate the public, one of the critical aspects of leadership. As well, he seemed to be out of touch with the concerns of ordinary Americans, as the recession was growing in severity in 1991, and he lost his re-election bid to Bill Clinton in 1992.

---

[11]Ibid., 183.

[12]Ira Challef, *The Courageous Follower: Standing Up To and For Our Leaders*, 2nd ed. (San Francisco, CA: Berrett-Koehler Publications, Inc., 2003).

Bill Clinton thrived in politics. He decided on a political career at the age of sixteen and never looked back. Clinton clearly understood the political challenges that awaited him in the White House. He was poised for leadership in 1992, as the first Democrat to occupy the Oval Office since 1980, and wanted to assure a hold on the office by evolving a non-conventional approach to power. Clinton floundered in his early days in the White House due to staking out an unnecessarily strong position on allowing gays in the military, but recovered from his early mistakes to achieve a significant win on his economic reform package that consisted primarily of tax increases. Resisting pressure from the left wing of his party, this New Democrat staked out a position as a deficit hawk and helped build a better economic condition for America. Like Reagan, Clinton orchestrated an intense and ultimately successful legislative persuasion effort to gain buy-in to his economic programs; nevertheless, his support came almost exclusively from the Democratic side of the aisle. He was also successful in passing the North American Free Trade Agreement (NAFTA) and a major overhaul of the welfare system, attracting Republican support as well.

But Clinton stumbled badly when he tried to reform health care. His campaign had been energized by the surprising senatorial victory of Democrat Harris Wofford in Pennsylvania, defeating the much better known candidate, Dick Thornburgh, who had been in George H. W. Bush's cabinet. Responding to the concern of Pennsylvanians over health care, Clinton's political consultants—James Carville and Paul Begala—convinced Wofford of the importance of health care. They also helped convince Clinton to embrace health care as a central part of his campaign; subsequently, Clinton appointed his wife, Hillary Clinton, to lead the effort and champion the legislation for health care reform. Regrettably, Hillary violated almost every principle of effective persuasion and change management in her approach to the issue. Favoring a comprehensive, complex legislative proposal that was the product of health care "experts" and had been fashioned in secret and without input from critical stakeholders, Hillary attempted to browbeat her opponents into submission and refused to even consider compromise on key aspects of the plan. The effort failed miserably, and President Clinton suffered a significant political defeat, which led in almost a direct way to the Republicans, led by Newt Gingrich, taking control of the House of Representatives, in the 1994 elections, for the first time in forty years.

Demonstrating his impressive resiliency, however, Clinton recovered by moving back toward the center, under the influence of his longtime political consultant, Dick Morris. Clinton rebuilt his political momentum in the course of budget negotiations with Gingrich, when the president showed resolve in refusing a Gingrich-inspired federal budget, and then in negotiating with the liberals in his party who opposed his support of a largely conservative welfare reform bill. Clinton prevailed in both cases; however, during the 1994–1995 furlough, he started an affair with a White House intern, Monica Lewinsky, that lead to impeachment hearings and the near destruction of his presidency.

George W. Bush had succeeded in Texas politics by preferring a strongly bipartisan approach. He gave strong indications that he would continue that practice in the White House, and in his early days he did. In one of his first legislative initiatives, No Child Left Behind, he reached across the aisle and attracted the strong support of Senator Edward Kennedy; Bush achieved passage of a significant bill with considerable Democratic support. But he was unsuccessful in preventing Vermont Senator James Jeffords from leaving the Republican Party and becoming an independent, thereby losing control of the Senate to the Democrats. Though Bush was tempted to negotiate with Jeffords, he was apparently discouraged from doing so by his very powerful vice president, Dick Cheney. This event was symptomatic of the broader reality of Cheney's pervasive and historically unparalleled influence as a vice president.

The terrorist attacks of September 11, 2001, strengthened Bush's resolve and clarified his vision; it also gave him an incredible boost in popularity (attaining a 92 percent approval rating in October 2001), and an edge in Congress. President Bush showed strong resolve and determined leadership in the days and weeks after the terrorist attacks. Congress was tremendously supportive of President Bush post-9/11, giving him almost everything he solicited—authorization for war in Afghanistan, a huge financial aid package for New York City, the USA Patriot Act—in record time and with bipartisan support. But when Bush determined to transform American foreign policy to position of preemption, and when he began to plan an attack on Iraq, he lost considerable support among the public and among members of Congress. Encouraged by Cheney and Defense Secretary Rumsfeld, his administration took on more of a marketing approach and a permanent campaign, and he seemed to forsake his interest in bipartisanship. Still the atmosphere of fear was pervasive, Bush won congressional authorization for the war in Iraq, the Democrats were defeated in the mid-term elections of 2002, and Bush was re-elected by a strong margin in 2004. And yet, as the war in Iraq become increasingly unpopular, and leadership incompetencies were on full display at all levels of government during the unprecedented Hurricane Katrina, the continued success of Bush's (and Karl Rove's) fear tactics wore thin. The Republicans and George Bush suffered a resounding defeat at the polls in the 2006 congressional elections.

Politics is the bridge between a president's vision and reality. A president must use his vision to guide his legislative proposals and must place experienced and competent people in the roles of helping him sell his programs. A president cannot really avoid retail politics, nor consider himself above or bound by it. It is the essence of leadership. The relationship with Congress must be sustained and certainly nourished, abetted by a comprehension of the real political pressures and tensions members in all congressional districts face.

Moreover, it is important that a president develops a clearly focused and limited agenda. He has only four years to demonstrate his achievements, and the clock begins to tick early on. Many presidents since Roosevelt have been determined to show their accomplishments within the first 100 days; however, it is clear that that may be an artificial (and unrealistic) benchmark. In any case, a president is more likely to succeed if he takes on fewer issues simultaneously and organizes the resources at hand—his legislative support people, his supporters in Congress, the media, and the public—toward their accomplishment. Carter's attempt to achieve over thirty policy goals was overly ambitious, whereas Reagan's focus on only three major goals seems sensible. Clinton chose to deliver on a campaign promise—getting gays in the military—too early, and went about health care reform in an inefficient manner, though he did lower the deficit by making it a huge priority. George H. W. Bush wanted to manage people's expectations, but refused to "go public" in explaining his seeming about-face on the matter of raising taxes.

Finally, although the partisan divisions between Republicans and Democrats have widened during the past several years, it remains important for a president to seek bipartisan approaches to policy making. George W. Bush won considerable acclaim for this aspect of his leadership as a Texas governor, and seemed to embrace it in his early White House days; but after 9/11, as he sought elevated powers to protect America, he tended to rely on hardball tactics to bring the Democrats down. Although effective for two electoral cycles (2002, 2004), the strategy ultimately backfired in 2006, when the Republicans, and George W. Bush, were substantially defeated at the polls.

STRUCTURE: MANAGEMENT

A president is largely free to organize the White House according to his design, which is an important aspect of presidential leadership. After all, the White House staff, along with the executive branch of government, help implement the president's programs.

The five presidents studied in this book have taken vastly different approaches to management. A good deal of their approaches relate to the people they chose to work with. The Reagan people liked to say, "People are policy."[13] Carter chose to surround himself with his friends and associates from Georgia, the so-called Georgia mafia. Like Carter, the people he chose were mostly Washington, D.C., outsiders and they had a great deal to learn about the political culture of the nation's capital. Carter managed them fairly closely, as his engineering and technical background inclined him to do, and forced them to concentrate on the achievement of multiple policy proposals that were highly complex and lacking priority order. As well, Carter was eager to break away from the tendency of the White House, especially under presidents such as Nixon, to dominate the executive branch and to guarantee that their cabinet secretaries and agencies were always in sync with the president's program. Accordingly, Carter released the strict controls White House staff had exerted over cabinet agencies and proclaimed he would run his government in a style of "collective collegiality."

---

[13]Gergen, 169.

The overly loose sense of supervision of executive branch agencies created problems, however, as cabinet secretaries floated trial policy balloons that created great unease in Washington. In addition, Carter's early attempt to operate in the White House with no chief of staff proved problematic, and he was forced to correct this flaw in the later years of his presidency.

Reagan was almost Carter's total opposite. Unlike Carter, he was largely ignorant of the details of policy. As expressed by his biographer, *Washington Post* reporter Lou Cannon, "The paradox of the Reagan presidency was that it depended totally upon Reagan for its ideological inspiration while he depended totally on others for all aspects of governance except his core ideas and powerful performances."[14] Reagan was bored by the "everydayness" of governance, and did not really understand the details of a budget or the nuances of a legislative proposal.[15]

Accordingly, Reagan appointed Washington insiders to key positions and he delegated power and authority to them to do the heavy lifting on behalf of the president's programs. As he had been very clear on the nature and order of his priorities, his staff clearly understood what the boss wanted done and enjoyed the freedom to do so through delegation from the president. This was if anything a culture of macro-management in the Reagan White House, according to journalist Francis Fitzgerald.[16] Reagan was a 9-to-5 president, who spent quality time with his beloved wife, Nancy.

Reagan's staff acted with efficiency and effectiveness in lobbying Congress and achieving success in the president's program for economic recovery. They did so by using Reagan when they needed him, but not allowing him into areas he was unfamiliar with. Reagan's presidency was a highly scripted one; however, as his biographer Lou Cannon reminds us, Reagan wrote the script.

Reagan's macro-management, however, also had limitations, which were especially apparent during the second term. His ease in making important personnel changes, his lack of responsible leadership in the Iran-Contra affair, and his growing distance from the details of governance became problematic. The Tower Commission that investigated the Iran-Contra situation concluded that Reagan's advisers had traded arms for hostages in violation of official U.S. policy, and singled out Chief of Staff Donald Regan for criticism.[17] But the Tower Commission also criticized President Reagan, in particular, for the deficiencies in his management style. The commission said:

> The president's management style is to put the principal responsibility of policy review and information on the shoulders of his advisors. Nevertheless,

---

[14]Lou Cannon, *President Reagan: The Role of a Lifetime* (New York: Simon and Schuster, 1991), 94.

[15]Ibid., 55.

[16]Francis Fitzgerald, *Way Out There in the Blue: Reagan, Star Wars and the End of the Cold War* (New York: Simon and Schuster, 2000).

[17]Bob Woodward, *Shadow: Five Presidents and the Legacy of Watergate* (New York: Simon and Schuster, 2000), 120.

with such a complex, high risk operation and so much at stake the President should have ensured that the NSC (National Security Council) option did not fail him. He did not force his policy to undergo the most critical review of which the NSC participates and the processes were capable.[18]

George H. W. Bush was a deeply experienced political leader who had easily managed political professionals and respected the culture of government managers in a way that no other president did. One of the earliest speeches he gave as president was to an assembly of federal managers. As an insider, Bush surrounded himself with people who were highly experienced in the policy process at high levels, and he deferred a great deal to their expertise. But he led them on a series of tactical, not strategic adventures and focused on the accomplishment of incremental change. He occasionally leapt forward, such as his active support for the Americans with Disabilities Act, but more generally presided over a government calibrated on small steps forward.

The competency of his foreign policy team proved to be a significant resource in Bush's mostly successful initiatives, including, most dramatically, the Persian Gulf War. He had established a sense of meaningful personal contacts with leaders throughout the world, and his deputies were similarly known to allies of the United States. He also appointed experienced hands to leadership positions in the domestic agencies, but they lacked the same level of guidance and direction as their diplomatic colleagues. In addition, Bush elevated a political ally, New Hampshire Governor John Sununu, to the position of chief of staff; however, Sununu lacked the delicacy and finesse to perform with maximum effectiveness.

Bill Clinton did not seem to devote as much attention to organizing his White House as he did to the great issues of the day. He was slow to staff his administration during the transition and he was still naming his team a week before the inauguration. Clinton selected a combination of insiders and outsides, and strove to have a cabinet that "looked like America" in terms of its diversity. There was a decidedly youthful cast to his White House staff, and there was a more casual atmosphere in the White House than in most other administrations. Moreover, Clinton placed many of his campaign staff into high-level positions in the White House, which according to Gergen and other observers did not serve the president well. Clinton gave great leverage and influence to Al Gore and Hillary Clinton. As mentioned earlier, Hillary's outsized influence occasionally hindered the president's success.

The president's lack of discipline reinforced the lackadaisical atmosphere that soon existed in the White House, and Clinton recognized that he needed help. He turned to experienced hands such as David Gergen and others to increase the order and efficiency of White House operations. To some extent, Clinton faced the Carter problem of trying to obtain many policy victories in many different directions, without a good sense of priority and sequencing.

---

[18]Tower Commission, *President's Special Review Board Report* (New York: Bantam Books, 1987), 79–80.

George W. Bush prided himself on his MBA training and believed he could instill business principles into his White House and a sense of accountability into the executive branch of government. His White House was populated with people of great experience and surprising diversity (at least in superficial characteristics such as race and gender), and had a much more buttoned-down feel than Clinton's White House. Bush intended that his team operate like a business, with a great emphasis on efficiency, clear decision making, and a strong "no leaks" policy.

If Bush professed to be an exemplar of the professional administrator who eschews the intrusion of politics into administration, the reality was quite different. As the administration became more convinced of the need to go to war in Iraq, and as that orientation proved to be somewhat unpopular, Bush and his colleagues began to rely on a marketing campaign to browbeat opponents into submission, as detailed by his press secretary Scott McClellan and political scientist James Pfeiffer.[19] Bush lost a great deal of objectivity as a public administrator when he decided to take the country to war against Iraq in the summer of 2002. Administration was subordinated to politics. Although almost every other president has politicized the executive branch of government, few have gone as far as Bush in doing so, as reflected in the creation of the Department of Homeland Security and the dismissal of several U.S. attorneys in the Department of Justice.

A president must have a serious orientation to the administrative excellence of the branch of government that he presides over. He must assemble an "architecture of execution, a culture and process for executing, promoting people who get things done."[20] He cannot control the Congress, even when the majority of its membership represents the same political party he does, and he definitely cannot control the judiciary. Federal judges, appointed for life, fiercely guard their independence and have proven, time and again, that they are willing to bite the hand that fed them. The president can exert a semblance of control over only the executive branch of government.

PROCESS: DECISION MAKING

Carter had the mind of an engineer. He analyzed problems carefully, comprehended the details and nuances for various solutions, and chose the one that was most logically correct. Politics was a secondary consideration, because Carter believed that he could convince citizens and members of Congress to do the right thing. His energy proposals were developed almost solely by Carter in consultation with Energy Secretary James Schlesinger. He did not

---

[19]James P. Pfiffner, "The First MBA President: George Bush as Public Administrator," *Public Administration Review*, January/February 2007; and Scott McClellan, *What Happened: Inside the Bush White House and Washington's Culture of Deception* (New York: Public Affairs, 2008).

[20]Larry Bossidy and Ram Charan, *Execution: The Discipline of Getting Things Done* (New York: Crown Business, 2002), 28.

open the formulation of policy to widespread and diverse input from members of Congress, or the public. Carter chose policies that were correct analytically, but did not consider how they would affect important constituencies.

Carter had an absorbent mind and could contemplate multiple issues simultaneously. He spent a great deal of time reviewing the intricate details of policy. But he never chose his priorities in a consistent manner, nor did he calculate that the volume of legislation he sent to Congress could literally overwhelm the legislative process, particularly as many of his bills ended up before two major committees: Senate Energy and Commerce and House Ways and Means.

Carter had the capacity to recognize flaws in his decision-making process and he occasionally sought to diversify his sources of input. But he possessed a great deal of confidence in his decision-making capability and intuition and truly believed he was on a path of truth and righteousness. He had profound religious convictions that influenced him to see the good in people and to try and address their needs. At times this conviction served him well, as it did dealing with the Middle East peace process. But he seemed tone-deaf to staff expressions of political concern on some policy issues and frequently antagonized important congressional leaders, including the leadership of his party.

Reagan's decision making was tied to his values. He used his vision to guide his decision making and favored policies, programs, and proposals that would advance his core beliefs of smaller government, lower taxes, and strong defense. Sometimes on the edge of absolutism in his embrace of his core values, he nonetheless surrounded himself with experienced, astute political professionals, such as James Baker, who could temper Reagan's vision by explaining the political realities on the Hill and save Reagan from his worst instincts. Reagan would occasionally override his advisers and stick to his guns, but he would always listen to their opinions. Reagan was keenly aware of his limited knowledge of policy details and was happy to defer to experts.

The clarity of Reagan's vision helped ease the decision-making process in his administration. His aides approached Capitol Hill leaders with confidence, claiming they had a mandate for change. But the vision occasionally bumped up against reality; for instance, Reagan's belief in "Star Wars" was widely refuted by the scientists of his day—he went on believing and investing in it anyway.

Finally, Reagan's decisions were lacking perspective at times. Although Reagan may have been in contact with poverty early in his life, he lost touch with people in America struggling to pay their bills or eking out an existence on a welfare check or dealing with the devastation of an illness such as AIDS. His sunny optimism would not quite penetrate the despair of some Americans. His attempt to emulate his hero, Franklin Roosevelt, came up short in this way.

George H. W. Bush was the beneficiary of an Ivy League education and the tutelage of a highly successful political family. In a sense, some things were decided for him. On the other hand, Bush showed great independence when he decided to leave the comfort and security of New England for the uncertainty and risk awaiting him in Texas. Later in life he chose China as his diplomatic posting, instead of the more familiar venues of Europe that were also dangled before him.

President Bush had an ease with making decisions that emerged from his long and deep experience in government. When he needed advice, he consulted the highly sophisticated network of friends and associates he had built up over the years. He was usually decisive, and equally confident that once a decision was made it would be implemented with efficiency by the professional managers and experienced administrators who staffed his White House and agencies.

Bush built an especially impressive foreign policy team that possessed the maturity and sophistication to help him manage the transformation of the Soviet regime and the end of the Cold War, as well as the organization and execution of the Persian Gulf War against Saddam Hussein. Deliberations were cordial, highly professional, and largely private. As well, Bush's network of contacts facilitated his ability to build impressive and mostly stable coalitions of international partners for U.S. policy. The Gulf War was truly a cooperative effort of many sovereign nations aligned against the expansionist behavior of Saddam Hussein.

On the other hand, Bush seemed to be devoid of fresh ideas, and overly reliant on shibboleths and lofty words such as a "thousand points of light" to guide his domestic policy. He made decisions to move forward in some areas, such as protecting the rights of disabled Americans, and protecting the environment. But he bowed to the pressures of a political campaign to deliver a promise—no new taxes—that he couldn't keep. In doing so, he repudiated the advice of senior advisers, such as his future Budget Director Richard Darman, who understood the growing budgetary deficits and the problems they would create. He boxed himself into a corner and his decision-making abilities were severely constrained.

Like Reagan, Bush was not really in tune with a wide spectrum of the American public other than his professional associates and, mostly, wealthy friends. His decision making was competent but not always totally informed.

Bill Clinton was reputed to have difficulty making decisions. He tended to allow his staff to engage in lengthy policy debates, sometimes lasting through the wee hours of the night, and often accompanied by pizza deliveries to the White House. Clinton was often in the middle of the policy discussions and, apparently, took great delight in them. Perhaps, Clinton had the mind and heart of a professor; he had, after all, taught at the University of Arkansas Law School. Apparently, Richard Nixon once quipped that "Bill Clinton confuses conversation with decision making."

There were signs of Clinton's discomfort with decision making. Because he possessed a keen intellect and could see many sides of an issue, and because he constantly remained aware of the political dynamics surrounding an issue, he could become paralyzed. Or he could enunciate polices that seemed inconsistent. During the 1992 presidential campaign, George H. W. Bush accused

Clinton of being spotted in more places on an issue than Elvis.[21] Clinton certainly had an open mind, and was eager to hear his staff argue over budgetary shortfalls and foreign policy options.

On the other hand, once he made a decision, Clinton understood how to sell his idea and how to achieve legislative victory. He showed this particular skill on the overhaul of his early economic reform package, on NAFTA, and on the welfare reform program. When he decided to invest himself heavily into an issue—as he did with the 2000 Camp David peace process between Israelis and the Palestinians—he proved himself to be quite determined and committed to success, though never inflexible about the meaning of success.

George W. Bush called himself "the Decider," and exuded great confidence in his competence as a decision maker. He proclaimed his comfort in making clear, often quick decisions, and disparaged those who got bogged down with seeing too many sides of an issue, saying "We don't do nuance in Texas!"

In some ways, his ease with decision making served him well. His agenda in the early days of the White House seemed to move forward, and he had little trouble making decisions in education reform, tax policy, and social security, among other things. Bush had a group of highly experienced professionals and seduced many journalists and political scientists into believing that the White House had become an exemplar of efficiency and was a good reflection of the nation's first MBA president.

But a president faces issues that are not always clear-cut and that are nuanced. Bush's search for clear choices and unambiguous decisions came at a heavy price. For one thing, he progressively narrowed the range of options he would consult; for instance, the most vocal internal policy challenges in his first administration—Secretary of State Colin Powell, Environmental Protection Agency (EPA) Administrator Christine Todd Whitman, Secretary of Treasury Paul O'Neill—either left office before the end of the first administration or were not invited back for the second. Furthermore, Bush became strongly convinced of the need for a paradigm shift in foreign policy—from containment and deterrence to preemption—and embraced that vision with the alacrity of a fanatic, and not the skepticism of an analyst. Finally, Bush proved particularly reluctant to examine the consequences of his decisions. He was determined to persevere in the war in Iraq, almost in spite of the consequences. As political scientist Joseph Nye suggests, perseverance can become emotional stubbornness that "hinders learning and adjustment." According to Nye, "Like Woodrow Wilson before him, Bush's stubborn commitment to his vision inhibited learning."[22]

To summarize, the styles of the five presidents considered in the book are significantly different, as expressed in the following chart:

---

[21]R. Cutler and A. Pennebaker, *The War Room* (United States: Cyclone Films, 1993).

[22]Nye, 71.

	Policy (vision)	Politics (strategy)	Structure (management)	Process (decision making)
Jimmy Carter	Thematic campaign based on themes of honesty and integrity, an outsider focus. Promised to give America a government as "good as its people" and to avoid imperial tendencies of Richard Nixon. Little preview of exact policy direction or ambition.	Disdain for "politics as usual," and an attempt to soar above the deal-making ways of retail politicians. Embraced of a huge policy agenda without priority order. Little guidance provided to staff who were mostly Washington outsiders. Difficult congressional relations. Most major policy initiatives failed. Big success, however, in the Camp David Peace Accords between Israel and Egypt.	Management style and structure emanated from the desire to de-imperialize the presidency. Stripped White House aides of many perks of office. Instituted a "spokes-of-the-week" management structure and "collective collegiality" approach to decision making.	Had an engineer's analytical approach to decision making. Made decisions based on analytical soundness and ethical proclivity but discounted political fallout. Built in a great deal of diversity, especially in the foreign policy operation, but had trouble managing bitter conflicts between two top foreign policy advisers. Attempts to blend positions did not succeed. Collective analytical approach to policy proposals, but an absence of strong policy preferences and priorities.
Ronald Reagan	Programmatic campaign based on principles of lowering taxes, cutting the welfare state and reducing the size and reach of government, and increasing	First administration marked by a competent and successful congressional relations effort and by strong retail politics on Reagan's part.	A macro-manager, who painted in broad strokes and delegated the details of implementation to his highly qualified staff. This worked well in Reagan's	Was effective in the dramatic and public relations aspects of the presidency and appreciated the symbolic uses of power and leadership. Restored

U.S. military prowess so the United States could influence the Soviets to come to the bargaining table. Very strong on projecting capable leadership and rescuing the presidency from the shrinkage of the office caused by Jimmy Carter. Very strong on principle, notably weak on the details of policy and governance.

White House aides included an impressive blending of conservative ideologues and Washington insider pragmatists who could help get this done. Limited policy agenda to the main principles of Reaganism and Reaganomics.

Second administration hurt by the personnel changes easily approved by Reagan, especially the shift of jobs between James Baker, his highly effective first-term chief of staff, and Donald Regan, the first-term treasury secretary. Regan lacked the political acumen of Baker, and the president lost his cover against his errors in judgment. Major crisis of Iran-Contra.

first administration, when he aligned staff closely to purpose and had help in monitoring events and personalities and exercising damage control when necessary. However, in the second administration, with a less politically savvy management team, Reagan became embroiled in huge problems, such as the Iran-Contra affair, without fully comprehending the implications.

faith in the office. Gave strong ideological focus and coherence to the administration, but avoided the details of implementation. Hired competent staff and gave them freedom and led by macro-management. He was uncomfortable resolving staff conflict and never became particularly close to those who worked for him.

continued

	Policy (vision)	Politics (strategy)	Structure (management)	Process (decision making)
George H. W. Bush	Did not have a vision and operated in the context of friendships and relationships. Nevertheless, aimed for maintaining stability in international relations (conservative internationalism) and small leaps forward in domestic policy (disjointed incrementalism). Understood the profound changes occurring in the Soviet Empire and sought to manage the transformation of power in a responsible manner. Comprehended the threat posed by Saddam Hussein's invasion of Kuwait and dealt with it.	Very much of an insider, who had held almost every important position in American government. Reached out to Congress in a conciliatory manner and sought bipartisan solutions to political challenges. Experienced a significant setback when his nominee for secretary of defense, Senator John Tower, was defeated in the Senate, and was unable to deliver on his no new taxes promise. His preference for insider negotiations underestimated the need to go public and explain his policy reversal.	Hired an unusually talented and experienced foreign policy team and a slightly less impressive group of domestic advisers. Many of his staff were insiders and understood how Washington works. Developed a strategy to competently manage other managers and respected the competence of White House staff. The foreign policy team deftly managed the dissolution of the Soviet Empire and the emergence of capitalistic democracies in Eastern Europe as well as in the Persian Gulf War.	Decisions were easily made by experienced and competent professionals. The president trusted his advisers and cabinet heads and gave them only general directive and guidance. The heavy-handed style of the chief of staff created challenges, and the president did not respond quickly enough.
Bill Clinton	New Democrat orientation helped challenge Democratic	Difficult start with an overly aggressive attempt to	Staffed White House with several inexperienced,	Impressive intellectual dexterity and analytical

orthodoxies and launched him on a path of deficit reductions, welfare reform, and economic revitalization following the 1990–1991 recession. Activity in the Democratic Leadership Conference and several political campaigns helped convince him of the need for change.

allow gays into the military, directly challenging the military leadership and Armed Services Committee chairman, Senator Sam Nunn. Persevered in the effort to improve economic conditions and prevailed in a tough fight to pass a deficit reduction policy. On economic programs he won without Republican support, but in his subsequent leadership on NAFTA attracted Republicans to his cause. Knew how to lobby from the Oval Office, when the issue is of significant importance. Stumbled badly on health care and the excessive grant of power to First Lady. Recovered from defeat—Republican takeover of the House in 1994—and

youthful campaign aides and provided only loose supervision. Realized this was a problem and reached out to David Gergen and others for help. Developed a more structured and routinized White House. Outsized influence of First Lady and vice president continued.

complexity allowed Clinton to see nuance and complexity of policy decisions. Long, inconclusive policy deliberations took place in the White House, with the president a full participant.

continued

	Policy (vision)	Politics (strategy)	Structure (management)	Process (decision making)
		reclaimed his middle-of-the-road, New Democrat approach with the welfare reform legislation of 1996.		
George W. Bush	Domestically described himself as a compassionate conservative who wanted to give free reign to faith-based groups to supplement, and in some ways supplant government provided welfare services. At first shied away from an active orientation in foreign policy, but was deeply influenced by the events of 9/11 to reorient American foreign policy to a paradigm of preemption.	Operated as governor in a notably bipartisan manner, which carried into early months in the White House. Suffered a significant setback when Vermont Senator Jeffords switched parties, giving the Senate back to the Democrats. Took strong decisive and impressive leadership actions after 9/11, and gained tremendous support among citizens and Congress. Leveraged high support to elevate presidential powers and worked collaboratively with Vice President Cheney.	Presented himself as the first MBA president and imposed a business atmosphere into White House procedures and operations. Emphasized efficiency, teamwork, and loyalty. The buttoned-down business-like atmosphere gave way to an emphasis on marketing and selling the president's programs, especially war in Iraq. The introduction of a large new bureaucratic structure—Department of Homeland Security—became as much a political as management initiative.	Bush called himself "the Decider" and was comfortable making quick and clear decisions. This helped him move his agenda along. But he consulted an increasing narrow range of opinions and failed to examine the consequences of his decisions.

Which of the five post-Watergate presidents was the best leader? Was it the austere, moralizing, well-informed but occasionally politically naïve former Georgia governor? Was it the charismatic, visionary, verbally fluid, politically talented, but policy detail–challenged former actor and California governor? Was it the scion of a powerful, affluent, politically connected family who had thrived on friendships and relationships as he attained almost every significant political office the government has to offer? Was it the intellectually brilliant, sometimes ethically challenged, former Arkansas governor who lifted himself out of difficult family background and achieved great political success, while revitalizing the Democratic Party? Or was it the feisty, sometimes sardonic business entrepreneur who benefitted from family contacts, but on his own grit defeated a popular incumbent governor and ascended all the way to the White House with a few "big ideas" and a reputation for bipartisan political effort?

The five post-Watergate presidents performed with varying levels of success in the four dimensions of leadership considered. They came to the White House with different backgrounds to prepare them for leadership: four were governors with little Washington experience, one was a true Washington insider, but had never faced the challenges associated with being the chief executive of a state government. Two were born to privilege, two to generally poor families, and one was more or less middle class. Four had impressive higher education credentials, including post-graduate degrees, and one had only gone as far as obtaining an undergraduate degree. Two came from a politically active and connected family, and three had to make it on their own. Three were relatively young, one middle-aged, and one older. Four campaigned as outsiders, and one could not help but campaign as an insider.

None of the above factors seems to have profoundly influenced the performance of these five men in the Oval Office. As President Barack Obama expressed in a November 2009 interview with the *U.S. News & World Report*, "I don't think anything prepares you for the presidency."[23]

What matters more than family pedigree, formal education, social standing, and age is the leadership acumen of the president. Success seems to be tied to the president's ability to chart a clear vision, goal, or purpose that can energize his party, the citizenry, and Congress (policy); his capacity to select talented people for his staff, especially those who comprehend the nuances of developing effective relationships with Congress (politics); his attention to designing a management structure in the White House and cabinet agencies that will faithfully execute the president's policies and programs (structure); and his ease and comfort with decision making and skill in listening to multiple viewpoints, but announcing clear and unambiguous decisions (process).

People will argue for years to come over which of the five presidents covered in the book was the most effective leader. It is hard to combine the

---

[23]Interview with Kenneth T. Walsh, *U.S. News & World Report*, November 2009, 23.

conclusions of what a particular leadership framework yields in measuring success, with what history ultimately judges. Nevertheless, by the measures used in this book, it is clear that Ronald Reagan in his first term, Bill Clinton in his first term, and George H. W. Bush were more effective presidents *overall* than Jimmy Carter or George W. Bush. As many others have concluded, second terms seem to present particular challenges to presidential leadership, and the research of the book supports that view. But, again, the author offers these evaluative summaries with humility.

Although U.S. citizens have rejected the idea of an imperial president such as Richard Nixon, or to a lesser extent George W. Bush, they have also made it clear that the polity depends on a strong chief executive, one who can lead the nation with determination, vision, and energy, while staying within the boundaries of the U.S. constitutional framework and traditions. The author's hope is that future presidents will lead the nation in this fashion with the guidance of the four critical areas of leadership.

INDEX